Can Democracy
Be Designed?

About the Series
Democratic Transition in Conflict-Torn Societies

Series editors
Anne Marie Goetz and Robin Luckham

This three-book series explores the politics of democratic transition in conflict-torn countries in the developing South and post-communist East, focusing upon the interplay between democratic institutions and democratic politics. The different volumes in the series identify the institutional arrangements and political compromises, which can assure democratic control of military and security establishments, facilitate the peaceful management of conflict, and enhance the participation of excluded groups, particularly women.

VOLUME 1
Governing Insecurity: Democratic Control
of Military and Security Establishments
in Transitional Democracies
edited by
GAVIN CAWTHRA AND ROBIN LUCKHAM

VOLUME 2
Can Democracy be Designed?
The Politics of Institutional Choice
in Conflict-Torn Societies
edited by
SUNIL BASTIAN AND ROBIN LUCKHAM

VOLUME 3
No Shortcuts to Power:
African Women in Politics and Policy Making
edited by
ANNE MARIE GOETZ AND SHIREEN HASSIM

Can Democracy Be Designed?

The Politics of Institutional Choice in
Conflict-Torn Societies

Edited by

SUNIL BASTIAN AND ROBIN LUCKHAM

Zed Books
LONDON & NEW YORK

Can Democracy Be Designed? was first published in 2003 by
Zed Books Ltd, 7 Cynthia Street, London N1 9JF, UK and
Room 400, 175 Fifth Avenue, New York, NY 10010

www.zedbooks.demon.co.uk

Cover designed by Andrew Corbett
Designed and set in 9½/12 pt Photina
by Long House, Cumbria, UK
Printed and bound in Malaysia

Distributed in the USA exclusively by Palgrave, a division of
St Martin's Press, LLC, 175 Fifth Avenue, New York, NY 10010

A catalogue record for this book
is available from the British Library

US Cataloging-in-Publication Data
is available from the Library of Congress

ISBN   Hb 1 84277 150 7
       Pb 1 84277 151 5

Contents

About the Contributors

Sunil Bastian is a Research Fellow at the International Centre for Ethnic Studies, Colombo. His work has focused on the relationship between Sri Lanka's ethnic conflict and development. He has published widely and is the editor of *Devolution and Development: the Case of Sri Lanka* (1994). At present he is working on a project centred on globalisation, foreign aid and conflict.

Vesna Bojicic-Dzelilovic is a Research Fellow at the Centre for the Study of Global Governance, London School of Economics and Political Science. She has published on the economics of civil war, sanctions, international assistance and post-war reconstruction in South-east Europe. Her recent publications include 'World Bank, NGOs and the Private Sector in Post-war Reconstruction' in E. Newman and A. Schnabel (eds.), *Recovering from Civil Conflict – Reconciliation, Peace and Development* (2002).

Radhika Coomaraswamy is Director of the International Centre for Ethnic Studies, Colombo. Her principal areas of research have been Constitutional Law, Gender and Ethnicity, and Women's Studies. She has numerous articles to her credit on these subjects and is the author of *A Crisis of Legitimacy: the Anglo-American Constitutional Tradition in Sri Lanka* and *Ideology and the Constitution: Essays on Constitutional Jurisprudence*. She is also the United Nations Special Rapporteur on Violence against Women.

Marcus Cox is Senior Editor of the European Stability Initiative (www.esiweb.org), an independent research institute based in Berlin which analyses political, economic and social developments across South-eastern Europe. He is a former legal adviser to the United Nations High

Representative to Bosnia–Herzegovina, specialising in refugee return and property issues, and has acted as a consultant to various international missions in Bosnia and Kosovo. His PhD in international law at Cambridge University focused on the dissolution of the former Yugoslavia and the creation of the state of Bosnia–Herzegovina.

Jon Fraenkel is a senior lecturer in Economic History at the University of the South Pacific in Suva, Fiji. He also specialises in Pacific electoral systems and in Fiji's political history.

Anne Marie Goetz is a Fellow of the Institute of Development Studies, University of Sussex. She has worked on feminist political theory and conducted research in South Asia and Southern and Eastern Africa on the politics of promoting gender equity in development policy, and on gender and political party development. She is also studying movements of the poor to combat corruption in South Asia. She is the author of *Women Development Workers: Implementing Credit Programmes in Bangladesh* (2001), editor of *Getting Institutions Right for Women in Development* (1997) and co-author of *Contesting Global Governance: Multilateral Economic Institutions and Global Social Movements* (2000). She has also co-edited *No Shortcuts to Power: African Women in Politics and Policy Making* (2003).

Aaron Griffiths was a Research Assistant at the Institute of Development Studies, Sussex, UK, and currently works at Conciliation Resources in London.

E. Gyimah-Boadi is Associate Professor in the Department of Political Science at the University of Ghana. He is also Executive Director of the Accra-based independent policy research think-tank, the Ghana Centre for Democratic Development (CDD-Ghana).

Shireen Hassim lectures in Political Studies in the School of Social Sciences, University of the Witwatersrand. She has recently completed a PhD dissertation on the political history of the women's movement in South Africa (1980–99) and has published widely in the area of gender politics. She is co-author of *South Africa: a Country Gender Analysis* and co-editor of *No Shortcuts to Power: African Women in Politics and Policy Making* (2003). She was a member of the Gender and Elections Reference Group coordinated by the Electoral Institute of Southern Africa and a member of the editorial group of the *Election Bulletin* published by womensnet.org.za

Mary Kaldor is currently a Professor at the Centre for the Study of Global Governance, London School of Economics, and Co-Chair of the Helsinki Citizens Assembly. Her many publications include *New and Old Wars: Organised Violence in a Global Era* (1999).

James Katalikawe read Law at the London School of Economics and Political Science, Harvard Law School, the Fletcher School of Law and Diplomacy and the School of Oriental and African Studies. He is currently Senior Lecturer in Law at Makerere University, Kampala, Uganda.

Kishali Pinto-Jayawardena practises public law in the appellate courts in Sri Lanka and is also a legal consultant for the Colombo-based *Sunday Times* newspaper, for which she writes a weekly column on law, gender, minority rights and human rights concerns. She holds senior consultancies at the International Centre for Ethnic Studies and at the National Human Rights Commission, and is presently reading for her MPhil/PhD at the Faculty of Law, University of Colombo on 'Safeguarding Representative Government and the Principle of Democratic Legitimacy in Pluralistic Societies'.

Robin Luckham is a Research Associate at the Institute of Development Studies, University of Sussex. His publications include *The Nigerian Military: a Sociological Analysis of Authority and Revolt 1960–67* (1971). He co-edited *Democratization in the South: the Jagged Wave* (1996) and *Governing Insecurity: Democratic Control of Military and Security Establishments in Transitional Democracies* (2003).

David Pottie is a senior programme associate in the Democracy Program at the Carter Center in Atlanta, USA. He holds a PhD in Political Science from York University, Canada. He has lectured in politics at York University, and also at the University of Natal, Rhodes University and the University of the Witwatersrand in South Africa. He has published on democracy, governance and elections in Africa, and on housing in South Africa.

Preface

This book is dedicated to the memory of two people who were, in their different ways, its inspiration: Neelan Tiruchelvam and Gordon White. Neelan was assassinated in July 2000 because of his principled stand as an advocate of peaceful solutions to Sri Lanka's conflict. He was a prominent scholar, legal practitioner and activist, and for many years was the moving force behind the International Centre for Ethnic Studies, Colombo. Gordon died on April Fools' Day 1998, which happened to be the starting date of our research programme. No doubt this would have appealed to his dry sense of humour. He was an especially respected colleague at the Institute of Development Studies and was very much the intellectual progenitor of our entire research programme and of this book in particular. His ideas are to be found in many places in the book.

Our research programme on Democratic Governance in Conflict-torn Societies was funded by the Social Science Research Unit (SSRU) (formerly ESCOR), the research-funding wing of the British Department for International Development (DFID). We are deeply grateful for its support for our work and its responsiveness to our concerns, not least by funding research partnerships with institutions in the South and East. Two of these institutions – the International Centre for Ethnic Studies, Colombo and the Law Centre, Sarajevo – hosted the two workshops at which our findings were discussed. We wish to thank them for their warm hospitality, and for exposing our work to some penetrating but sympathetic criticism.

Our thanks are due to Radhika Coomaraswamy, who not only contributed intellectually to the project but also supported it once she became the Director of ICES after the demise of Neelan, and to Nicky Bastian who assisted in the Sri Lankan component of the project. Thanks are also due to Vivian Hart of the University of Sussex and Martin Doornbos, who acted as advisers to this project, attended the final Sarajevo workshop, and provided very helpful comments on our drafts. Mark Robinson, like Gordon White, was one of the original team responsible for the research programme. Richard Crook, although he has not contributed to this particular volume, has been a supportive critic and colleague and is partly responsible for the success of the research programme as a whole. Aaron Griffiths has been an especially helpful and creative research assistant, contributing to the intellectual content of the book as well as co-organising the workshops and undertaking editorial tasks. Alison Ayres has also contributed to the book through her important inputs to the IDS working paper on which Chapter 1 is based. With Robert Muggah, she prepared an extremely comprehensive initial bibliography, and organised our initial writing workshop. Invaluable secretarial and editorial assistance at the IDS was provided at various stages by Kim Collins and Julie McWilliam. We wish to thank them all.

Abbreviations

ACDR	Association of Committees for the Defence of the Republic
ADF	Alliance of Democratic Forces
ALTA	Agricultural Landlords and Tenants Act
ANC	African National Congress
APLA	African People's Liberation Army
APSCFE	All Party Select Committee on Franchise and Elections
AV	Alternative Vote system
BiH	Bosnia–Herzegovina
CA	Constituent Assembly
CEDAW	Convention on the Elimination of All Forms of Discrimination Against Women
CGE	Commission on Gender Equality
CODESA	Congress for a Democratic South Africa
COSATU	Congress of South African Trade Unions
CP	Conservative Party (Chapter 3)
CP	Communist Party (Chapter 7)
CPP	Convention Peoples Party
CRC	Constitutional Review Commission
CWC	Ceylon Workers' Congress
DFID	Department for International Development
DRC	Democratic Republic of Congo
ESCOR	Economic and Social Committee on Research
EUAM	European Union Administration of Mostar
FAP	Fijian Association Party
FLP	Fiji Labour Party
FP	Federal Party
FPTP	First-past-the-post
GEAR	Growth, Employment and Redistribution
GNU	Government of National Unity
HDI	Human Development Index

HRC	Human Rights Commission
HSM	Holy Spirit Movement
HVIDR	Association of Croat War Invalids of the Homeland War
ICES	International Centre for Ethnic Studies
ICTY	International Criminal Tribunal for Yugoslavia
ICVA	International Council of Voluntary Agencies
IDEA	International Institute for Democracy and Electoral Assistance
IEBL	Inter-Entity Boundary Line
IFI	International financial institution
IFOR	Implementation Force
IFP	Inkatha Freedom Party
IGG	Inspector-General of Government
IMF	International Monetary Fund
IPAC	Inter-Party Advisory Committee
IPTF	International Police Task Force
JVP	Janatha Vimbukthi Peramuna
KY	Kabaka Yekka Party
KZN	KwaZulu–Natal
LRA	Lord Resistance Army
LSSP	Lanka Sama Samaja Party
LTTE	Liberation Tigers of Tamil Eelam
MAI	Multilateral Agreement on Investment
MK	Umkhonto we Sizwe
MPNP	Multi-Party Negotiating Process
NAL	National Alliance of Liberals
NATO	North Atlantic Treaty Organisation
NCD	National Commission on Democracy
NDC	National Democratic Congress
NEDLAC	National Economic and Development Labour Council
NFP	National Federation Party
NGO	Non-governmental organisation
NLC	National Liberation Council
NP	National Party
NPP	New Patriotic Party
NRA	National Resistance Army
NRAC	National Resistance Army Council
NRC	National Redemption Council (Ghana)
NRC	National Resistance Council (Uganda)
NRM	National Resistance Movement
NVTLP	Nationalist Vanua Tako Lavo Party
OHR	Office of the High Representative
OSCE	Organisation for Security and Cooperation in Europe
PA	People's Alliance
PAC	Pan-African Congress
PAC	Public Accounts Committee

PANU   Party of National Unity
PIP   Public Investment Programme
PAMSCAD   Programme of Actions to Mitigate the Social Costs of
           Adjustment
PNDC   Provisional National Defence Council
PNP   People's National Party
PP   Progress Party
PR   Proportional representation
RC   Resistance Council
RDP   Reconstruction and Development Programme
SACP   South African Communist Party
SADF   South African Defence Force
SANCO   South African National Civic Organisation
SANDF   South African National Defence Force
SDP   Social Democratic Party
SDU   Self-defence unit
SFOR   Stabilisation Force
SFRY   Socialist Federal Republic of Yugoslavia
SLFP   Sri Lanka Freedom Party
SMC   Supreme Military Council
SSRU   Social Science Research Unit
STRAWN   Sinhala–Tamil Rural Women's Network
SVT   Soqosoqo ni Vakavulewa ni Taukei
TALDI   Tuzla Agency for Local Development Initiatives
TC   Tamil Congress
TEC   Transitional Executive Council
TULF   Tamil United Liberation Front
UBSD   Union of Bosnia–Herzegovina Social Democrats
UDIVDR   Association of Volunteers and Veterans of the Homeland War
UDM   United Democratic Movement
UGP   United Generals Party
UK   United Kingdom
UN   United Nations
UNLA   Uganda National Liberation Army
UNLF   Uganda National Liberation Front
UPC   Uganda People's Congress
UPDF   Uganda People's Defence Force
USA   United States of America
VLV   Veitokani ni Lewenivanua Vakarisito
VORADEP   Volta Regional Development Corporation
WEREMUD   Western Region Movement for Unity and Development
WNC   Women's National Coalition

Introduction
Can Democracy Be Designed?

SUNIL BASTIAN AND ROBIN LUCKHAM

We live in an era when political systems based on liberal democracy and economic models promoting global capitalism enjoy almost unchallenged hegemony. Western donors and international financial institutions promote political liberalisation in tandem with economic liberalisation – regarding both as preconditions for full participation in the global economy. The case for liberal democracy is reinforced by the claim that it facilitates the peaceful management of the violent conflicts which have been a prominent feature of the post-Cold War era. At the same time liberal democracy has spread, not just because it is promoted by the West, but also because it taps into the political aspirations of citizens in states in the developing South and post-communist East, who had felt themselves excluded and oppressed under the previous authoritarian systems.

However, the triumphalist vision of democracy as a universal panacea for the world's problems has increasingly come into question. Democracy, it would appear, is Janus-faced. As well as empowering citizens, overcoming exclusion and contributing to good governance, it can also become the tool of powerful economic interests, reinforce societal inequalities, penalise minorities, awaken dormant conflicts, and fail in practice to broaden popular participation in government – as exemplified by its troubled history in countries like Sri Lanka, the longest established of the six democracies or transitional democracies considered in this book.

In this book we neither treat democracy as a general panacea, nor as simply an adjunct of capitalism, nor as just a device for engineering solutions to political and social problems, including conflict. One cannot of course disregard its close historical interconnections with capitalist development, nor its enduring contradictions as a system of governance.

1

Yet in an era of globalisation, when powerful actors, who control capital, have disproportionate influence within modern states, democracy can still (within limits) provide the powerless and the underprivileged with channels for collective political action to challenge their subordination and exploitation.[1]

In sum we regard democracy as a value in its own right – whilst recognising its contradictions – and see it as a universal entitlement of citizens in all modern states. We stand on the side of democracy and emphasise its emancipatory and even subversive potential (see Luckham 1998: 309–16).

There are a number of ways to view the seeming contradictions of the democratic project. First, they may be little more than problems of transition, occurring because democratic norms and practices are not yet fully established. Second, they may arise from specific and remediable defects in democratic institutions, for instance when the latter are biased by unchecked majoritarian or centralising tendencies. Third, they may reveal inherent limitations of democracy itself, or at least of the paradigmatic liberal multi-party representative form it takes in contemporary democracies. Lastly they may be inherent in the nexus between liberal democracy and global capitalism, as when elected governments are hostage to global markets and control a diminished public sphere in which to act on behalf of their citizens.

In this book the emphasis is placed upon how democratic institutions can be reformed to ensure they deliver democratic governance – and do not worsen poverty and inequality, or aggravate conflict. We shall consider some of the ways modern democratic Machiavellis[2] may redesign democratic institutions to create safeguards against the excessive concentration of power under 'winner-takes-all' electoral democracy; to increase the rights protection and political representation enjoyed by minorities; to bring government closer to the people by decentralisation; and to increase the responsiveness of democratic governments to the political demands of poor and socially marginalised groups.

Yet democratic institutions are never introduced in a political, economic and social vacuum. They come into being within specific historical contexts, national societies and cultures. We hope the varying national experiences of democracy considered in this book will contribute to a better historical understanding of the conditions which have given rise to demands for democracy, shaped its institutional forms, influenced whether it is consolidated, and determined how and on behalf of whom it functions in each national context. Democratic institutions and elected governments, as we shall show, may or may not open spaces for democratic politics; they may or may not be responsive to the political demands of the poor, women and minorities; they may or may not facilitate the management of conflicts.

The aspirant democratic Machiavellis, who introduce or reform democratic institutions in specific historical situations, are just as likely to be swayed by short-term political priorities and demands from narrow political constituencies as by strategic visions of the nature and purposes of democratic governance. Furthermore, the institutional devices selected by constitution makers seldom function quite in the way intended: a case in point is how an electoral system designed to foster inter-ethnic accommodation had the precisely opposite effect in Fiji, discussed in Chapter 8.

This is why our book starts with the *question* 'Can democracy be designed?' – rather than assuming that it can. To answer this question, we asked authors to provide focused empirical analyses of the politics of institutional design in six countries: South Africa, Uganda, Sri Lanka, Bosnia-Herzegovina, Ghana and Fiji.

The first four of these have emerged from, or continue to be immersed in, major armed conflicts. In South Africa and Uganda there have been simultaneous transitions from war to peace and from non-democratic to democratic governance – although in Uganda's case both transitions are arguably far from complete. In Bosnia-Herzegovina a kind of peace has been imposed from the outside, but there is no real democracy, and the conflict has been frozen rather than resolved. Sri Lanka is just beginning the process of negotiating an end to conflict. Uniquely among the six countries it has remained a liberal democracy ever since its independence from colonial rule. Both Ghana and Fiji have experienced periods of military rule and isolated episodes of political violence – but in contrast to the four other countries have been fortunate enough to avoid major armed conflict.

Authors were asked to undertake their analysis at three main levels. First, they were to examine how broad principles of democratic governance, as well as the desire to prevent conflict, were translated into specific institutional choices in particular national contexts. What were the political *processes* through which choices were made? Who made them and how? Was political reform driven by dominant interests, including those of state élites, large corporations or international donors? Or was it a response to broad popular constituencies or reform alliances, pressing for transformations from below? Was it externally driven and shaped by imported models of democratic governance, or was there genuine national ownership of the democratisation process? Did the pressures for change stem from crises in the legitimacy of existing political institutions, or even from violent conflict itself, opening the space for political reform (as arguably in South Africa)? Or did crises and violence harden social divisions, and make political transformations even more difficult to bring about?

Second, authors were asked to outline the structure of the new or newly redesigned democratic institutions and how in reality they functioned. In what ways did they open spaces for democratic politics, and how were they in turn reshaped by the latter? Was institutional reform mainly formal, or did it have a real impact on government accountability, popular participation or conflict resolution? To what extent were institutional changes reinforced (or undermined) by parallel changes in political and civil society? How far did institutional choices, for instance among varying power-sharing formulas or between different electoral systems, make a real *difference* to the norms and practices of politics?

Third, they were requested to assess the impact of democratic reforms. Did these reforms broadly speaking achieve what they were supposed to achieve? Or did they have non-anticipated or even counter-productive results: for instance sharpening rather than diminishing ethnic conflicts; promoting group cultural or religious rights at the expense of gender equality; or discouraging collective political action by women, minorities or the poor?

Fourth, they were asked to situate reforms in the wider historical context of a changing global political economy. How far was the impact of reforms shaped by political, economic and social forces beyond the control of constitution makers and elected politicians, such as exposure to global markets, long-term processes of economic growth or decline, or the spread of conflicts across national boundaries? Indeed, in all the countries examined in this book the complex politics of adjustment to a changing global economy has remained an important sub-text of the democratisation process.

In sum, the analysis of the national experiences considered in this volume is based on empirical accounts of how democratic institutions were introduced, and of how they have interacted with democratic – and not-so-democratic – politics. It takes into account the constraints and contradictions of democratisation in contexts of globalisation, poverty and violence. And it explores differences in the historical situations and experiences of the countries studied, and how they have shaped the politics of institutional choice.

The approaches followed by individual authors in pursuing these issues are not, however, uniform. Some have confined their analyses to the way particular institutional devices, such as electoral systems (in Fiji and Sri Lanka) or decentralisation (in Bosnia-Herzegovina), have been introduced, changing or failing to change political behaviour. Others have focused on the impact of institutional choices upon specific groups, including (in Sri Lanka and South Africa) women. Others, again, have painted a more broad-brush picture of constitutional and institutional change during transitions to democracy and from conflict.

The book starts with a conceptual chapter on democratic institutions and democratic politics by Robin Luckham, Anne Marie Goetz and Mary Kaldor. It argues that democracy tends to be constructed around three creative tensions. The first of these is that between democracy as a universal aspiration for popular self-rule and as a historically bounded form of governance in modern states, formed in the context of global capitalism ('liberal democracy', in other words).

The second is the relationship between democratic institutions and the diverse forms and discourses of democratic politics in particular national contexts. The chapter argues that democratic institutions only flourish if they are supported by active and broadly based democratic politics. But conversely the design and structure of democratic institutions also make a difference, by creating spaces for democratic politics and shaping how elected governments deal with substantive issues of participation, socio-economic justice and conflict.

The third creative tension, the authors argue, is between democracy and conflict. On one hand, conflicts over the allocation of values and resources are what democratic politics are all about. On the other hand, unresolved conflicts often exclude, disempower and breed violence, thus weakening or destroying democracy. Democracy can contribute to the prevention and resolution of violent conflict both through democratic institutions and through democratic politics. Institutions can create procedures under which conflict can be managed through negotiation and debate, rather than violence. Democratic politics can pose democracy, along with social justice, more inclusive government, the rule of law and other values as substantive political demands, to counter the narrower agendas of the conflicting parties.

How these creative tensions are resolved is greatly dependent upon the historical experience, socio-economic structure and political institutions of individual polities. The remainder of the book is devoted to case studies of the specific national contexts in which democracy was introduced or redesigned, and of the complex ways in which democracy facilitated the non-violent management of conflicts, or (in some cases) failed to do so.

The transition in South Africa, described by Shireen Hassim and David Pottie, brought to an end a protracted armed conflict stemming from the political exclusion of the black majority under the apartheid system. It was an especially clear-cut case of the entire political settlement being renegotiated in the institutional form of a new constitution. Among our case studies it presents the clearest relative 'success story' of both democratisation and conflict resolution. Yet the transition looks much smoother and more trouble-free with the benefit of hindsight than it was in reality: there were a number of critical junctures at which the whole process could easily have unravelled.

The chapter focuses upon the conditions which made this success story possible. The process of forging a new democratic constitution was crucial: the constitution was largely shaped through negotiation and compromise among local actors carrying different ideological histories and different political cultures, rather than imposed from above or unduly influenced by external actors. Bargains had to be struck with representatives of the outgoing apartheid regime, so as to end the political violence. Yet democratisation was made easier because political institutions were relatively well established (despite their exclusionary nature) and because there was already a vibrant civil society. The constitution-making exercise involved much popular consultation, and drew strength from strong traditions of grassroots politics engendered by the struggle for a non-racial democracy led by the African National Congress (ANC). It produced an inclusive constitutional framework which satisfied almost all the country's racial and ethnic groups, without parcelling up political authority among them, as in plural societies like Bosnia or Fiji. It also began, under considerable pressure from women's organisations, to address gender inequality in the public sphere.

In sum, the three most important ingredients of successful transition in South Africa were the relatively favourable internal political and societal conditions, the internally driven character of the process, and its relatively inclusive and participatory character. Even so, an enormous amount remains to be done to overcome the immense economic and social inequalities inherited from the apartheid system. Moreover, the reinsertion of the country into the circuits of the global economy acts as a further serious constraint on the capacity of democratic institutions to alleviate poverty and respond to emergent sources of insecurity and conflict.

The next two chapters present case studies of Uganda by Aaron Griffiths and James Katalikawe and of Ghana by E. Gyimah-Boadi. New constitutions were adopted following protracted authoritarian rule in both countries, as well as civil war in Uganda. In both, moreover, earlier attempts to reintroduce democratic governance had come to grief, though only in Uganda had this led to large-scale political violence.

These two countries present a story with many parallels in other developing countries. In each, governments pursued strategies of nation building and conflict resolution in multi-ethnic societies. These strategies depended heavily upon statist models of development and authoritarian modes of governance, under both military and civilian regimes. Statist economic policies were used to redistribute resources and buy the loyalty of diverse ethnic-regional and other political groups; authoritarian coercion was used to suppress dissent, notably when failing economies ceased producing the economic surpluses required to sustain redistributive programmes. However, a central question for comparative inquiry is why Ghana, despite many similarities to Uganda (a multi-ethnic state, agrarian discontents, a troubled political history of coups, military rule and failed constitutions, etcetera) has nevertheless escaped the large-scale major violence that has cast a deep shadow over the latter's post-colonial history.

In both countries, populist governments came to power in the 1980s – in Ghana through a coup and in Uganda by means of an armed insurrection – and implemented economic liberalisation programmes followed by political liberalisation. Both are considered 'success stories' by the donor community (though not necessarily by all their own citizens).

The constitutional settlement in Uganda involved a more elaborate process of popular consultation than its counterpart in Ghana, and arguably came up with a more innovative document. But it had certain crucial limitations, notably the continued prohibition of multi-party political competition, the *de facto* preservation by the National Resistance Movement (NRM) of its monopoly of power and the inability to settle the ongoing conflict in the North. In clear contrast, the outgoing Provisional National Defence Council (PNDC) government in Ghana not only orchestrated a return to multi-party democracy in 1992, but also held relatively freely contested multi-party elections, and was prepared to hand over power when the opposition eventually defeated President Rawlings in 1999.

The political dramas of constitution making in Uganda and Ghana were played out in tandem with externally driven market-oriented economic adjustments, as in South Africa. International donors attempted to shape the political reform process – although their influence had limits, illustrated by their inability to persuade the Museveni government in Uganda to modify its model of 'movement' or 'no-party' democracy. In

7

both countries economic adjustments have come with heavy social costs, potentially affecting their ability to consolidate democratic governance over the longer run. And, in both, elected governments have come under some pressure to play the old game of ethnically and regionally redistributive politics, with adverse impacts on their development policies.

President Museveni's argument has been that Uganda's 'no-party system' makes it easier to resist such pressures. The authors of the chapter on Uganda suggest that it may merely mean that redistributive politics takes place non-democratically, behind closed doors, in what has become a personalised presidential system – which may make it harder to ensure political stability and consolidate democratic governance in the longer run.

The central section of the book consists of three chapters on Sri Lanka, a country of especial interest because it is one of the post-colonial world's longest-established democracies. Universal franchise was introduced in 1931 and government changes have been achieved through the electoral process a number of times since independence in 1948. In addition Sri Lanka was for long considered an outstanding example of socially just, poverty-reducing development policies. Yet neither democracy nor relative social justice seem to have averted societal violence and civil war. The chapters on Sri Lanka explore the reasons why.

In her chapter Radhika Coomaraswamy provides an overview of the history of constitution making in Sri Lanka. Since independence the country has had three constitutions; and at present proposals for a new constitution are being debated, in order to resolve the armed conflict which has divided the country over the past two or three decades. She argues that each of the earlier efforts at constitutional reform has been politically partisan – designed by the government and party in power to produce political outcomes conducive to their interests, clouding the legitimacy of the constitution and undermining the principle of constitutionalism.

In addition to being politically partisan, the country's constitutions have been based on borrowed Western models. The Sri Lankan state and its politics have been majoritarian in both form and content, reinforced by the tendency of Sinhalese nationalist politicians to see democracy as a winner-takes-all system. A mono-ethnic constitutional design has denied political and ethnic minorities an effective voice in government, and aggravated the political conflicts of a multi-ethnic society.

Hence although Sri Lanka was often seen as a successful democracy, it has actually been characterised by the politics of exclusion, not only of minorities, but also of the country's alienated youth. This politics of exclusion has fostered two major class-based youth insurrections, together with a protracted secessionist war waged against the state by armed militants from the Tamil minority since the 1970s.

The chapter reviews a number of attempts to resolve these ethnic and class-based conflicts through constitutional and political reform. It questions how far such reform is now sufficient to resolve conflicts deeply embedded in the fabric of society by thirty years of violence, during which the 'politics of force' has become a prominent feature of Sri Lankan society. It thus casts doubt upon what can be achieved purely through constitutional design, and highlights some of the difficulties that may be faced by Sri Lanka's current peace process.

The second Sri Lanka chapter, by Kishali Pinto-Jayawardena, attempts to explain why Sri Lanka's redistributive social policies have largely failed to empower women, despite their visible presence in a handful of high-profile positions, including the presidency. It documents the very low representation of women in both national and provincial legislative bodies. It suggests that this under-representation of women stems from the interaction of a number of factors, including male biases in political parties and trade unions, societal expectations about the roles of women, and the perceptions of politics by women themselves, including leading women politicians. The widespread political violence has reinforced these biases, making it even more difficult for women to enter mainstream politics. Nor has the introduction of an electoral system based on proportional representation made any impact upon women's legislative representation – in sharp contrast to South Africa, where the impact of PR has been reinforced through affirmative action by political parties in selecting party lists.

Pinto-Jayawardena illustrates the problems faced by women in politics with the example of the Sinhala–Tamil Rural Women's Network (STRAWN) – a women's organisation which grew out of community development work and tried to contest the 1999 provincial elections with its own list of candidates. STRAWN faced immense difficulties running an electoral campaign, including threats of violence against its leaders. Not only did it fail to win many votes, but its participation in elections posed problems for its development work – illustrating the difficulties of civil society organisations in trying to influence mainstream politics.

The final chapter on Sri Lanka by Sunil Bastian deals with the political economy of electoral change in Sri Lanka, where proportional

9

representation was introduced in 1978 as part of a package of political reforms meant to concentrate political authority and facilitate the establishment of liberal capitalism in the economy. The establishment of capitalism, he argues, is an essentially political task, and the electoral system plays a crucial role both in élite competition for resources and in managing the social forces present in the electorate and represented in the legislature.

In his detailed analysis of electoral trends, Bastian demonstrates that the previous first-past-the-post system posed certain barriers to the further development of Sri Lankan capitalism. In Sri Lanka it tended to have a spatial bias against the core areas of capitalist development; it weakened the hold of political parties over their parliamentarians, resulting in political instability bringing governments down before their terms were over; it promoted 'manufactured' majorities, which favoured state capitalist economic policies; and it expanded the representation and power of the intermediate classes in the legislature. By the late 1970s these class forces were aligned behind a relatively extreme version of state capitalism, which tended to isolate Sri Lanka from the world economy.

But from 1977 the centre-right government, which won the elections in that year, began to introduce now-familiar structural adjustment policies in order to facilitate economic liberalisation and economic growth. Along with these economic reforms it also effected significant changes in the political system. These changes included a presidential rather than parliamentary form of government and a version of electoral proportional representation (PR), both of which Bastian argues were intended to break the previous political deadlock, which had impeded market-oriented capitalist development.

Hence the political and economic logic behind PR electoral reform was completely different from that in South Africa, where it was linked to the post-apartheid political project of creating a more inclusive polity. To be sure, Sri Lanka's reforms were brought in at more or less the same time that the alienation of the Tamil minority was coming to a head and escalating into armed conflict. They also had some impact on the trajectory of the conflict, in so far as they facilitated the concentration of state power, economic liberalisation and social inequality. But they were not introduced with the prime purpose of averting conflict; nor did they in fact stop it from spreading – if anything the reverse.

In contrast, Jon Fraenkel's case study of electoral reform in Fiji provides a poignant example of the perils of trying to avert potentially violent conflict – between the country's ethnic Fijian and Indo-Fijian communities – by constitutional engineering alone. Fiji is also a case where academics, who have become prominent in donor-supported efforts to design electoral institutions to dampen down ethnic conflict in plural societies, played a significant role in designing new electoral institutions – although the new constitution introduced in 1997 was also based on broad-based consultation of local stakeholders from all the country's communities, and reflected a widespread disenchantment with the politics of ethnic extremism. The 1997 constitution's electoral arrangements were based on a modified alternative vote (AV) system, designed to foster pre-election vote-pooling alliances and robust political coalitions among the more moderate parties representing Fijians and Indo-Fijians, whose representation in the legislature would thereby be enhanced.

Fraenkel starts his critique of this attempt at electoral engineering by questioning the assumptions behind the Constitutional Review Commission's analysis of the defects underlying the earlier system, and showing how this questionable analysis led to the proposals to introduce the AV preferential voting system. He then goes on to show that the new electoral system achieved none of the goals that the electoral engineers expected. The 1999 election elected a legislature that was not only far from representative relative to the different parties' share of the vote, but also defeated the moderates and brought to power an extremely unstable alliance between extremist parties from both the country's major communities.

This created a political impasse, which provided the pretext for the 2000 putsch by armed ethnic Fijian extremists. In the end further escalation of ethnic violence was averted by negotiations within and between the main communities, mainly outside the formal framework of political authority. Constitutional governance was restored under a modified version of the constitution, although the AV electoral system has been retained, and the political privileges of ethnic Fijians have been reinforced.

The chapter examines the reasons for this perverse outcome of institutional design. Fraenkel describes the complexity of the existing ethnic polarisation, and the reasons for the ability of the more extreme parties to manipulate the system. He argues that it was existing ethnic fractions that produced ethnically polarised politics; electoral arrangements had relatively little to do with it. And he suggests that there are no neat institutional or electoral arrangements for securing multi-ethnic systems of governance; a more appropriate and 'a more modest goal is an electoral system which does not exacerbate divisions'.

11

The final section of the book is devoted to two case studies of attempts to build democratic institutions capable of managing conflicts at the national and the local levels in Bosnia–Herzegovina. The Dayton Agreement, examined in a chapter by Marcus Cox, is a supreme example of constitution making from outside. Pressure from the international community to end hostilities dominated the process. Almost no attempt was made to secure popular or parliamentary endorsement; and the constitution entered into force as an annexe of the Agreement itself – in other words, as part of the peace treaty.

The Dayton Agreement created a loose federal structure with a minimum of central authority. Vast gaps opened up between two parallel constitutional systems: on one hand, the Dayton provisions, which were a 'compendium of contemporary thinking on conflict resolution'; on the other hand, the real politics of the three war-time para-states, which continued to be run by ethnic nationalist parties, mafias and military structures, with very little in the way of democratic accountability. The international mission set up to implement the Agreement has responded to the lack of progress in democratisation or peace building by intervening in all aspects of political life to break the influence of war-time structures, creating a *de facto* international protectorate. The latter has been double-edged – opening up limited spaces for ethnic reintegration and institution building, yet creating new obstacles to the emergence of genuinely democratic politics.

An important feature of the Dayton Agreement is its extraordinarily complex arrangements for the decentralisation of power between the different entities, cantons and municipalities of the new multi-ethnic state, considered by Vesna Bojicic-Dzelilovic. Federalism and decentralisation are widely seen as ways of bringing government closer to citizens and of managing conflict. But in Bosnia–Herzegovina they also tended to reinforce the societal cleavages responsible for the conflict, and arguably in some instances completed the work of ethnic cleansing.

The chapter contrasts power-sharing arrangements in two multi-ethnic municipalities: Mostar, where they failed to overcome hostility between members of the Croatian and Muslim communities; and Tuzla, where they were more successful. It shows how in Tuzla a beneficent cycle, in which cooperation among members of the different ethnic communities, a municipal economy relatively unaffected by the war, active civil society organisations, citizen participation in municipal government and the relative absence of political violence became mutually reinforcing. Decentralisation in Tuzla also helped preserve the political spaces in which this beneficent cycle could serve as a rallying point for efforts to create alternatives to ethnic politics and violence elsewhere in Bosnia-Herzegovina.

The contrasting experience of Mostar, however, questions the view that institutional design, the allocation of resources to local communities and the introduction of accountability mechanisms are enough by themselves to make decentralisation work. As the comparison with Tuzla suggests, other factors – such as the configuration of competitive party politics, the vitality of civil society and the strength of the local economy – will determine whether institutions can function as instruments of inter-ethnic accommodation.

References

Luckham, R. (1998) 'Are There Alternatives to Liberal Democracy?' in M. Robinson and G. White (eds.), *The Democratic Developmental State: Politics and Institutional Design*, Oxford: Oxford University Press.

Luckham, R. and G. White (eds.) (1996) *Democratization in the South: the Jagged Wave*, Manchester, Manchester University Press.

White, G. (1998) 'Constructing a Democratic Developmental State', in M. Robinson and G. White (eds.), *The Democratic Developmental State: Politics and Institutional Design*, Oxford: Oxford University Press.

Wood, E. M. (1995) *Democracy against Capitalism: Renewing Historical Materialism*, Cambridge: Cambridge University Press.

Notes

1 The dual character of democracy in both empowering and constraining subaltern groups in the context of capitalist development is emphasised by Wood (1995: Chapter 7), although she suggests that it may be only by reviving Athenian notions of direct or participatory democracy that its emancipatory potential can be realised.

2 This conception of the 'designers' of democratic institutions as modern Machiavellis is explored in Luckham and White (1996: 278–82) and in the context of the democratic developmental state by White (1998: 32–47); the latter in particular provides the initial conceptualisation upon which our programme of research was based.

13

1

Democratic Institutions and Democratic Politics

ROBIN LUCKHAM, ANNE MARIE GOETZ
AND MARY KALDOR

The last two decades have witnessed a dramatic increase in the number of countries describing themselves as democracies. Nearly everywhere, it has been argued, liberal representative democracy has been accepted as the best method of managing political affairs. This is, as Francis Fukuyama (1989) put it, the 'End of History'.

Yet the spread of democracy has been far from smooth. Authoritarianism, poverty, conflicts about identity and human rights violations are still the dominant characteristics of politics in large parts of the world. With a few exceptions, the spread of democratic institutions has been accompanied by public scepticism, even apathy, expressed in low voter turn-out, low membership of political parties and pervasive distrust of politicians.

Some of the challenges faced by both new and established democracies have to be understood, at least in part, in the context of globalisation. Liberal representative systems of governance are typically associated with the nation state and a definition of citizenship that is territorially bounded. Yet what appears to be the universal acceptance of such systems occurs at a moment when the efficacy of territorially based polities is called into question by the interconnectedness of political, social, and economic relationships across national boundaries.

In this chapter, we draw a distinction between institutions and politics and we argue that the spread of democratic institutions does not necessarily mean the spread of democratic politics.[1] The argument is organised around the following concerns which arise in contemporary debates on democracy:

- The meaning of democracy, including the distinction between democratic institutions and democratic politics;

- The extent or 'depth' of democracy. We consider how far the actual practice of democracy is consistent with aspirations for democracy, especially in terms of the way disadvantaged groups experience citizenship;

- The relationship between democracy and social equity. We ask whether democracy as a system can reconcile conflicting expectations regarding redistributive policies and economic growth;

- The conflict-management effectiveness of democracy: its capacity to promote the resolution of conflicts, through democratic institutions and debate, rather than violence.

Meanings and models of democracy

The term democracy, deriving from classical Greek, means rule (*Xratos*) by the people (*demos*). From the beginning, it has been a contested concept, arising historically from struggles against despotic rule and social injustice. That is, it was democratic politics which produced democratic institutions. Yet at the same time the institutions most associated with modern democracy – free elections, political and civil rights protected under the rule of law, and so on – were shaped through the efforts of dominant groups to regulate popular participation. They wished to ensure that democracy did not interfere with emerging capitalist markets, and did this by making a sharp distinction between the public sphere of politics and administration and the private sphere of the economy and family life (Wood 1995).

In the contemporary era, the democratic institutions of Western liberal democracies have assumed an increasingly paradigmatic character. In democratising countries in the East and South they are now widely (and in our view problematically: Parekh 1993) seen as the starting point for the construction of democratic politics, rather than the other way around.

Democratic institutions have been created in varying degrees to meet the following goals:

- To enable participation either directly or through elections;

- To avoid tyranny by autocratic rulers and (in some democratic systems) by the majority;

- To promote open and fair competition for power on the basis of the popular vote;

15

- To ensure the accountability of governments;

- To provide a forum for rational discussion of political problems and settlement of conflicting social interests.

Different models have maximised different goals. Broadly speaking, one may distinguish between popular or direct models of democracy, for which Athens is the paradigmatic example, and liberal representative models, for which the US constitution is the reference point.[2] The latter emerged at the end of the eighteenth century, and put the emphasis on political contestation, on rational discussion, and on avoiding tyranny. It was sometimes known as the republican model because it drew on the experience of republican Rome and the city states of Renaissance Italy more than democratic Athens. Kant, writing at the end of the eighteenth century, insisted that republicanism, which he contrasted with democracy, was the necessary condition for perpetual peace. He viewed England and America as republican, in contrast to post-revolutionary France. Republicanism meant checks and balances; democracy he equated with despotism.

The liberal representative model thus put far more emphasis on institutions than the Athenian model. Tyranny was to be avoided by control of the executive assured through the separation of powers and emphasis on individual rights. Citizenship was a more passive notion than under direct democracy. Citizens enjoyed rights to security, private property and liberty, but primarily as individuals rather than as members of groups and communities. The main form of participation was through elections. Rational discussion was to be achieved through the election of representatives who would debate the important issues of the day on behalf of the citizens.

Twentieth-century democracy brought about a sometimes contradictory fusion of the institutions of the liberal state with the politics of participatory democracy. In this sense it is the product of the two overlapping historical revolutions which established 'modern' polities.[3] The first was the bourgeois revolution, the second the political mobilisation of the broad mass of citizens, including the urban working class and women, behind demands which included the extension of the franchise to all adult citizens.

As Huber *et al.* (1997) have argued, this second democratic revolution not only increased citizen involvement in the affairs of government, but expanded the concept of citizenship itself to cover economic and social as well as political entitlements. That is to say, it introduced the idea of social democracy, not as an alternative system of rule to liberal representative democracy, but to ensure the responsiveness of the latter to demands for social justice. At the same time, the growth of mass political parties fostered new forms of active citizenship. Yet political parties were also electoral machines, channels for political patronage and vehicles for the political organisation of powerful socio-economic interests.

In societies where liberal institutions failed to take root, parties were frequently transformed into instruments of control. In the communist East, the second, 'popular' democratic revolution swallowed the first, 'liberal' revolution. The mass of citizens was mobilised by revolutionary parties, only to be subordinated by the latter without liberal institutions to protect against tyrannical governance. Hence post-communist countries face the formidable task of building liberal institutions as well as democracy, complicated still further by transitions from command to market economies.

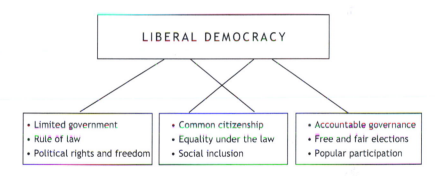

Figure 1.1 Liberal democracy

In partial contrast, most countries in the developing South gained their independence under the formal institutions of liberal democracy. This was not just because the latter were bequeathed by departing colonial powers, but also because their citizens demanded them. They were at least in part the product of democratic politics, as well as of the 'institutional transfer' of Western models. Even where displaced by authoritarian rule, the principle of democratic governance was never entirely abandoned. Frequently military dictators recognised their lack of popular legitimacy by proclaiming their support for constitutional government, the rule of law and eventual 'return to civilian rule'.

The collapse of the so-called 'people's democracies' in the East, and of

17

'developmental dictatorships' in the South has left no credible systemic alternative to liberal representative democracy. It has also changed the terms in which the latter is to be judged. Defenders of liberal democracy can no longer rest their argument on the narrow claim that it is the 'least bad' form of government. Instead it finds itself tested against the standards of the 'vast body of normative democratic theory and in the expectations of millions of ordinary citizens' [including their] 'long-subordinated ideals of equality, participation, accountability, responsiveness, and self-realization' (Schmitter 1994: 57)

According to our definitions, institutions are a socially constructed set of arrangements routinely exercised and accepted. Democratic institutions are in essence a set of arrangements for organising political competition, legitimating rulers and ensuring accountable governance, typically through free elections to determine the composition of the legislature and of the government (in other words, representative rather than direct democracy). They also imply a liberal state and limited government (hence *liberal* democracy: see Figure 1.1), in which the basic rules of governance are established by the constitution and the rule of law. Furthermore, democratic institutions are underpinned by common citizenship, in which the rights and freedoms of all citizens are equally protected under the law.

The dominant Western tradition of analysis holds that these institutions are the building blocks of democracy. According to Schumpeter, one of that tradition's most seminal thinkers, democracy is not 'an end in itself [but] a mere method that could be discussed rationally like a steam engine or a disinfectant' ... [being an] 'institutional arrangement for arriving at political decisions in which individuals acquire the power to decide by means of a competitive struggle for the people's vote' (1965: 284, 269). In this view, political contestation is the very crux of democracy, being the political counterpart of competition in the economy (Przeworski 1991). In the current conventional wisdom the test of the superiority of democracy is its capacity to deliver what Western donor institutions now term 'good governance' (World Bank 1992) – that is, to assure political stability, make rulers accountable, regulate the market and provide the collective goods citizens desire.

This Schumpeterian view can be distinguished from the notion that democracy is an end in itself: a creative and sometimes subversive process through which the aspirations of citizens can be expressed (Luckham 1998: 307–16), in which democratic politics and active citizenship are as crucial as democratic institutions. The distinction between democratic institutions and democratic politics parallels the distinction between formal or procedural democracy and substantive democracy, originally introduced by de Tocqueville. Formal democracy refers to the institutions, procedures or routines of democratic systems. Substantive democracy refers to the redistribution of power – the degree to which citizens can participate in the decisions which affect their lives (Kaldor and Vejvoda 1997).

Politics can be defined as the struggle or competition for power or for access to rulers and collective goods. Yet not all forms of politics are democratic, even inside the formal structures of democratic institutions. According to Beetham (1994), democratic political practices require not only political contestation, but also that contestation be tempered by certain basic moral and political principles, including popular control (over governments and political élites) and political equality (among all citizens). That is to say, they aim to hold democratic institutions to their democratic promise, by:

- ensuring open and effective challenges to governments and their policies through free and fair elections, the party system and other forms of political contestation;

- increasing citizen participation, so that the exercise of power at all levels of political authority is based so far as possible with citizens;

- maximising the accountability and transparency of the holders of political power and bureaucratic office, at all levels of government;

- guaranteeing equal political and civil rights for all citizens, together with the basic social and economic entitlements that enable them to fully exercise these rights;

- ensuring fully inclusive citizenship, based on respect for gender, cultural and other differences;

- providing accessible procedures through which these rights and entitlements can be guaranteed, not just through the courts, but also in day-to-day relationships with agents of the state;

- assuring effective citizen redress against infringements of rights by private (especially corporate) interests as well as by the state;

- increasing the accountability of such corporate interests, above all where they impinge upon the public domain and citizens' rights.

Democratic politics as thus defined include, but are broader than, the processes of political contestation which animate liberal democracies.

19

They depend upon a culture of participation, including a range of mechanisms – pluralistic media, an active civil society, competing political parties, etcetera – through which all citizens can, if they want, acquire a political voice. It is through democratic politics that governments and, more broadly, democratic institutions acquire legitimacy, are made accountable to their citizens, and can in turn regulate powerful private interests.

This definition of democratic politics includes the capacity of citizens (acting independently or through government) to hold powerful private interests as well as agents of the state to account,[4] for three main reasons. First, in a globalised world the traditional distinctions between state and market, public and private, around which liberal democratic institutions have been constructed, have become blurred as corporate interests have rolled back the frontiers of the public domain (Wood 1995; Held 1997). Second, democratic politics cannot be confined to the terrain of national government, when the real levers of political power may lie elsewhere – for instance in the corporate economy, mass media and international financial institutions. Third, recent years have seen the emergence of new forms of democratic politics linking grassroots campaigns across national boundaries and developing norms of 'global governance' in order to influence the behaviour not only of national governments, but also of transnational corporations and international institutions.[5]

But here we add some notes of caution. First, neither democratic politics nor democratic institutions can be replacements for each other. The pitfalls of engineering democratic institutions are amply illustrated in the case studies presented in this book. But equally, attempts to construct popular or participatory 'alternatives' to liberal democracy based on grassroots empowerment of ordinary citizens, as in Tanzania, Nicaragua and Uganda, have not proved sustainable when they have neglected democratic institutions (Luckham 1998; Oloka Onyango 1989, 1995). Hence, although we stress the role of democratic politics, the crucial issue is how it can enliven democratic institutions; and how the latter can in turn foster democratic politics.

A further caveat is that different strands of democratic thought emphasise different aspects of democratic politics, and these may clash. Some, as we have seen, regard political contestation as the essence of democratic politics; others emphasise inclusion and participation. Some, again, would confine democratic rights and freedoms to the political or public sphere – in contrast to those who argue (as we do) for an expanded conception of rights under which freedom from poverty and gross social inequality are seen as basic entitlements of democratic citizenship.

Finally, in a politically and culturally diverse world, in which globalisation recreates social differences as fast as it breaks them down, there is not, and probably cannot be, universal agreement on the goals of democratic politics, nor on the institutions which can best express them. Western liberal democracy, to be sure, is currently the paradigmatic form of democratic governance. But there are immense dangers in imposing it uncritically on non-Western societies with scant regard to the latter's own historical experience of struggles against tyrannical rule and efforts to develop their own forms of democratic politics.

Democratising democracy:[6] the politics of inclusion

It is quite possible to have accountability in ... the high politics of the state, honest rulers and free elections, and yet profound injustice or irresponsibility in the deep politics of society, that is, the relations between rich and poor, powerful and weak. (Lonsdale 1986: 130)

Existing literature on democratisation tends to give pride of place to the high politics of state rather than the deep politics of society. It also tends to concentrate more on consolidation of democratic institutions than on democratic politics in the sense outlined earlier. Institutional development tends to be seen as a good in itself. Élite pacts defining 'rules of the game' are given more attention than the political struggles of marginalised groups, including women, minorities and the poor. The latter enter the picture mainly when they can disrupt the 'normal' functions of democratic institutions and hence have to be accommodated by the latter. Their incorporation has tended to be seen as a solution to the problems of political order or governability in fledgling democracies, rather than as a requirement of democracy *per se*.

Such a preoccupation with stabilising democratic contestation among élites makes a certain amount of sense in fragile democracies emerging from authoritarian governance or armed conflict. Yet it is not the approach followed here. Instead democratisation is approached the other way around – by starting from the deep politics of society[7] and asking what they imply for the high politics of the state. Of course, one should not ignore the difficulties of consolidating institutions, nor the problems of assuring stable, effective governance, including how it may be complicated by democratic politics itself. But we prefer to take the politics of inclusion as our starting point, rather than starting with

21

institutions and asking what residual spaces are left in which citizens may exercise their entitlements. Hence, we focus on four main questions:

- How can the basis of citizenship be expanded to give citizens (especially women, the poor and the unorganised) a more effective political voice and stake in government?

- How can the accountability of governments and their responsiveness to citizens' interests and needs be increased?

- How can democratic institutions be designed so as to create expanded spaces for political contestation and debate?

- How, at the same time, can democratisation from below be harmonised with stable, effective governance, without which it is difficult to translate the entitlements of citizenship into policies that actually benefit the mass of citizens?

There are both negative and positive reasons for giving priority to these issues. On the negative side there is an apparent chasm between democratic aspirations and democratic practice in most real-world democracies. The well-known 'democracy deficits' of established Western democracies include under-representation of women, voting systems which skew electoral outcomes, majoritarian governments which ignore minority interests, non-accountable, non-transparent bureaucracies, and the diminished policy space available in globalised economies (Beetham 1994; Beetham *et al.* 2002). Cynicism about democracy, voter apathy and the decline of the traditional mass parties have become so widespread that they seem to call the entire democratic project into question at the moment of its triumph.

Democratisation in the developing South and post-communist East, too, has largely failed to live up to its initial promise. In a distressingly large number of cases, it has merely created what Collier and Levitsky (1997) term 'democracies with adjectives': 'low intensity democracy', 'patrimonial democracy', 'democradura' ('hard' democracy), 'illiberal democracy', 'no-party democracy', 'guided democracy', 'tutelary democracy', 'semi-democracy', etcetera.[8]

In some cases democracy is diminished by the absence of one or another of its formal attributes, such as full political contestation or civil liberties. In others the formal attributes are in place but there is a lack of substantive democracy, due for instance to political corruption, clientalism or the absence of a culture of participation. Often there are elected governments which lack the effective power to govern, either because real political power lies elsewhere (for instance with the military in some transitional democracies), or because they are hemmed in by external economic constraints (such as IMF/World Bank conditionalities), or because of political instability and violent conflict.

All this raises fundamental questions about the meaning and quality of democracy, not just in fragile, contested new democracies like Mozambique, Guatemala or Russia but also in longer-established ones like Sri Lanka, India[9] or even the USA[10] – where democratic institutions may coexist with political violence, human rights abuses, discrimination against minorities, excessive influence of military and security services and non-accountability of public officials.

An important tradition of 'democracy realism' in democratic theory holds that such deficits are normal features of representative democracy. Being above all a system of political competition, the latter does not encourage, nor is it intended to encourage, high popular participation in the affairs of government, so it is argued.[11] To be sure, governments are legitimised by submitting themselves to the vote. Elections, together with a constitutional state and the rule of law, prevent tyranny. Yet democratic institutions do not stand or fall by their success or failure in empowering citizens, enabling participation or assuring economic and social justice. On the contrary, disputes generated by the unequal distribution of wealth and power have always been the stuff of democratic politics. What distinguishes the latter from other forms of politics is that these disputes are settled through the competitive struggle for the people's vote and not through coercion or violent conflict.

'Development realists' like Leftwich (1996) likewise downplay the democratic shortcomings of real-world democracies, but for slightly different reasons: that democratic contestation itself may undermine the political and macroeconomic stability required for growth, by precipitating frequent government changes, or through populist mobilisation against economic stabilisation and adjustment policies. The cause of economic growth is best served, so it is argued, by limited democracies, controlled for long periods either by a dominant ruling party (as in Botswana and Singapore) or by stable coalitions (as in Malaysia or Mauritius), even though these systems do not necessarily live up to the (allegedly unrealistic) standards of Western models.

Paradoxically, democracy and development realists share common ground with certain radical critiques which highlight the limited scope for democratic politics in contemporary liberal democracies. These latter argue that democratic institutions are configured around a divide between the state and the capitalist marketplace, which severely limits the room for manoeuvre of elected governments, particularly in a globalised world economy. Far from being a benign or neutral space in which the interests of the poor and powerless can be articulated, civil society often reproduces the class, gender and racial hierarchies of capitalist states. Moreover, systems of representation are explicitly designed to exclude as well as to include by restricting political choice to voting in periodic elections.[12]

Such critiques are salutary correctives to the tendency to see liberal democracy and civil society as universal panaceas. They highlight the problems of measuring democratic performance against over-idealised models of democracy. And they call attention to potentially difficult trade-offs between democratisation and other goals like development, social justice or indeed the stability of democratic institutions themselves.

Nevertheless, they may create unwarranted pessimism about democracy and its capacity to open spaces for debate and ensure government accountability and responsiveness to citizens. It may therefore be preferable to start from a more disaggregated (and realistic) analysis of how democracy works. Sklar (1983, 1987) invented the term 'democracy in parts' to characterise the survival of democratic spaces in authoritarian systems due, for instance, to semi-autonomous courts and legal systems; to non-intimidated press and media; or to civil society organisations still able to challenge government. He used the concept both to question the idea that authoritarianism was monolithic, and to initiate a discussion of how democratic politics could commence without waiting for the formal establishment of democratic institutions.

A somewhat different approach is called for now that liberal democracy has become the paradigmatic form of governance almost everywhere. The idea of democracy in parts may be used to provide a differentiated account of the quality of real-world democracy, based on an inventory of 'democracy deficits', as provided in Table 1.1 (pp. 26–7). The first two columns of the table distinguish between the deficits of formal democratic institutions and those associated with the lack of democratic politics. The rows of the table identify four broad levels at which deficits may appear.

First, democracy means little to ordinary citizens ('hollow citizenship') if they do not enjoy equal rights and entitlements as citizens: either because constitutional and legal arrangements fail to guarantee these rights; or because they are excluded from the public sphere due to gender discrimination,[13] societal inequality, lack of organisation, cultures of intolerance or violence.

The inability of citizens to hold governments and political élites accountable for their use of power (weak vertical accountability) is a second crucial form of democracy deficit. This may stem from procedural defects such as may occur in voting systems or decentralisation provisions. Or it may reflect weak societal support for democracy – citizens may have little effective choice between alternative political programmes; civil society may be weak and divided; or the power of dominant economic interests may be disproportionate.

A third type of democracy deficit is on the terrain of high politics and manifests itself in the weak horizontal accountability (O'Donnell 1998) of overpowerful and potentially tyrannical executives *vis-à-vis* the legislature or judiciary. This may be due to weak constitutional and legal checks and balances – but it may also be because they are circumvented by government patronage, corruption, judicial inertia, weak opposition parties or coopted media.

Fourth are the international accountability dilemmas associated with globalisation. Both national governments and indeed international institutions often lack the formal mandate to deal with pressing global issues. Moreover, the policy space within which they can take decisions has shrunk due to global economic forces or the power of multinational enterprises, making it even more difficult for citizens to hold them to account.

If these democracy deficits tend to be less glaring than those of authoritarian systems, democracies nevertheless vary between those where deficits are so deep that democratic institutions are little more than a formality, and those whose governments remain (despite their shortcomings) in some real sense accountable to their people.

Where, then, can democratic politics start? How can it begin to close these deficits? Liberal democracy's own institutions and procedures provide an entry point, in that they create spaces for political debate and decision. But they are not the only spaces that are open. How they are used depends on whether citizens themselves can be mobilised for collective political action.

As shown in the third column of Table 1.1, there are several forms of democratic politics and many different political arenas in which they arise. First there are those forms of collective action and organisation that constitute individuals as equal, active and responsible citizens. The notion of citizenship is at the core of discussions about participation in democratic societies, and articulates the defining features of the relationship between individuals, the state and the market.

In its purely formal sense, citizenship vests in individuals the right to participate in electoral processes – to choose leaders through the ballot,

Table 1.1 Democracy Deficits and Democratic Politics

	Democracy Deficits		Spaces for Democratic Politics
	In formal constitutional and political arrangements	In Substance or Practices of Power	
Citizenship	• Socially or ethnically exclusive definitions of citizenship • Poorly protected civil and political rights • Legal/political barriers to freedom of expression and organisation • Non-recognition of social and economic entitlements • Access to legal and administrative systems skewed against minorities, the unorganised, the poor	• Major social inequities (class, gender, regional, religious, ethnic etc). • Exclusion from the public sphere of women, minorities etc. • *De facto* disenfranchisement of the poor due to lack of resources and organisation • Uncivil society: cultures of intolerance, lack of respect for difference • Violence, intimidation, especially against marginalised groups	• Grassroots organisation (in villages, slums, of women etc.) • Both class-based (e.g. TUs, peasants) and new (gender, environment etc.) social movements • Non-exclusive identity politics (minority rights or ethnic associations etc.) • Participatory development initiatives • 'Islands of civility' in conflict zones
Vertical Accountability of Rulers to Citizens	• Elections not free and fair • Electoral systems distort outcomes or disenfranchise minorities • Weak or absent formal accountability procedures • Over-centralisation of constitution and structures of governance • Few contact points between civil society groups and political/administrative structures	• Electorates have little effective choice between alternative political programmes • Few autonomous, effective, broadly based civil society groups • Weak interest aggregation by political parties, especially of interests of the poor and marginalised • Civil and political society reproduce hierarchies of class, gender, race etc. • Political processes weakened and social capital destroyed by violent conflict	• Consensus on rules of political game • Issue-based, non-zero sum politics, not based on gender, racial or ethnic hierarchies • Synergies between strong civil society groups and political parties • Effective, internally democratic parties • Inclusive forms of corporatism, responsive to pressure from below • Robust regional/local/municipal democracy

Horizontal Accountability	• Majoritarianism: politics as a zero sum game • Non-recognition by constitution of major regional and social diversities • Weak constitutional checks and balances • Rule of law absent or weak • Executive not sufficiently accountable to legislature • Governmental secrecy, lack of transparency • Weak democratic control of military, police and intelligence bodies	• A narrowed public domain: diminished scope for collective political action • Patrimonial politics: government manipulation via patronage, ethnicity etc. • Endemic corruption • Political processes suborned by élite economic and social interests • Judiciary weak or co-opted • Weak opposition parties • Media lacking in independence • Legacies of military/authoritarian governance	• Societal consensus supporting supremacy of constitution, rule of law • Robust parliamentary processes • Plural sources of wealth, status and power • Strong traditions of regionalism • Civil society groups able to articulate democratic values (rights groups, anti-corruption campaigns etc.) • Independent, broadly based media
International Accountability	• Key decisions made by largely unaccountable international bodies (IMF, World Bank, UN Security Council, major corporations etc.) • Democracy deficits within these international bodies • Constraints on national sovereignty built into non-renegotiable ainternational greements (e.g. World Trade Organisation)	• Vulnerability in international markets • Hegemony of international firms • Exposure to capital flight • Donor pressure via conditionality etc. • Difficulties of aggregating democratic politics across national boundaries	• Donor support for political reform (despite its contradictions) • International human rights law and practice • Embryonic global civil society (e.g. human rights, development and environment NGOs) • South–South and South–East political alliances

to stand for public office – and vests in the state the power to tax, control the armed forces and govern. But such a formulation does not conceive of participation as an ongoing process of discursive debate and real contestation. The reshaping of democracy during the twentieth century to encompass a broader set of entitlements that individuals could claim as part of their citizenship rights highlighted citizenship as practice rather than mere status. It also began to challenge existing conceptions of the public sphere and its reinforcement of gender and other hierarchies.

Citizenship both determines and is shaped by the political opportunities for citizens to gain access to the public sphere and hold governments and state élites accountable. This is clearly easier where there is broad consensus on the rules of politics, where it is not seen as a zero-sum game, and where it is not dominated by gender, racial or ethnic hierarchies. Government accountability not only depends on the organisation of the public sphere itself – how far there is open government, whether power is decentralised, and so on. Even more, it depends on the ability of citizens to insist upon accountability when governments resist it. This is normally facilitated by factors such as the existence of civil society groups, organised and internally democratic political parties, and robust traditions of local democracy.

Third, plural sources of political power and legitimacy can counter-balance the power of governments and state élites. This is easier where there are well-established constitutional and legal systems and/or robust traditions of parliamentary and political debate. Independent civil society groups like human rights or anti-corruption groups, willing and able to stand up to the state and to insist on standards of public morality, accountability and performance, are also vital (White 1996: 185–6). Some would argue that state power can only be kept in check if there exists a strong 'bourgeois' civil society based on independent concentrations of wealth, status and power that are not excessively dependent upon the state. But these in turn tend to reinforce social and economic inequalities, which conflict with democracy's premise of equal citizenship. Contradictions between political pluralism and political equality – and their societal preconditions – are enduring sources of tension in most real-world democracies.

Finally, the international system can also create spaces for democratic politics. Developments in international law, together with cross-national political alliances between NGOs and civil society groups, can be used to counteract some of the otherwise negative impacts of globalisation. International support for capacity building in civil society, or for human rights bodies, may foster internally based struggles for democracy, especially if it eschews the common donor preoccupation with formal democracy and the heavy-handed use of political conditionality.

Democracy and entitlements: the politics of pro-poor policies

Below we consider the policy effectiveness of democracies from the point of view of the poor. In other words, how far does the more egalitarian distribution of political power implied by democracy lead to state action to provide resources and opportunities to the poor? We focus on the politics of promoting redistributive policies through institutions and political processes which are linked to dominant class interests – the politics of scheming for the poor, in Ascher's phrase (1984), which has an obvious resonance with our own conceptualisation of democratic politics.

There is a huge literature, both theoretical and empirical, on 'developmental democracy', including relationships between democracy and growth, and democracy and equality.[14] Democracies in the developing world are just as capable of creating the conditions for capitalist growth as authoritarian regimes, but, as Moore and Putzel observe, they may be 'no better than the non-democracies at poverty reduction' (1999: 7). However, Dreze and Sen's (1989) well-known finding that famines do not occur in democracies (what they call systems of political pluralism) suggests that competitive politics and liberal rights and freedoms do at least facilitate public action against the most extreme expressions of human deprivation.

The policy effectiveness of democracies for the poor depends upon how governments manage the familiar 'growth versus equity' tension. Goldsworthy describes the tension between 'order' and 'participation' as an enduring political dilemma in development: 'if, as is not implausible, concentration of power is an aid to growth but dispersal of power is an aid to distribution, how can we try to resolve the two?' (1984: 567). Phrased differently, this is about a tension between efficient governance and responsive governance. It is not possible to have responsiveness to the poor without the generation of wealth. But in some democracies, it is perfectly possible to have strong institutional capacity and wealth creation without social equity, up to a limit imposed by the social instability which widespread destitution can cause.

Despite democracy's commitment to equal citizenship, there is an inherent élite bias in state economic and social policies, given the

29

political weakness of the poor in competing for power and demanding responses to their needs. Analysts of public administration have always pointed out that any policy to redistribute resources away from privileged groups attracts more bureaucratic and social opposition than purely regulatory policies or policies which distribute resources from a new or external source (Lowi 1964; Thomas and Grindle 1990). This problem has received particular attention in discussions of land reform (Ascher 1984; Kohli 1986), or of pro-poor spending as part of economic reform and structural adjustment agendas (Nelson 1989).

As Nelson suggests, resistance by privileged groups to pro-poor measures increases to the degree that:

- the proposed resource transfer is seen as zero-sum (taking power, privilege, or resources from the rich), long-term, and large (hence there are very few convincing examples of land reform in democracies);

- the target group is large (as opposed to small or 'deserving' but powerless, as in the case of children, widows or the disabled);

- extensive institutional change is proposed (such as reorienting agricultural extension services to address the needs of women farmers);

- there are no opportunities to use pro-poor measures for political patronage. Thus universal social welfare programmes are less appealing than targeted programmes which provide a package of benefits which local leaders can deliver to their constituencies.

However, in their recent analysis of élite perceptions of poverty, Moore and Putzel (1999: 21–8) posit that economic divisions do not mechanically dictate political interests. Élites may develop a commitment to poverty reduction, depending upon:

- their recognition of poverty reduction as a public good, because of an appreciation of the relationship between poverty and corrosive social problems which affect élites – such as crime, disease or social unrest;

- whether deprivation is conceptualised purely in income terms, or in terms of morally laden ideas about national integrity and a caring society, which are more likely to attract élite support;

- whether common interests are recognised between groups of the poor and élites, for instance on the basis of ethnic or religious affinities;

- whether there is political mileage to be had from generous national pro-poor gestures.

The point is that effective redistributive measures are not simply a matter of the poor generating enough political pressure to demand redistribution. They require ruling classes which are open to social equity concerns, and a state with the institutional capacity to break the connections between venal politicians, rapacious business interests and compliant bureaucrats. Indeed, the efficiency, coherence and probity of the state determine whether associations of subalterns will see any profit in engaging with the state at all. Public policies to promote the productivity, rights to land, employment or welfare of the poor can create an enabling environment within which the poor can mobilise to secure their access to these rights and work together to hold the state accountable (Moore and Putzel 1999: 12–17).

In sum, democracy's capacity to resolve tensions between 'order' and 'participation' so as to respond to the needs of the poor cannot be assumed; it must be organised. It often requires changes in a wide range of administrative and political institutions. It involves the state in correcting for market 'failures' – or compensating for the fact that markets can thrive on certain levels of social inequality. Below we consider some of the institutional and other conditions which can foster such politics of 'scheming for the poor'.

The nature and institutional make-up of the state

At issue here is the 'strength' or capacity of the state to act against vested interests at all levels of policy making and implementation, in order to take up mandates for social equity and generate coherent social policies, whilst maintaining macroeconomic stability and growth.

Leadership is crucial and plays differing roles under presidential and parliamentary systems of governance in constructing popular mandates for social equity policies. Strong presidential government can sometimes avoid the dilution and erosion which come through protracted debate and interest-group pressure. A recent example from Uganda is President Museveni's bold universal primary education initiative in 1997. Although one can question the initiative's financial, let alone pedagogic, soundness, it sliced through what might otherwise have been years of political debate and bureaucratic footdragging.

At the same time, there are enormous risks to over-centralised leadership and 'delegative democracy'. Parliamentarianism, in contrast, combines executive and legislative power, helps to organise consensus

31

and can give pro-poor politics a more enduring institutional basis than presidential initiatives. Yet some variants of parliamentarianism (like the British) can be just as prone to centralisation as presidential systems. Others, in contrast, can produce stalemated governance, lacking clear lines of accountability, especially where there is a fragmented party system, as in India.

In theory, administrative decentralisation provides local communities with more direct access to service providers, and decentralised politics strengthens the relationship between voters and their representatives. This should make government more responsive to the priorities of local communities, contributing, although somewhat indirectly, to poverty reduction. But decentralisation alone does not address the political weakness of the socially excluded. Away from the scrutiny of central authorities, local class, ethnic, racial or patriarchal tyrannies can sometimes be more extreme. As suggested in a recent study of governance and poverty in Uganda:

> poorer people usually have as little influence in their local settings as they do in the national political arena, and sometimes substantially less ... largely obscured from the scrutiny of either the media or public advocacy groups, local political environments frequently reduce the incentives for élites to reorient their priorities. (Goetz and Jenkins 1998: 10)

Paradoxically, a certain degree of 're-centralisation' may be required to ensure that the needs of the poor are not neglected, and, indeed, such a process is occurring now in Uganda. In some cases where decentralisation is seen to be responding to the interests of the poor, this may reflect the influence of other factors: for instance, in the Indian states of West Bengal and Kerala, the organisation of the poor through a relatively disciplined centralised socialist party has contributed to their capacity to resist the control of local overlords (Bardhan 1998: 192).

Policy choices and implementation systems in policy areas like tax reform, social policy, labour policy (Weyland 1997, 1996) and land reform (Ascher 1984; Kohli 1986) are generally seen as crucial to equity-enhancing efforts. Taxation both raises revenue for pro-poor spending, and engages wealthy groups in supporting broader social development goals in the interest of national stability and social equity. Land reform and social and labour policies can increase the productive capacities of the poor, compensate for market failures and promote the human capital development of the poor. For such policies to favour disadvantaged groups, they need to bring them disproportionate benefits – and this is done through progressive taxation, targeted social spending, minimum wage measures, and land reform which gives priority access to the poor.

But, as noted earlier, policies which involve resource transfers tend to arouse great resistance. Progressive taxation thus requires the politically engineered consent and cooperation of wealthier groups. Coherent labour policy which benefits most poorer producers, as opposed to privileged skilled workers, requires pressure from broad-based labour associations as well as politically effective associations of poor farmers, informal sector workers, domestic workers, and so on. Targeted social spending – whether it is increased welfare payments for subsidised school fees or childcare for poor working women – requires greater state capacity than systems of universal benefits. Moreover, benefits from targeted programmes are easily captured by state élites for use in clientalistic networks.

The general coherence of the public administration is key to poverty reduction. Without it, the pursuit of narrow departmental interests can lead to the neglect of broader state goals such as fiscal responsibility and social equity, and lead to what Weyland (1997) characterises as 'every agency for itself, and the Finance Ministry against all', in which demands from politically powerful ministries such as defence prevail over politically weaker areas like education, health or agriculture.

Democracies have a range of institutions to enforce accountability measures, and to influence government in the long stretches between elections; but typically these are beyond the reach of the poor. The poor rarely have the means to prosecute their grievances through lobbying of politicians or through the legal system. It is particularly difficult for them to challenge corrupt practices, which are among the greatest obstacles to the efficient delivery of development resources, dramatically limiting the impact of anti-poverty programmes. Reform initiatives which seek to tackle corruption by transferring power from state to market agents are not always successful (Harriss-White and White, 1996); more to the point, they can end up transferring costs of basic service delivery to the poor.

However, there are institutional and procedural choices which can help empower the poor to participate in policy debates, to challenge corruption, and to demand accountability. The current Right to Information Campaign in India demonstrates that asserting the public's right to information about government spending is a potentially powerful means of breaking both bureaucratic secrecy and corruption at the local level (Jenkins and Goetz 1999). Transparency in the posting of local budgets, recruitment measures, and local tenders can help engage citizens in monitoring public sector probity. Public hearings, for instance on the environmental or social impact of industrial or commercial developments, can enable groups to engage with policy makers more directly than through the formal political process.

The strength of subaltern groups and the organisation of political competition

Constraints on collective action by the poor are imposed by their lack of material and political resources. A range of different forms of organisation, not necessarily overtly political, can, however, improve their chances of influencing decision making, at least at the local level. Village cooperatives and development committees, or urban unions of informal sector traders or transporters, for instance, can stand up to the interests of the rich, particularly since they have some leverage within the production system. But, for all that many activists and writers continue to insist on wide political participation by the poor as the key to effective policy in their interests, many also recognise the limitations of efforts which put the full onus on the poor to defend their own interests. As Harrison (1980: 297) noted two decades ago:

> it is not easy to organise the poor to take their share in decision making....
> The culture of silence is deep-seated. Even if grassroots organisations are
> formed they are easily dominated by the professionals, managers, and
> bureaucrats.... People may become active around one particular urgent
> issue, yet lapse into apathy when it is solved.

Political parties can offer subaltern groups a voice in decision making, depending on their class constitution and ideology. Party systems determine important features of a state's capacity to provide a stable regulatory environment, efficient institutions, and responsiveness to the poor. Where parties have broad memberships and can organise across a range of social interests, they can generate more inclusive agendas which take the interests of the poor on board; but where they have narrow social bases and identity-based interests, this can exacerbate social conflict and generate clientalistic politics. Much depends upon the broader political culture, and on whether there is a shared basis of liberal democratic values in political competition. The number of parties also makes a difference to the capacity of party systems to produce effective policy. Too many competing parties, unless they are able to form stable and majority coalitions, can make the definition and implementation of long-term policies more difficult. Coalitions have electoral incentives to promote national goals rather than catering to specific sectors, regions, or class fractions, as small parties with limited bases of support are tempted to do (Weyland 1997). They can provide the executive branch with the support necessary for policy reforms favouring underprivileged groups, and release it from having to buy support through patronage.

Corporatist alliances and policies of social inclusion

Certain corporatist arrangements can provide subaltern groups with an effective voice in policy making. Those featuring in Chile's democratic transition have been held up as a model route to both growth and social equity. Key to their effectiveness has been the broad social base of official representatives of both business and labour. On the business side, this has promoted compliance with policies such as tax increases to finance social spending and, eventually, social stability. On the labour side, it has encouraged wage restraint and enabled labour to moderate long-repressed demands, and hence helped the government avoid a populist trap. Desire to increase union membership to make up for the years of union suppression under Pinochet has focused the attention of labour peak associations on poorer workers. This has broadened their membership base, strengthened their bargaining power and legitimacy, and enabled them to pursue policies (such as a minimum wage) with a major impact on poorer sections of the labour force (Weyland 1997). Corporatist negotiations have been facilitated by a broad and stable ruling coalition of centre and left parties which has prioritised equity-enhancing reforms in the context of healthy economic growth.

However, corporatism is rarely so effective in developing countries. Weyland (1996) contrasts Chile with Brazil, where fragmentation and rivalry characterise not just business and labour, but the entire party system as well. The absence of encompassing organisation has meant that each group has pursued narrow self-interests at the expense of collective social goals, with sectoral business associations unwilling to contemplate equity-enhancing sacrifices such as tax reform and targeted social policy. A fragmented and unstable party system has oriented politicians to protecting their personal political turf rather than focusing on longer-term, collective problems. All parties have sought privileges through special concessions from the state, transforming a corporatist system into a clientalistic one.

The extent to which corporatist negotiations can generate poverty-reduction policies depends upon the breadth of interests spoken for by labour representatives, the organisational coherence of parties to corporatist negotiations, and, more generally, the importance of industry

35

in the country's economy. In most developing countries, labour unions represent just a fraction of the country's workers, rarely the poorest, and rarely rural workers. Nor do they represent other major social groups that are typically low on political influence, such as women or ethnic minorities. In South Africa, efforts have been made to acknowledge such groups in a fourth chamber of the National Economic and Development Labour Council (NEDLAC), the country's corporatist negotiating forum. However, the NGOs and other civil society groups in this fourth chamber do not have the same rights of negotiation and veto as business, government, or labour. Nor, since they do not have as much control over their memberships as do fee-paying member organisations, can they make meaningful threats or promises in negotiations.

External policy intervention versus state promotion of pro-poor policies

Another factor shaping the path democratic governments steer between efficiency and responsiveness is the extent to which they are subject to policy interference from external actors. Mkandawire argues that IMF and World Bank economic stabilisation and adjustment packages in Africa have created 'choiceless democracies' in which 'the uniformalisation of what are considered "fundamentals" in economic policy limits the range of policy options for democratic regimes' (1999: 119). Features of globalisation such as the mobility of capital, shifts in the terms of trade and growing debt burdens constrain national creativity in addressing poverty problems. There is often pressure to pander to business interests by cutting corporate taxes, curbing employment rights, or limiting the state's obligation to provide social protection. Some observers play down such problems and insist that the pressures for democratisation which accompany globalisation discourage governments from succumbing to pressures from capital to abandon social concerns (Moore and Putzel 1999: 7). Indeed, the international financial institutions (IFIs) and donors themselves promote poverty reduction programmes – sometimes, however, with scant regard to the capacity of governments to implement and win popular support for them. In Africa in particular, the combination of globalisation and economic stabilisation tends to rule out the 'many intricate political compromises that may not always meet the exigencies of economic rationality' but which are critical to democratic politics and to poverty reduction (Mkandawire 1999: 121).

One of the basic points about democratic political practices is that what they can make, they can unmake too. Social consensus in favour of equity can be overturned by passing political events, as well as by factors beyond the control of individual governments, such as international financial flows, recessions or market shifts. Coalitions can dissolve, powerful leaders can be lost. Reforms which provide socially excluded groups with resources can end up creating new policy élites that will try to monopolise access to their new-found privileges. The few important cases that do stand out of democratically achieved, broad-based social welfare and equity are proof of this. In Sri Lanka, Costa Rica, Jamaica and the state of Kerala in India, policy gains for the poor have had to be struggled over and won back periodically. And in Sri Lanka at least, both pro-poor policies and subsequent market-oriented economic adjustments have been implemented in ways that have reinforced the conflict between the country's Sinhala majority and the Tamil minority.

Democracy and identity-based conflicts: problem or solution?

Do identity-based conflicts pose particular difficulties for democracy?

For long periods of its history Europe answered the question of state formation through the nation state paradigm: a nation is a cultural community living on a common territory, and its self-determination requires that it should create its own state. However, as Mamdani notes, 'in the making of nation states, Europe went through an entire history of ethnic cleansing. Where it did not, it branded cultural minorities as permanent "national minorities" alongside the cultural majority as the "nation"' (1996: 29).

Multi-ethnic states in the East and South have faced immense difficulties building states, let alone democracies (Horowitz 1985, 1993). And the global spread of democracy itself has proven more conflictual than anyone could have imagined when it began. The collapse of communist regimes and patrimonial dictatorships opened the way to democratisation in some countries. But in many others it merely brought more decentralised forms of oppression and the escalation of political violence. States, it is argued, are especially at risk from political violence whose 'structural root causes' are to be found in power struggles between 'different identity groups' (Commission of the European Communities 1996). According to the International Institute for Democracy and Electoral Assistance (IDEA 1998: 4) some 80 per cent of 'major conflicts' in the 1990s had a clear identity component.

37

Is the simultaneous spread of democracy and rise in identity-based violent conflicts a historical accident? Or are they causally interconnected? Many have seen democratisation as a major cause, or at the very least precipitant, of political violence, holding that 'the opening of democratic space throws up many groups pulling in different directions, that it causes demand overload, systematic breakdown and even violent conflict' (summarised by Ake 1997: 8). Political contestation organised around non-negotiable identity claims poses severe difficulties for democracy. And by helping politicise these claims, democracy can contribute to political polarisation and ultimately violence (Baker 1996; Stewart and O'Sullivan 1998).

In this chapter, we start from the contrary position: that democracy can be see as a reversal of Clausewitz's dictum, that is: 'Politics is the prosecution of war by other means' (Sartori 1987: 42). The resolution of conflict is best sought on an 'oratorical battleground', unlike the warlike approach to politics under which 'force monitors persuasion, might establishes right, and conflict resolution is sought in the defeat of the enemy' (ibid.). Democracy thus can be understood as a system for the peaceful management of conflicts. It provides a non-violent method for selecting rulers, a forum through which conflicts can be debated and resolved, and an opportunity for inclusive participation. To be sure, 'democratic states suffer from conflicts just as others do, and the presence of democracy is no guarantee of a society without political violence.... [But] democratic societies tend to develop the institutions, resources and flexibility, in the long term, to peacefully manage these kinds of conflict' (IDEA 1998: 13).

Nor are there convincing reasons why democratic institutions should not in principle be capable of handling identity-based conflicts. To endorse the claim that plural societies are incompatible with democratic values

> seems to imply that 'plural societies' the world over are condemned to an undemocratic future simply because of their plural composition. If this is correct, it would appear that democratic aspirations are a futile fantasy for the vast majority of humankind. (Bose 1995: 90)

The roots and dynamics of identity conflicts are of course an enormously disputed topic, which we explore in a companion paper (Kaldor and Luckham 2001). Such conflicts cannot be understood and addressed solely in terms of 'identity politics'. The latter normally fit within complex skeins of causation, interacting with other factors such as rivalries among political élites, global economic dislocations, uneven development, competition for scarce resources, or international intervention (Mayall and Simpson 1992).

Yet neither can identity politics be safely ignored. As Mamdani (2001: 21–4) insists, in many instances such political identities as those based on race, religion or ethnicity are historically embedded in the state, institutionally reproduced and (sometimes) legally enforced.[15] Of course, by no means all identity conflicts are in the same sense 'about' identity, as Young (1976) has pointed out. Some express the hegemonic projects of politically dominant groups (like Serb nationalists in ex-Yugoslavia, Sinhala nationalists in Sri Lanka or Islamicists in Sudan). Others arise from minority struggles against discrimination, or to realise self-determination. Some ethnic constituencies have pursued claims upon the state, such as access to state-distributed jobs, patronage and resources. Elsewhere, ethnic identities are simply manipulated to advance the ambitions and interests of warlords or state élites, as in the conflicts in Liberia, Sierra Leone or the Congo.

Violence itself, once unleashed, becomes a historical catalyst for intensified ethnic polarisation. Ignatieff (1999) writes eloquently of the 'narcissism of minor difference': the fratricidal obsession with the markers of identity that can develop among groups with relatively little to separate them culturally and linguistically (like Tutsi and Hutu in Rwanda, or Serbs, Croats and Muslims in Bosnia). Once created, these fratricidal legacies cannot easily be wished away.

When such identities become inscribed in the history and institutions of states, the latter are seldom completely neutral arbiters, as shown in our case studies of Bosnia, Fiji and Sri Lanka. Enloe (1980) has analysed how ethnic identities are deployed by security bureaucracies as tools of state policy, or to keep political élites in power. Because democratic institutions, too, belong within the ensemble of state institutions, they cannot be assumed to be neutral forums for conflict management. This does not mean they cannot help to resolve or transform conflicts. But the legitimacy of existing democratic institutions may be precisely one of the things that is challenged.

Two developing countries in which political violence has been most systematic, protracted and resistant to settlement, Sri Lanka and Colombia (Pearce et al. 1990), happen to be long-standing democracies, where there are multi-party elections, vocal legislatures and (in theory at least) constitutional and legal protections for human rights. India and the UK, both paradigmatic liberal democracies, also have dismal records of managing conflict in Kashmir and Punjab and in Northern Ireland.

On the other hand, democracy can make a virtue of plural systems by providing a framework through which cross-cutting social and ethnic cleavages can balance each other and through which grievances and discontents can be expressed and sometimes rectified. India could be said to be to be a living example of this point. Although identity-based politics (and violence) have grown in importance in recent years, the survival so far of democracy in a very poor country can be explained both by an active civil society and by the myriad of cross-cutting social, religious, regional, caste and linguistic loyalties (Manor and Segall 1998: 61).

Obviously, therefore, the relationship between democracy and conflict is far from simple, and there is little point in polemical disputes about whether democracy promotes conflict or resolves it. Rather, it is better to shift the terms of the debate to *how* democracy can encourage non-violent management of conflicts. If, as we have argued, ethnic, religious and other faultlines tend to become embedded in the history and institutions of the state, transitions to democracy provide windows of opportunity when wise leadership, inclusive forms of politics and institutional choices can realise democracy's potential as a system for the peaceful transformation of conflicts.

Peace-building and democratisation

Both democratic transitions and the 'new wars' can be seen as contrasting responses to profound crises in political authority (Kaldor and Luckham 2001). Such crises have taken different forms in different national contexts, and one may distinguish between three main situations.

1 In some crises of democratic transition, 'incompetent, parochial, fragile, and authoritarian governments that fail to satisfy basic needs' (Azar and Moon 1990: 10) have been brought down – permitting democratisation, but often increasing the risk of violence by retreating authoritarian élites, or by those who feel themselves excluded from the new political dispensation. Thus the political and institutional choices made during transitions are crucial and can make all the difference between democratic consolidation and regression to non-democratic rule or violent conflict.

2 The shortcomings of existing democratic institutions, including their inability to manage political violence, are another less often con-sidered source of conflict. Sometimes the problem may not be with democracy as such, so much as with the lack of democratic politics within façade democracies (see above). Governments may not respond to the demands of excluded groups, or may fail to protect citizens from violence, because they are in pawn to special interests like the

ex-communist *nomenklatura* in parts of Eastern Europe, or the military– business mafias that have 'captured' democratic institutions in some African and Latin American states.

More troubling issues arise, however, when more established democracies seem incapable of resolving conflicts, as in Sri Lanka or Northern Ireland. As we shall argue below, the main problem is often with particular forms of democratic contestation, notably under majoritarian 'winner-takes-all' institutions. However, sometimes the problems may be even more fundamental. Stewart and O'Sullivan (1998: 20–7), for instance, argue that Sri Lanka's post-independence history not only refutes the simple proposition that democracy abates conflict but starkly illustrates the limits of constitutional engineering undertaken to blur the edges of majoritarian politics and encourage political alliances across ethnic boundaries. Hence, constitutional reform by itself is insufficient. It must be supported by more inclusive politics and by government policies to address the differential economic advancement between communities and regions, which often shapes inter-ethnic hostility.

3 In some crises violence has become politically and socially embedded through conflict, blunting the impact of constitutional reform and diminishing the capacity of democratic institutions to respond creatively to conflicts. For political violence tends to transform the rules and practices of politics: by normalising force as a way of allocating power and resources; by reinforcing ethnic polarisation; and by undermining the legitimacy of the state and of democratic institutions. Its legacies do not usually vanish when conflicts 'terminate', and indeed can re-ignite conflicts again and again, as in Colombia, the Sudan, Bosnia or the Congo.

Moreover, peace building may require Faustian bargains in which ex-dictators, warlords or guerrillas secure immunity from prosecution, or even gain control of the state. The central dilemma is that concessions made to the men of violence dilute accountability for human rights violations, and may even give them an effective veto over democracy. Cases in point are the Hun Sen government in Cambodia and the Taylor government in Liberia, both of which have used their control of the means of violence to intimidate opponents and frustrate any real democratic contestation.

Sometimes indeed, the requirements of conflict management and of democratisation clash (Baker 1996). In former Yugoslavia, the Trans-caucasus region or Rwanda, the introduction of elections led to brutal

41

campaigns to eliminate ethnic contenders for rule. In Rwanda, it is argued that 'the imposition of a narrow concept of democratisation based on a Western-style multi-party system ... was a major contributory factor to the political dynamics leading up to the events of 1994', including the genocide (Woodward 1996: 24).

Mamdani therefore warns against the notion

> that multi-party democracy can lead to democratic outcomes regardless of context, for this can only be when all participants accept the rules of the game. Logically and historically, the creation of a political community must precede multi-party competition. The creation of a political community requires a minimum consensus within that community – of all, not just a majority. (1996: 29)

Especially after conflicts, complex trade-offs must be made between the compromises needed to bring all the major political and military players on board, and the long-term requirements of sustainable and popularly based democracy. The potentially divisive impact of democratisation is often counteracted through power-sharing arrangements, as under the Government of National Unity in South Africa.

But the crucial issue in the longer term is how to constitute diverse cultural communities into a single political community based on broad consent and inclusive notions of common citizenship. This requires more than power sharing at the top. Minorities must acquire a real stake in democratic institutions, and a durable consensus must be built from the bottom up as well as from the top down.

Yet to foster a broad-based consensus it may not be enough just to strengthen secular, civic or 'modern' forms of citizenship – especially in societies where the *wananchi* (Swahili for 'ordinary people') have become deeply alienated from remote public institutions, which are not responsive to their needs or are outright oppressive. Preferably, democracy should build on organisations and institutions citizens can understand and to which they can relate. In Africa, for instance, this could include the 'second public' of village, town and community associations, clan and ethnic networks, religious and communal bodies which Ekeh (1975 and 1990) argues are more inclusive moral communities than the 'first public' of the nation state. It might also include some rehabilitation of grassroots-based communitarian 'alternatives' to Western models of liberal democracy (Luckham 1998).

One must remember that in as much as people turn to ethnic, religious, or other group-based organisations for assistance, protection, and identity, these are everyday concerns which matter to ordinary citizens – along with jobs, food, housing, health – and lie at the heart of substantive democracy. Recognition of their importance builds on what Saul (1997a) labels the 'political economy of democratisation' approach, rather than the 'thin' democracy of the 'political science of democratisation'.

Horses for courses? Majoritarian democracy and its alternatives

According to the Carnegie Commission on Preventing Deadly Conflict:

> In societies with deep ethnic divisions and little experience with demo-cratic government and the rule of law, strict majoritarian democracy can be self-defeating. Where ethnic identities are strong and national identity weak, populations may vote largely on ethnic lines. Domination by one ethnic group can lead to a tyranny of the majority. (1997: 100)

Below we discuss the relative merits of majoritarian democracy and the alternatives proposed to it. Following Reynolds (1999: Chapter 4)[16] we subdivide majoritarian systems (see Table 1.2) into (1) classic majori-tarian democracy, and (2) qualified majoritarianism, in which insti-tutional constraints are introduced in order to modify majoritarianism's winner-takes-all tendencies. We also distinguish between (3) consocia-tionalist power sharing between cooperating but autonomous groups, and (4) integrative power sharing, aiming to transcend group differences by encouraging groups to cooperate around common political goals.

1 *Majoritarian democracy* refers to those forms of democratic government which concentrate power in the hands of executives elected by a majority of the popular vote. Political competition is heavily emphasised over the other functions of democracy referred to earlier in this chapter. The institutional forms most often favouring majoritarianism include (a) strong presidential rule or parliamentary systems in which prime ministers control strong parliamentary majorities; (b) first-past-the-post electoral systems, which tend to produce such majorities; (c) unicameral legislatures or bicameral legislatures with weak second chambers; (d) relatively weak constitutional divisions of powers between the branches of government; and (e) unitary, centralised state and administrative structures.

A number of empirical studies seem to demonstrate that these institutional components of majoritarianism individually or in combina-tion can foster ethnic polarisation, political instability and violent conflict (Reynolds and Sisk 1998; Reynolds 1999; and, on presidential government, Stepan and Skach 1993). Yet, in our view, the waters have

Table 1.2 Institutional design: systems of governance and conflict management in conflict-torn societies

Constitutional & legal Arrangements	Advantages	Disadvantages	Considerations
Majoritarian systems include: (1) Classic majoritarianism, where 'winner takes all'. (2) Qualified majoritarianism, moderated by institutional arrangements to improve representation of minorities and ensure plural centres of power.	• They encourage coherent, single-party executives and effective governance. • Competition for power keeps governments on their toes and responsive to public opinion. • Strong, legitimate opposition institutions provide channels for the disaffected to express grievances and encourage commitment to the constitutional order. • Qualified majoritarianism can help modify defects such as exclusion of minorities and over-centralisation of power.	• Majoritarian systems can consistently exclude minorities from power, and create situations whereby they may turn to violence. • They can be destabilising where 'winner takes all' and loss of political office is equated with social and economic exclusion. • Majoritarianism can be particularly damaging in semi-democracies, fostering arbitrary, non-accountable governance.	• How can short-term confidence building be combined with longer-term political integration? • Does the institutionalisation of ethnic and other differences facilitate resolution of identity based conflicts, or harden lines of social division? • Are ethnic, racial, religious etc. differences the most salient divides, or are there other faultlines, such as socio-economic inequality, which may cut across identity politics and minority concerns? • Are forms of power sharing temporary or permanent? • Are they informal or inscribed into constitutional arrangements?

- Power-sharing systems are based on the ethos of inclusion rather than exclusion:
  (3) Consociationalism: 'grand coalitions' among autonomous cultural communities with minority vetoes written into constitutional settlements.
  (4) Integrative power sharing between all significant political forces including ethnic minorities, encouraging cross-cutting political alliances.

- They ensure political power is shared between majority and minority groups.
- Decision making by consensus fosters conflict resolution and political stability.
- Inclusive governance fosters broad-based support for government policies.
- Integrative power sharing encourages political alliances on issues rather than ascriptive communal traits, reducing the political salience of the latter.

- Power-sharing agreements are not always sufficient to resolve deep-seated conflict and can entrench ethnic/racial/religious etc. divides.
- Consociational systems are based on élite pacts and reinforce ongoing power monopolies, in which minorities acquire a subordinate-cum-spoiler role.
- Consensus politics can result in political immobilism and failure to tackle issues like poverty.
- Not enough political space for opposition can breed political complacency and non-accountable governance.

- How can integrative tendencies be encouraged, while retaining the key inclusive confidence-building mechanisms needed in the short term?

Sources: Adapted from A. Reynolds (1999) *Electoral Systems and Democratization in Southern Africa*, Oxford: Oxford University Press, and Institute for Democracy and Electoral Assistance (IDEA) (1998) *Democracy and Deep-Rooted Conflict: Options for Negotiators*, David Bloomfield and Ben Reilly (eds.), Stockholm: International IDEA.

been muddied by the tendency to lump all majoritarian systems together for the purposes of comparative analysis.

One should distinguish between (a) functioning democracies in which strong rule by majority-supported executives is the intended product of constitutional arrangements; and (b) 'democracies with adjectives' as described earlier, where strong majoritarian tendencies largely reflect strongman rule by non-accountable executives, and thus the relative *absence* of democracy.

Functioning majoritarian democracies in turn subdivide into two groups: (a) fully competitive systems where there is regular alternation among different parties in power, as in the UK or Sri Lanka; and (b) single-party-dominant systems in which, although elections are freely contested, one party or a stable coalition controls the executive for long periods, as in Botswana, Malaysia, Japan or (previously) Sweden.

The basic case for majoritarian democracy is that it is conducive to stable, effective governance; especially under single-party-dominant systems (White 1998; Leftwich 1998). The case against is that it consistently excludes minorities from power and offers them insufficient protection from hegemonic majorities. Thus there is a seeming trade-off between majoritarianism's tendency to exacerbate societal cleavages and its ability to assure effective government. Yet some would question whether there really is such a trade-off. Strong majority governments – with the capacity to deliver political stability, law and order and pro-poor policies – may also be more able to respond to minority grievances, especially in single-party-dominant systems like those of Botswana or Uganda.

However, in many non-Western systems, majoritarianism tends to reinforce the accumulation of power in the hands of populist presidents endorsed through plebiscitory elections, and largely unconstrained by any 'horizontal' accountability toward other democratic institutions, including parliament, the constitution and the judiciary. This is what Latin American social scientists have termed 'delegative' democracy (O'Donnell 1994). Non-accountable populist presidencies are also widely regarded as one of the main political legacies of communist rule in Eastern Europe. The crux of the matter is the absence of democratic politics. Democracy deficits more than majoritarianism *per se* may be why disaffected minorities have taken up arms against the state in so many new democracies.

2 Under *qualified majoritarianism* or *democratic counter-majoritarianism* (Devenish 1993) a range of devices may be wheeled in to remedy the

defects of majoritarianism. The less radical accept the basic principle of majority rule, but modify it to assure better political representation of minorities and more plural, decentralised centres of power. There is, however, no single recipe for constitutional engineering, which should take account of a country's history, socio-economic structure and depth of inter-group polarisation. The following is a menu of the constitutional, legal and political options that might be considered by a democratic Machiavelli aiming to curb the political excesses of majoritarian governance.

- *Strong, constitutionally guaranteed human rights protections:* these are both desirable in their own right, and can reduce minority fear of discrimination and state persecution. Whether they should include group rights is more debatable, since the latter can sometimes undermine individual rights and reinforce the isolation of minority communities (Young 1990; Devenish 1993).

- *Affirmative action measures* to reverse legacies of discrimination, or to assure inter-communal 'balance' – as under the 'federal character' principle supposed to govern the allocation of political and administrative appointments in Nigeria (Ekeh and Osaghae 1989).

- *Forms of electoral representation* to ensure that political office holders are representative of all or most politically organised groups, especially minorities. The most widely canvassed is *proportional representation* (PR) (Sartori 1997; Reynolds and Sisk 1998; Reynolds 1999). However, there exist many other electoral devices designed to encourage electoral appeals across inter-communal divisions – the Single Transferable Vote (STV), a variant of PR, for example – or to assure the representation of particular excluded groups (electoral quotas, for example – though under PR this may also be achieved through party lists).

- *Spatial decentralisation of power,* aimed at creating plural centres of power and multiple decentralised points of access of citizens to the state, including different forms of administrative devolution, federalism and confederalism (see European Union, EC Somalia Unit (1995) for a comparison of their appropriateness in Somalia). Some forms of decentralisation are deliberately configured in ethnic or communal terms, so as to allow previous minorities to become majorities in particular regions. The system of 'ethnic federalism' implemented by the government of Ethiopia post-1994 is a pertinent example (Cohen: 1997) and another is the extreme devolution of powers to cantons and municipalities in Bosnia. Both cases, however, reinforce Ghai's observation that 'spatial decentralisation rarely resolves all minority fears, as it may help to create new minorities – the problem of minorities within minorities is well known' (1998: 64).

- *Corporate decentralisation* treats members of communities as collectives vested with cultural or political rights; rights to substantive entitlements; or vetoes over policies having a negative impact on the community in question. But as Ghai notes, corporate decentralisation, 'based on ethnic markers, tends to enhance ethnic values at the expense of national ... all national decisions have to be ethnically negotiated, so ethnic politics are at the heart of national politics, and the problems of consensus and governance are compounded by mutual vetoes' (Ghai 1998: 60–1). Fiji's constitutional and electoral devices, designed to protect the political supremacy of indigenous Fijians, provide a pertinent example of the pitfalls of such an approach.

- *Horizontal accountability* (O'Donnell 1998) of the executive to the legislature and (via an independent judiciary) to the constitution can help restrain government tendencies to resort to populist electoral appeals in disregard of minority rights.

- *The embedded autonomy of state bureaucracies* (Evans 1995) is another important protection against the arbitrary use of power by majoritarian governments, providing an inbuilt capacity to resist attempts by governments to impose discriminatory policies and practices, construct patronage systems and engage in corruption.

- *Democratic control over the armed forces and police* is often crucial in ensuring they are not used as partisan political instruments, or do not engage in human rights abuses and fan the flames of conflict (Stepan 1988; Cawthra and Luckham, 2003).

3 *Consociationalism* (Lijphart 1977) in essence refers to efforts to restructure the entire political system around the principle of corporate decentralisation. Its central premise is that communal cleavages in plural societies run so deep that constitutional tinkering with majoritarian democracy is not enough. The basic model of consociationalism comprises four elements (Reynolds 1999: 110-3): (a) *grand coalitions* to ensure executive power sharing among élites representing all significant ethnic and other groups; (b) *segmental autonomy* or internal political and cultural self-regulation for all these groups; (c) *proportionality*, including

proportional electoral representation and allocation of public funding and of government jobs on a communal basis; (d) *mutual vetoes*, granting all groups significant powers to block decisions on vital issues.

Many recent post-conflict agreements have been consociational in intent. However, they have differed between those where power sharing has been seen as a short-term expedient to build peace and facilitate democratic transition, as in South Africa, and those where it is made a permanent feature of constitutional design, as in Fiji or post-Dayton Bosnia. Lijphart himself (1996 and 1998) has recently claimed that Indian democracy and South Africa's post-apartheid constitution embody the 'spirit' of consociationalism, despite constitutions which would appear to enshrine more orthodox versions of liberal democracy.

It seems doubtful whether consociationalism is capable of tackling the basic social inequities which so often fuel conflict. It is too reliant on political cooperation among ethnically based élites. It may sometimes be explicitly anti-democratic, as in Malaysia, where it reinforces *bumiputera* ('sons of the soil') political ascendancy, for instance by excluding other ethnic groups from key military, police and bureaucratic posts. 'Power sharing' in such cases may be something of a misnomer, since even if power is shared it is shared unequally. Moreover, democratic politics may become hostage to the spoiling tactics of groups (like Inkatha in South Africa, Taukei in Fiji or Serb ethno-nationalist politicians in Bosnia), which play the ethnic card to the hilt. And it can also result in political immobilism, owing to the difficulty of negotiating consensus concerning important government decisions.[17]

4 By *integrative power sharing*, we mean forms of power sharing constructed to reinforce shared democratic principles and to avoid consociationalism's tendency to harden societal cleavages within constitutional formulas. The goal is thus to encourage cross-cutting coalitions transcending communal cleavages, rather than to entrench the latter. Some of the same political devices – such as proportional representation and affirmative action – may be used, but power sharing itself is made self-liquidating, and leaves space for new forms of non-communal politics to emerge when the wounds of conflict heal. A good example is South Africa, where the Government of National Unity which formed during the post-apartheid transition was dissolved after the constitution-making exercise was complete – but not before there had been heated debate between advocates of longer-term power sharing (Koeble and Reynolds 1996) and those who argued it would stifle democratic contestation and make governments less accountable (Jung and Shapiro 1995; 1996).

49

What matters is the overall commitment to political and social inclusion, rather than the particular political formulas by which it is brought about. Thus in some political systems *de facto* power sharing has been facilitated through constantly shifting alliances among parties, as in Thailand and some countries in continental Europe. In others, party alliances have been maintained over the long term, as in Colombia or Mauritius. In yet others, dominant but integrative political parties – like the ANC in South Africa, Chama cha Mapinduzi (CCM) in Tanzania or (until the 1970s) the Congress Party in India – have been the vehicles for coalition building.

Integrative power sharing may sometimes be facilitated by explicit recognition of cultural differences, for instance through language and education policies and variations in personal law, or by affirmative action to redress historical imbalances between regions, ethnic groups or religions. Yet the ultimate goal is to depoliticise these differences and insulate them from partisan political debate – and to place increasing reliance on universal guarantees of human rights and constitutional checks and balances to protect minority interests and build inclusive democracy.

Hence, integrative power sharing can draw upon much the same menu of constitutional and political choices as democratic counter-majoritarianism, but with some difference in emphasis: for instance, voting systems like the STV or the alternative vote (AV), which encourage electoral appeals across particular ethnic constituencies. In contrast to consociationalism, integrative power sharing assumes that only in the more extreme cases are political parties ethnically exclusive and elections simply ethnic censuses, so that parties mobilise across as well as within ethnic boundaries, and voting reflects complex inter-actions between ethnicity and other variables (Young 1993; Reynolds 1999; Reynolds and Sisk 1998).

Nevertheless integrative power sharing may be open to some of the same objections as consociationalism (see Table 1.2): including an over-emphasis on élite politics, insulation of governments from opposition criticism and tendency to political immobilism. In Colombia, for example, *de facto* power sharing among the main political parties did not enable governments to take the hard decisions needed to tackle the country's conflicts, including curbing the prerogatives of the armed forces and paramilitaries (Hartlyn 1993). In Fiji, the adoption of AV had the precise opposite effect to that intended; polarising the vote in favour of the extremist ethnic parties. Where redistributive politics occurs behind closed doors, as in many multi-ethnic states, mutual suspicion among different ethnic constituencies can fester and be even more intense than where it is open to public scrutiny and debate. Government room for manoeuvre may be severely constrained by the need to play different ethnic and regional constituencies off against each other, diminishing their capacity to govern effectively and to push through redistributive policies.

Power sharing, in sum, should be seen as a tool of democratic politics rather than as a goal in its own right. It can be a valuable aid to confidence building, encouraging politically organised groups in divided societies to cooperate and resolve their disputes peacefully. Yet democratisation should eventually be able to make power sharing redundant, by ensuring that disputes are resolved through the democratic process itself, and that the rights and freedoms of all, including minorities, are equally protected under the rule of law.

Conclusion

This chapter has focused on four contemporary debates about democracy, namely: what does democracy mean; how far do democratic values and institutions penetrate society; how far do democracies provide conditions for effective anti-poverty policies; and how far do they help resolve – or provoke – new forms of conflict. Cutting across each of these discussions has been a distinction between democratic institutions and democratic politics. This distinction is a reminder that democratisation is not just a process of implanting formal institutions of liberal democracy, but a project of norm creation and cultural change.

We have chosen to address dilemmas of unequal citizenship, poverty and conflict because contemporary governance debates are burdened with assumptions about the positive contribution of democracy to civil and political equality, poverty reduction and conflict resolution, in spite of the inconclusiveness of the empirical evidence. When one begins, as we have done, with the 'deep politics of society' (social relations and conflict) rather than the high politics of the state, a range of democratic deficits are illuminated. These deficits are not always immediately apparent in governance debates which focus upon the formal institutions of democracy.

One of the enduring dilemmas about democracy is whether political institutions will catalyse the development of a democratic political culture and democratic politics, or whether it is the other way around. We quoted earlier a conviction expressed by Mamdani, that multi-party competition cannot lead to democratic outcomes without the creation of a political community embracing all members of society. It is possible to debate endlessly on the 'chicken or egg' question of whether institutions or a political culture come first. One thing is for sure: where democratic institutions do establish themselves, in however nascent a way, they often create incentives to shape the behaviour of political élites to be inclusive in their politics, and to challenge excessive concentrations of power. As Geddes notes for Eastern Europe:

> Among the dynamics inherent in even seriously flawed competitive systems are the tendency of aspiring political leaders to mobilise previously excluded groups into the political system to support their own challenges to established leaders and the tendency of leadership competition within parties to result in party cleavages.... As a result, even narrow and flawed democracies contain within them forces that often lead to more inclusive and competitive systems in the long term. (1996: 35)

Democratic institutions, then, can create incentives for democratic politics. They can also build conditions to resolve problems of inequality and conflict. In a formal sense, liberal democratic institutions sustain expectations of social equity because of liberal civil and political rights which the poor can use to promote their interests. Democracies raise expectations about policy effectiveness because institutions for accountability create expectations about public sector probity, and political competition allows for rational debate and the introduction of new ideas, needs and interests. And democracies are expected to provide avenues for the peaceful resolution of conflict because plural systems allow for compromise and balance between contesting interests through institutions for the redress of grievances and discontent. Actually existing democracies rarely meet these expectations, and we should not be excessively sanguine about the ability of institutions to entrench democratic politics in today's fragile democracies. But, as we have seen, there is enormous potential for constructive institutional design, policy choice, and changes to the culture of politics, which can make democracy more responsive to problems of inequality and conflict.

References

Ake, C. (1997) 'Why Humanitarian Emergencies Occur: Insights from the Interface of State, Democracy and Civil Society,' *Research for Action*, 31, UNU/Wider.

Amnesty International (1997) *Amnesty International Report 1997*, London: AI.

Amnesty International (1998) *Amnesty International Report 1998*, London: AI.

Ascher, W. (1984) *Scheming for the Poor: the Politics of Redistribution in Latin America*, Massachusetts: Harvard University Press.

Azar, E. E. and C. Moon (eds.) (1990) *National Security in the Third World: the Management of Internal and External Threats*, University of Maryland at College Park, Center for International Development and Conflict Management, Aldershot: Edward Elgar.

Baker, P. H. (1996) 'Conflict Resolution versus Democratic Governance: Divergent Paths to Peace' in C. A. Crocker, F. O. Hampson and P. Aall, *Managing Global Chaos: Sources and Responses to International Conflict*, Washington, DC: US Institute of Peace Press.

Bardhan, P. (1998) 'The State Against Society: the Great Divide in Indian Social Science Discourse', in S. Bose and A. Jalal (eds.), *Nationalism, Democracy and Development: State and Politics in India*, Delhi: Delhi University Press.

Bayart, J.-F., A. Mbembe, and C. Toulabor (1992) *Le Politique par le bas en Afrique Noire: contributions a une problématique de la démocratie*, Paris: Karthala.

Beetham, D. (1994) 'Conditions for Democratic Consolidation', *Review of African Political Economy*, 21, 60: 157–72.

Beetham, D., S. Bracking, I. Kearton and S. Weir (2002) *International IDEA Handbook on Democracy Assessment*, The Hague: Kluwer Law International.

Bose, S. (1995) 'State Crisis And Nationalities Conflict In Sri Lanka and Yugoslavia', *Comparative Political Studies*, 28, 1: 87–116.

Brass, P. (1995) *The Politics of India since Independence*, Cambridge: Cambridge University Press.

Carnegie Commission on Preventing Deadly Conflict (1997) *Preventing Deadly Conflict: A Final Report*, Washington, DC: Carnegie Corporation.

Castañeda, J. G. (1994) *Utopia Unarmed: the Latin American Left after the Cold War*, New York: Vintage Books.

Cawthra, G. and R. Luckham (2003) *Governing Insecurity*, London: Zed Books.

Cohen, J. M. (1997) 'Decentralization and Ethnic Federalism in Post-Civil War Ethiopia', in Krishna Kumar (ed.), *Rebuilding Societies after Civil War: Critical Roles for International Assistance*, Boulder: Lynne Reinner.

Collier, D. and S. Levitsky (1997) 'Democracy with Adjectives: Conceptual Innovation in Comparative Research', *World Politics*, 49 (April): 430–51.

Commission of the European Communities (1996) Communication from the Commission to the Council, 'The European Union and the Issue of Conflicts in Africa: Peace-Building, Conflict Prevention and Beyond', Brussels: SEC, 96, 32.

Devenish, G. (1993) 'Democratic Counter-Majoritarianism: Protecting Ethnic Minorities in a Liberal Democracy with Special Reference to South Africa' in P. Nherere and M. d'Engelbronner-Kolff (eds.), *The Institutionalism of Human Rights in South Africa*, Copenhagen: Nordic Human Rights Publications.

Dreze, J. and A. Sen (1989) *Hunger and Public Action*, World Institute for Development Economics Research, Oxford: Clarendon.

Ekeh, P. P. (1975) 'Colonialism and the Two Publics in Africa: a Theoretical Statement', *Comparative Studies in Society and History*, 17 (January): 91–112.

Ekeh, P. P. (1990) 'Social Anthropology and Two Contrasting Uses of Tribalism

53

in Africa', *Comparative Studies in Society and History*, 32: 660–700.

Ekeh, P. P. and E. E. Osaghae (1989) *Federal Character and Federalism in Nigeria*, Ibadan: Heinemann.

Enloe, C., 1980, *Ethnic Soldiers: State Security in Divided Societies*, London: Penguin.

Escobar, A. and S. E. Alvarez (1992) *The Making of Social Movements in Latin America: Identity, Strategy and Democracy*, Boulder, CO: Westview Press.

European Union, EC Somalia Unit (1995) 'A Study of Decentralised Political Structures for Somalia: a Menu of Options', paper prepared by consultants at the London School of Economics and Political Science.

Evans, P. (1995) *Embedded Autonomy: States and Industrial Transformation*, Princeton: Princeton University Press.

Fukuyama, F. (1989) 'The End of History?' *The National Interest*, 16: 3–18.

Geddes, B. (1996) 'Initiation of New Democratic Institutions in Eastern Europe and Latin America', in A. Lijphart and C. H. Waisman (eds.), *Institutional Design in New Democracies: Eastern Europe and Latin America*, Boulder, CO: Westview Press.

Ghai, Y. (1998) 'Decentralization and Accommodation of Ethnic Diversity', in C. Young (ed.), *Ethnic Diversity and Public Policy: a Comparative Inquiry*, UNRISD, Basingstoke: Macmillan Press.

Goetz, A. M. and S. Hassim (2003) *No Shortcuts to Power: African Women in Politics and Policy-Making*, London: Zed Books.

Goetz, A. M. and R. Jenkins (1998) 'Creating a Framework for Reducing Poverty: Institutional and Process Issues in National Poverty Policy, Uganda Country Report', commissioned study for DFID and SIDA, Sussex: IDS mimeo.

Goldsworthy, D. (1984) 'Political Power and Socio-Economic Development: Two Polemics', *Political Studies*, 32: 551–69.

Harriss-White, B. and G. White (eds.) (1996) 'Liberalisation and the New Corruption', *IDS Bulletin*, Special Issue, 27, 2 (April), Brighton: Institute of Development Studies.

Harrison, P. (1980) *The Third World Tomorrow*, Harmondsworth, London: Penguin Books.

Hartlyn, J. (1993) 'Civil Violence and Conflict Resolution: the Case of Colombia' in Roy Linklider (ed.), *Stopping the Killing: How Civil Wars End*, New York: New York University Press: 37–61.

Held, D. (1987) *Models of Democracy*, Cambridge: Polity Press.

Held, D. (1993) 'Democracy: from City States to a Cosmopolitan Order?', in D. Held (ed.) *Prospects for Democracy. North, South, East, West*, Cambridge: Polity Press.

Held, D. (1997) 'Democracy and Globalisation', *Global Governance*, 3, 3: 251–67.

Hirst, P. (1990) *Representative Democracy and its Limits*, Cambridge: Polity Press.

Horowitz, D. (1985) *Ethnic Groups in Conflict*, Berkeley: University of California Press.

Horowitz, D. (1993) 'Democracy in Divided Societies', *Journal of Democracy*, 4, 4: 18–38.

Huber, E., D. Rueschemeyer, and J. D. Stephens (1997) 'The Paradoxes of

Contemporary Democracy: Formal, Participatory and Social Dimensions', *Comparative Politics*, 29, 3: 232–42.

Ignatieff, M. (1999) 'The Narcissism of Minor Difference', in his book *The Warriors Human: Ethnic War and the Modern Consciences*, Vintage: 34–71.

Institute for Democracy and Electoral Assistance (IDEA) (1998) *Democracy and Deep-rooted Conflict: Options for Negotiators*, David Bloomfield and Ben Reilly (eds.), Stockholm: International IDEA.

Jenkins, R. and A. M. Goetz (1999) 'Accounts and Accountability: Theoretical Implications of the Right-to-Information Movement in India', *Third World Quarterly*, 20, 3: 603–22.

Jung, C. and I. Shapiro (1995) 'South Africa's Negotiated Transition: Democracy, Opposition, and the New Constitutional Order', *Politics and Society*, 23, 3: 269–308.

Jung, C. and I. Shapiro (1996) 'South African Democracy Revisited: a Reply to Koeble and Reynolds', *Politics and Society*, 24, 3: 237–47.

Kaldor, M. and R. Luckham (2001) 'Global Transformations and New Conflicts', *IDS Bulletin*, 32, 2: 48–69.

Kaldor, M. and I. Vejvoda (1997) 'Democratization in Central and East European Countries', *International Affairs*, 73, 1: 59–82.

Koeble, T. and A. Reynolds (1996) 'Power-Sharing Democracy in the New South Africa', *Politics and Society*, 24, 3: 221–36.

Kohli, A. (ed.) (1986) *The State and Development in the Third World*, Princeton: Princeton University Press.

Leftwich, A. (ed.) (1996) *Democracy and Development*, Cambridge: Polity Press.

Leftwich, A. (1998) 'Forms of Democratic Developmental State: Development Practices and Development Capacity' in M. Robinson and G. White (eds.), *The Democratic Developmental State: Political and Institutional Design*, Oxford: Oxford University Press: 17–51.

Lijphart, A. (1977) *Democracy in Plural Societies: a Comparative Exploration*, New Haven: Yale University Press.

Lijphart, A. (1996) 'The Puzzle of Indian Democracy: a Consociational Interpretation', *American Political Science Review*, 90: 258–68.

Lijphart, A. (1998) 'South African Democracy: Majoritarian or Consociational', *Democratization*, 5, 4: 144–50.

Lijphart, A. and C. H. Waisman (eds.) (1996) *Institutional Design in New Democracies: Eastern Europe and Latin America*, Boulder, CO: Westview Press.

Lonsdale, J. (ed.) (1986) 'Political Accountability in African History', in Patrick Chabal (ed.), *Political Domination in Africa: Reflections on the Limits of Power*, Cambridge: Cambridge University Press.

Lowi, T. (1964) 'American Business, Public Policy, Case-Studies and Political Theory', *World Politics*, 16 July: 677–715.

Luckham, R. (1998) 'Are There Alternatives to Liberal Democracy?' in M. Robinson and G. White (eds.), *The Democratic Developmental State: Politics and Institutional Design*, Oxford: Oxford University Press.

Mamdani, M. (1996) 'From Conquest to Consent as the Basis of State Formation: Reflections on Rwanda', *New Left Review*, 216: 3–36.

Mamdani, M. (2001) *When Victims Become Killers: Colonialism, Nativism and the Genocide in Rwanda*, Oxford: James Currey.

Manor, J. and Segal, G. (1998) 'Taking India Seriously', *Survival*, International Institute for Strategic Studies.

Mayall, J. and M. Simpson (1992) 'Ethnicity is not Enough: Reflections on Protracted Secessionism in the Third World', *International Journal of Comparative Sociology*, 33, 1–2: 5–25.

Mkandawire, T. (1999) 'Crisis Management and the Making of "Choiceless Democracies"', in Richard Joseph (ed.), *State, Conflict and Democracy in Africa*, Boulder, CO: Lynne Reinner.

Moore, M. (1995) 'Democracy and Development in Cross-National Perspective: a New Look at the Statistics', *Democratization*, 2, 2: 1–19.

Moore, M. and J. Putzel (1999) 'Politics and Poverty: a Background Paper for the World Development Report 2000/1', mimeo, Brighton: Institute of Development Studies.

Mouffe, C. (ed.) (1992) *Dimensions of Radical Democracy: Pluralism, Citizenship, Community*, London: Verso.

Nelson, J. (1989) 'The Politics of Pro-Poor Adjustment', in J. Nelson (ed.), *Fragile Coalitions: the Politics of Economic Adjustment*, Washington, DC: Overseas Development Council.

Newell, P. (2002) 'Globalisation and the Future State', *IDS Working Paper* 141, Brighton: Institute of Development Studies.

O'Brien, R., A. M. Goetz, J. A. Scholte, and M. Williams (2000) *Contesting Governance: Global Economic Institutions and Global Social Movements*, Cambridge: Cambridge University Press.

O'Donnell, G. (1994) 'Delegative Democracy', *Journal of Democracy*, 5, 1: 55–69.

O'Donnell, G. (1998) 'Horizontal Accountability in New Democracies', *Journal of Democracy*, 9, 3: 112–26.

Oloka Onyango, J. (1989) 'Law, Grassroots Democracy and the National Resistance Movement in Uganda', *International Journal of Sociology of Law*, 17.

Oloka Onyango, J. (1995) 'Constitutional Transition in Museveni's Uganda: New Horizons or Another False Start?' *Journal of African Law*, 39, 2: 156–72.

Parekh, B. (1993) 'The Cultural Particularity of Liberal Democracy', in David Held (ed.), *Prospects for Democracy: North, South, East, West*, Cambridge: Polity Press.

Pateman, C. (1970) *Participation and Democratic Theory*, Cambridge: Cambridge University Press.

Pateman, C. (1985) *The Problem of Political Obligation: A Critique of Liberal Theory*, Polity Press: Cambridge.

Pearce, J., S. Cohen, and J. Ferguson (1990) *Colombia: Inside the Labyrinth*, London: Latin America Bureau.

Przeworski, A. (1991) *Democracy and the Market: Political and Economic Reforms in Eastern Europe and Latin America*, Cambridge: Cambridge University Press.

Reynolds, A. (1999) *Electoral Systems and Democratization in Southern Africa*, Oxford: Oxford University Press.

Reynolds, A. and T. D. Sisk (1998) 'Elections and Electoral Systems: Implications for Conflict Management', in Timothy D. Sisk and Andrew Reynolds, *Elections and Conflict Management in Africa*, Washington, DC: US Institute of Peace Press.

Robinson, M. and G. White, (eds.) (1998) *The Democratic Developmental State: Political and Institutional Design*, Oxford: Oxford University Press: 17–51.

Rueschemeyer, D., E. Huber and J. D. Stephens (1992) *Capitalist Development and Democracy*, London: Polity Press.

Sartori, G. (1987) *The Theory of Democracy Revisited*, New Jersey: Chatham House.

Sartori, G. (1997) *Comparative Constitutional Engineering: an Inquiry into Structures, Incentives and Outcomes*, Macmillan, second edition.

Saul, J. S. (1997a) 'Liberal Democracy vs. Popular Democracy in Southern Africa', *Review of African Political Economy*, 72: 219–36.

Saul, J. S. (1997b) '"For Fear of Being Condemned as Old Fashioned": Liberal Democracy vs. Popular Democracy in Sub-Saharan Africa', *Review of African Political Economy*, 73: 339–53.

Schmitter, P. C. (1994) 'Dangers and Dilemmas of Democracy,' *Journal of Democracy*, 5, 2: 57–74.

Schumpeter, J. A. (1965) *Capitalism, Socialism and Democracy*, London: Routledge.

Sklar, R. L. (1983) 'Democracy in Africa', *African Studies Review*, 26, 3–4.

Sklar, R. L. (1987) 'Developmental Democracy,' *Comparative Studies in Society and History*, 29, 4: 686–714.

Stepan, A. (1988) *Rethinking Military Politics: Brazil and the Southern Cone*, Princeton: Princeton University Press.

Stepan, A. and C. Skach (1993) 'Constitutional Frameworks and Democratic Consolidation: Parliamentarianism Versus Presidentialism', *World Politics*, 46, 1: 1–22.

Stewart, F. and M. O'Sullivan, (1998) 'Democracy, Conflict and Development – Three Cases', *Working Paper* No. 15, Oxford: Queen Elizabeth House.

Thomas, J. W. and M. S. Grindle, (1990) 'After the Decision: Implementing Policy Reforms in Developing Countries', *World Development*, 18, 8: 1163–181.

Weyland, K. (1996) *Democracy Without Equality: Failures of Reform in Brazil*, Pittsburgh, PA: University of Pittsburgh Press.

Weyland, K. (1997) '"Growth with Equity" in Chile's New Democracy?', *Latin American Research Review*, 32, 1: 37–67.

White, G. (1996) 'Civil Society, Democratization and Development', in R. Luckham and G. White (eds.) *Democratization in the South: the Jagged Wave*, Manchester: Manchester University Press: 178–219.

White, G. (1998) 'Constructing a Democratic Developmental State', in M. Robinson and G. White (eds.), *The Democratic Developmental State: Political and Institutional Design*, Oxford: Oxford University Press: 17-51.

Wood, E. M. (1995) *Democracy Against Capitalism: Renewing Historical Materialism*, Cambridge: Cambridge University Press.

Woodward, D. (1996) *The IMF, the World Bank and Economic Policy in Rwanda: Economic, Social and Political Implications*, Oxford: Oxfam.

World Bank (1992) *Governance and Development*, Washington: World Bank.

Young, C. (1976) *The Politics of Cultural Pluralism*, University of Wisconsin Press.
Young, I. M. (1990) *Justice and the Politics of Difference*, Princeton: Princeton University Press.
Young, T. (1993) 'Elections and Electoral Politics in Africa', *Africa*, 63, 3: 299–313.

Notes

1 This chapter originally arose from a writing workshop at the Institute of Development Studies in November 1998. An earlier (and longer) version was published in 2000 as IDS Working Paper No. 104. In addition to the three principal co-authors, written and other contributions were made by Alison Ayers, Sunil Bastian, Emmanuel Gyimah-Boadi, Shireen Hassim and Zarko Puhovski. Thanks are also due to Martin Doornbos for comments, to Alison Ayers and Robert Muggah for research assistance; to Kim Collins and Julie McWilliam for their patience in typing additions and maintaining version control; and to Aaron Griffiths for editorial assistance.

2 These and other models are discussed by Held (1987 and 1993).

3 See in particular Rueschemeyer *et al.* 1992, Wood 1995.

4 See the important but neglected tradition of thinking on popular, participatory or radical democracy (Pateman 1970; Mouffe (ed.) 1992; Escobar and Alvarez 1992).

5 See Newell 2002 and O'Brien *et al.* 2000, in relation to the labour, environment and women's movements.

6 To use a phrase popularised by Castañeda (1994) in Latin America.

7 What French scholars, such as Bayart *et al.* 1992, term 'la politique par le bas'.

8 All these terms refer to one kind or another of diminished democracy. They therefore differ from distinctions made between qualitatively distinct types of democracy, such as that made by Sklar (1983) between 'liberal', 'guided', 'social', 'participatory', 'consociational' and 'developmental' democracy.

9 Although India is generally regarded as the most successful Third World democracy, parts of the country have spent long periods under military administration characterised by systematic abuses of human rights (Brass 1995: 223).

10 Criticised in Amnesty International reports (1997, 1998) for a poor record of human rights protection in regard to black and Spanish-speaking minorities.

11 Schumpeter (1965) is the founding father of this tradition of analysis. A persuasive statement of the case for democracy realism may be found in Przeworski (1991).

12 See Hirst (1990), Pateman (1985) and Wood (1995), and the similar arguments of Saul (1997a and 1997b) concerning the pitfalls of democracy in Africa.

13 Gender is an enormously important factor, both in structuring the public sphere and in determining exclusion from it. We do not deal with it in detail

here only because it is the focus of a separate volume in our series: Goetz and Hassim, 2003.

14 See Sklar (1987), Moore (1995), Leftwich (1996) and White (1998) for recent reviews.

15 This position transcends the traditional distinction between those who see identity conflicts as rooted in the primordial 'givens' of kinship, community, tribe, religion and nation; and those who emphasise their constructed and mutable nature.

16 However, Reynolds includes a third species of majoritarianism, termed 'integrative majoritarianism'. Our fourth category of 'integrative power sharing' in effect fuses the latter and what Reynolds terms 'integrative consensual power sharing'.

17 None of these, however, are the *inevitable* result of consociationalism and there are important exceptions, as Reynolds (1999: Chapter 4) argues.

The Politics of Institutional Design in the South African Transition

DAVID POTTIE AND SHIREEN HASSIM

By 1990, the crisis of apartheid had reached unmanageable proportions for the ruling National Party (NP). Escalating violence – near civil war in Natal – forced an illegitimate government to maintain power through increasing repression. In black townships, the structures of the local state had been rendered virtually non-functional by residents' refusal to pay exorbitant rents and service fees, and their rejection of 'puppet leaders' appointed by the apartheid state. There was massive poverty resulting both from the exclusion of the majority of the population from access to state resources and the racial structuring of labour markets which kept black workers' wages low. In addition, the economy was in a critical state, with negative growth rates, spiralling inflation and lack of investment. Nevertheless, over the next few years, South Africa avoided the threat of full-blown civil war and economic collapse, and created the conditions for economic and political stability through a process of multi-party negotiation over a new democratic system.

This transition to democracy offers a valuable opportunity to study processes of democratisation in a context in which political institutions were relatively well established (despite their exclusionary nature), civil society was strong and local technical and legal capacity was highly developed. Here, institutional design was neither imported nor entirely top-down, but shaped by local actors carrying different ideological histories and different political cultures. The design of new institutions was a matter of intensive debate about trade-offs between and even within different parties, in which democratic demands and expectations from below mitigated against minimalist, formal interpretations, and foregrounded demands for substantive democracy. Indeed, the political party with the largest support base, the African National Congress (ANC), argued that the revolutionary project of 'transformation' would

60

be pursued within the framework of a social-democratic constitutional state. The extent to which institutions could at the same time act as both stabilising instruments and as vehicles for state-led radical change is therefore a central consideration in the consolidation of democracy in South Africa.

This chapter seeks to examine the politics of institutional design in South Africa, focusing on the ways in which the design of institutions accommodated or neglected the imperatives of political stability and redress of inequalities. We focus on four sets of institutions: the constitution, the electoral system, the form of government, and the national machinery for women. These institutions were designed in a deliberate and extended process of multi-party negotiation in 1992–4, during which there was considerable public debate over the desirability of various institutional options. The chapter outlines the key political factors which influenced the choice of institutions. An underlying concern is the extent to which the design of these institutions has facilitated the political participation of disadvantaged social groupings in both national political discussions and the policy formulation process.

The chapter also argues that, given apartheid's legacy of exclusion and the sophistication of institutions of control and repression, the development of institutions of democracy and inclusion is vital. Key political principles are participation, accountability and governance. We focus on the impact of the formal institutionalisation of politics on the ability of civil society organisations – particularly those whose primary constituency is relatively marginal to national politics – to articulate their interests within broad policy formulation. If 'hyper-institutionalisation' undermines the ability of social groupings to articulate interests and challenge fundamental assumptions of government policy, then the possibilities of eliminating major social and economic inequalities – in South Africa, those of gender, class and race – are weakened. As Waylen points out, 'institutional democratisation does not necessarily entail a democratisation of power relations in society at large' (1994: 328).

Institutional design

In South Africa, the handing over of political authority from the apartheid regime to a popular government was tied to discussions about mechanisms to ensure the longer-term sustainability of democracy. Partly this was a response to the realisation of right-wing parties that demands for separate institutions of representation and veto powers for minority groupings would not succeed. In part, though, it demonstrated

61

the ANC's view that the long-term legitimacy of the democratic government among whites, as well as local and international investors, lay in an explicit commitment that majority rule would not 'descend' into the 'African pattern' of one-party rule and uncurbed presidential power. The outcome was a strong institutional focus on multi-party negotiations. Rules and procedures clearly *did* matter.

Comparative transition theorists have identified three reasons for the importance of institutional design. First, institutionalisation of party systems is regarded as a key factor in determining the stability of democracies (Bartlett and Hunter 1997: 90). The concern here is that political parties are able to organise and represent constituencies with some degree of legitimacy and within the rules of electoral contestation, containing political conflicts within a stable frame. Yet, second, it is argued by some that well-developed state institutions can generate consensus about policy issues in ways that are unlikely if debate is only conducted through political parties. Consensus building with regard to policy making reduces the likelihood of opposition taking on radical popular forms such as riots and demonstrations. Third, institutional development is seen as crucial to providing mechanisms for holding governments accountable, both directly to citizens and to democratic norms and values enshrined in constitutions, etc. (Schedler, Diamond and Platter 1999). The central value of institutionalising the relationship between the state and various interest groups is thus seen to lie in its ability to enhance the conditions for the consolidation of democracy.

In the initial phase, the processes of institutional design focus on inclusivity of all political actors, but especially those with disruptive power, such as organised ethnic groupings. The degree of inclusion – who gets a place at the table – shapes both the nature and scope of institutions under negotiation, as well as their long-term legitimacy. Formal negotiations tend to favour political and social groupings that are already organised at national level, or have access to national actors. Poorly organised and resourced groupings, such as women and the rural poor, tend to be absent from institutional decision-making processes.

In South Africa, the ANC was seen to be broadly representative of the poor and the working class. In its alliance with the South African Communist Party (SACP) and the Congress of South African Trade Unions (COSATU) it appeared that the eradication of both racial and class inequalities would be central to negotiations. Women were less obviously represented as a constituency, although the ANC at least had a well-developed history of recognising women's demands. Women managed to insert themselves into the negotiations by a combination of moral suasion and multi-party organisation. This presence broadened the design of institutions to include addressing gender inequalities, expanding the conceptions of equality and rights enshrined in the constitution. As this chapter will argue, however, the capacity of these institutions to facilitate the narrowing of gender inequalities has been more limited. As in the case of class inequalities, good institutional design *per se* is insufficient for the consolidation of substantive democracy.

Procedural democracy can, however, enhance the legitimacy of democratic governments and clear the way for them to advance substantive democracy. From this perspective, three key features of institutional design determine the consolidation of democracy, and inform the principles of participation, accountability and governance. These are:

- the shifting power relations in society;

- the technical, legal and institutional design of the political system; and

- the distributive consequences of that design.

Many authors have tried to explain the necessity of the South African political transition on the basis of an enduring, and intractable, crisis in the apartheid regime (Saul and Gelb 1996; O'Meara 1996; Murray 1994). Nevertheless, one cannot simply read off the terms and character of the eventual transition as an inevitable outcome. This balance of forces produced neither armed revolution nor perpetuation of the *status quo*, and the eventual outcome owed much to political agency by the various actors. Their role has been variously analysed in terms of rational choice (Sisk 1995), élite pacting (Friedman 1993), and the character of the liberation forces (Marais 1998; Murray 1994; Sparks 1994; McKinley 1997).

The negotiations both emerged from and reconfigured shifting power relations in the period of transition. The search for inclusion and 'moderation' across the racial and geographic divides also (conveniently, for some) moved the ideological spectrum of politics to the centre through the elimination of radical options, including both the socialist transformation hoped for by some of the movements associated with national liberation struggles, and a far-right-inspired civil war. In some accounts of the South African transition, the role of élites and élite pacting were at the heart of the shifting relationship between the two protagonists, the apartheid government and the ANC-led alliance, particularly in the period when the multi-party talks broke down in

1992. At that time a 'channel' was opened between two of the top negotiators (NP member Roelf Meyer and ANC member Cyril Ramaphosa) and much has been made of the special relationship between them.

But this was only part of the story. SACP general secretary Joe Slovo argued that compromise would be essential for the ANC to take elected office, for without the existing civil service it would be unable to govern (Slovo 1992). Moreover, the ideological shift to negotiations generated a wide-ranging emphasis on process, and the creation of bodies for discussion, debate and interim government. The negotiations reflected a broad-based mobilisation of interests and organisations from both the state and civil society, even while actual decisions were made by a considerably smaller group. By contrast, both the Pan-Africanist Congress (PAC) and the Inkatha Freedom Party (IFP) generally remained out of the talks, with the PAC's armed wing, the African People's Liberation Army (APLA), persisting in armed attacks and the IFP's leader, Mangosuthu Buthelezi, preferring to dictate his terms from outside the negotiating process. Moreover, political violence continued during the entire negotiations period. While falling short of outright civil war, the death toll continued to rise throughout 1992 and 1993, and the resolution of the political deadlock was given added urgency.

The ANC's shift from revolutionary movement to negotiating partner with the apartheid government was also accompanied by a number of discursive shifts. Looking towards a future as party in government, the ANC shifted from the 1980s policy of ungovernability, in which illegitimate organs of apartheid power were rejected (through the campaign to boycott the payment of rents and services to local authorities, for example), to a discourse of 'democratic governance' and a focus on creating the conditions for macroeconomic and political stability, based on majority rule. Building a culture of democratic governance required the wholesale transformation of decision-making authority within the South African state. This shift was in part enabled by the ANC's long-standing commitment to consultation within its own structures, whilst in exile, during negotiations and after 1994. After 1994 the ANC reminded its supporters of the movement's historic commitment to non-racialism and democracy, with the attainment of state power as but one phase in what the ANC termed an ongoing national democratic revolution (ANC 1997: 8). Against the background of apartheid South Africa, the period 1990–4 ushered in a host of alternative dimensions of power where formal state structures were less relevant or had been rejected as illegitimate.

Given the structured inequality of economic and political life in South Africa, the ANC concern for redressing apartheid inequality was reflected in the emergence in tandem with the negotiations of a policy discourse of development. The resulting policy framework, the Reconstruction and Development Programme (RDP), was premised on meeting basic needs and established targets for the achievement of delivery in areas such as housing, water and electricity. For the ANC, the RDP both reflected a shift in discourse from ungovernability to development, and was itself a product of internal bargaining with its alliance partners. The RDP involved a reconfiguration of state decision making, since the RDP Office involved itself in budget decisions and became a central clearing house for the coordination of development expenditures across departmental lines. As well as being a state programme, the RDP was largely premised (at least in rhetorical terms if not always in practice) on the revitalisation of state–civil society relationships. As an approach to governance, it involved a populist appeal to deliver people-driven development, with beneficiaries gaining a say in how their communities would be developed. Thus the development process was treated as an important element in redressing the structured inequality of the apartheid regime.

These discursive shifts could modify but not wholly transform the power relations of a society emerging from a history of deep and entrenched conflict. These power relations obviously influenced the institutional choices made during the negotiations. At the same time, the institutional choices, once made, had their own distributive conse-quences. Moreover, the new institutions then became an important locus of power in their own right. Five methodological issues relevant to the remainder of this chapter flow from this conceptualisation of institu-tional transformation.

First, political transitions do not have a clear-cut end point where democratic consolidation magically begins, and South Africa is no exception. The formal aspects of procedural and electoral democracy have been established in South Africa, but the debate about the goals and substance of the democratic process in the country still continues.

Second, there are multiple streams of transition. South Africa has achieved a remarkably successful political transition, but the type of economic transformation that might have been expected in the early 1990s has not accompanied it. The privileging of the political moment in South Africa's transition was hard-fought, and the gains with respect to basic human rights and political representation are not to be dismissed.

However, there are also signs that important trade-offs have compromised the ability of the ANC to pursue progressive economic transformation. The ANC's linkage of democracy and development through its embrace of the RDP in 1994 signalled its intentions to advance the interests of the poorest of the poor. In the RDP, development was understood not only in terms of service and infrastructure delivery to redress apartheid inequalities, but also as a promise to alter the decision-making structures that sustain the flow of development. Equally important, the RDP was drafted through a consultative process between the alliance partners, and its status as election manifesto of the ANC appeared to confirm the values of inclusivity and accountability of the government to the ideals and values of the democratic movement.

Contradictions soon appeared as the RDP policy process was embedded in a macroeconomic programme that emphasised deficit reduction, state restructuring and fiscal sustainability. The resulting policy expression of this approach, the Growth, Employment and Redistribution (GEAR) strategy, was released in 1996 as the RDP Office was shut down. For critics of GEAR, the ANC was not merely stalling on its redistributive promises, but undermining its very capacity and will ever to deliver. The non-negotiable, all-or-nothing stance taken over GEAR by the Minister of Finance was a startling retreat from the politics of consensus represented by the RDP. The developmental state currently on offer in South Africa may well prove its worth in the future, but, for now, it is not of the type envisaged in the negotiation era and before.

Third, state reform occurs at an uneven pace. The negotiations process was characterised by advances and retreats, by consensus building and renewed political violence. Whereas some areas of debate were characterised by considerable public participation (the constitution, for example), others (such as defence) were not. Whist the basic structure of national government was set in 1994, the local government reform process proceeded throughout the remainder of the decade. After 1994 all levels of government in South Africa now shared a difficult balancing act between the twin imperatives of fiscal sustainability and enhanced service delivery.[1]

Fourth, the transition process conditions the character of political actors. The ANC has transformed itself from a liberation movement into a mass political party and it has embraced the policy process through an emphasis on consensus building. By contrast, the NP struggled to define a post-apartheid role for itself as an opposition party and it has not been able to create a national profile for itself remotely resembling that of the ANC. Where once it could negotiate from a position of strength because of its control over the state apparatus and the support of the economic élite, it is now very much a junior partner.

Fifth, political actors are in part conditioned and captured by institutional processes. This phenomenon is as true for trade unions and civic organisations as it is for political parties. Where civic organisations gear themselves for community consultation they can become captured by local élites, and where they interact with state-led processes of development they soon learn to structure their activities around the timing of state budgets and elections. On a more ominous note, they can also face the demobilisation of their membership and appeal. In the case of the tripartite alliance, the SACP and COSATU have counted on gaining access to the policy process through representation in national government. This alliance has strengthened their public profile, but generated considerable debate within their ranks over the costs and benefits of participation in government with the ANC.

Participation and negotiation, 1990–4

South Africa's long transition offered considerable opportunities for the reinsertion of popular politics into the country's social fabric. This process began with the unbanning of the ANC and the signing of the Groote Schuur Minute between the NP and the ANC in 1990, and went through a number of phases before a National Peace Accord was agreed to by political parties and interest groups in September 1991 (see the chronology of the transition in Table 2.1 on p. 68).

The Congress for a Democratic South Africa (CODESA) first met on 20 December 1991 and was attended by 19 political groups and governments (Friedman and Atkinson 1994; Davenport 1998). Almost 400 delegates met in a committee-based negotiating process. Several working groups were set up to negotiate five sets of issues: principles and structures of a new constitution, transitional government, creation of a climate conducive to peaceful political participation, constitutional future of the homelands, and the implementation of agreements reached at CODESA. The absence of women on the negotiating teams galvanised the newly formed Women's National Coalition (WNC), a coalition of women's organisations across race and party lines, into launching a national and highly visible campaign to raise gender issues in the negotiations.

Government footdragging in the face of ongoing violence was another feature of the negotiations. One NP strategist suggested during CODESA that the longer the transition the better the chances of the NP to win over black support (Mattes 1994: 4). For this participant, the ANC had

Table 2.1 Schema of South Africa's political transition, 1990–4

1990

February –	F. W. de Klerk announces release of Mandela, unbanning of ANC
May –	Groote Schuur Minute between NP and ANC
September –	Goldstone Commission is formed to inquire into ongoing violence

1991

February –	Exemption of Umkhonto we Sizwe (MK) from national peace accord
May –	ANC breaks ties with government, citing ongoing violence
June –	ANC holds first national consultative meeting
September –	National Peace Accord is signed by all parties
December –	CODESA meets

1992

March –	NP wins referendum to continue negotiations
April –	Government opens talks with PAC
May –	CODESA closes
June –	Boipatong massacre, 47 killed
June –	August – ANC engages in rolling mass action campaigns
September –	Bisho massacre, 29 killed
September –	ANC and NP sign Record of Understanding to resume multi-party talks

1993

April –	Chris Hani assassinated
April –	Multi-party Negotiation Process
June –	Conservative Party, KwaZulu government and IFP pull out of talks
July –	Constitutional principles adopted
September –	Transitional Executive Council (TEC) Bill approved in Parliament
November –	Interim constitution finalised
December –	Constitution adopted and first meeting of Transitional Executive Council

1994

Jan.–April –	Joint rule under TEC
March –	Afrikaner Weerstand Beweging (AWB) foray into Bophuthatswana
27 April –	First democratic multi-party elections

not returned from exile to take immediate power and the longer the transition, the greater the chance for disillusion with the ANC to set in. But as Friedman argues, CODESA was never meant to be a constitutional conference, only the means to prepare one, and South Africa's search for a negotiated settlement through 1992 and 1993 was characterised by alternating waves of hope and despair (Friedman 1993: 171).

Disagreements over NP demands for power sharing and a veto rather than majority rule, amongst other factors, led to the collapse of CODESA in May 1992. After the collapse, the ANC engaged in a sustained campaign of 'rolling mass action' to reaffirm the support of the majority of South Africans. Political violence remained a fact of life throughout the negotiations period. For example, there were over 3,000 political fatalities in 1992 and almost 4,000 in 1993, threatening to scuttle any chance of a return to negotiations.

Government complicity in the killings further threatened to undermine any return to negotiations. In September 1990 the NP government had established the Commission of Inquiry Regarding the Prevention of Public Violence and Intimidation (hereafter referred to as the Goldstone Commission, after the head of the Commission, Judge Richard Goldstone). The Goldstone Commission examined, *inter alia*, the possible involvement of security forces in acts of violence against South African political activists. This involvement came to be known as 'third force' activities, the 'third force' being defined as 'a sinister and secret organisation or group that [committed] acts of violence in furtherance of some nefarious political aim' (SAIRR 1993: 28). In its second interim report in 1992 the Commission said that it found no evidence of a third force. Instead the sources of political violence were many and complicated, including the actions of security forces, the sudden and unexpected unbanning of political organisations, and the existence of a climate of political intolerance combined with economic deterioration.

In the dark days when negotiations broke down, the ANC sought to demonstrate through its reliance on mass action that negotiations worked in tandem with the balance of power outside the negotiating room. Joe Slovo claimed that the negotiations demonstrated that they are 'a terrain of struggle which, at the end of the day, depend[s] upon the balance of forces outside the process. It was the link between the negotiations and our mass struggle that played the absolutely key role' (Slovo 1992: 7). But mass killings at ANC events in Boipatong in June and Bisho in September 1992 seemed to push the chances of a settlement further away than at any other time since 1990.

Nevertheless, it was also clear that neither side could secure a settlement on its own. ANC leader Nelson Mandela and President F. W. de Klerk of the NP government signed a Record of Understanding that committed each party to resume negotiations through a Multi-Party Negotiating Process (MPNP), although it was not until early 1993 that talks began again.

Ultimately, the second round of negotiations at Kempton Park took the form of two-way bargaining between the ANC and the NP, with other smaller parties lining up behind one or the other. The IFP continued to argue that the table had three sides, remaining a wildcard in the search for a political settlement. It (and to a lesser extent the Conservative Party) could hold other parties hostage by walking away from the table, only to return at the last minute to enable a settlement. While it could not entirely dictate the pace of events on its own, the threat of its non-participation became its strongest bargaining tactic.

However, both the ANC and the NP had reasons to worry about negotiations dragging on too long. By April 1993, the ANC wanted an election date to be set before any other issues were settled. From its side the NP feared that once an election date was set the ANC would stall on negotiating until after the elections and then decide matters on its own (Mattes 1994: 5). However the NP also worried about losing their constituency to the Conservative Party and the Inkatha Freedom Party as talks dragged on. Thus, despite fears from both sides about the structure and results of elections, both sides had more to gain from contesting them. But violence continued to threaten this result. Soon after the resumption of talks in April 1993, SACP leader Chris Hani was assassinated. In June 1993 the Conservative Party, the IFP and the KwaZulu government pulled out of the talks. In the same month armed and uniformed members of the far-right Afrikaner Weerstandbeweging (AWB) smashed the doors of the conference centre with a tank and occupied the lobby. Despite all the emphasis on compromise and conciliation, significant acts of aggression threatened to derail each phase of the negotiations process.

But even if the main contenders for power could agree on the process of negotiations, they still had to find sufficient common ground over the definition and nature of the state they would build. Here, the negotiations, focusing on consensus building, ultimately achieved a broad political and ideological convergence over the basis of state power. By privileging the political moment of the transition over the economic one, the ANC had accepted certain important parameters. Negotiations could therefore focus on the post-apartheid state structure and how far the distribution of political power would either break with the past or maintain continuity.

By June 1993 there was agreement on a two-phase transition process which would begin with the installation of a Transitional Executive Council (TEC), placing executive and legislative power in the hands of a non-elected body as an interim measure. The TEC would comprise all governments, political parties and organisations represented at the MPNP. The second phase of the transition would begin with an election in April 1994 to elect a constitution-making body to draft a constitution.

The government had conceded that an elected constitution-making body should draft and adopt the final constitution, while the ANC agreed that such a body should function as the legislature, and there should be an interim Government of National Unity to provide continuous constitutional government throughout the transition (Welsh 1994: 93). Following the 'shaming' of political parties by the WNC in the CODESA round, all negotiating teams included women. A women's caucus was formed to ensure that women had 'voice' within the negotiations, and to formulate common approaches to issues. Within the ANC, the concept of gender equality was accepted as central to the new constitution (Albertyn 1995).

Demonstrating inclusivity was increasingly important to the legitimacy of the negotiations. Agreement on an interim constitution was a crucial step towards building the formal structure of popular participation through democratic elections. The negotiations over the 1993 interim constitution tied any future political or constitutional dispensation to 34 constitutional principles (Constitution of RSA 1993: schedule 4). These were adopted as building blocks for the new constitution and would serve as the measure by which a proposed Constitutional Court would have to certify it. The principles addressed, *inter alia*, the separation of powers between the judiciary, executive and legislature (principle 6), the principle of both exclusive and concurrent powers for the national and provincial levels of government (principle 19), the entrenchment of basic human rights, linguistic diversity and non-discrimination, the recognition of traditional authority, and the objective of a non-partisan public service. These principles came to establish the basis for the 'normalisation' of South African politics, but would also become the focus of a highly charged debate during the drafting of the 1996 constitution.

The Kempton Park negotiations also created the Government of National Unity (GNU) to function as a transitional government over the next five years. This reflected how far the ANC had come on the road to

71

transforming itself into a legal entity prepared to work within the structures of state power. An essential element of the GNU was a sunset clause that would protect the security forces and civil servants from a wholesale purge when the ANC assumed political office. The ANC therefore acknowledged a balance of power in which the NP retained control of the state apparatus and security forces until the elections, and thereafter the basic personnel of those structures would remain unchanged. By agreeing to the GNU the ANC was converting its broad support from the people (expressed through mass action and insurrection) to electoral support for the ANC in state office.

The process and content of the negotiations era would structure basic political relationships far beyond 1994. The privileging of the political transition over economic transformation eroded the position of trade unions and civic associations in the negotiations. To be sure, a range of innovative practices such as the consultative forum process was instituted to bring trade unions, civic associations and other elements into discussion and debate. But these also marked the institutionalisation of civil society, as we shall show below with respect to both local government and gender. Political transition also demanded compromises from both the NP and the ANC, which became a focus for intra-party differences. Yet the most obvious success of the negotiations was to produce general agreement on the democratic process and pave the way for South Africa's first democratic elections in 1994.

Making peace

While the 1994 elections were the cause of much celebration in South Africa and around the world, making peace was never a foregone conclusion. Neither the South African Defence Force (SADF) nor the armed wings of the liberation movements trusted one another. After all, ongoing violence was a significant feature of the negotiations period and the future loyalty of the South African security forces remained a crucial issue for both the apartheid regime and the liberation movement. And yet, while the complicity of the armed forces in ongoing violence gained considerable attention, the debate about the future of the military remained out of public sight (the military dimensions of the negotiation process are discussed in a companion volume: Cawthra 1995). Only broad parameters were discussed at the CODESA negotiations, including: a commitment to the peaceful settlement of political disputes, that the security forces be bound by the principle of constitutional supremacy, that they be politically non-partisan, that they respect human rights and that they should strive to be representative of society as a whole (Fine 1993: 50).

The ANC decision to suspend the armed struggle in August 1990 effectively sidelined MK militancy and the potential for the revolutionary dimension of the mass struggle (Rantete 1998: 187). While the government argued that the ANC must suspend all forms of activity except negotiations, the ANC vigorously claimed for itself the right to continue mass action if not armed struggle. Mass action was dependent on the revitalisation of ANC branch structures, and between mid-1990 and early 1992 public enthusiasm for such activities appeared to wane. However, it was reinvigorated in 1992 by the collapse of the CODESA negotiations, with major protests following the Bisho massacre of ANC supporters by the Ciskei security forces and mass stay-aways from work.

Throughout this period MK recruitment continued, and the armed branch of the ANC sought to establish itself through the formation of community-level self-defence units (SDUs), although in the end these were not formed throughout the country, with KwaZulu the notable exception. Many MK cadres felt abandoned by the ANC's turn to negotiations, or they fell victim to targeting by the government security forces (Rantete 1998: 187; Seegers 1996: 277). And yet the overall numbers of MK recruits raised the MK's composition from fewer than 6,000 at the end of the 1980s to over 24,000 by late 1994 (Seegers 1996: 277), when they were integrated with the SADF along with security forces of the former homelands, to form the new South African National Defence Force (SANDF).

In addition to the institutional integration of the security forces, political relations among parties in conflict also required attention. From the perspective of the ANC, the IFP had acquired the reputation of being a disruptive force (Davenport 1998: 45). Its complicity with the NP and the security police further tainted its reputation after it was revealed that the latter had paid it to organise anti-ANC rallies after Mandela's release from prison (Nathan and Philips 1992: 119), and had funded an IFP-created trade union. These and many other links between the IFP and the NP strained attempts to create new institutional structures in the name of national unity.

Moreover, while political relations were governed at national level by such agreements as the National Peace Accord, conflict resolution in strife-torn areas fell to regional and local dispute resolution committees. Here, at the committee level, the real work of trying to forge peace was undertaken. Despite many high-level meetings between Mangosuthu

73

Buthelezi and Nelson Mandela, violence between followers of the IFP and ANC continued. An effective peace could only be built in civil society and it was precisely at the community level that apartheid and IFP–ANC political rivalry had so effectively created enduring divisions (Asmal *et al.* 1996). Nevertheless, the worst fears of covert action, and of destabilisation of the 1994 election process, never materialised.

Structuring inclusion: elections

The diverse strands of negotiations at national and local level laid the groundwork for the 1994 elections. The right-wing threat never materialised and the SADF provided security for the elections, which were roundly hailed as a great success.

The basic agreement on the structure of the South African electoral system was one means through which institutional design most influenced the parameters of political participation. One of the fears in the 1994 elections was that the ANC would win the two-thirds majority in the National Assembly that would enable it to change sections of the interim constitution without consulting other parties.[2] Such an outcome could threaten the previous years' efforts to build a balance of power. In the end such fears were unrealised, as the ANC's 62.5 per cent share of the seats fell just short of that mark. As Reynolds notes, even President Mandela expressed relief that the ANC had not reached the two-thirds majority because 'the government of national unity should in no way be an "empty shell" for opposition parties' (Reynolds 1994: 182). The 1999 elections, which formally ended the power-sharing arrangement, revealed that fears of a two-thirds ANC majority continued to be present among white voters, although again the final result found the ANC one seat short of the mark.

The post-1994 National Assembly consists of 400 members elected through a system of proportional representation set out in schedule 2 of the 1993 constitution. Candidates are selected from their party lists, with 200 of the candidates for the National Assembly selected on the basis of regional lists and the other 200 from national lists. Provincial legislatures are also elected on the basis of proportional representation. Elections for both national and provincial legislatures were held concurrently with separate ballot papers for each election. This electoral system was retained in the 1996 constitution.

Initially, the ANC did not endorse PR since it feared that it would necessitate government coalitions by over-representing minority interests, its previous thinking having supported a first-past-the-post constituency system. Mattes (1994: 7) argues that when the ANC endorsed PR in October 1990, they were partially encouraged to do so on the basis of opinion poll data that showed they would not be hurt politically. Moreover, demarcating small, non-racial constituencies for a plurality system would have been practically impossible given the background of apartheid geography. The ANC was extremely concerned that racial and ethnic politics should be undermined as far as possible without authoritarian regulations or limits on party organisation. In the end, the negotiators opted for a system of PR with the nation forming a single electoral district for the National Assembly. The parties could have, but did not choose to build a system of constituency representation into the PR system.[3] The central list system gave all parties the ability to control the nomination of candidates and ensure their loyalty in Parliament. For the NP and other smaller parties, the PR system was preferred as the best means to ensure maximum representation in the new assembly – and, indeed, the threshold of votes needed to get seats in Parliament was extremely low. In 1994 a total of seven parties won parliamentary seats. The NP was second with just over 20 per cent of the vote and the IFP was third with just over 10 per cent. The remaining four parties represented in the National Assembly each received 2 per cent or less of the vote (in 1999 the number of elected parties increased to 13). Represented parties benefit from access to public funding, under a constitutional provision in support of multi-party democracy.

An unintended consequence of the acceptance of the PR with List system was the room it offered women's organisations to demand the inclusion of women in the new legislature. Within the ANC, the Women's League spearheaded a demand for a quota of women on party lists. After heated debate, a 30 per cent quota was accepted for provincial and national electoral lists, although the demand for quotas in the ANC's internal structures was defeated. The outcome was the election of a relatively high number of women in both the first and second democratic elections (after the latter in 1999, women comprised 29.6 per cent of the members of parliament, placing South Africa among the top ten countries of the world). At the local level, the Municipal Structures Act of 1998 reformed the local government electoral framework and called for political parties to ensure that 50 per cent of the candidates on their lists are women and that men and women are evenly distributed on the lists (a voluntary target, reached only by the ANC).

The 1994 election therefore stood as a crucial, and bold, test for the legitimacy of the new electoral system and the principles of free and fair

75

elections as the basis of political power. However, the long-running contestation over the terms of the transition, the ongoing political violence, and fears of possible military or right-wing attempts to disrupt the electoral process all posed uncertainties about the success of the democratic transition.

At provincial level the ANC won a majority in seven of the nine new provinces. The NP won in the Western Cape and the IFP won in a highly contested result in KwaZulu–Natal. In the case of the IFP the party had only joined the electoral process five days before the elections but its controversial victory there gave the party a regional base and its share of the national vote brought IFP leader Mangosuthu Buthelezi to national politics.

On the basis of this thumbnail sketch of the results it is evident that it was still possible for political parties to play the regional and ethnic card in elections. The IFP was the most successful party in this regard, with over 85 per cent of its national votes coming from KwaZulu–Natal, overwhelmingly from ethnic Zulus. The white right was mobilised on similar terms, with General Constand Viljoen forming the Freedom Front (FF) early in 1994. The FF won approximately 400,000 votes at national level and over 600,000 votes in provincial elections on the basis of its call for the creation of an Afrikaner *volkstaat* (homeland). While the latter remained an unlikely prospect, the FF nevertheless attracted sufficient electoral support to defuse the possibility of widespread extra-parliamentary activity from the far right. And both the IFP and the FF had earned their places for the next round of negotiations in the shaping of the country's final constitution.

Structuring inclusion: constitutional government since 1994

The 1994 elections therefore set the stage for continued political transition with all the normal trappings of state power. The GNU was a multi-party government designed to be inclusive, democratic and representative. Parties winning over 20 seats were entitled to a cabinet post. Cabinet was to be comprised of no more than 27 ministers and each party participating in the GNU was to be represented in a proportional way. The first cabinet had eighteen ANC members, six from the NP and three from the IFP.[4]

The parliamentary rules were not spelt out in the constitution so the GNU inherited the rules of the former tricameral Parliament. The rules, however, were adapted, and the committee system was dramatically reformed with an increase in the number of committees and their opening up to the public. This degree of institutional change was obviously a challenge for MPs, most of whom had never sat in a legislature before. Building the new rules, transforming the demographic composition of senior staff and developing the research capacity to support MPs has been an uneven process (Jacobs 1998: 8).

The ANC's overall imperative to transform the legislature into a 'people's parliament' facilitated the demands of women MPs to make parliament more women-friendly. Women MPs drew attention to aspects of the workings of Parliament that they considered 'masculinist', including the shortage of washroom facilities, the lack of crèches and scheduling of debates in the early evenings. Addressing these obstacles to women MPs' effective participation became a priority in the first two years of the new government. Women's organisations are also guarding against representational losses due to changes to the electoral system. The Commission on Gender Equality has called for 'all political parties to introduce voluntary fifty per cent quotas for women candidates in future elections.... There is overwhelming evidence to suggest that women stand a better chance of getting elected under proportional representation, as opposed to constituency based electoral systems' (CGE press statement, October 1999). However, feminist activists have also noted that the PR system has undermined processes of accountability, another key value of the women's movement (Hassim 2003).

Attempts to link MPs to constituencies through the allocation of parliamentary grants have not succeeded. Although the South African PR system was designed to avoid bloc voting on the basis of race and region, it does affect legislative–executive relations. The voter has no direct sanction over individual candidates, and the MPs in turn lack a constituent power base in their dealings with the party and the executive. As a result, few MPs have made much use of the constituency grants. Issues of accountability were central to electoral debates in the 1999 election.

Aside from the successful creation of a multi-party government, the biggest achievement of the GNU was the passage of the 1996 constitution, taking up most of the MPs' time in the first two years of Parliament. The Constitutional Assembly which, in accordance with chapter 5 of the 1993 interim constitution, drafted the 1996 constitution, was comprised of a joint sitting of the National Assembly and the Senate. While the Constitutional Assembly was mandated to renegotiate the constitutional framework, much of the basic architecture had already been set out in the interim constitution. The new constitution was to comply with the

77

34 principles set out in schedule 4 of the interim constitution and was subject to the certification of the Constitutional Court.

Federalism posed a major stumbling block in the adoption of a new constitution. The IFP boycotted much of the constitutional negotiations owing to its concern that provincial power would not be entrenched. IFP leader Buthelezi called the proposed constitution an 'advanced death certificate of pluralism, federalism and freedom of a country which, constitutionally speaking, is committing suicide by instalments' (Reagan 1996). The IFP and the NP maintained that principle 19 of the 1993 constitution provided for entrenched provincial autonomy since it stated that 'powers and functions at national and provincial levels of government shall include exclusive and concurrent powers'. Principle 20, however, also linked those powers to financial viability, functional requirements and effective public administration.

In addition to the work of the Constitutional Assembly itself, the drafting of the 1996 constitution was also a broadly participatory and consultative process. The Assembly received more than two million submissions on the working draft from members of the public.[5] It relied on a media campaign with regular radio, press and television pro-grammes supplemented by a series of community and national level sectoral meetings to consult and inform the public. While it is difficult to assess the impact of public participation on the drafting process, the high public profile of the negotiations underscored the legitimacy of the new constitution.

Taken together, the various levels of debate around the constitution demonstrated that the drafting process was essentially political. Each theme committee charged with the technical aspects of the constitution had at least three expert advisers but the political parties drove the process. Moreover, unlike the Kempton Park negotiations in which the NP was under pressure to succeed, now the ANC had to serve as facilitator, since the NP, IFP and FF adopted hardline stances on issues that resonated with their supporters (federalism for the NP and IFP, creation of an Afrikaner *volkstaat* for the FF).

Foremost attention was placed on the Bill of Rights in chapter 2 of the constitution. Here, basic political rights and freedoms were expressed as well as economic rights. The right to strike for labour and the right to private property were included in the Bill of Rights. The developmental challenges facing post-apartheid South Africa were also recognised through clauses addressing basic rights to housing, health care, food, water, education, language and culture and social security. Rights of arrested, detained and accused persons were extensively specified, given the long history of repression and detention throughout the apartheid era.

Beyond the Bill of Rights the constitution addressed the form and structure of the new state, the responsibilities of the various spheres of government, and provided for the creation of state institutions to support constitutional government.[6] The adoption of these bodies emphasised the importance assigned to arm's-length institutions and the implementation of checks and balances beyond the simple designation of the executive, judicial and legislative branches of government. These features of the constitution were seen as necessary responses to avoid the apartheid era centralisation of power in the executive. The constitution therefore introduced an element of horizontal accountability into the ongoing business of government to complement the vertical accountability of the electorate through elections.

Structuring inclusion: alliance politics in power

An additional feature of government since 1994 has been the continued existence of a tripartite alliance involving the SACP, COSATU and the ANC. This alliance has retained and formalised their long-standing relationship during the struggle against apartheid and through the negotiations era. However, an important challenge for the ANC is that it must balance these constituencies against its claims to govern in the national interest. It must also fend off criticisms from the other political parties that it is captured by these 'special' interests.

The tripartite alliance has endured significant stresses and challenges arising from the policy shifts of the ANC government. The June 1996 introduction of the government's macroeconomic and fiscal policy in the GEAR document strained alliance relations. Members of the SACP and COSATU complained that they had not been consulted and that the ANC had simply introduced GEAR as a non-negotiable policy framework. In addition, critics of GEAR felt that it heralded the abandonment of the RDP, whose progressive orientation was based, in part, on submissions from COSATU and the South African National Civic Organisation (SANCO).

The introduction of GEAR seemed to them a reversal of the consensus-building approach, with government imposing limits to state action on the basis of fiscal arguments about the constraints on state spending and by extension, state capacity. For its part, the ANC denied that the RDP had been forgotten, being relocated to the line departments rather than remaining a single coordinating ministry. But at another discursive

79

level, the ANC embraced what it saw as the harsh reality of yet one more accommodation to structural adjustment to the prevailing global economic order. However, there has been no serious discussion of a split in membership, and in the run-up to the 1999 elections COSATU once again endorsed the ANC platform and released senior members to join Parliament.

Elsewhere the policy-making process also reflected a commitment to consultation and tripartism. For example, the National Economic and Development Labour Council (NEDLAC) is a tripartite policy body, launched in February 1995 to promote more inclusive decision making and consensus seeking in the economic arena. It structures the inter-action of labour, government and business on many economic issues. NEDLAC is divided into four chambers, each dealing with a separate policy area (public finance and monetary policy, trade and industry, labour market and development). The Development Chamber provides for the participation of a fourth constituency, civic organisations.

However, none of the institutions designed to facilitate participation in policy formulation were able to intervene in the key policy shift represented by GEAR. The Cabinet's position was non-negotiable, and neither NEDLAC nor the national machinery for women was privy to the Cabinet's deliberations as macroeconomic policy issues are outside their terms of reference. The South African Human Rights Commission, whose brief is to monitor the government's implementation of the socio-economic rights clause of the constitution – arguably undermined by GEAR – also did not intervene. Instead, NGOs and church groups formed an Anti-Poverty Coalition that sought to create pressure on government from the outside. These developments suggest that institutional design *per se* will not guarantee positive outcomes for poor people or weakly organised constituencies.

But in this apparent reversal the ANC has to face other institutional processes and dynamics. For example, just as the ANC has moved to embrace the policy arena it has found itself increasingly embroiled in bureaucratic and technocratic considerations. As a result, the ANC has become implicated in the inherited institutional and regulatory networks of the state, even as it engages those relationships with an eye to transforming them. The balance of the chapter deals with efforts to redress two such legacies. The first deals with the constitutional debate over the form of government in South Africa so as to address regional identities and inequalities through the creation of nine provincial governments. The second policy sphere deals with the attempt to create national machinery to enhance women's political participation.

Governance after 1994: provincial government

The current make-up of provincial government is a result of the pre-election negotiations over the form of the post-apartheid state. The negotiators settled on a three-tiered system of national, provincial and local government. Regional politics were acknowledged both in the party list structures for the National Assembly as well as in the adoption of a federalist form of government (a key compromise between the ANC and opposition parties). In the pre-1994 negotiations, the NP and the IFP were the strongest proponents of strong regional government and a federal state structure for South Africa. As Lodge (1999: 13) has written:

> The case for South African democracy's assuming a federal form was based chiefly on the supposed political benefits of a multi-centred political dispensation in ethnically divided societies. Dividing executive authority between central and regional government would give minorities, defined in different ways, a stake in the system.

Both the NP and the IFP felt that they would be able to protect their regional power bases through the promotion of decentralised state power. The prospect of gaining regional office was therefore a strong drawcard for parties that could not hope to achieve political power at national level.

While federalism did not appear among the 34 constitutional principles that laid the groundwork for the interim constitution of 1993, it was nevertheless implied in at least ten of the principles and in the division of concurrent and exclusive powers for national and provincial government (Davenport 1998: 64). The federalist theme was also retained in the drafting of the 1996 constitution, although designed along cooperative rather than competitive lines. The model of co-operative government was adopted to promote coordinated governance instead of allowing the provinces to 'compete with each other and the national government for power and resources' (Speed 1995: 9).

But the emerging politics of federalism in South Africa have not necessarily fostered strong and effective provincial government. In fact, the experience of provincial government since 1994 has been marked by financial instability, political turmoil and calls from some quarters to re-think its role and purpose. Ironically, the liberal Democratic Party, whose predecessors were key promoters of a federal system of government, are criticising provincial legislatures as incompetent and wasteful, and as arenas for the ANC to reward party loyalty.

81

The establishment of provincial government posed a number of administrative and financial challenges. Nine new provinces had to be demarcated for electoral and administrative purposes. In some cases former homeland administrations had to be integrated with the previous regional structures of the apartheid era and the new provincial legislatures had to be established from scratch. In May 1994 the central government assumed the powers of the four former provinces and the homelands. In effect, the new provinces did not have any power and would only receive their powers as central government determined that the new provinces had established new administrations capable of exercising it. Some premiers began to complain that they had assumed offices without power (SAIRR 1995: 351).

The restructuring and amalgamation of former homeland administrations posed an additional immediate challenge. For example, the creation of Eastern Cape province involved the amalgamation of the former homelands of Transkei and Ciskei with part of the former Cape Province. As a result:

> The legacy of the old Transkei and Ciskei to the new Eastern Cape government was chaos. More than a dozen reports by various auditors-general indicate that no reliable accounts were kept from about 1987. So many records have been destroyed or lost that it is now virtually impossible to find out where the money went, to construct asset registers for inherited offices, or to hold anybody accountable for the mess. (*Daily Dispatch*, 26 August 1997)

Even the selection of provincial capitals posed a major challenge. Five cities in the Eastern Cape claimed capital status with the matter eventually being settled in favour of Bisho, the former capital of Ciskei. In KwaZulu–Natal a different solution was found, with Ulundi and Pietermaritzburg serving as dual capitals and the provincial legislature rotating between the two cities.

Each provincial legislature is elected through proportional representation, with an executive council headed by a premier, who is elected by the provincial legislature. The GNU rules meant that consensual politics and proportional representation were to play a role in the composition of the executive and the distribution of cabinet portfolios: a party required at least 10 per cent of the seats in the provincial legislature to be represented by a member in the executive council.

The 1994 elections resulted in the ANC gaining provincial power as the majority party in seven of the nine provinces. The NP became the majority party in the Western Cape and the IFP won in KwaZulu–Natal.

The position in KwaZulu–Natal remained unchanged following the 1999 election. In the Western Cape, the NP experienced a dramatic loss of support, and is now only able to govern the province as part of a coalition with the Democratic Party (DP).

Under the 1996 constitution, provincial government has relatively few areas of exclusive legislative competence. Provinces have executive authority only to the extent that they have the necessary administrative capacity and national government may, under some circumstances, take over functions that a provincial government cannot properly perform (Constitution of RSA, 1996). The national Parliament was given the power to intervene in areas of exclusive provincial jurisdiction by passing legislation which is necessary to: (a) maintain national, economic unity or essential national standards; (b) establish minimum standards for service provision; and (c) prevent unreasonable action being taken by a province prejudicial to the interests of another province or the country as a whole (Constitution of RSA, 1996: schedule 5). The lines of distinction between national and provincial areas of competence are blurred since the constitution envisages shared or concurrent powers in many areas, including education, housing, welfare, environment, health, tourism, agriculture and trade, with provincial governments also having powers related to local government.

Against this background, the flow of legislation emanating from provincial governments has been slow, partly due to their restricted areas of exclusive legislative competence. As a result, most laws passed by provincial governments have been of a technical nature, designed to bring various provincial practices in line with national legislation or the constitution, or to provide the regional enabling frameworks for national legislation. Provincial legislatures have met for relatively few days each year. For example, the KwaZulu–Natal legislature only sat for 27 days in 1996, passing 12 pieces of legislation. In response, the ANC complained that: 'This is totally unacceptable. We cannot get bills through the House because we spend half our time correcting technical mistakes' (*Daily News*, 4 December 1996).

Yet, provincial government remains a coveted prize for the political parties. Provincial politics in KwaZulu–Natal especially was conditioned by the years of struggle, and the province remained wracked by political violence with 1,464 political fatalities in 1995, though this declined to 226 by 1997 (SAIRR 1998: 52–3). During the run-up to the 1999 national and provincial elections, the peace process remained as vital as ever. Political relations in the province continued to fracture, with the arrival of a new opposition party, the United Democratic Movement

83

(UDM), and long-standing rivalries revived through community power struggles fought in terms of support for the three parties, ANC, IFP and UDM. However, as a sign of some progress on the path to peace in the province, a KZN Peace Process Code of Conduct was signed by the IFP and the ANC in May 1999. Municipal elections held in December 2000 were peaceful.

Political parties have continued to show an interest in electoral contest at provincial level for several reasons. First, provincial government offers the opportunity for parties other than the ANC to exercise executive power. This factor is an important consideration following the end of the GNU era, since it contributes to meaningful multi-party politics. Second, provincial government offers the opportunity for smaller parties to contest political office, some on the basis of regional or ethnic mobilisation, others not. Third, chapter 3 of the constitution entrenches cooperative government, and as such provincial governments are likely to remain partners, albeit unequal ones, in the immediate post-transition structure of South African politics.

Governance after 1994: national machinery for women

In this section, we explore the extent to which the creation of institutions to address gender inequalities has facilitated the participation of women in key national policy debates, and shaped the overall policy priorities of the democratic government. The pressure for gender-focused institutions came from women within political parties (in particular the ANC), and the non-partisan Women's National Coalition. The WNC was formed in 1992, and may itself be seen as a product of transition. Yet women's organisations, although vociferous during the transitional negotiations, have not had the disruptive power of organisations like trade unions. Rather, the commitment to redressing gender inequalities became a marker to how far the ANC remained committed to its poorest constituents.

It can be argued that the package of arrangements designed into the constitution and the new democratic structures 'institutionalised' women's politics by drawing it into formalised structures and processes of interaction with other 'stakeholders' which are routine, repeatable and formalised. The intention is to ensure that gender concerns are 'mainstreamed' into the everyday work of government – procedures, policy formulation, and service delivery. Thus women's concerns are channelled inside government through the Office on the Status of Women (OSW), and in civil society through the Commission on Gender

Equality (CGE). Constituencies of women are formally organised in the Parliamentary Women's Group, and through the Joint Standing Committee for Improving the Quality of Life and Status of Women. In effect, what has been instituted is a 'gender pact'. As has been noted by numerous commentators, the achievement of this comprehensive set of institutions was a major victory for the women's movement (Kemp *et al.* 1995; Hassim and Gouws 1998; Cock 1997) .

One central consequence has been to 'open' the state to the consideration of gender issues both in its internal operation as well as in policy formulation. The role of the OSW, in particular, is to 'conceptualise a national gender policy and provide guidance on its implementation' by working with line ministries, provinces and public bodies in mainstreaming gender into all policies and programmes (CGE 1997: 53–4). Part of its brief is to liaise between the NGOs that deal with women's issues, and the Office of the Deputy President, as well as with Parliament. The location of the OSW in the Office of the Deputy President is widely regarded as giving it 'the necessary clout' (CGE 1997: 53).

Yet at the same time civil society women's organisations, most notably the WNC, were demobilised to the extent that their public profile diminished and their interventions in key processes, in particular in the formation of social policy, were limited. This does not mean that women's issues were off the agenda, but rather that many of the articulators of those interests shifted into the state. The departure of many highly skilled women organisers and leaders from civil society into government 'has harmed existing networks and organisations of civil society, and placed increased pressure on the human, technical and financial resources of non-governmental organisations' (Albertyn 1995: 11). Thus the shift to 'engaging' the state has in some respects had the direct, albeit unintended, consequence of weakening women's organisations, most notably the WNC.

With the effects of GEAR beginning to emerge in 1996, the budget allocated to both the CGE and the OSW was small, in both cases covering only personnel and not programme costs. The Democratic Party questioned whether a separate Gender Commission was necessary, and its protection in the constitution proved a major asset in this debate. As a result of its small budget, the OSW struggled to define an appropriate role for itself. Energies were taken up with finalising a National Gender Plan, a draft of which had already been drawn up as part of the RDP process. This task was confined to a small group of consultants, and women's organisations did not develop close linkages with this aspect of the national machinery. Although located within

85

government at the highest level, the OSW has not played a key role in pressurising government to address issues of gender inequality.

By contrast, the CGE, with donor support, embarked on consultations with women's organisations to define a role for itself. Funding crises symbolised the fragility of the national machinery, and drew allies within the women's movement closer to the CGE. While the CGE was not designed primarily to fulfil a policy role, it nevertheless became the fulcrum around which women's organisations pivoted. A series of 'Gender Dialogues' on key national issues (such as HIV/Aids, reproductive rights and electoral participation) reinforced this aspect of its work.

The key structure in terms of increasing women's access to and leverage within the state has been the Parliamentary Committee on Improving the Quality of Life and Status of Women, originally established to monitor government's commitments within the Convention on the Elimination of all Forms of Discrimination Against Women (CEDAW) agreement. It has developed a much more extensive role, however, identifying priority legislation and lobbying to fast-track it through the parliamentary rosters. In addition, it has used its status as a portfolio committee to invite submissions from a range of women's organisations, and to call ministers and senior civil servants to report on specific gender-related aspects of their work. As a result of its energies, three significant pieces of legislation were passed: the Choice on the Termination of Pregnancy Act, the Domestic Violence Act, and the Maintenance Act, all significantly improving women's legal rights and status.

The Committee was instrumental in driving forward a project to analyse the implications of the national budget for different sectors of women. However, neither the Committee nor women Cabinet members were able to challenge the Cabinet on the gender implications of its macroeconomic policy. While legislative changes were relatively successful, policy shifts were harder, despite the existence of a well-designed national machinery for women.

Hence, the development of institutions inside and outside government to make and influence social policy from a gendered perspective, as well as changing political priorities more generally, has shifted the terrain of politics more squarely into the state rather than civil society. Nevertheless, the role of civil society remains crucial, especially given the weakness of the state's national machinery for women. A recent study of how far the state has been 'engendered' found that the most crucial gains in the first government were the linkages between civil society and government, often outside of the context of the national machinery.

With regard to violence against women, reproductive health and customary law, the study found that pressure from 'outside' tended to be more decisive than that of institutions within the state (Albertyn 1999). The national machinery for women proved to be an ally rather than an initiator of policy change.

Engagement with policy has offered women's organisations the opportunity to engage with the difficult business of translating broad demands into implementable policy recommendations. In this policy process, however, women's organisations with a national presence and with sufficient resources are privileged over smaller women's organisations. This narrowing of civil society's policy focus reduces the likelihood of debate on the fundamental assumptions of political choices and institutional design, thus limiting the ambit of politics and of institutional change (Goetz 1998).

Conclusion

Emerging from a conflict-ridden past, the ANC sought to challenge the inherited structure of South African society. In the end it did so not on the basis of violent revolution but through negotiations and compromise. Process became a central feature of the operation of South African politics. At times this process has been consultative, democratic and participatory, whereas at others it has relied on élite pacts and bilateral deals. Nevertheless, the constitution bears witness to an emphasis on the entrenchment of the values of transparency and accountability. Against those goals we must continue to evaluate the resulting changes in South Africa on three main counts that have figured in this chapter: changes in the structure of the state, changes in the character of governance and changes in the decision-making process.

This chapter has examined the character of the negotiations era and the immediate time frame around the 1994 elections. A shifting balance of political forces brought about the incorporation of the liberation forces into state power and the ultimate political ascendancy of the ANC, demonstrated in its election victory. But the ANC's consolidation of political power also manifested itself in institutional and policy development. Through its accommodation to the market (GEAR) and power brokerage in the political realm (GNU, tripartite alliance, Constitutional Assembly debates, NEDLAC), the ANC demonstrated its ability to broker deals across a number of fronts, bringing in other stakeholders to share in the emerging political and economic dispensation of post-1994 South Africa.

Yet the institutionalisation of these interests has tended to assume a particular character. Despite the mobilisation of civil society through the civic movement in the 1980s, there was less entrenchment of civic organisations in the national policy arena than one might have expected. Civic and women's organisations have been accorded a relatively narrow role in the Development Chamber at NEDLAC. There have been various consultative initiatives within government departments but these have so far not substantially recast the decision-making structures of the state.

Even so, given the volatility and uncertainty of the negotiations period, the ANC has consolidated its hold on political power and the state apparatus with astonishing speed. Certainly, major inequalities persist with respect to the racial distribution and skills of state personnel. But the ANC has enthusiastically embraced the policy process, issuing a steady flow of discussion papers and legislative proposals to reform the state apparatus. Consultation and participation initiatives have taken place against the context of government policy statements, increasingly emphasising 'delivery' (of water, houses, health care, etcetera) to meet the 1994 promises of the RDP. The previous emphasis on process, so important for the negotiated political transition, has given way to an emphasis on efficient government.

It may be too early to judge the success of South Africa's transition to democracy. On the core assumption that an orderly transition with high legitimacy and inclusivity would lay the basis for peace and stability, the negotiators were successful. The PR electoral system has generated enthusiastic participation from all political parties, yielding diverse representation in the national and provincial legislatures. The ANC's commitment to gender representation is manifested in a women's 30 per cent quota of the party list. Hence in terms of multi-party participation and gender representation, the electoral system, as a product of the negotiated transition, may be assessed positively. Two successful elections, with high voter participation, decreasing violence and only minor irregularities suggest that the constitutional values of multi-partyism, and respect for political diversity are entrenched in the popular imagination. The design of institutional checks and balances on the executive authority has proved workable. The constitution and the Constitutional Court have been important sources of legitimate authority. The successful integration of the various statutory and non-statutory military forces into the SANDF has removed any possibility of military coups from the right, or violent insurrection from the left.

Less easily measurable are the impacts of institutional design on delivering development with democracy. Poverty levels in South Africa have risen in the period of ANC government. While the ANC has achieved macroeconomic stability, even in the face of crises in global markets, its relationship with organised labour has been increasingly strained. Alliance partners in the education, health and public sectors have used their rights to strike and demonstrate, leading to stand-offs between government ministers and unions. Legislation regulating working conditions negotiated within NEDLAC is under threat of revocation following investor complaints of a rigid labour market. The future of NEDLAC itself is uncertain, as participants lose faith in whether its agreements are binding. The sophisticated gender machinery has not significantly increased women's policy leverage, leading to disillusionment with state 'femocrats' and a call for a more autonomous women's movement.

These developments would suggest that the process of institutional design is not clearly bounded, nor are institutions always able to produce the outcomes that designers might wish for. Rather, the politics of contestation over policy formulation and outcomes will challenge how far institutions in themselves facilitate democracy.

Other institutional features of South Africa's transition are also difficult to assess categorically. Provincial government is a case in point. While the nine provincial governments remain important in political and electoral terms, their administrative contribution is less clear. They are important sources of employment, providing the majority of public service jobs – not unimportant in a country with official unemployment over 30 per cent. But provincial government may find itself on the receiving end of public service retrenchments, and in unofficial competition with strong metropolitan government at the local level.

Finally, the overall record of popular participation in South Africa's new democracy remains uneven. Where inclusion has succeeded in the creation of well-structured forms of political participation, the trade-offs against sustained activity in civil society, social forums and other non-state forms of politics are beginning to show. South Africa has succeeded reasonably well in building a politics of inclusion through institutional design. However, good institutional design *per se* is insufficient to consolidate substantive democracy.

References

African National Congress (1997) 'Draft Strategy and Tactics Document', ANC 50th Consultative Conference.

Albertyn, C. (1995) 'National Machinery for Ensuring Gender Equality', in S. Liebenberg (ed.), *The Constitution of South Africa from a Gender Perspective*, Cape Town: David Philip.

Albertyn, C. (1999) *Engendering the Political Agenda: a South African Case Study*, Johannesburg: Centre for Applied Legal Studies, University of the Witwatersrand.

Asmal, K., L. Asmal and R. S. Roberts (1996) *Reconciliation Through Truth: a Reckoning of Apartheid's Criminal Governance*, Cape Town: David Philip.

Bartlett, D. and W. Hunter (1997) 'Market Structures, Political Institutions and Democratization: the Latin American and East European Experiences', *Review of International Political Economy*, 4, 1.

Cawthra, G. (1995) 'Defence and Development: Dangerous Liaisons?', in P. Fitzgerald *et al.* (eds.) *Managing Sustainable Development in South Africa*, Cape Town: Oxford University Press.

Cock, J. (1997) 'Women in South Africa's Transition to Democracy', in J. Scott, C. Kaplan and D. Keates (eds.), *Transitions, Environments, Translations: Feminism in International Politics*, New York: Routledge.

CGE (1997) *Annual Report*, Braamfontein: Commission on Gender Equality.

Constitution of the Republic of South Africa, *Act 200 of 1993*.

Davenport, T. R. H. (1998) *The Transfer of Power in South Africa*, Cape Town: David Philip.

Fine, A. (1993) 'Working Group One' in S. Friedman (ed.) *The Long Journey: South Africa's Quest for a Negotiated Settlement*, Johannesburg: Ravan Press.

Friedman, S. (ed.) (1993) *The Long Journey: South Africa's Quest for a Negotiated Settlement*, Johannesburg: Ravan Press.

Friedman, S. and D. Atkinson (eds.) (1994) *The Small Miracle: South Africa's Negotiated Settlement*, Johannesburg: Ravan Press.

Goetz, A. M. (ed.) (1998) *Getting Institutions Right for Women in Development*, London: Zed Books.

Hassim, S. and A. Gouws (1998) 'Redefining Public Space: Women's Organisations, Gender Consciousness and Civil Society in South Africa', *Politikon*, 25, 2.

Hassim, S. (2003) 'Representation, Participation and Democratic Effectiveness: Feminist Challenges to Representative Democracy in South Africa', in Anne Marie Goetz and Shireen Hassim (eds.), *No Shortcuts to Power: African Women in Politics and Policy Making*, London: Zed Books.

Jacobs, S. (1998) 'Parliament's Post-Election Performance', in W. James and M. Levy (eds.), *Pulse. Passages in Democracy Building: Assessing South Africa's Transition*, Cape Town: Idasa.

Kemp, N. Madlala, A. Moodley and E. Salo (1995) 'The Dawn of a New Day: Redefining South African Feminism', in A. Basu (ed.), *The Challenge of Local Feminisms*, Boulder, CO: Westview.

Lodge, T. (1999) *South African Politics since 1994*, Cape Town: David Philip.

Marais, H. (1998) *South Africa: Limits to Change, the Political Economy of Transformation*, London: Zed Books.

Mattes, R. (1994) 'The Road to Democracy: from 2 February 1990 to 27 April 1994', in A. Reynolds (ed.), *Election '94: the Campaigns, Results and Future Prospects*, Cape Town: David Philip.

McKinley, D. (1997) *The ANC and the Liberation Struggle: a Critical Political Biography*, London: Pluto.

Murray, M. J. (1994) *The Revolution Deferred: the Painful Birth of a Post-Apartheid South Africa*, London: Verso.

Nathan, L. and M. Philips (1992) 'Security Developments Under de Klerk' in G. Moss and I. Obery (eds.), *South African Review 6: from Red Friday to CODESA*, Johannesburg: Ravan Press.

O'Meara, D. (1996) *Forty Lost Years: the Apartheid State and the Politics of the National Party, 1948–1994*, Johannesburg: Ravan Press.

Rantete, J. (1998) *The African National Congress and the Negotiated Settlement in South Africa*, Pretoria: J. L. van Schaik.

Reagan Information Interchange (1996) 'A Pause in South Africa's March Toward "Suicide by Installments?"' (accessed 9 September 1996).

Republic of South Africa (1996) *Constitution of South Africa*, Pretoria: Government Printers.

Reynolds, A. (ed.) (1994) *Election of '94: The Campaigns, Results and Future Prospects*, Cape Town: David Philip.

SAIRR (1993, 1994 and 1995) *Race Relations Surveys, 1992/3, 1993/4 and 1994/5, 1996/7*, Johannesburg: South African Institute of Race Relations.

Saul, J. and S. Gelb (1996) *The Crisis in South Africa*, New York: Monthly Review Press.

Schedler, A., L. Diamond and M. F. Plattner (eds.) (1999) *The Self-Restraining State: Power and Accountability in New Democracies*, Boulder, CO: Lynne Rienner.

Seegers, A. (1996) *The Military in the Making of Modern South Africa*, London: Tauris Academic Studies.

Sisk, T.D. (1995) *Democratization in South Africa: the Elusive Social Contract*, Princeton: Princeton University Press.

Slovo, J. (1992) 'Negotiations: What Room for Compromise?' *African Communist*, Third Quarter.

Sparks, A. (1994) *Tomorrow is Another Country: the Inside Story of South Africa's Negotiated Revolution*, Johannesburg: Struik.

Speed, S. (1995) 'A Step Closer to Lasting Democracy', *Mayibuye, Journal of the African National Congress*, 6, 1.

Waylen, G. (1994) 'Women and Democratization: Conceptualising Gender Relations in Transition Politics', *World Politics*, 46.

Welsh, D. (1994) 'The Making of the Constitution', in H. Giliomee, L. Schlemmer and S. Hauptfleisch (eds.) *The Bold Experiment: South Africa's New Democracy*, Halfway House: Southern Book Publishers.

Notes

1 Although no cabinet minister resigned between 1994 and 1999 for 'non-delivery', many scandals were covered in the press, particularly in housing, health care, education and social services. It is estimated that half a million jobs were lost. Despite the fact that a majority of the electorate ranked job creation as their number one priority, the ANC was re-elected with an improved majority. It would appear that the electorate was not yet prepared to punish the ANC for its inability to link democracy to development.

2 Section 62(1) of the interim constitution stated that bills amending the constitution require a two-thirds majority of all members of both the National Assembly and the Senate.

3 The only element of constituency representation is within the regional list, whose 200 names are allocated across the nine provinces on the basis of names suggested by party branches and officials in these provinces.

4 In June 1996, the NP withdrew from the GNU, losing its cabinet positions and effectively becoming the opposition. Although the IFP had stayed away from most of the Constitutional Assembly debates, it did join at the last minute, remaining in the GNU and retaining its cabinet posts.

5 Most were petitions and standardised letters organised by lobby groups. For example, the proponents of an Afrikaner homeland sent one million sub-missions, and the lobby to retain Parliament in Cape Town sent over 750,000. Nevertheless, over two hundred thousand other submissions were received: *Mail and Guardian*, 30 June–6 July 1995.

6 These included the Office of the Public Protector to investigate the activities of government; the Human Rights Commission; the Commission for the Promotion and Protection of the Rights of Cultural, Religious and Linguistic Communities (important, given the recognition of eleven official languages); the Commission for Gender Equality; the Auditor-General; the Independent Electoral Commission; and the Independent Authority to Regulate Broad-casting (Republic of South Africa, 1996).

The Reformulation of Ugandan Democracy

AARON GRIFFITHS AND JAMES KATALIKAWE

By the time Yoweri Museveni and the National Resistance Army (NRA) took Kampala in January 1986, Uganda had become known as the 'sick man of Africa'. There had been long periods of violent political conflict and military misrule, and the post-independence political and constitutional arrangements were in tatters. Since 1986, however, Uganda has been transformed. Under the National Resistance Movement (NRM), relative stability has been enjoyed by much of the country. A lively civil society has blossomed, the state's organisational capacity has increased, the army and police force have been shaped into more disciplined forces, and Uganda is a favourite of the international donors.

These successes came under the strong leadership of Museveni, and the NRM's 'movement political system', which made all Ugandans members of the movement, severely restricted party activity and promoted non-party local democracy. Notable innovations in grassroots political participation were accompanied by an ambivalence toward wider democratic reform stemming from the considerations of maintaining socio-political order and establishing legitimacy and authority after the long period of conflict and political flux. Increasingly, the workability of the movement system (and the role of constitution making in legitimising it) has been questioned. What was initially justified as an interim measure for reconstruction quickly became rationalised as the preferred form of political system. The contradictions emerged as a transitional regime proved to be an enduring one and an open, all-encompassing regime proved to be increasingly exclusive. Violent conflict has festered away in the North and shows no sign of ending. The perception of the NRM as a Southern-based organisation has never been dispelled in some parts of the country.

In the light of these ambiguities in the NRM's reformation of Uganda, this chapter will examine how both the movement system and the 1995 constitution have addressed the problems in Uganda's political system.[1] Briefly stated, this chapter takes the normative view that democratic politics are inclusive and based on discussion, accountability, and a non-exclusive conception of power, which in turn are ultimately required to create a sustainable peace. But democracy itself can be formulated in many different structures and institutions, all with their own problems (especially when misapplied), some of which may actually provoke conflict where institutional arrangements do not cross-cut political identities to promote coalition building. In assessing the efficacy of institutional design, the question to be asked is how far the choices made by the NRM since 1986 have embodied a political logic with a proven or likely positive impact in resolving or moderating the violent potential of Uganda's long-standing conflicts.

The historical context and the roots of conflict

A discussion of the NRM's choices needs to be set in historical context. Both the colonial and the nationalist governments failed to find structures to accommodate politicised ethnic group difference and the ambitions of 'tribal leaders' in a democratic polity. It is a problem that colonialism (both in the longer term and in the reforms it attempted in its dying hours) bequeathed to much of Africa, but in most places the experience led to less bloodshed and volatility than in Uganda. Since independence, tensions have persisted between different parts of the country, especially the developed central part and undeveloped North. Northern dominance in the military and inter-ethnic conflicts between different factions in the army only added to the strife. Depending on who is in power, some consider themselves central to the country's mainstream political activity, while others feel marginalised and out of the reckoning.

The ethnic and tribal variation underlying Uganda's cleavages (56 ethnic groups, four different linguistic categories and over 30 different dialects) does not mean that it is therefore impossible to forge a harmonious society within a stable nation state. Political institutions often failed in Uganda because they mediated these cleavages in a polarising rather than a cross-cutting way. The potential for Acholi Catholics to ally with Baganda Catholics, for example, thus reducing North–South polarisation, has rarely been realised, except in the early years of independence when the religious division of parties did give some cross-ethnic unity.

The roots of the problem must be traced to Uganda's colonial experience, which left damaging military, economic, religious and political legacies. The British favoured recruitment from the 'martial races' of the northern Acholi and Langi, a tradition and military model which continued after independence. Northern soldiers, whenever trouble has erupted, 'were usually over-zealous in restoring order among the southerners' (Furley 1987: 2). On the other hand, the British preferred to grow their cash crops in the more fertile South, which developed the best infrastructure. The North and West did not share in colonial economic development. Finally, the rivalry between the competing branches of Christianity persistently materialised as violence. During the early crystallisation of political parties, the Democratic Party (DP) emerged as mainly Roman Catholic, while the Uganda People's Congress (UPC) became mainly Protestant – both parties marked more by these characteristics than by any concerted ideology.

The political legacy of the colonial state was a narrow relationship with society, one of domination rather than representation, that left it unsuited to being a legitimate institution at the moment of independence. Further, the British formed differing relationships with the different tribal–political groups they encountered, and the governments they variously called kingdoms, territories and districts 'had no socio-political or economic network linking them to one another' (Odongo 2000: 33). The British relationship with Buganda was to be particularly significant. The *Uganda Agreement 1900* had appeared to set Buganda apart from the rest of Uganda and conferred on the Kabaka (the King of the Baganda) and his chiefs 'special privileges' in return for their cooperation. It set the scene for the disunity of Uganda when in the 1950s the Baganda resisted reforms of the Legislative Council: instead of agitating for more African representation they sought assurances that the Council would not affect the Agreement. This led to the abrogation of the latter, the declaration of a state of emergency in Buganda and the deportation of the Kabaka (who returned two years later). The idea of a unitary form of government for Uganda, which the British authorities supported, was in shambles, and no mass African nationalist movement emerged, as it did in Tanzania or Kenya, to counterbalance the sectarian nature of political groupings.

Independence in 1962 marked Uganda's first attempt at constructing a democratic polity. The 1962 constitution was largely based on the recommendations of the Relationships Commission, under the chairmanship of the Earl of Munster, which in turn reflected earlier agreements under which Uganda had already been functioning since the mid-1950s.

It suggested 'a composite state containing a single federal Kingdom (Buganda), in association with the rest of the country, which would be governed unitarily' (Munster Commission 1961: 55). Three other kingdoms not so far along the road to secession (Ankole, Bunyoro and Toro) were to be given semi-federal status 'in order to emphasise their traditional characteristics' (ibid.). This was not necessarily the best possible institutional solution, but reflected the realities on the ground, as the Munster report admitted:

> This cannot [the Commission observed] be said to be an ideal balance of forces, since it gives a unique position to Buganda, at present a disruptive element in the country. On the hand, the union of the rest of the country will be a powerful force to offset Buganda's powers and privileges, and to hold in check her inherent bias toward secession, so long as it may last. (Ibid.)

As one of the architects of the independence constitution has put it: 'it would have been a reckless disregard of realities not to relax the anxieties of [the] Kingdoms by providing some measure of federalism' (Ibingira 1973: 152–3). But it also produced anomalies and inconsistencies, such as the paradox of a unitary state with federal states contained within it, and the paradox of a republic whose first President was the hereditary ruler of Uganda's largest kingdom, even though the country as a whole was not a monarchy (ibid.).

The new fragile constitutional order, buttressed by a government coalition between the UPC and the Buganda-based Kabaka Yekka (KY) Party, worked until 1966, when the 20-year period of political instability and violence began. The immediate cause of the breakdown was the Buganda problem, which the 1962 constitution had tried unsuccessfully to accommodate. There were conflicting interpretations of the constitutional provisions relating to Buganda's autonomy. Then there was the 'Lost Counties' controversy concerning the return to the Bunyoro of two counties previously annexed by Buganda: the Kabaka refused to give his assent to referendum legislation and then refused to accept the results, triggering a political crisis. This, together with the growing tensions within the UPC, brought about the demise of the UPC–KY alliance, the censure of the Obote government, the arrest of five cabinet ministers at a cabinet meeting, the suspension of the 1962 constitution and the introduction of the 1966 interim constitution.

In retrospect, it can be seen that independent Uganda had a difficult and dangerous legacy to deal with, despite the optimism felt at the time. Ocitti describes the Lost Counties referendum as 'merely the spark that set off the time bomb' (2000: 401). That the independence constitution did not last or live up to its expectations had relatively little to do with the way in which it was made: by the standards of post-colonial constitutions it involved quite broad-based consultation, and made a serious effort to find solutions to the problems of a plural society. Rather, it failed because of the burden of colonial history and also because its post-colonial custodians proved unequal to the task. The President's refusal to assent to the Referendum Act of 1964 and his subsequent refusal to accept the results of the 'Lost Counties' plebiscite were not only provocative but also unconstitutional. Obote was not slow to pick up on this theme, and blamed the fact that:

> Parliament was [turned into] a forum for tribal representatives [who then proceeded] to frustrate any legislation which would curtail the powers of the rulers, tribal governments and tribal law making bodies. (Obote 1968: 9)

What he referred to as the 'surgery' to remove this problem involved a new interim constitution in 1966 which was shortly afterwards superseded by the republican constitution of 1967, the object of which was the removal of the perceived causes of the 1966 political crisis. But instead of a unifying constitutional settlement, Obote proceeded to prescribe a highly centralised constitutional regime. In lieu of the 1962 mishmash there would be one system of local government throughout the country. The constitution abolished the offices of the traditional rulers, the heads of district administrations, and sought to minimise tribal tensions by providing for a uniform system of local government with some decentralisation of government powers and functions. The federal and semi-federal status of the kingdoms having been dispensed with, there was to be an executive President, with wide discretionary powers. But the idea of a unitary system of government was overshadowed by the political realities of Obote's declining legitimacy. The 1966 crisis had left Buganda leadership alienated and bellicose, and no amount of political patronage could repair the damage. These spreading tensions soon engulfed the army, and in 1971 contributed to Idi Amin's military coup.

Life under Amin was nasty, short and brutish, and there was no room for constitutional niceties. The atrocities committed by Amin's regime have been graphically retold elsewhere (see Report of the Commission of Inquiry into violation of Human Rights, UPPC, Entebbe, 1994). Nor did Amin's Tanzanian-backed downfall in 1979 mean the end of Uganda's political problems. With the economy in tatters and

97

Table 3.1 Historical landmarks

Date	Event
1894	Territory made a British protectorate.
1900	Buganda Agreement.
1953	Kabaka of Buganda, King Mutesa II, exiled (returns two years later).
1962	Full independence. Milton Obote (UPC) as Prime Minister.
1963	Republican status on a federal basis assumed. King Mutesa II becomes President.
1966	Obote leads coup to depose King Mutesa and become head of state. Federal status withdrawn.
1967	New constitution.
1969	Opposition banned. One-party state.
1971	Coup led by Idi Amin.
1979	Tanzanian troops join with the Uganda National Liberation Army (UNLA) to defeat Amin, who flees to Libya. Dr Yusuf Lule is named President, and replaced two months later by Godfrey Binaisa.
1980	Army overthrows Binaisa and makes arrangements for elections. Obote returns to power following controversial elections.
1982	Tanzanian troops leave. The NRM and its military wing, the NRA, led by Lule and Yoweri Museveni, step up offensives.
1985	Obote loses control of army and is ousted by General Tito Okello.
1986	(January) Okello flees after short-lived power-sharing arrangement with the NRA. Museveni sworn in as President.
1988	National Resistance Council (NRC) passes bill establishing a Constitutional Commission to draft a new constitution.
1989	NRM extends its term of office till 1994 to allow time for a new constitution to be drafted.
1992	Political parties formally suspended by the NRC.
1993	(March) Draft constitution published. (July) The four tribal monarchies reinstated, with the kings' roles defined as traditional and cultural leaders.
1994	(March) Constituent Assembly elected to debate draft constitution. (December) NRM interim period extended until after next election.
1995	(June) Multi-party advocates walk out of Constituent Assembly after losing motion to delete movement system from the constitution. (October) New constitution promulgated.
1996	Museveni wins presidential elections. Uganda's long involvement in Democratic Republic of Congo commences as troops enter (the then) Zaïre.
1997	Movement Act comes into law.
1998	Political Organisations Bill is devised, but does not pass into law.
2000	Referendum result extends movement system. Over 90 per cent vote for it, on 51 per cent turn-out.
2001	(March) Museveni wins presidential elections. Runner-up Besigye files petition for annulment to Supreme Court which is narrowly defeated. Besigye flees Uganda.
2001–	Constitutional Review Commission.

most governmental institutions in terminal decline, there followed yet another period of great uncertainty and confusion. The Uganda National Liberation Front (UNLF) leadership, having ousted their common enemy from power, had nothing else in common, and their attempts to form a government of national unity were bedevilled by dissension and jockeying for ministerial positions and influence. Many lost both, and that paved the way for the infamous 1980 general elections, widely considered to have been rigged, that brought Milton Obote back to power and sent some disgruntled opponents, Yoweri Museveni among them, into the bush to begin the five-year 'bush war'. Many more massacres took place, notably in the Luwero triangle where the NRA had much support, before Museveni finally won power on 26 January 1986.

It was within this context of collapsed authority and violence that the new regime's choices were conditioned.

From Army to Movement, 1985–9

The process of shaping Uganda's new democratic polity occurred under exceptional circumstances: the violent overthrow of the previous regime by a rebel army comprising several competing dissident groups. The NRA/M leaders were then able to maintain enough of a consensus in favour of their right to exercise political authority (while successfully keeping their remaining military opponents at bay) to give them time to take advantage of their exceptional opportunity. They would build fresh state institutions and establish lasting control over all except the northern fringes of the country (particularly Acholiland). The political arrangement they used was no-party government, and below we sketch out how this model developed through the early period.

After prolonged bloodshed, the country was gasping for a new opportunity for peace, and the NRA/M's behaviour promised much. In this context the NRA/M gained a great deal of legitimacy by successfully articulating the promise of a revived and tangible democracy. While promoting it as essential for Uganda's future, the regime was less explicit about the form democracy would take. The argument for a movement system developed later. The Ten-Point Programme proudly proclaimed that the restoration of democracy was the NRM's top priority. Further, 'for democracy to be meaningful and not a mockery, it must contain three elements: parliamentary democracy, popular democracy and a decent level of living for every Ugandan' (The Ten Point Programme, 1985: 6).

This revealed a more comprehensive and participatory democratic

99

vision than a narrowly liberal one based primarily on representation in parliament, or a 'realist' view of democracy as a purely institutional arrangement. Yet this approach did not itself lead to the hybrid form of movement democracy that Museveni – 'a pragmatist rather than an ideologist' (Furley 1987) – developed. There was no real theory or strategy regarding how the parliamentary and the popular levels of democracy would combine, although both would operate without parties. With the attainment of power the question of the kind of democratic politics that would function at both levels was tempered by the requirements of setting up a stabilising interim government. Retrospectively, Museveni wrote that the interim period had two main aims, both of them state-building ones: rehabilitation of the country's collapsed infrastructure and economy, and laying a firm foundation for security, political stability and orderly succession of political authority, including reform of the army, police, judiciary and constitution (Museveni 1997: 192). Neither of these aims was deemed compatible with an immediate return to multi-party democracy. Instead, at the parliamentary level, state reform was to be overseen by a kind of government of national unity – not a coalition of parties, but a cabinet consisting of members of different parties. Museveni's first cabinet was drawn from all four corners of the country, and all ethnic, political, and religious affiliations, and varying shades of opinion were represented.[2] The concept of 'broad-basedness', a key part of the legitimation of having a 'movement', was endorsed.

Broad-based movement government was to function instead of multi-partyism. The NRM presented itself as what the country needed: consensual, inclusive, less confrontational, open to all comers, and giving pride of place to women and hitherto marginalised minorities. Because the Movement was broad-based and inclusive, and not prone to the flaws of competitive party systems, it was advanced as the only political system likely to serve the ends of national unity, reconciliation, political stability, security and development. It defined itself against the dismal record of the country's political parties, which, being largely based on ethno-religious affiliations rather than political ideology, were blamed for all the country's past political conflicts. There is certainly some historical substance in this argument. The parties that sprang up just before independence were geared towards not the consolidation of democracy but the struggle to decide 'who was to inherit the mantle of power from the departing colonialists and what security there would be for each of the diverse ethnic groups in the new state' (Grace Ibingira, cited by Mugaju 2000: 18). By 1964, following the decision of many opposition MPs to cross the floor and join the UPC, Uganda was a *de facto* one-party state (*ibid.*). With the eventual return to multi-partyism (1980 and 1985) came further violence and conflict.[3] Museveni would later rationalise this by arguing that the Ugandan peasantry were not ready for an organised pluralist form of democracy, not having been industrialised and allowed to crystallise into classes. Such a conception of democracy had deep roots in African nationalist and postcolonial discourse. It is based on mass mobilisation, rather than political pluralism and representation, and on consensus rather than opposition, attempting to address the problem of the diminished and alien public sphere that politics operated in under colonial rule. On the other hand, Museveni's hybrid version had more typically liberal democratic elements. It stressed constitutionalism and elections, and 'the power to change your leaders through a secret ballot held at regular intervals' was held to be the key to democratic self-governance (Museveni 1995).

It is arguable that the Movement was the most promising political organisation Uganda had yet seen. But as for why it emerged, it may be that rather than emerging from a clear antecedent political vision, it was because an attack on pluralist democracy would help obscure the NRM's country-wide support deficit. Museveni did not have enough highly qualified and experienced comrades to call upon in forming his government, nor did he have country-wide assured support. The NRA/M's political organisational base was narrow and it had to contend with the reality that the UPC and DP had deep historical roots and established claims over the political allegiances of Ugandans. They also had to deal with their allies who had fought alongside them against Obote and Okello, but perceived the NRA ascendancy as a brief interlude before the return of multi-party democracy. Before long, though, the Movement was defined not only as a congregation of forces, but – and this infuriated its critics – as a political system, narrowing the scope for potential opponents to withdraw their cooperation with their legitimate political status intact. The weak foundations of the regime led to increasing tensions and a spate of arrests of leading politicians in 1986. Broad-based rhetoric aside, Museveni's first cabinet was dominated by trusted members of the NRM, and in November 1986 the few non-NRM members from the UPC and CP (but not the DP) were demoted to junior functions to appease Movementists (Ocitti 2000: 339–40).

Alongside this attempt at creating broad-based government, Museveni's early moves also involved securing key powers and putting the NRM in control. One of the first things Museveni did was partially to suspend the 1967 constitution. Legal Notice No. 1 of 1986 (amended by Legal Notice

No. 1 of 1987) declared that the NRA leadership was an interim government to be in power for four years, and placed all legislative powers in the hands of the executive National Resistance Council (NRC). All political party activities were suspended for an interim period (as some claim was informally agreed in a gentlemen's agreement with all the parties). These arrangements also left all supreme executive powers, including control of the army, in the hands of the President, in keeping with the suspended 1967 constitution.

While the NRM's preferred form of *parliamentary* democracy was broad-based and party-less, the *popular* level of democracy was also being used by the NRM to establish a stable and legitimate power base by building grassroots support through local democracy. A participatory form of local government was introduced – the Resistance Council (RC) system – in which local communities participated fully in the election of their local leaders. It had its roots in the bush war. Well before achieving power, Movement cadres had formed 'Resistance Councils and Committees' modelled on Mozambican and Libyan examples (similar Tanzania-derived bodies were briefly tried in Uganda during the days of the National Liberation Front, 1979–80). Here, the work was done by the NRM cadres who, while the NRA was fighting, 'were going round the country, explaining our mission and advising the people at the village level on the settling of their own Resistance Councils' (Museveni 1997: 134). Their system of organising local communities helped build alliances between the poor Baganda peasants and the Banyaruanda migrant labourers in the Luwero triangle. The NRM, indeed, prided itself on dismantling the institution of chiefship which under colonialism had become what Mamdani (1995: 115) calls 'decentralised dictatorship'. Mamdani has argued that this introduced an important innovation in the arena of rights: the right of peasants *as communities* to hold state officials accountable, breaking with the received liberal tradition of individual rights. Further undermining tribal authority, the NRA redefined the basis of rights from descent to residence: all adults could belong to the council in their place of residence (Mamdani 1996: 202–8).

The result was a hierarchy of Resistance Councils, from village (RC1) through parish, sub-county and county to district (RC5). The RC system was an important innovation, and has been called the single most important achievement of the NRM, for it dismantled the colonial legacy of indirect rule at the local level and replaced it with village self-governance (ibid.: 215). There were also weaknesses, including the lack of attention paid to social differentiation within communities, and a tendency for the RCs to become instruments of the NRM, rather than the state or people. In this sense it could be seen as the consummate NRM reform – democratising the rural local setting, while keeping the representative aspects of democracy under its own control by restricting the kind of political organisation allowable, and making the highest level of local government (the district) still relatively small (and thus insignificant on the national stage).

While democratic decentralisation was a fundamental and lasting reform, the existence of a movement system was initially supposed to last for a few years, after which, the political parties having been freed, the government would go to the country. In the event, this did not happen. The interim period was extended in 1989 by another five years without much protest (only one member of the NRC resigned his seat, and he later returned to the fold). The country was for the first time in decades enjoying relative peace and the majority were prepared to let Museveni continue. The initial interim nature of arrangements became subsumed in a long constitution-making process that would ultimately formalise the movement system on a much more permanent basis.

Throughout this period, the NRM governed with the army close by its side. In 1986 the supreme authority of the government was vested in the NRC, the membership of which included representatives of the NRA (Legal Notice No. 1 of 1986). Legal Notice No. 1 of 1989 for the first time in the history of Uganda gave to the army a formal share of legislative authority. 'From the NRM perspective, it is impossible to exclude the army from the process of decision making, because after all, they "liberated the country from fascism"' (Oloka-Onyango 1992b: 100). Army participation in the governance of the country was also enhanced by a declaration that the Army Council, acting jointly with the NRC, would prepare and enact the new constitution, have the power to appoint and remove the President, and be able to declare states of emergency or insurgency (Legal Notice No. 1 of 1989).

The making of the new constitution, 1989–95

Rather than simply amend the 1967 constitution, restore the 1962 independence constitution, or appoint constitutional experts to prepare a draft constitution for promulgation by the NRC, the government chose a more original course. A Constitutional Commission was to be appointed to collect the people's views and prepare a draft constitution, which would then be submitted to a specially elected Constituent Assembly for approval and promulgation. This replaced the arrangement under which the National Resistance Army Council (NRAC) and the NRC were to act, in concert, as a Constituent Assembly. According to the then Army Commander, the reason for the change of plan was that the people participated in the constitution-making process, making it a more legitimate and lasting institution (*New Vision*, 5 April 1993).

In 1988 the 21-member Odoki Commission was appointed by the President, in consultation with the Minister of Constitutional Affairs. It was headed by a distinguished High Court judge (now Chief Justice), Benjamin Odoki, and included members from all ethnic and religious backgrounds, although 'almost to a person, it comprised strong adherents of the movement system, incorporating therein both the Political Commissar of the NRM as well as his counterpart in the NRA' (Oloka-Onyango 1998: 21). It reflected the usual method of NRM 'consultation' established from the first days of 'broad-based' government: hand-picked, individual and non-competitive selection (Oloka-Onyango 2000: 45).

The Odoki Commission began work in February 1989 and submitted a draft constitution in 1993, two years late. As mandated, the Commission toured the whole country, holding public meetings, debates, seminars and workshops and canvassing public opinion on a wide variety of constitutional issues. Many NGOs played a crucial role in assisting the submission of written comments. However, many question how genuine the consultative process really was. There were reports of agendas being fixed, controlled discussions, and ˙rumours that the constitution had already been drafted (Furley 1999; see also Furley and Katalikawe 1997). In a country with very high levels of illiteracy, a preponderance of élite participation could well be assumed. Museveni alleged something along these lines himself when he argued that the Commission was imposing its views, acting as a 'temporising force' which was 'watering down' the views of the people who, he claimed, did not want the return of parties for a long time (Museveni 1997: 94).

The Commission's final report rejected a one-party system but suggested periodic referenda through which people could choose between the movement system and a multi-party system. Its proposals set the framework for debates in the Constituent Assembly. It is fair to say that the Commission was not just a rubber stamp, even if it did produce a document largely consistent with NRM philosophy.

The elections for the Constituent Assembly (CA) were used as a trial run for the parliamentary elections that would follow. For the first time the NRM functioned 'almost as if they were a political party' and Museveni campaigned for 'NRM' candidates (Regan 1995: 178). The restrictions on political activity by parties during elections was at last formalised in the Constituent Assembly Election Rules, which included measures to prevent party activities, such as banning public rallies and other demonstrations in support of candidates. These provisions sharply restricted meaningful political debate, although Regan claims that there was in fact active party campaigning in many areas (*ibid.*).

Many complained that the rules on candidates' meetings were not conducive to effective debates. The 20-minute slot per candidate, for example, was in most cases inadequate for thorough analysis of the draft constitution. Many aspirants used money to buy votes, and many did not raise any constitutional issues during their campaigns. Oloka-Onyango (2000: 51) claims the electoral process was pushed underground – in a variety of forums including funerals and fund-raising events – and that it shifted the debate from issues to personalities and their proximity to the President. It is doubtful whether this would necessarily have been better under a party arrangement, but the polarisation between move-mentists and multi-partyists was carried over from the election to the CA itself, as noted below.

The CA elections were duly held in March 1994 and, as expected, the Movement supplied most of the delegates among the 211 returned at the polls – three delegates having been returned unopposed. In addition there were ten delegates appointed by the President; one woman delegate from each of the 39 districts, elected by an electoral college; ten army delegates; two trade unionists; eight multi-partyists; four youth delegates; and one delegate representing the disabled. There was applause for measures that allowed the hitherto disadvantaged and downtrodden to be involved in government for the first time in their country's history. Critics, however, suggest that virtually all the 39 women district delegates were Movement supporters, and that the same was true of the presidential nominees and the army delegates.

In practice, the ensuing constitution-making process only addressed most controversial issues (pluralism, federalism, and the hereditary kingdoms) within the boundaries set by the NRM and their control over the Constituent Assembly, and some of the issues were being pre-empted by the actions of the NRM regime before the constitution was complete. During the CA deliberations there were complaints that the multi-partyists were systematically ignored and their ideas were rejected, leading some to storm out of the deliberations on the extension of the movement system in 1995 (Ssenkumba 2000: 11). The debates over article 269 on political parties caused many CA delegates to walk out, while two sympathetic NRA delegates, Major-General Tinyefuza and Lieutenant-Colonel Serwanga Lwanga, abstained from voting. Oloka-Onyango concludes that it was the last nail in the coffin of the concept that the NRM was founded on broad-basedness, and the last point in the transition of the Movement from temporary arrangement to permanent fixture in Ugandan politics (2000: 52).

The constitution was finally enacted in 1995, with the movement system given a five-year term before being put to a referendum. While consolidating the position of the NRM's political system, this constitution puts political parties in a straitjacket. Under article 269 it allows parties to exist, but prohibits them from having branch offices, holding delegates' conferences or organising public rallies. Furthermore it prohibits them from 'sponsoring or offering a platform to or in any way campaigning for or against a candidate for any public elections', or 'carrying on any activities that may interfere with the movement political system for the time being in force'. Article 270 allows only for parties which were already in existence, restricting the creation of new ones. In effect, because the old parties cannot hold delegates' conferences to elect new leaders, old discredited leaders like Obote have been stuck in place, much to the advantage of the NRM.

Under article 70, the movement political system is described as 'broad-based, inclusive and non-partisan' and it is said to foster 'participatory democracy, accountability, transparency' and 'individual merit'. In contrast, the multi-party political system is not defined, yet severely restricted. Thus political parties are required to 'have a national character', may not 'be based on sex, ethnicity, religion, or other sectional division' (article 71), and must, regarding internal organisation, observe certain democratic principles such as regular elections of office bearers, and must ensure accountability for their resources, funds and assets. The Movement is exempt from all these stringent restrictions.

The constitution-making process is an example of the NRM's deft political management. While infusing itself with legitimacy through the consultation process, it managed to suppress demands that had previously riven Ugandan politics such as those for federalism and secession. Interestingly, apart from the movement system arrangements, the constitution is largely liberal democratic in form. Ottaway (1999) concludes that 'All told, the constitution has not created a monolithic system despite the absence of party competition.' It features extensive checks and balances, some pluralism of representation, and both horizontal and vertical dispersion of power. There is a Human Rights Commission (HRC), an Audit Commission, an Inspector General of Government (IGG), Director of Public Prosecutions, the Inspector General of Police, the Electoral Commission, the Board of the Central Bank, and a Public Service Commission. Many of these, especially the

IGG, have become independent and effective agencies (*ibid.*: 44). Since 1996 the HRC (based on an earlier NRM innovation) has been credited with some successes and given a lead on human rights issues, in some cases strongly criticising the security forces. Its work has been stymied by lack of adequate funding and lack of cooperation, but it has shown a positive commitment to its task. It has not dared deal with civil and political rights, though, or directly addressed the movement system (Human Rights Watch 1999).

The Movement entrenched, 1995–2001

Before some of the key issues in Ugandan democracy are discussed, this section will review some key events in the 1995–2001 period. The year after the enactment of the constitution saw the first presidential elections. DP leader Paul Ssemogerere was easily defeated by Museveni. Museveni (1997: 202) believes it was because of the record of the NRM in achieving peace and building the economy, while opponents complain it was thanks to the use of state machinery. There was some cause for encouragement in that Ugandans seemed to be looking beyond their own regional affiliations. Paul Ssemogerere did best in the North, although he is Muganda. There were also signs of less sectarianism on religious lines: the Katikiro (PM of Buganda) is a Catholic, unheard of before.

In the following years, complaints continued to increase that the Movement was continuing to consolidate its position as a political organisation to the detriment of the stated principles of no-party democracy. By late 1994, 42 of 48 ministers were staunch 'NRM supporters' (that is, not multi-partyists). Museveni's notion of broad-basedness became more selective as debates over multi-party politics and Baganda demands for a federal state threatened to become more divisive, and as elections were fought. By 2000, according to Barya (2000: 37), no pluralist could be found in any arm of the executive: '[t]herefore the all-inclusive non-partisan character – that is the little that existed in the 1986–1994 period – has vanished'.

In late 1996 a bill 'to make provision for the movement political system, to create the organs of the movement and to define the roles of those organs pursuant to article 70 of the constitution' was drawn up. The ensuing 1997 Movement Act created a political organisation with structures distinct from government (except in funding), framed in a manner that duplicates the RC system. But – as Colonel Kiiza Besigye, Museveni's erstwhile NRA colleague and ultimate opponent in the 2001 elections, complained – instead of calling it a political organisation, its makers called it a 'political system' (*Sunday Monitor* 5 November 2000: 33). Critics claim that the Act has several consequences: it reaffirms the NRM's monopoly of political activity and its hegemonising tendency since the transitional period was extended; it sets up political units and sub-units of the organisation and compels them to pay homage to a particular kind of ideology; and it creates a state within a state (Oloka-Onyango 2000: 57). This all follows from the debate over whether RCs are organs of the state, or organs of the NRM.

The Political Organisations Bill, aimed at removing the restrictions on political parties in article 269 to open up more space for them before the referendum, had been scheduled for December 1998, but was repeatedly withdrawn, even until after the referendum. The Bill was finally passed by Parliament in 2001, but the President sent it back, unhappy that parties would be allowed to operate outside Kampala and below the district level.

When the referendum of 2000 finally came around it was boycotted by many political opponents, and the Movement won with a vast majority of the votes cast. The turnout was around 50 per cent of registered voters, which is arguably not low compared to votes on constitutional matters in other countries.[4] The most concentrated levels of support for the Movement were in the South-west, and the weakest areas were those affected by the Lord's Resistance Army (LRA) insurgency, in the homeland of party figures Obote and Cecilia Ogwal, and in provincial urban areas (Armon 2000).

The Movement's electoral successes continued when, in the presidential elections of March 2001, Museveni won with 69.3 per cent of the votes cast ahead of Colonel Kiiza Besigye's 27.8 per cent. On a 70 per cent turnout (a good showing, although it was lower in Besigye-supporting areas), Museveni's national support increased marginally from the previous year's referendum. He took seven out of ten votes (of all registered voters including no-shows) in the West, and two out of every ten in the North. Apart from the North, Museveni remains most vulnerable in urban areas and those recently affected by conflict (except Karamoja) (Armon 2001). Besigye's petition to have the results annulled was narrowly defeated in the Supreme Court. Two out of five judges ruled that fraud and intimidation in the elections were sufficient to have affected the results.

There was undoubtedly harassment of opponents. Besigye was subject to travel bans and obtrusive surveillance before fleeing the country. Winnie Byanyima (MP for Mbarara municipality and Besigye's wife) was dismissed as Director of Information at the NRM Secretariat in

1999 for taking a position contrary to the party line, and is due to answer charges for treason and unlawful possession of a firearm (though she is not expected to be convicted on either count). Besigye's election-time youth mobiliser Rabwoni Okwir was unlawfully arrested, detained and 'manhandled'. Despite the new model constitution, certain anti-quated laws are still on the statute book, and are invoked against the press and non-Movement MPs. Members of the press have frequently been charged with sedition, treason and the publication of false news (*The Monitor*, 13 November 1999. Journalists frequently required to visit the CID include Wafula Oguttu and Charles Onyawga-Obbo of *The Monitor*). During the election campaign, some students were arrested and beaten up for committing the offence (still in the penal code) of 'annoying the President'.

In the midst of the presidential campaign a Constitutional Review Commission (CRC) was set up in a most precipitate manner, and many argue it was designed to steal Besigye's thunder. The CRC has a very broad mandate and its report (supposedly due in August 2002) will set the tone for political developments in the run-up to 2006. Its content, and the President's response, may give some clues about if and how the succession and liberalisation promised before 2006 may or may not proceed. As yet, the President has often asserted that the succession and liberalisation will occur according to schedule, but has given few clues as to how this will be achieved.

Discussion: democracy and the Movement

In summary, the NRM/Movement record since attaining power is in many ways positive. Along with economic growth, there are some signs of poverty reduction and improved social indicators. On the negative side, conflict continues to fester as it has throughout Museveni's rule. From the beginning, the NRA had been a disciplined force in the South and West, but was more brutal when sent into the North and East following 1986, being seen by some as part of a 'conquering mission' (*Weekly Topic*, 1 April 1987).[5] While other parts of the country have been pacified, the North has suffered continued fighting. Museveni has not been able to bring peace to Acholiland, where conflict has become entangled with cross-border problems with Sudan. The West also has border problems, although for a long time it appeared Museveni was not kept informed as to their extent.

The government's record shows a 'confluence of good governance and illiberalism' (Armon 1995). It might be argued that the latter is coming ever more to the foreground as, now that re-democratisation has been achieved, tensions build over Uganda's long-term future. The Movement looks set to stay for some time, and its democratic credentials are gradually eroding owing to its increasingly party-like characteristics (a party, that is, at the helm of a one-party state) and its harassment of opponents. In the light of the continuing troubles, the constitutional arrangements designed to moderate political conflicts are now regarded by many as self-serving – as no more than strategies for monopolising political power – and as such more likely to fuel than defuse the country's long-standing internecine conflicts. As one critic puts it:

> From the original fusion of moral and material goals of seeking a purified political system and greater equality of economic rewards, the NRM has turned into a powerful state-institution dominating all political and social groups, either turning them into auxiliaries or effectively neutralising or constraining their political influence. (Ssenkumba 2000: 2)

In this section, three problematic issues for Uganda's democratic institutions and politics are discussed: the degree to which power is concentrated with the army and the President (a long-time concern in Uganda, as Gingyera-Pinycwa 1991 stresses); questions around the movement system's ability to manage ethnic politics as the Movement behaves more like a dominant party; and the debate over whether some kind of federalism is a necessary form of power sharing in Uganda.

Concentration of power: army and President

Democratic institutions can only have limited impact where real political power remains in the person of the President and in the military, with little scope for holding them accountable. Power has long been concentrated in the hands of the Ugandan President. The 1967 constitution had instituted a strong president who could appoint or remove persons from public office without parliamentary approval, severely undermining the powers of various public offices and the legislature and judiciary (Oloka-Onyango 1992: 54). The 1995 constitution remains presidential in certain respects, but with perhaps more parliamentary and judicial autonomy, and with its presidentialism tempered by the IGG, Public Accounts Committee (PAC), a relatively free press, and decentralisation. Yet, as Kjaer (1999: 102) summarised the situation:

> there has not been a qualitative jump from personal to institutional rule. Museveni as a person embodies the movement, and he is the single most important guarantor of the sustainability of the present political system.

Museveni appears to dictate policy after consultation with a very tight old-army circle; the caucus and secretariat appear to be ineffective. From time to time he deploys a *de facto* 'whip system' in Parliament. The 'Movement caucus' intermittently allows him to ensure his core interests are served. Key examples include the passing in breakneck speed of a second Referendum Bill in 2000 when it became clear that the first would be ruled unconstitutional by the judiciary,[6] the equally swift amendments to the constitution effected when judges ruled that the voting procedures that had been being employed in Parliament were unconstitutional, and the 2001 Parliamentary Elections Amendment Bill.

The strength of the President is related to the continuing importance of the military. Under Obote, military power constituted the ultimate source of formal state power (Ocitti 2000: 47). It has remained so under Museveni in a somewhat less threatening form. The President is the Chairman of the Movement, the Chairman of the Army High Command, the Commander-in-Chief of the Uganda People's Defence Force (UPDF) and the Chairman of the Army Council. He was also for a long time – and unconstitutionally – Minister of Defence. Problems might stem from the fact that the NRM has retained some of the militarist ethic that helped it achieve power, and its attempts to deal with the situation in the North have reportedly been heavy-handed. On the other hand, the body of the army itself has been successfully reformed. In ten years Uganda succeeded in first absorbing rivals into the NRA, renamed the Uganda People's Defence Force (UPDF), and then demobilising much of the large army that remained with a donor-supported programme. However, in the late 1990s many demobilised men were reintegrated into the army for the Congo campaigns.

The army remains intimately close to Museveni and, more than any region, the army is Museveni's power base. Museveni in turn has kept it connected to the centres of power. The politicisation of the army is promoted in the constitution. Article 78(1) provides that Parliament 'shall consist of ... (c) such numbers of representatives of the army ... as Parliament may determine'. (This is subject to review ten years after the coming into force of the 1995 constitution, and then every five years.)

Given Uganda's history, Museveni may well be justified in his dedication to the military. Some would argue that politicising the army is a promising strategy for buying the military into the idea of stable government. Mudoola argued that the Ugandan military would be domesticated effectively by accepting it as an interest group rather than denying it an extra-military role (Mudoola 1991).

111

Despite its political role, the army has sometimes asserted its independence of the presidential power nexus. Army officers have been able to say deeply controversial things about, for instance, the Amnesty Act of 2000, relations with Rwanda and Sudan, and the restoration of the Ankole kingdom. It is when they touch on certain kinds of issues, however, as in Besigye's critique of Movement politics, that big problems arise. It is as yet unclear what effect continued involvement in the Democratic Republic of Congo and tensions with Rwanda and Sudan will have on the military's internal politics.

In sum, Uganda is far from being a military regime dominated by an ex-army President, but there is cause to doubt whether its democratic institutions have been institutionalised enough to guarantee that they will thrive if Museveni is succeeded by a less capable figure.

Movement or parties

The debate over the merits of the no-party movement system rages on. In our view, although there is a basis for arguing that no-party is a legitimate alternative to party democracy, the behaviour of the Movement as an organisation undermines the legitimacy of the system. In practice, the Movement only partially conforms to the model it advocates. It professes to be inclusive, but some perceive the government as waging war in the East and the North (Kasfir 1994: 149). Much of the leadership comes from the West, drawn especially from the Bahima of Ankole district. Official development programmes have been concentrated in the West, while many government institutions, especially security, are seen as Western-dominated, as are the Revenue Authority, Investment Authority and Uganda Railways (*Africa Confidential*, 1 March 1996).

Movement dissident Colonel Kiiza Besigye put forward three convincing reasons for the downfall of the original broad-basedness: some of the politicians from other parties in the NRM government sought to undermine the NRM or strengthen themselves, thus falling out with the leadership; original NRM politicians did not accept those who were in government as a result of the broad-based policy; and the NRM's growing belief that its grassroots support had grown enough for it to dispense with the broad-based elements (in *Sunday Monitor*, 5 November 2000: 32).

Museveni's furious reaction when Besigye announced his candidacy for the presidential elections (without consulting the correct organs of the Movement) betrayed how he appears to view the Movement as a party-like structure rather than an association of all Ugandans, any of whom could stand for office on the basis of individual merit. The

Movement principle of individual merit suffered further blows when the President successfully prevailed upon the Movement's national executive committee to endorse his candidature for the presidential elections; when he put pressure on the Movement to put forward only one candidate in all parliamentary seats where multi-partyists had a chance; and when he toured the country in the run-up to the parliamentary elections actively campaigning for, and against, particular candidates. The President's actions, and those of the Movement as an organisation, are undermining the movement system that was endorsed by 90 per cent of those who voted in the referendum.

The NRM no longer has legitimate grounds on which to criticise parties: 'if the parties have turned into breeding grounds for individuals who turn to politics as the quickest road to position and privilege, so is the NRM fast becoming so' (Mamdani 1993: 44). Further, if the Movement is meant to be the main political organisation in Uganda's democracy, it remains internally undemocratic. Before 1995, the NRM had never held a national convention, never elected any of its officers and never systematically consulted its membership about its policies. Even now, the internal structures of the Movement remain opaque and informal. Without formal predictable structures, reform is likely to be problematic unless driven strongly by Museveni. Kasfir characterises the Movement below the strong centre as a weak, non-vibrant organisation. Democracy in Uganda may have been consolidated, but less so 'movement democracy' (Kasfir 2000: 73–6).

If parties were to be allowed back, a first step would be to allow the Movement to become a party. Indeed there have been calls from its liberal wing to turn the Movement into a political party. But when Bidandi Ssali, Local Government Minister and a key (if liberal) bulwark of the Movement, suggested after the parliamentary elections (2001) that the movement should consider transforming itself into a party and opening political space to compete with other parties, Museveni's response was vitriolic public condemnation. In late 2001, Eriya Kategeya, Interior Minister, first Deputy Prime Minister, Movement stalwart and lifelong friend of Museveni, was also condemned by Movement hardliners when he made a similar statement.

Nor have the parties done all they can to make their return more likely. The opposition parties refuse to exploit the limited democratic space Museveni has allowed them, playing the politics of absolute principles instead. In other words, they refuse to engage with the existing political system and make few gains. NGOs, on the other hand, bring about some change by focusing more on the policy-making process than on the preferred principles for political competition (see Ottaway 1999: 44). Mamdani has argued that the movement system is to blame for artificially protecting the weak and shallow pre-1986 parties (Mamdani 1995: 122). Elements of the parties cooperated readily early on. The DP was a conspicuous presence in the early NRM governments. But the parties may feel they have more to gain by setting up a party–movement polarisation, while the differences between policy alternatives remain narrow.

To conclude, the movement system has not functioned as promised: to sustain a broad-based Movement requires a favourable political consensus, a Movement whose upper echelons do not appear to be drawn from a narrow base, and whose actions do not appear to be those of a dominant party harassing its political opponents.

Decentralisation of power and the 'federo' question

The devolution of power is often held up as a means of power sharing that can deepen democracy and help prevent conflict in plural societies like Uganda. Crook notes that one of the most important variables that determines whether this can work is the extent to which the regime can tolerate – or is forced to tolerate – regionalised political power bases. If it has reason to be nervous about providing an institutional base for ethnic rivals, it may try to fragment potential local power bases into smaller, less politically significant units (Crook 2001: 10).

The NRM response has been to ignore calls for a federalist system, opting instead for more fragmented decentralised bodies. The conclusion of the constitutional debate on the matter upheld the NRM's incipient policy: that power was to be decentralised to the districts, rather than to the provincial level as was desired by Buganda and other former kingdom states. The aim was to delimit local areas to divide the main ethnic power bases. There are no directly elected bodies between the District Councils and the national level: 'The intention is very clear; it is to diffuse and fragment any institutional bases around which ethnic or sub-national political identities could re-form themselves. Even the District boundaries have been demarcated in such a way as to sub-divide any traditional ethnic "political fiefdoms" or kingdom areas' (Crook 2001: 10).

The NRM fears federalism as an issue that could ruin its unifying project. Museveni purged his cabinet of 'pro-federo' ministers in 1994 because the issue was threatening to tear the NRM apart (National Analyst, 4 May 1995: 7). One former CA delegate claims the government has not only consistently gone out of its way to block any meaningful public discussion of federalism, but it carefully managed CA discussions to make sure decentralisation was designed with as little federal character as possible, despite evidence of considerable public support (Nabudere 2000). Instead, the constitution resurrects monarchism, albeit in a modified form (the kings are not to 'meddle' in politics, and the government has prevented the former Ankole Kingdom from reinstating its traditional ruler). The monarchical issue had threatened to be a troublesome one in the constitutional debates, and by giving way to the Buganda monarchists especially, the NRM succeeded in uniting all Baganda factions behind the constitution-making process.

The Local Council (formerly Resistance Council) system is the arena in which the NRA/M made most immediate progress in realising their own non-liberal-democratic form of democracy. It is an essential part of the new political system in a country that long suffered from oppressive state power wielded from the centre. Some argue that being NRM creatures the local bodies subverted democracy by acting primarily as NRM propaganda machines. While they gave expression to grassroots and popular aspirations during the years of struggle, under the NRM government they were increasingly deployed as instruments of the state to prohibit popular mobilisation (Mamdani 1991). Yet in 1998 three quarters of incumbents were removed in the local elections, suggesting decentralisation was at least making some headway in terms of accountability (Ottaway 1999: 37). Services such as education and health, which are largely delivered through the local government system, have also improved greatly since the mid-1980s.

However, it may be the case that Museveni's evolving strategy of undermining federal aspirations and boosting his own support with decentralisation could partially backfire. The number of districts increased from 39 in 1994 to 56 in 2001. Many argue that new districts come into being where the President perceives his interests may be best served through the fragmentation of certain ethnic or regional blocs. New districts have also tended to come into being around election time, and the President is usually rewarded with high levels of electoral support in the new districts. In some places, however, the electoral returns from creating new districts appear to be diminishing: new districts in the West registered inordinately high support for Museveni in the 2001 presidential elections, but in the North and around Kampala new districts registered lower support for him than their 'parent' districts (Armon 2001). The increase in the number of districts also raises the number of 'special interest' (and Movement-beholden) MPs in Parliament. The fact that the President 'sent back' the Parliamentary Elections Bill in 2001 and ensured the removal of a clause seeking to make the special interest

115

elections full-franchise is significant. The increased number of Movement-beholden MPs should also make it more straightforward for the President to amend the constitution during the course of the new Parliament. The setting up of new districts is costly and makes little sense in terms of the efficiency of the public sector, a point made by the World Bank. This policy also carries the risk that the demand for new districts among local élites could get out of hand.

Conclusion

Uganda, under the Movement, improved its socio-political situation dramatically, but has seen its earlier democratising momentum peter out. The NRM leadership has balanced an opening of democratic spaces on a level unprecedented in Uganda with a strong controlling hand that has narrowed the scope for effective opposition. Uganda has built a range of democratic institutions, but has not seen a full materialisation of democratic politics. The Movement allowed the blurring of its identity between state institution and party-like political organisation, weakening the credentials of its alternative form of democracy. Uganda's constitution building has been a success, but the stakes remain too high to allow democratic politics its full expression.

The Movement's monopoly of legitimate political space may retard progress towards stable, inclusive and accountable government. Without more effective opposition, the no-party system will not deliver. The story of Ugandan democratic politics is that of failed opposition to power. Not only has power been exercised unchecked, but it has managed to coopt potential sources of opposition if it has not engaged in violent conflict with them. In the 1960s the practice of 'crossing the floor' left the opposition to Obote in tatters. From the outset of the Museveni era, opposition has been discredited and stifled. Yet opposition exists in some form everywhere power is exercised, and we would argue that institutionalised opposition is an essential part of democratic politics. When repressed it is less likely to take forms consistent with democratic values. The lesson is that real politics cannot be legislated away. Mamdani's conclusions still holds: 'Neither consensus nor accountability ... can be legislatively decreed; both must be arrived at through struggle. Both need to be the outcome of political practices.' Consensus must be dynamic (Mamdani 1993).

References

Armon, J. (1995) 'A State of Developmental Democracy? Assessing Ten Years of Decentralisation and Constitutional Reform under the National Resistance Movement in Uganda', unpublished MPhil thesis, Institute of Development Studies, Sussex.

Armon, J. (2000) 'Referendum 2000 – Key Facts', mimeo, Institute of Development Studies, Sussex.

Armon, J. (2001) 'Uganda Presidential Elections 2001 – Key Facts', mimeo, Institute of Development Studies, Sussex, 5 November.

Barya, J.-J. (2000) 'Political Parties, the Movement and the Referendum on Political Systems: One Step Forward and Two Steps Back?', in J. Mugaju and J. Oloka-Onyango (eds.), *No-party Democracy in Uganda: Myths and Realities*, Kampala: Fountain Publishers.

Bratton, M. and G. Lambright (2001) 'Uganda's Referendum 2000: the Silent Boycott', *African Affairs*, 100, 400: 453–67.

Crook, R. (2001) 'Strengthening Democratic Governance in Conflict-Torn Societies: Civic Organisations, Democratic Effectiveness and Political Conflict', Sussex: Institute of Development Studies, *Working Paper* 129.

Furley, O. (1987) *Uganda's Retreat from Turmoil?*, Conflict Studies No. 196, Centre for Security and Conflict Studies.

Furley, O. (1999) 'Democratization in Uganda', unpublished paper presented at the Biennial Conference of the African Studies Association of the UK, School of African and Oriental Studies, University of London, 14–16 September 1999.

Furley, O. and J. Katalikawe (1997) 'Constitutional Reform in Uganda: the New Approach', *African Affairs*, 96.

Gingyera-Pinycwa, A. G. G. (1991) 'Towards Constitutional Renovation: Some Political Considerations', in H. G. Hansen and M. Twaddle (eds.), *Changing Uganda: the Dilemmas of Structural Adjustment and Revolutionary Change*, London: James Currey.

Hansen, H. G. and M. Twaddle (eds.) (1991) *Changing Uganda: the Dilemmas of Structural Adjustment and Revolutionary Change*, London: James Currey.

Human Rights Watch (1999) *Hostile to Democracy: the Movement System and Political Repression in Uganda*, New York: Human Rights Watch.

Ibingira, G. S. K. (1973) *The Forging of an African Nation*, Viking Press.

Kasfir, N. (1994) 'Uganda Politics and the Constituent Assembly Elections of March 1994', in H. G. Hansen and M. Twaddle (eds.), *From Chaos to Order*, London: James Currey.

Kasfir, N. (2000) '"Movement" Democracy, Legitimacy and Power in Uganda', in J. Mugaju and J. Oloka-Onyango (eds.), *No-Party Democracy in Uganda: Myths and Realities*, Kampala: Fountain Publishers.

Kjaer M. (1999) 'Fundamental Change or No Change? The Process of Constitutionalizing Uganda', *Democratization*, 6, 4.

Mamdani, M. (1991) 'Social Movements and Constitutionalism in the African Context' in I. Shivji (ed.), *State and Constitutionalism: an African Debate on Democracy*, Harare: Sapes Books.

Mamdani, M. (1993) *Pluralism and the Right of Association*, Kampala, CBR

Publications, Working Paper 29.

Mamdani, M (1995) *And Fire Does Not Always Beget Ash: Critical Reflections on the NRM*, Kampala: Monitor Publications Ltd.

Mamdani, M. (1996) *Citizen and Subject*, Kampala: Fountain Publishers.

Mudoola, D. (1991) 'Institution-building: the Case of the NRM and the Military 1986–9', in H. G. Hansen and M. Twaddle (eds.), *Changing Uganda: the Dilemmas of Structural Adjustment and Revolutionary Change*, London: James Currey.

Mugaju, J. (2000) 'An Historical Background to Uganda's No-Party Democracy', in J. Mugaju and J. Oloka-Onyango (eds.), *No-Party Democracy in Uganda: Myths and Realities*, Kampala: Fountain Publishers.

Mugaju, J. and J. Oloka-Onyango (eds.) (2000) *No-Party Democracy in Uganda: Myths and Realities*, Kampala: Fountain Publishers.

Munster Commission (1961) *Report of the Uganda Relationship Committee*, Government Printer, Entebbe.

Museveni, Y. K. (1995) 'What Did the Buganda Gain from the New Constitution?' Address by Yoweri Kaguta Museveni to Resistance Councillors at Mpigi District Headquarters, 16 September 1995.

Museveni, Y. K. (1997) *Sowing the Mustard Seed*, Macmillan: London.

Nabudere, D. W. (2000) *Uganda Referendum 2000: Winners and Losers*, Kampala, Monitor Publications.

Obote, A. M. (1968). 'The Footnotes of Uganda's Revolution', *East African Journal*.

Ocitti, J. (2000) *Political Evolution and Democratic Practice in Uganda 1952–1996*, African Studies 51, Lewiston: Edwin Mellen Press.

Odongo, O. (2000) *A Political History of Uganda: the Origin of Yoweri Museveni's Referendum 2000*, Kampala: Monitor Publications.

Oloka-Onyango, J. (1992a) 'Judicial Power and Constitutionalism in Uganda', Kampala Centre for Basic Research, Working Paper No. 30.

Oloka-Onyango, J. (1992b) 'Governance, Democracy and Development in Uganda Today: a Social Legal Examination', *African Study Monographs*, 13, 2.

Oloka-Onyango, J. (1998) *Governance, State Structures and Constitutionalism in Contemporary Uganda*, Kampala: Centre for Basic Research.

Oloka-Onyango, J. (2000) 'New Wine or New Bottles? Movement Politics and One-partyism in Uganda', in J. Mugaju and J. Oloko-Onyango (eds.), *No-Party Democracy in Uganda: Myths and Realities*, Kampala: Fountain Publishers.

Ottaway, M. (1999) *Africa's New Leaders: Democracy or State Reconstruction?* Washington, DC: Carnegie Endowment for International Peace.

Regan, A. J. (1995) 'Constitutional Reform and the Politics of the Constitution in Uganda: a New Path to Constitutionalism', in P. Langseth, J. Katorobo, E. Brett and J. Munene (eds.), *Uganda: Landmarks in Rebuilding a Nation*, Kampala: Fountain Publishers: 155–90.

Ssenkumba, J. (2000) 'NRM Politics, Political Parties and the Demobilisation of Organised Political Forces', Centre for Basic Research, Kampala, Working Paper No. 59.

Therkildsen, O. (2002) 'Uganda's Referendum 2000: the Silent Boycott. A Comment', *African Affairs*, 101, 403: 231–41.

Notes

1 We are grateful to Jeremy Armon, Martin Doornbos, Richard Crook and the editors for their comments on this chapter at various stages in its writing. The views expressed and errors contained in it remain ours.

2 It should be noted that this was not an entirely new idea. Most governments since independence have been both politically 'broad-based' and formed according to the doctrine of 'tribal balancing'. The first Obote government consisted of two parties – the UPC and the KY; by the time it was overthrown, it had several DP members in its ranks. Similarly, the Idi Amin military government was to some degree a coalition of forces, and more so the short-lived UNLF government and the Okello administration. As well as encouraging potential opponents to toe the line, broad-basedness helps to legitimise the old technique of using patronage to fill important political positions (Kasfir 2000: 65). Other critics attack it for giving the impression that recruitment is on a regional and ethnic basis rather than on merit (see discussion in Barya 2000).

3 Museveni has continued to present parties and opponents as 'wrong and doubtful' people 'with no ability to manage a nation', and claims that it would be suicide for Uganda to 'hand over power to people we fought and defeated', even if the constitution is supposed to allow them to compete for power (Museveni addressing a rally, *East African*, 12 February 2001).

4 Some believe that there was an effective 'silent boycott' by many sympathetic to multi-partyism – many Ugandans being ill-informed about the referendum and subject to political and social cross-pressures during the campaign. Others dispute these findings (see Bratton and Lambright 2001 versus Therkildsen 2002).

5 In 1987 the Holy Spirit Movement (HSM) emerged under Alice Lakwena, combining Northern (especially Acholi) nationalism, religious–moral crusade and belief in magic (Ottaway 1999: 34) and proceeded to wreak havoc in the North. Following its defeat, Joseph Kony's Lord Resistance Army (LRA) emerged, borrowing some elements of the Holy Spirit Movement but being more a political organisation entangled in the enmity between Uganda and Sudan. Although the LRA is unpopular because of its extreme brutality, support for the government remains low (*Weekly Topic*, 1 April 1987).

6 The former Speaker who lied under oath in defence of the first Referendum Act has recently been appointed Attorney-General. The Prime Minister and then-Minister for Parliamentary Affairs also lied under oath, with no detrimental impact on their subsequent careers.

Ghana
The Political Economy of 'Successful'
Ethno-regional Conflict Management

E. GYIMAH-BOADI

Like most countries in Africa, Ghana is a multi-ethnic, multi-religious and multi-cultural society. Not surprisingly, ethno-regional divisions and tensions have persisted in the postcolonial period. However, under both military and elected civilian administrations, ethnic, regional, religious and other social conflicts have been held in check. Since the early 1990s Ghana has gone through a process of political liberalisation and return to democratic rule, as have other countries in the sub-region. Political parties have been legalised, a new liberal democratic constitution has been promulgated, independent media are flourishing and civil society has surged. But, unlike other countries in the sub-region – notably Liberia, Sierra Leone, and until recently Nigeria – the process of democratisation in Ghana has not been accompanied by or degenerated into violent conflicts and instability. Moreover, widespread fears of an ethno-regionally driven implosion in the aftermath of a return to multi-party constitutional rule and after eleven years of authoritarian rule under the quasi-military Flight-Lieutenant Jerry Rawlings and the Provisional National Defence Council (PNDC) proved unfounded.

Why has Ghana not become as politically polarised and violent as other countries, despite its ethnic and cultural diversity, economic problems and vicissitudes? Why has the country escaped the violence and instability that have plagued democratisation elsewhere in Africa? How has Ghana managed ethnic, regional and other endemic social conflicts and prevented them from escalating into violence, especially under liberal political conditions? What are the prospects that peace and stability will continue to hold in Ghana's Fourth Republic and liberal constitutional order? These are some of the issues addressed in this chapter.

Ethno-regional profile of Ghana

Ghana is a country of about 19 million people comprising a variety of socio-cultural groups, of which the most important are the Akans (sub-divided into Asante, Fante, Akwapim, Brong, Akim, Nzema and other smaller units), who make up about 44.1 per cent of the population, the Mole-Dagbani (15.9 per cent), the Ewe (13 per cent), the Ga-Adangbe (8.3 per cent), the Guans (3.7 per cent), the Gurma (3.5 per cent), and other groups (11.4 per cent).

There is a rough coincidence of ethnicity and administrative region, though each region is also home to a sizeable number of 'strangers' and others who might have migrated out of their 'home' regions. The Ashanti, Brong Ahafo, Eastern, Central and Western regions are generally peopled by Akans; the Mole-Dagbani and Gurma are in the Northern, Upper West and Upper East regions; while the Volta Region is mainly home to the Ewe. Southern Ghana in general, and the Akan groups in particular, have enjoyed relative economic and political dominance in both colonial and postcolonial times. In addition to considerable ethnic rivalry, there have also been conflicts between the populist and élitist tendencies in Ghanaian society and polity.

Inter-group conflicts, including sporadic violence, have been recurrent themes in the Ghanaian political experience. Brong-Akans and Asante-Akans have feuded persistently over whether or not the latter is a 'vassal state' of the Asante Kingdom. Kokomba and Nanumba ethnic groups in the Northern Region, Akan settler farmers and their hosts in the pre-dominantly Akan cocoa-growing areas in the Eastern Region, and Ashanti settler farmers and their hosts in the Western Region have clashed over settler rights versus landlord claims. Inter-group conflicts have occurred under all types of regimes in Ghana – civilian authoritarian, civilian elected, military and quasi-military. Ga, Ewe and Akan rivalry pervaded the military government of the National Liberation Council (1966–9) (Dowse 1975). An Ewe irredentist movement had surfaced in the early 1970s under the Acheampong–NRC government.[1] And in the late 1970s and early 1980s class conflicts appeared to emerge as a leading form of inter-group conflict involving the popular classes (urban workers, the lumpenproletariat and, to some extent, the rural poor). This turmoil cohered around the person of Flight-Lieutenant Jerry John Rawlings and a group of left-wing intelligentsia who attacked the Ghanaian political, social and economic establishment.[2] The attempted coup of 15 May 1979, the successful coup of 4 June 1979, a three-month populist interregnum, as well as the 31 December 1981 coup and its immediate aftermath represent the high point of overt class conflict in postcolonial Ghana. During that period, there was an attempt to pursue economic measures and to institute political arrangements more responsive to the needs of the subordinate classes and to the disadvantage of the middle and professional classes as well as the traditional rulers.[3]

Ethno-regional tensions have seemed to escalate during the short-lived episodes of democratic rule. For instance, the first competitive electoral contests in the 1950s saw the emergence of ethno-regionally based political parties – the Ashanti-based National Liberation Movement, the Ewe-based Togoland Congress Party and the Mole-Dagbani-Gurma-based Northern Peoples Party.[4] There was a resurgence of ethnic tensions between Akans and Ewes in the late 1960s around the multi-party elections of that period and under the Busia–Progress Party (PP) administration. The ruling Progress Party and the main opposition party, the National Alliance of Liberals (NAL), were widely regarded as respectively Akan- and Ewe-based. A number of developments helped to stigmatise the Busia–PP government as anti-Ewe: the absence of Ewes in its Cabinet, the perception that Ewes were over-represented among the senior public servants affected by the government's 'Apollo 568' retrenchment exercise, and the dominance of Akans in army command positions. The Busia government's reaction to a court ruling in favour of an Ewe public servant named Sallah who had been retrenched, as well as the recriminations arising from the debate in Parliament in which a leading minister in the government had accused Ewes of 'inward-looking tribalism', reflected intensified Akan–Ewe conflict in a multi-party political context.[5]

It is also true that the management of inter-group conflict and the promotion of national unity have been high on the agenda of post-colonial Ghana. This concern with national unity and the prevention of disintegration arose from a general recognition by the nationalist élite that national unity rested on shaky grounds for a multi-national entity put together by the colonial authorities without regard to ethnic affinities. But it was ethno-regional (and class) animosities, surfacing in the period immediately before independence, that gave much urgency to the project. Having been largely neglected and left relatively undeveloped under colonial rule, the Northern Region declared a social and economic distance from the rest of the country and its leaders argued that their people were not ready to be governed as part of independent Ghana without special protections. Having been colonised by Germany, and governed later on as part of the UN Trusteeship Territories together with Togoland, Ewes in South-eastern Ghana exerted irredentist pressures towards their 'cousins' in Togoland. And Asantes demanded special protections for their cocoa and mineral wealth as well as their culture (Austin 1964).

Postcolonial governments, especially that of the First Republic under Kwame Nkrumah, took energetic measures to promote national unity and integration. Arguing that economic development required maximum political and social peace, and that a degree of 'totalitarianism' was necessary to contain the otherwise fissiparous tendencies in ethno-regionally and culturally divided Ghana, the Nkrumah–Convention People's Party (CPP) government embarked on a process of democratic closure and the institution of authoritarianism. The process began innocuously enough, with the passage of laws forbidding the formation of political parties along ethnic, religious and regional lines (Avoidance of Discrimination Act, December 1957), which effectively suppressed all existing parties advocating federalism, such as the National Liberation Movement and the Togoland Congress Party. Indeed, the dissolution in March 1959 of the quasi-federalist interim Regional Assemblies established under the 1957 (independence) constitution seems to have put a permanent lid on the issue of federalism and, to all practical intents and purposes, decentralised local government. The process of democratic closure continued with the expansion of presidential powers, the elimination of constitutional checks on executive power and the formalisation of single-party rule in the Republican era between 1960 and 1966.[6]

Democratic closure in Ghana reached its apogee under the military regimes that ruled Ghana from 1966 to 1992. Under the National Libera-tion Council (NLC, 1966–9), the National Redemption Council/ Supreme Military Council (NRC/SMC, 1972–9), the Armed Forces Revolutionary Council (AFRC, 1979) and the Provisional National Defence Council (PNDC, 1982–93), constitutional rule was replaced by rule by decree, parliaments were disbanded, political parties were banned and citizens were detained without trial or tried in extra-judicial tribunals.

However, distribution and redistribution of economic and symbolic goods as well as bureaucratic and political appointments appear to have been the chief strategies used in the fight for national integration. Thus, efforts were made under both civilian and military, authoritarian and democratic regimes in Ghana to spread the provision of economic infrastructure (especially roads, bridges and post offices) and social services (clinics and health posts, schools, public measures, etcetera) in all regions. And special attention was paid to the historically dis-advantaged Northern regions. For example, in the field of education, in addition to the system of fee-free primary and middle school for all Ghanaians, special facilities were given to children from the North for secondary and university education. Even in the location of state-owned enterprises, ethno-regional considerations were tolerated, sometimes in violation of economic rationality; and a tomato factory was located in Tamale in the North even though it was far away from the main producer and consumer markets in Southern Ghana.[7] To keep ethno-regional conflicts in check and the urban middle and nascent working classes (and especially its fraction of new graduates from the country's educational institutions) politically quiescent, Ghanaian governments pursued a policy of full employment in the state enterprises in particular, and the expanding public sector in general. This policy led to the creation of over 300 state-owned enterprises and a bloated civil service by the 1970s, and made the government the leading employer in the formal sector.[8] The pursuit of similar goals also led successive Ghanaian governments to maintain controls on the market and especially on the prices of popular consumer items, and to provide direct and indirect subsidies on various consumer items and social services. In addition, Cabinet, bureaucratic and technocratic positions in government and the public service, as well as membership of ruling military councils, were informally balanced to reflect the cultural and ethnic diversity of the country (see Table 4.1, p. 140).

On the whole, the system of rough equity in the distribution of government-controlled resources and high-level bureaucratic and appointive positions, complemented by centralisation of political power, worked reasonably well in the first 30 years of independence. Relative to other countries in the sub-region such as Nigeria, Ghana did not experience major eruptions of ethno-regional conflict, and relationships between the social classes and religions remained relatively amicable. Before the economic recovery of 1983, strategies of economic distribution[9] (either in the form of Nkrumah's 'state socialism' in the late 1950s and early 1960s, or General Acheampong's 'capturing the commanding heights of the Ghanaian economy' in the 1970s, or Rawlings's economic populism in 1979 and the early 1980s) have been at the core of the efforts made by postcolonial governments to reduce ethno-regional generational and nascent class conflicts, and to promote national unity. Thus, the failure to develop an efficient internal market during that period,[10] and the consequent economic, social and political distortions, could be taken, at least in part, as the price paid for the equally pressing imperative of nation building in an unformed nation.

The problem with Ghana's strategy of conflict management and nation building through the distribution of the national product, however, is that it worked best under conditions of relative economic buoyancy. Moreover, there were severe limitations on the ability of the Ghanaian economy, which was never strong in the first place, to sustain such distribution-driven programmes. By the early 1980s, the strategy had become untenable as the Ghanaian economy had hit rock bottom – with export production precipitously down, foreign exchange acutely scarce and the country's international credit rating very low; with a chronic shortage of spare parts, consumer goods and other supplies; and with its economic and social infrastructure in decay.

Additionally, the strategy of centralised control and distribution of the national economic product was inherently unsustainable. It fostered neo-patrimonialism and its accompanying political and economic logic – in which Ghanaian regimes and their leaders raided their own treasuries, engaged in reckless fiscal behaviour, and brutally exploited the most productive socio-economic sectors – especially the export crop rural producers – in order to secure their hold on political power.[11]

But how have the major changes in the direction of economic policy in Ghana in the 1980s impacted on national unity in general and, in particular, on the postcolonial model of nation building and conflict management through economic distribution?

Problems in the transition from distribution to economic rationalisation

Faced with acute economic crisis, social decay and political instability in the early 1980s, the PNDC was compelled to abandon the postcolonial model of economic development. Led by Flight-Lieutenant Jerry Rawlings, the PNDC embarked on an economic recovery programme along World Bank/IMF lines in 1983. The focus of this programme, at least initially, was on economic stabilisation, rationalisation and the rehabilitation of infrastructure. However, with the strong emphasis on economistic principles and goals (such as a quick return on investment and comparative advantage) initial investments in the structural adjustment programme (SAP) went into the rehabilitation of Ghana's export sector and the supporting infrastructural base of roads, railways and harbours. Thus the cocoa, timber and mineral-producing areas in the Ashanti, Brong Ahafo and Western regions, the port cities of Tema and Takoradi, the national capital Accra (home of most of the country's manufacturing establishments) and the Ashanti capital Kumasi were showered with attention in the SAP reconstruction exercise. By contrast, the historically disadvantaged and economically depressed areas, especially the Northern, Upper East and Upper West regions, appear to have suffered neglect during most of this period.[12]

It is true that SAP-induced austerities affected all segments of the Ghanaian population and socio-economic groups. But some evidence suggests that the urban low-wage earner and unemployed, as well as the poor in the historically disadvantaged and economically depressed areas, were among the most negatively affected groups. The urban working class suffered job losses under the labour retrenchment exercise in which at least 36,000 persons were laid off in the lower ranks of Ghana's education system and civil service between 1987 and 1990. In addition, their real incomes stagnated as the government imposed restraints on wages and allowed the cost of living to skyrocket through massive currency devaluations, price decontrol and the withdrawal of subsidies on health, education and potable water. Some analysts suggested that they could see a link between the outbreak of the guinea worm epidemic in Northern Ghana in the mid-to-late 1980s and the introduction of user charges on potable water under the SAP within the same period. Other studies documented declines in hospital attendance and enrolment in primary and middle schools in some of Ghana's historically disadvantaged (Northern) and economically depressed (Central and Volta) regions.[13]

Neo-liberal economic reforms and political consequences

As in many other countries in Africa, Ghana's SAP provoked widespread negative public reactions. While ethno-regional reactions to the SAP were muted and largely indirect, class reactions were sharp and direct. The strongest opposition came from working-class elements and labour unions – notably the Industrial and Commercial Workers' Union (ICWU), students and radical intelligentsia. Workers and their unions protested over wage restraints, removal of subsidies and cost recovery measures, as well as a threat to cancel leave allowances and labour retrenchment. Student agitation arose over the reduction of student allowances and the threat to impose charges on student services, while the radical intelligentsia charged that the PNDC had betrayed its anti-imperialist and populist ideology by consorting with World Bank/IMF neo-orthodoxy.

The adjusting regime in Ghana appeared to recognise the uneven impact of the programmes across social and ethno-regional groups and attempted to compensate losers directly and indirectly. The most direct attempt to compensate SAP losers came under the Programme of Actions to Mitigate the Social Costs of Adjustment (PAMSCAD). The programme earmarked US$84 million for community-initiated projects in health, education, housing and sanitation: poor farmers in the Northern and Upper regions, the impoverished, and those who had lost their jobs in the labour retrenchment exercise were targeted for assistance. Additionally, an effort was made to give special attention to job creation in the infrastructural rehabilitation activities under the Public Investment Programme (PIP, 1986–8). Furthermore, the extension of the national electricity grid through Brong-Ahafo to the Northern regions of Ghana, as well as the general spillover from the SAP such as improvements in roads, railways, telecommunications and supplies, could be regarded as indirect compensations to SAP losers.[14]

It is important to note, however, that these limited governmental concessions to social class and ethno-regional anti-SAP pressures constituted a deviation from the SAP. They came only as an afterthought and from a resolutely neo-liberal perspective were 'slippages' and intolerable breaches of the conditionalities imposed by the World Bank, the IMF and other relevant international financial institutions and bilateral donors.[15] The penalties for such offences ranged from deliberate delays in disbursing pledged donor assistance and reduction in donor support to outright suspension of the SAP and accompanying aid. Fear of incurring the wrath and provoking the sanctions of powerful IFIs and other external actors imposed severe restrictions on the ability and inclination of the PNDC government to use economic redistribution to appease ethno-regional and class interests, and/or to maintain ethno-regional and class coalitions.

Determined to stick with painful neo-liberal economic reforms, and afraid of taking measures that might incur the wrath of donors, the PNDC government became severely constrained in its ability to provide relief from austerities to affected social groups and ethno-regional interests. Thus, the regime resorted to a combination of authoritarianism and ethnic solidarity to underpin its political base.

The institutions and practices introduced earlier under the banner of revolutionary populism, such as the extra-legal public tribunals and National Investigations Committees, arbitrary arrests, detention without trial, disregard for due process, cruel and unusual punishment, and retroactive decrees, were retained and readily used to repress opponents of the regime. The PNDC government maintained tight control over the print and broadcast media and used them as tools for government

127

propaganda. In addition, it established a pattern of political violence in which alleged subversionists were tortured and tried in kangaroo courts, and not infrequently executed. It also kept a proliferating network of paramilitary and security organisations such as the Civil Defence Organisations, Commandos and Panthers, which served the government as vigilantes and enforcers.[16]

This PNDC authoritarianism was complemented by quasi-corporatist arrangements that involved state-supported private and public organisations such as the 31st December Movement, the June Fourth Movement, Committees for the Defence of the Revolution, Mobisquads of the National Mobilisation Programme, the armed forces (through the Office of the PNDC Chief of Staff and the Armed Forces Directorate) and the Ghana Private Road Transport Union.

This intense and prolonged political repression gave rise to the state of affairs in Ghana in the late 1980s aptly described by a PNDC official as the 'culture of silence'. Repression had become necessary as an instrument for the political management of an unpopular economic programme, state contraction and much-diminished opportunities for state patronage and clientalism. And it is instructive to note that PNDC authoritarianism was in full swing by the late 1980s, when robust autocrats in Africa and other parts of the world were in full retreat.

The adoption of neo-liberal economic reform was, at least in part, a causal factor in the isolation of the Rawlings government within a narrow ethnic compound. The reforms and their austerity and ideological implications caused alienation between the PNDC regime and its original support base of urban workers, students and radical intelligentsia. At least one major political outcome of this was dislocation in the ruling coalition and at the level of the political leadership. It led to the ethno-regionally significant departure from the regime of the 'Northern radicals' (Chris Bukari Atim, Sergeant Alolga Akata Pore and Zaya Yeebo, who had been big supporters of radical populist policies) and a spate of attempted coups. More significantly, it marked the beginning of the isolation of the Rawlings government and its inability to expand its social base beyond a narrow Ewe/Volta Region core and a few old friends. A critic of the PNDC government drew attention to this fact in a public lecture in 1988 when he asked:

> Is it not strange and rather unfortunate that the Head of State, the Head of National Security, the Head of the Police Service, the Head of the Army, the acting Governor of the Bank of Ghana and the head of the National Investment Bank, and I am sure there are others – all happen to belong to

a single ethnic group or at least a single region of the country? (Adu Boahen 1989: 53)

It is instructive to note that, despite the unfavourable public commentary attracted by this perception, and the obvious political embarrassment it represented, the PNDC government remained unable to overcome this problem throughout the remainder of its tenure.

Heightened ethno-regionalism can also be inferred from the increase in the number and activities of ethno-regional and community-based voluntaristic cultural and economic development organisations in the era of structural adjustment. They ranged from the usual 'old boys/girls' and parent–teacher associations servicing schools at the elementary and secondary levels, to town and village development associations and ethnic-regional solidarity groups. Examples of the latter kinds of associations in this period include the Volta Region Social Development Association, whose activities were organised innocuously around a soccer team, the Volta Regional Development Corporation (VORADEP) and the Western Region Movement for Unity and Development (WEREMUD), whose formation attracted hostile government attention. While these developments could be regarded in a positive sense as the healthy emergence of community self-responsibility and the flowering of civil society institutions, they also represented centrifugal formations in the malintegrated and unformed Ghanaian nation. In the PNDC era and under SAP, individuals and communities appeared to have become inward-looking rather than nationalistic in their outlook and expectations.

Transition to constitutional rule and conflicts

With the tenability of state distribution/state patronage and mass social welfare sharply diminished by economic decline, neo-liberal reforms and state contraction, the PNDC–Rawlings regime came to rely mainly on authoritarianism as the main strategy for controlling centrifugal pressures and promoting nation building. Under growing internal and external pro-democracy pressures in the late 1980s and early 1990s, however, the PNDC was compelled to change its strategy of governance. Against the protestations of the regime and its supporters that political liberalisation would undermine economic reform and revive societal conflicts, preparations for a return to civilian constitutional rule began in earnest in late 1991.

On the face of it, the transition to constitutional rule in the early 1990s was no different from the previous ones (1969 and 1979). The

129

PNDC would look for a proximate and ideologically compatible group to whom it could hand over power or with whom it could negotiate a transfer of power – as the NLC had been able to do with the Busia–Progress Party in the late 1960s and the AFRC–Rawlings had been able to do with the Limann–Peoples' National Party (PNP) group in the late 1970s.[17] But the problem was much more tricky for the quasi-military PNDC–Rawlings. The regime had lasted longer than all previous regimes and was therefore more deeply entrenched in power. Moreover, it had antagonised the two main groups in the Ghanaian political establishment: the left-of-centre Nkrumahist group and the right-of-centre Busia–Danquah group. Its human rights record had been atrocious and it feared post-incumbency reprisals. Compounding the concerns arising from these factors was the fear of an anti-Ewe backlash, in the face of persistent public perception that Ewes dominated the PNDC–Rawlings government. Against this background, the PNDC was more strongly motivated to control the transition process than previous military regimes.

Thus, unlike previous military regimes, the PNDC refused to declare its political neutrality. Instead, it openly sought to control the entire transition process and to give itself maximum advantage. While it accepted the report of the National Commission on Democracy (NCD) to return the country to constitutional rule, it did not commit itself to any timetable. Instead it established a Committee of Experts to formulate proposals for constitutional proposals. The report of the Committee was then submitted to the Consultative Assembly, established by the PNDC to draft a new constitution for the country. The regime packed the transitional bodies, especially the Consultative Assembly, with its partisans, while limiting the participation of those known to harbour dissenting views. It refused to liberalise the chilly political setting within which the transition was taking place: repressive PNDC decrees stayed in place, as did state control of the media, strictures against the return of exiles and a ban on political party activities (finally lifted only six months before the presidential elections). Indeed, most key transition decisions such as the appointment of members of the Interim Electoral Commission were made unilaterally by the PNDC. And, in a further manipulation of the transition process, the PNDC sneaked into the draft constitution clauses that granted full immunity for all PNDC members and their actions.[18] Thus the 1992 transition could be described as having been effected by a combination of 'pacted' and IFI/donor-imposed conditionality – confirming the status of the PNDC as a bureaucratic, authoritarian government with strong neo-patrimonial tendencies.[19]

Notwithstanding the above limitations, the draft constitution approved overwhelmingly in a referendum in April 1992 was a fairly liberal democratic document – providing for a President, a National Assembly elected on a multi-party basis, and a wide range of freedoms with checks on executive power. Presidential elections were held in early November 1992, followed by parliamentary balloting in late December 1992. On 7 January 1993 Ghana launched its Fourth Republic under a liberal constitution, with Rawlings as the elected President and his National Democratic Congress (NDC) as the ruling party.[20] Significantly, several provisions of the 1992 constitution sought to affirm the desire to promote inclusive civic participation and national unity. For instance, both the Christian and Muslim groups in the country were given one representative on the National Media Commission, a body created to regulate the media; and each region was to elect a representative to the Council of State, the President's main advisory body. Article 35 (6b) of the constitution enjoined the State of Ghana to take appropriate measures to 'achieve reasonable regional balance in recruitment and appointment to public offices'; article 55 (4) provided that political parties must have a national character and that membership should not be based on ethnic, religious or other sectional divisions; and under article 55 (9), the members of the national executive of a political party had to be chosen from all regions of Ghana.

However, other provisions of the 1992 constitution did not help the cause of national reconciliation and may have sown the seeds of political instability. The clauses in the transitional provisions of the constitution, – such as those entrenching controversial PNDC structures like the public tribunals, and especially the ones providing blanket indemnity to the members of the PNDC for all their actions – removed any real possibility of effecting redress and restitution in favour of those who had been wrongfully punished under the AFRC/PNDC dictatorship. The sneaky manner in which the transitional provisions were inserted into the constitution raised considerable public outcry and frustrated the chance of open dialogue and reconciliation between the incumbent PNDC and its teeming detractors. Much of the opportunity to use the transition process to foster reconciliation between the PNDC and its opponents, and thus to secure future political stability, was thereby lost.

Indeed, the controversies generated by the indemnity clauses and the PNDC's tight manipulation of the transition process set the stage for intense political conflicts over the electoral process and its aftermath. Against the background of intense opposition suspicion that the PNDC was bent on self-succession, the election campaign was highly acrimonious and disputes arose over its outcomes. While some international

131

observers gave the transition elections a qualified approval, the opposition parties and their supporters charged that factors of an uneven playing field, over-exploitation of incumbency, the bloated voters' register, the pro-government election authority and a host of irregularities were responsible for the victory of Jerry Rawlings and his party in the presidential polls.[21]

The declaration of Rawlings as the winner triggered a spate of post-election violence, including the detonation of four bombs in different parts of Accra by a shadowy group called the Alliance of Democratic Forces (ADF), the politically motivated death by burning of the chairman of the Western Region branch of the ruling NDC, rioting by supporters of the main opposition party (New Patriotic Party, NPP) in many large cities, including Kumasi (Ghana's second-largest city, capital of the Asante Kingdom and opposition stronghold, where a dusk-to-dawn curfew was imposed and a state of emergency declared). The disputed election results also led to a boycott of the parliamentary elections by the main opposition parties. With no contest from the opposition, the NDC cleared 189 of the 200 parliamentary seats, and the remainder were won by former allies of the NDC or friendly independents – making the first Parliament of Ghana's Fourth Republic a de facto one-party parliament. Thanks to these disputes and their upshot, relations between the government and the extra-parliamentary opposition turned highly acrimonious; political society became sharply polarised, with the ruling NDC and its supporters on one side, and the older postcolonial élites on the other.

The NDC–Rawlings government and national unity

The quasi-military mode of governance was a considerable source of conflict between the PNDC government and the internal pro-democracy opposition, and the regime had been the target of numerous attempts to overthrow it violently.[22] But these were largely and successfully repressed, giving a general impression of national stability and peace. By contrast, political liberalisation and multi-party electoral competition in the early 1990s seemed to have disturbed this 'facile peace'. It seemed to have brought ethno-regional, class and ideological conflicts to the fore of Ghanaian society and economy. The relatively broad-based anti-Rawlings opposition and pro-democracy coalition centred around the Movement for Freedom and Justice splintered into the right-wing NPP and an assortment of parties claiming an Nkrumah–Convention People's Party heritage. The NPP became widely regarded as a mainly Akan/Ashanti party, while the NDC was seen as the Volta Region/Ewe party.

132

Perhaps the most telling indication of an ethno-regional character in party political activity at this time is found in the pattern of voting in the presidential elections of 1992 and 1996. The two leading presidential candidates scored heavily in the regions regarded as home regions by voters. While Rawlings received 93.3 per cent of the votes in the Volta Region, Adu-Boahen, the candidate for the NPP, received 60 per cent of the votes in Ashanti Region (his highest score in the entire contest). Hilla Limann, the President in 1979–81 and leader of the Nkrumahist People's National Convention, also received his highest votes in that election in his home area (Upper East and West Regions). This pattern of voting, in which Asantes generally voted anti-Rawlings and Ewe/Volta region voted pro-Rawlings, was all the more remarkable in view of the fact that the latter region had benefited least from the neo-liberal economic reforms and the gains derived therefrom, whereas the former counts among the regions that benefited the most from the same reforms.[23]

A similar pattern of voting was to emerge in the 1996 elections. Rawlings received 94.5 per cent of the presidential votes in his home region, while Kufuor, his main rival, made his strongest showing of 65.8 per cent in his home region of Ashanti. Indeed, in that election, both the ruling and the main opposition parties had flourished the ethnic card in the election campaign. With only a handful of leading figures in the Kufuor party and its allies claiming Ewe origins, and the NPP barely campaigning in the Volta Region, the Kufuor–NPP ticket was seen as an anti-Ewe ticket. And while the NDC sought support in all the regions, the most avid mining for votes was done in the migrant communities in the towns and villages and in the Volta Region, jokingly described by Rawlings as his 'World Bank' of votes.

The pattern of mobilisation of votes along ethnic and regional lines observed in 1992 and 1996 was largely repeated in the December 2000 elections (Gyimah-Boadi 2001). For example, to trump the NPP, the NDC appeared to have adopted a policy of selecting only Accra indigenes (native Ga) as parliamentary candidates to contest on the party's ticket, notwithstanding the cosmopolitan status of the capital city of Accra. NDC vans reportedly roamed neighbourhoods dominated by indigenes of Accra warning that a vote for the NPP would open the floodgates for Asantes and other non-indigenes to take over Accra lands. NDC supporters and indigenes of the Volta Region were allegedly subjected to election-related physical assaults in NPP strongholds in the Ashanti and Brong Ahafo regions. Not surprisingly, the results of the December 2000 elections were largely a repetition of the ethnic and regional pattern of voting seen in 1992 and 1996, albeit in a somewhat attenuated form.

For instance in the run-off stage of the presidential election John Kufuor of the NPP captured the plurality of votes in six regions of the country – including all the regions populated mainly by Akans (80 per cent in Ashanti, 62 per cent in Central, 61 per cent in Western, 62 per cent in Eastern, and 58 per cent in Brong Ahafo), while being rejected in favour of the NDC's John Mills in the Volta Region (88 per cent) and the three northern regions – Northern (51 per cent), Upper East (57 per cent) and Upper West (62 per cent). Similarly, in the parliamentary election there was substantial bloc voting for the NPP (31 out of 33 seats, with 2 going to the NDC) in Ashanti Region and for the NDC in the Volta Region (17 out of 19, 2 independents, and none for the NPP).

Indeed, the months immediately after the 1992 elections and the installation of the NDC–Rawlings government saw a spate of open accusations (publicly traded between Akans and Ewes in the state and private media) of Ewe domination in key or sensitive bureaucratic and political appointments. Serious recriminations arose over a so-called 'Ewe conspiracy' revealed in *The Ghana Revolution*, a book whose author – Kofi Awoonor – is an Ewe himself and a key insider of the Rawlings regimes. It is instructive to note that this book, published abroad in the mid-1980s, became widely noticed and discussed within Ghana only after the 1992 elections, the return to constitutional government and, especially, the relaxation of press controls.[24] But perhaps the most serious eruption of sectarian conflict in Ghana's young Fourth Republic was inter-communal violence between the Kokomba and Nanumba ethnic groups in the Northern Region of Ghana in February 1994. Within a few weeks of conflict over Kokomba demands for land and cultural rights, and Nanumba counter-claims of 'power of eminent domain', over 2,000 lives were lost, several villages were razed to the ground, and thousands of the area's inhabitants were displaced. In March of the following year, the conflict flared up again and over 100 people were reportedly killed.[25]

Notwithstanding the difficult circumstances of its birth, the elected NDC–Rawlings government, like its predecessors, remained committed, at least officially, to the promotion of national unity. It is important to note that lopsided voting in the Volta Region would never have been enough by itself to secure an electoral victory for Jerry Rawlings and his party. Victory reflected the ability of the NDC to create a relatively effective political machine out of the former 'popular organs' (with a presence throughout the country) such as the Association of the Committees for the Defence of the Revolution (ACDR) and the 31st December Women's Movement.[26] Moreover, the elected NDC govern-ment was careful to maintain an ethno-regional balance in appointments

134

to the Cabinet and the constitutionally designated bodies such as the Council of State, the National Media Commission, the Commission on Human Rights and Administrative Justice, and the National Commission on Civic Education. The first batch of ministerial appointments in the NDC–Rawlings administration was distributed as follows: Akans, 16; Northerners, 6; Ewes, 3; and Ga/Adangbes, 2. Deft handling of appointments certainly helped to blunt perceptions of Ewe/Volta Region political dominance – even if Ewe/Volta Region loyalists tended to hold key command positions in the military/security apparatus and in strategic institutions, such as the Bank of Ghana and the privatisation agency, and real power resided in the home region and main electoral base of President Rawlings. It is instructive to note that the new Kufuor–NPP regime has officially committed itself to a policy of an 'all-inclusive government'. Thus, the position of Vice-President in the new administration is held by a Muslim from the Northern Region, the new Speaker of Parliament is a Ga and the army chief is an Ewe. In addition, the President has been careful to ensure that all the ethnic and regional groups (including the Ewes who voted overwhelmingly in favour of the opposition NDC) are represented in the Cabinet (see Table 4.1).

Indeed, there are hardly any indications that ethno-regional tensions and conflicts have continued in the Fourth Republic. In fact, they have subsided considerably after the short-lived public preoccupation with the ethnic composition of the military, public services and ruling regime – without official censorship. In addition, the truce arranged between the Kokomba and Nanumba combatants has generally held. The leaders of the various parties have been restrained in exploiting the conflict for political advantage, and support for the mediation efforts of the government appears to be genuinely bipartisan. Thus, contemporary Ghanaian experience hardly validates the contention of postcolonial governments, especially the PNDC–Rawlings government, that pluralistic democracy promotes national disintegration.

Moreover, the elections in 1996 and 2000 proved to be a great improvement upon 1992. To be sure, the campaigns were vigorously fought, but the electoral process was largely peaceful and the results met with broad public acceptance. Election-related violence in the December 2000 polls in Bawku Central constituency in Upper West Region left over 50 people dead and several homes burnt down, but the conflict appears to have been successfully contained and peace-building efforts have been undertaken in the post-election period. Effective institutional design and innovative reforms in the electoral process enhanced transparency, reduced suspicions and associated tensions, facilitated the resolution of election conflicts, and engendered public acceptance. Institutional reforms included a relatively thorough clean-up of the voters' register, the introduction of photographic IDs for voters in the urban areas (where the problem of personation was thought to be greatest), transparent ballot boxes, and counting and declaration of results at the polling station in the presence of accredited agents of the political parties. Indeed, many of these innovations and reforms, undertaken in response to trenchant criticisms by the opposition parties in the 1992 elections, were worked out and agreed upon among the ruling and opposition parties between elections, using the forum of the Electoral Commission's Inter-Party Advisory Committee (IPAC). These reforms were reinforced by the active involvement of a coalition of domestic civil society in monitoring the election and vouching for its credibility.[27]

But if democratisation/political liberalisation has not necessarily undermined national unity, it has certainly complicated economic development in general, and neo-liberal economic reforms, notably structural adjustment, in particular. It is true that the elected Rawlings government continued to express a commitment to economic reform. Indeed, it announced plans to accelerate the privatisation of state-owned enterprises, divesting half of its shares in the Ashanti Goldfields Corporation in 1993. But by most conventional measures, economic growth in Ghana suffered a setback after 1992, when the concurrent processes of political liberalisation and democratisation got under way. At US$415 in 1998 and US$402 in 1999, *per capita* GDP rose from US$322 in 1994, but ended lower than its 1991 level of US$447.8. The real GDP growth rate declined from a seven-year (1985–91) average of 5.0 per cent to 4.4 per cent (1993–1999). Inflation (annual average) rose from 18 per cent in 1991 to 25.0 per cent in 1993, 24.9 per cent in 1994, 59.5 per cent in 1995, 46.5 per cent in 1996 and 27.9 per cent in 1997 (though it declined to 19.2 per cent and 13.2 per cent in 1998 and 1999 respectively). And the value of the local currency, the cedi, fell from 375 = US$1 in 1991 to 956 = US$1 in 1994, 1,637 in 1996, and 2,050 in 1997. By the end of 1999, the rate stood at over 4,000 cedis and was rising in 2000.[28] In addition, major public works and infrastructural rehabilitation programmes initiated before the return to constitutional rule were suspended after that event for lack of funds. And the privatisation process in general stalled.

To be sure, these apparent setbacks in economic renewal may reflect structural problems in the Ghanaian economy, unrelated to any political changes. Moreover, neo-patrimonialism, accompanied by manifestations such as patronage and entrenched official corruption, has remained persistent as a key factor undermining economic reforms, while political liberalisation has not been able to effect significant reforms in governance. Setbacks in economic management may also represent a temporary negative 'blip' or, as government spokesmen put it, 'a bad patch' in an otherwise upward trend in economic development. Indeed, the government was relatively restrained in its spending in election years 1996 and 2000, and the economy grew modestly in the late 1990s, though it slowed significantly in 1999. But the general reduction in the government's zeal for economic reform as well as growth reflects the loss of fiscal discipline in the run-up to the 1992 elections and after, as well as the growing ability of civil society to challenge the austerities in the neo-liberal economic reforms.

Political expediency seems to have overtaken economic management in the context of electoral competition, free expression and free association. Thus, in response to union and student unrest, and to secure the votes of urban workers in the 1992 elections, the PNDC–Rawlings government made across-the-board wage increases of between 70 and 100 per cent and annulled a planned increase in petroleum taxes; in response to popular pressures, it suspended planned public sector job retrenchments and increased student allowances in 1993 and 1994; more seriously, the value-added tax introduced in the 1995 budget was withdrawn after paralysing labour strikes and violent demonstrations against the measure. While the Bill was passed when reintroduced in Parliament in 1998, the rate was reduced from the 17 per cent proposed in 1995 to 10 per cent. Although the VAT Amendment Bill of 2000 revised the rate upwards to 12.5 per cent, persistent opposition to it appears to have delayed presidential assent and implementation.

Clearly, economic reform has suffered a setback under democratic pluralism. First, governments have found it difficult to resist the temptation to raid the national treasury to secure re-election. Second, the elected NDC–Rawlings government was unable to resort to strong-arm tactics to secure quiescence in the liberalised political setting. And, third, civil society (trade unions, student organisations, professional bodies, trader associations) is more able to articulate opposition to adjustment reforms and to mobilise constituencies in defence of earlier welfarist/distributionist policies – however unsustainable such policies may be.

Summary and conclusion

As Ghana is a multi-ethnic/multicultural country, management of ethnic, regional and other conflicts as well as nation building have been

137

very high on the agenda of the country's postcolonial governments. These tasks have driven or provided an excuse for the adoption of statist strategies of economic development and authoritarian modes of governance. Statist and socialist economic policies facilitated the welfarist/ distributionist programmes so important for securing loyalty and political quiescence from the diverse ethno-regional and other politically salient societal groups; authoritarian rule provided governments with the coercive instruments for keeping social conflicts under control.

The strategy of nation building via economic distribution worked reasonably well in the periods of relative economic growth and steady expansion of the state sector (1960 to 1980). It had become largely untenable by the late 1970s and early 1980s in the prevailing conditions of economic decline, neo-liberal economic reforms and, especially, the contraction of the state. At the same time, the externally and internally driven pressures for political liberalisation and democratisation in the early 1990s have imposed restrictions on the use of authoritarian modes of political management. These pressures have led to the liberalisation of authoritarian rule and an end to quasi-military and single-party rule in the country.

There is at least superficial evidence of a surge in ethno-regional and other social tensions in the new political era. The competing political groups have found themselves unable to resist playing the 'sectarian card', and voting patterns have followed at least mildly ethno-regional lines. However, politicians have been sensitive to the ethno-regional issues and have tried to balance the representation of the various societal groups in their cabinets and other key political and administrative positions. Thus, in ethno-regionally volatile societies, real power may be kept in the hands of trusted in-groups. But a more equitable distribution of nominal power and symbolic goods may help attenuate feelings of exclusion on the part of the other socio-cultural and political groupings, and render fissiparous tendencies manageable.

The relative success of the highly competitive second-transition elections of 1996 and 2000 suggests the possibility of reducing election and post-election conflicts through institutional design. Responding effectively to concerns about the electoral system and creating a transparent and verifiable election process facilitated the resolution of election conflicts. Constant dialogue between the election authority and the political parties (through IPAC) helped to reduce apprehensions and tensions in the process. And civil society involvement in monitoring the election and conducting independent verification of the results (Network of Domestic Election Observers and Ghana Alert in 1996, Coalition of

Domestic Election Observers, Forum for Religious Bodies, Ghana Legal Literacy Foundation and Ghana Alert in 2000) helped to induce greater public confidence in the electoral process and broad acceptance of its outcomes.

While democratisation and political liberalisation do not appear to pose a direct threat to national unity in Ghana, they do present serious challenges to both economic reform and the management of ethno-regional and other social conflicts. The opening up of the political system and relaxation of controls on civil society have brought opposition to economic reform to the fore, though new elected governments remain committed to such reforms. Ghana, like other African countries, continues to face the crucial challenge of how to combine sound and sustainable economic development with democratic governance and thereby create a solid basis for nation building. However, careful attention to symbolic representation and distribution of nominal power can help keep economically driven conflicts and other socio-political pressures under control.

Appendix

Table 4.1 *Breakdown of ministerial postings by ethnicity/region*

Administration	Akan	Ewe	Ga/Adangbe	North	Total
Nkrumah–CPP (1957)	8[29]	1	2	2	13
Nkrumah–CPP (1960)	8	3	2	0[30]	13
Nkrumah–CPP (1965)	9	1	2	2	14
Busia–PP (1969)	15	0[31]	1	3	19
Limann–PNP (1979)	8	2	2	2	14
Rawlings–NDC (1993)	15	3	2	7	27
Rawlings–NDC (1996)	12	2	3	6	23
Kufuor–NPP (2001–)[32]	25	3	4	5	35

References

Adu Boahen, A. (1989) *The Ghanaian Sphinx: Reflections on the Contemporary History of Ghana, 1972–1987*, Accra: Ghana Academy of Arts and Sciences.

Adu Boahen, A. (1997) 'Ghana: Conflict Reoriented', in I. William Zartman (ed.), *Governance as Conflict Management: Politics and Violence in West Africa*, Washington, DC: Brookings Institution Press: 99–148.

Afrifa, A. A. (1966) *The Ghana Coup, 24th February, 1966*, London: Frank Cass.

Ahiakpor, J. (1985) 'The Success and Failure of Dependency Theory: the Experience of Ghana', *International Organization*, 35: 532–55.

Akwetey, E. O. (1996) 'Ghana: Violent Ethno-Political Conflicts and the Democratic Challenge', in A. Olukoshi and L. Lasko (eds.), *Challenges to the Nation State in Africa*, Uppsala: Nordiska African Institute: 102–35.

Amenumey, D. E. K. (1989) *The Ewe Unification Movement: a Political History*, Accra: Ghana Universities Press.

Austin, D. (1960) *Politics in Ghana, 1946–60*, Oxford: Oxford University Press.

Austin, D. (1964) *Politics in Ghana, 1946–1960*, London: Oxford University Press.

Awoonor, Kofi (1984) *The Ghana Revolution: Background Account from a Personal Perspective*, New York: Oases Publishers.

Bates, R. (1981) *Markets and States in Tropical Africa*, Berkeley: University of California Press.

Brown, D. (1980) 'Borderline Politics in Ghana: the National Liberation Movement of Western Togoland', *Journal of Modern African Studies*, 18, 4: 575–609.

Byrdon, L. and K. Legge (1996) *Adjusting Society: the World Bank, the IMF and Ghana*, London: IB Tauris Publishers.

Danso Boafo, K. (1996) *The Political Biography of Dr Kofi Abrefa Busia*, Accra: Ghana Universities Press.

Dowse, R. (1975) 'Military and Police Rule', in Dennis Austin and Robin Luckham (eds.), *Politicians and Soldiers in Ghana*, London: Frank Cass: 16–36.

Drah, F. K. (1979) 'The Brong Political Movement', in Kwame Arhin (ed.), *A Profile Of Brong Kyempim*, Legon: Institute of African Studies: 119–70.

Frimpong Ansah, J. (1992) *The Vampire State in Africa*, London: James Currey.

Genoud, R. (1969) *Nationalism and Economic Development in Ghana*, New York: Praeger Publishers.

Gyimah-Boadi, E. (1990) 'Economic Recovery and Politics in the PNDC's Ghana', *Journal of Commonwealth and Comparative Politics*, 27, 3: 328–43.

Gyimah-Boadi, E. (1991) 'Ghana's Return to Civilian Rule', *Africa Today*, 28: 3–16.

Gyimah-Boadi, E. (1994) 'Ghana's Uncertain Political Opening', *Journal of Democracy*, 5, 2: 75–86.

Gyimah-Boadi, E. (1997) 'Ghana's Encouraging Elections: the Challenges Ahead', *Journal of Democracy*, 8, 2 (April 1997): 65–91.

Gyimah-Boadi, E. (1998) 'Managing Electoral Conflicts, Lessons from Ghana', in T. Sisk and A. Reynolds (eds.), *Elections and Conflict Management in Africa*, Washington, DC: USIP: 101–18.

Gyimah-Boadi, E. (1999) 'Institutionalizing Credible Elections in Ghana', in A. Schedler, L. Diamond and M. Plattner (eds.), *The Self-Restraining State: Power and Accountability in New Democracies*, Boulder, CO: Lynne Rienner.

Gyimah-Boadi, E. (2001) 'A Peaceful Political Turnover in Ghana', *Journal of Democracy*, 12, 2 (April 2001): 103–17.

Hutchful, E. (1986) 'New Elements in Militarism: Ethiopia, Ghana and Burkina', *International Journal*, 41, 4: 802–30.

Huq, M. M. (1989) *The Political Economy of Ghana, the First 25 Years*, London: Macmillan.

Killick, T. (1978) *Development Economics in Action*, London: Heinemann.

Luckham, R. *et al.* (2000) *Democratic Institutions and Politics in Contexts of Inequality, Poverty and Conflict*, Institute of Development Studies Working Paper 104, January.

Lyons, T. (1997) 'Ghana's Encouraging Elections: a Major Step Forward', *Journal of Democracy*, 8, 2 (April).

New Patriotic Party (1992) *The Stolen Verdict: Ghana's November 1992 Elections*, Accra.

Ninsin, K. (1996) *Ghana's Political Transition, 1990–1993: Selected Documents*, Accra: Freedom Publications.

Omari, P. (1970) *Kwame Nkrumah: the Anatomy of African Dictatorship*, Accra: Moxon Paperbooks.

Oquaye, M. (1993) 'Law, Justice and the Revolution', in E. Gyimah-Boadi (ed.), *Ghana under PNDC Rule*, Dakar: Codesria Books: 154–75.

Oquaye, M. (1995) 'The Ghanaian Elections of 1992 – a Dissenting View', *African Affairs*, 94, 375: 257–75.

Price, R. (1984) 'Colonialism and Underdevelopment in Ghana: a Reassessment', *Canadian Journal of African Studies*, 18, 1: 163–93.

Ray, D. (1986) *Ghana: Politics, Economics and Society*, Boulder: Lynne Rienner Publishers.

Rooney, D. (1988) *Kwame Nkrumah: the Political Kingdom and the Third World*, New York: St Martin's Press.

Rothchild, D. and E. Gyimah-Boadi (1988) 'Populism in Ghana and Burkina Faso', *Current History*, 88, 538 (May).

Songsore, J. (1989) 'The Economic Recovery Program/Structural Adjustment and the "Distant" Rural Poor in Northern Ghana', paper presented at the International Conference on Planning for Growth and Development in Africa, ISSER, University of Ghana, 13–17 March (mimeo).

Toye, J. (1989) 'Ghana's Economic Reforms and World Bank Policy: Conditioned Lending, 1983–1988', paper presented at a conference on Politics and Structural Adjustment, Institute of Development Studies, Brighton, Sussex, 1989.

UNICEF (1986) *Ghana: Adjustment Policies and Programs to Protect Children and Other Vulnerable Groups*, Accra, November.

Notes

1 For a useful account of the separatist movements in the period immediately before independence, see Austin 1960; for a summary of the history of Ewe irredentism, see Brown 1980 and Amenumey 1989; for the Brongs, see Drah 1979.

2 The emergence of radical, urban-based opposition to the Ghanaian establishment in the late 1970s and early 1980s, giving rise to a wave of populism and populist coups in Ghana, is discussed in Hutchful 1986; Rothchild and Gyimah-Boadi 1988.

3 For details see Rothchild and Gyimah-Boadi 1988; and Ray 1986.

4 For details, see Austin 1964.

5 For a somewhat tendentious analysis of perceived anti-Ewe bias in the Busia–PP administration, see Danso Boafo 1996: 97–102.

6 See Austin 1964 261–382; also Omari 1970 and Afrifa 1966.

7 A discussion of the distributionist and welfarist emphasis in the economic programmes of successive Ghanaian regimes before the neo-liberal reforms is found in Huq 1989; also see Killick 1978; Rooney 1988; and Genoud 1969.

8 See Killick 1978.

9 For details, see Frimpong Ansah 1992; also Huq 1989.

10 The political logic underlying the tendencies of African/Ghanaian governments to intervene in internal markets is analysed in Bates 1981.

11 See Bates 1981; Price 1984; and Ahiakpor 1985.

12 This is the thrust of the arguments advanced by Songsore 1989. See also Byrdon and Legge 1996.

13 See UNICEF 1986; for a recent assessment focusing on these issues, see Brydon and Legge 1996.

14 I am grateful to Kwasi Anyemadu of the Economics Department of the University of Ghana for pointing this out to me.

15 For a useful discussion of 'slippages' and the penalties attached to them, see Toye 1989.

16 For details of PNDC era repression and authoritarianism, see Gyimah-Boadi 1990; also Oquaye 1993 and 1995.

17 For details, see Gyimah-Boadi 1991 and 1994.

18 For a flavour of the angry reactions of the middle-class opposition to the PNDC's stage-managed transition, see statements from the Ghana Bar Association and National Union of Ghana Students on the transition programme in Ninsin 1996, especially Document 21, 'Statement by the Ghana Bar Association on the PNDC Transitional Program'; and Document 22, 'National Union of Ghana Students Statement on The Transition Provisions of the Constitution'.

19 For a typology of transitions to democracy, see Luckham *et al.* 2000: 16–18.

20 See Gyimah-Boadi 1994; also see Adu Boahen 1997.

21 See New Patriotic Party 1992.

22 Adu Boahen argues persuasively that disagreements over the most suitable mode of governance, especially military versus civilian, constitute the greatest source of political conflicts in postcolonial Ghana. See Adu Boahen 1997.

23 Colonel Osei-Wusu, a minister in the NDC–Rawlings government and an Akan, was to accuse Ashantis publicly of 'ingratitude' for their display of defiance and for not voting for Rawlings.

24 See various issues of the state and private newspapers in the first half of 1993, especially, *Ghanaian Times*, 'Anlo Tribalism, a Threat to the Heritage – a Rejoinder', 17 and 18 June 1993; and 'Who Was Who and Who Is Who in the Armed Forces', in the *Ghanaian Chronicle*, 7–13 June 1993, in which contending claims of Ewe domination are discussed. Kofi Awoonor's book, *Background to the Ghana Revolution*, had been a lightning rod for these public recriminations.

25 See Akwetey 1996.

26 For details of NDC electoral strategies in 1996, see Lyons 1997 and Gyimah-Boadi 1997.

27 For details of the reforms in the electoral process and the involvement of civil society in the 1996 elections, see Gyimah-Boadi 1998 and 1999.

28 Macroeconomic data cited in this section are taken from *Ghana: Policy Framework Paper, 1999–2001*, prepared by the Ghanaian authorities in collaboration with the staffs of the IMF and World Bank (April 1998); Republic of Ghana, *The Budget Statement* (1995 and 2000); and *Financial Times* (Supplement on Ghana), 4 November 1999.

29 The list of ministers includes the Prime Minister.

30 The omission in representation appears to have been corrected between 1960 and 1965.

31 A particularly controversial omission in representation in view of the fact that the titular President and Prime Minister were both Akan, and the Ewe opposition leader, Gbedema, was disqualified from taking that office by a court decision.

32 The list reflects the ministerial appointments as of April 2001. The ethnic and regional representation is more pronounced in the deputy ministerial appointments.

5

The Politics of Institutional Design
An Overview of the Case of Sri Lanka

RADHIKA COOMARASWAMY

It may be said that Sri Lanka is a multi-ethnic polity with a mono-ethnic institutional design. This contradiction is the primary reason for the crisis of constitutionalism in one of Asia's most vibrant democracies. The brutal internal conflict and the extraordinary violence it has perpetuated revolve around debates on institutional design. How have successive constitutions attempted to satisfy the fears of Sinhalese majorities? How will future constitutions fulfil the aspirations of the Tamil community? There is at present a general consensus among the predominantly Sinhalese parties on the contours of other important chapters of the constitution such as fundamental rights, electoral systems, the power of the judiciary, and a parliamentary executive. It is the ethnic conflict that still challenges the legitimacy of this national consensus. The main debate turns on the parameters of a constitutional package that will give territorial autonomy to the predominantly Tamil areas of the country. The future structure of the Sri Lankan state remains highly contested. The final social contract that will settle the future institutional design of the country has yet to be worked out.

For most of its post-independence history, the Sri Lankan state and its politics were majoritarian in both form and content. For many Sinhalese nationalists, democracy was seen as majority rule – the winner takes all. Political and ethnic minorities were denied an effective voice in governance or the formulation of policy. The extremely adversarial nature of political contestation inhibited the growth of consensual political decision making. The unitary Westminster model adopted from the British appeared to foist a polarised polity on Sri Lankan reality. For this reason, many early scholars commented on the fact that democratic politics may have actually accentuated conflict, destroyed democratic institutions and created intractable ethnic conflict (Wriggins 1960). Others have argued

145

that the Westminster model simply accentuated existing perceptions about the structure of the state and the need for a strong unitary centre committed to defending the Sinhalese Buddhist nation (Roberts 1979). Whether it was democratic politics or ethnic nationalist visions, based on a reading of the past, which contributed to divisiveness and conflict in Sri Lanka remains a matter of debate. However, there is no doubt that majoritarian democracy as it unfolded in Sri Lanka, without a strong bill of rights or a federal structure, was a major cause of ethnic conflict. It is not democracy in general that needs to be interrogated in the Sri Lankan context, but the majoritarian form of democracy that does not give space for the sharing of power with ethnic and political minorities.

The relationship of institutional design to the nationalist imaginations of the Sinhalese and the Tamils is another consideration that merits discussion. Many scholars have pointed to the fact that Sinhalese nationalism recognises Sri Lanka as a Sinhalese Buddhist state, united under a central monarch whose duty it is to protect and foster Buddhism (Obeyesekere 1979). The politics of Sinhalese nationalism therefore required that the imperatives of majoritarianism be entrenched. Any formula that attempted to suggest a non-majoritarian approach to democracy was treated with scorn, whether it involved power sharing at the centre or at the periphery. Tamil nationalist writing, on the other hand, saw the Tamil community as a co-equal partner, later articulated as a second nation within the boundary of one country. This two-nation theory called for the Sri Lankan state to be structured with a great deal of power being devolved to the Tamil periphery, as well as measures for power sharing among communities at the centre. These contradictory imaginations have led to political acrimony and vicious, open warfare. Their resolution remains the most pressing issue for the future of Sri Lankan politics.

The other important problem for the stability of the Sri Lankan constitutional order is the fact that institutional designs drawn from Western Europe and the USA have little to contribute with regard to the problems of underdevelopment, poverty and class injustice. While the 1972 constitution attempted to deal with this issue by strengthening the welfare state, later constitutions written in an era of globalisation abandoned any constitutional provisions for social equity and class equality. The dramatic growth of the private sector and the resultant job opportunities for the English-speaking élites led to a great deal of class frustration among those left behind, especially in the 1980s. As a result social forces associated with class anger often used extra-constitutional means in expressing dissent. The violent uprisings of the Janatha

Vimukthi Peramuna (JVP) in 1971 and 1989 directly challenged the existing constitutional order. Though their alternative vision of society was not spelt out clearly, the liberal democratic order was dismissed as one that supports the interests of the feudal and urban élite (Gunasekera 1998). Despite this JVP challenge and the report of the youth commission set up by the government to identify the causes of the unrest, there have been hardly any attempts to deal with issues of underdevelopment and poverty at the level of institutional design.[1] There is a belief that pragmatic economic policies are the only remedy for the type of instability generated by economic and social injustice. It is important to note that Sri Lanka, like many other Third World countries, has been forced to abdicate much of its sovereignty with regard to economic planning. The World Bank and the IMF continue to play a vital role, and national manoeuvrability on economic policies to address class anger is correspondingly limited.

This chapter attempts, first, to analyse the politics of institutional design by outlining the contours of Sri Lanka's three constitutions and the draft proposals for a new constitution. It goes on to discuss, second, how issues of institutional design have been conditioned by the politics of exclusion, in the context of ethnic nationalism and minority resistance. Third, it considers the problems of underdevelopment and economic injustice and the challenges they pose for the constitutional order. Finally, there is an analysis of the present constitutional proposals and the role of civil society in evolving an institutional design that will potentially generate a more comprehensive social contract.

A tale of three constitutions

Before independence there was much debate on the nature of the constitutional order that should govern an independent Sri Lanka. The debates centred on the safeguards given to minorities, both ethnic and political. Initiatives such as the Donoughmore Proposals aimed at consensual politics by establishing a committee system of government based on all-party decision making at the executive level (Wickremasinghe 1995), but did not feature in the final negotiations for self-government. In addition, proposals for a federal structure of government were put forward by Tamil parties as well as Kandyan leaders and even the future Prime Minister of Sri Lanka, S. W. R. D. Bandaranaike (Bandaranaike 1926). These were not adopted, either. Finally, there were proposals for power sharing through special representation of minorities in Parliament, with 50 per cent of the seats to be kept for the majority community

147

and 50 per cent for all the minorities. However, the drafters of the first constitution rejected all these proposals for power sharing.

The first constitution of Sri Lanka (1948) attempted to replicate the Westminster model of Britain in a model colony. Drafted by the renowned English jurist Lord Ivor Jennings, it envisioned a unitary state, with Parliament being supreme. The head of state was the governor, the representative of the English monarch. It envisaged a powerful centre, without any effective sharing of power by the provinces. The judiciary was subordinate to Parliament in that judicial power was seen as being exercised by Parliament through the courts. As in Britain there was no Bill of Rights. The public service, however, was strong, with an independent Public Service Commission. The drafters expected that the customs and practices of the British Parliament would be followed and so the constitution was a minimalist one, leaving a great deal of flexibility for political interpretation.

The choice of a parliamentary over a presidential system ensured that the principle of checks and balances with regard to the legislature would not operate. Parliament was the most important institution of government, symbolising the complete sovereignty of the people. This emphasis on Parliament resulted in the triumph of majoritarian democracy, and what sometimes seemed to be the tyranny of the Assembly. It was the ethnic majority that determined the direction of postcolonial politics, and there was no concerted effort to woo the minorities or respond to their grievances. As long as the constitution ensured that the political base of the two major parties rested on the votes of the majority Sinhalese ethnic community, this constituency dominated the politics of institutional design. In addition, governments determined by parliamentary majorities ensured a lack of continuity between governments and a degree of instability which might have been prevented if a limited presidential system had been adopted.

The adoption of a first-past-the-post representational system was another legacy of Westminster. However, its operation in a heterogeneous society was problematic. On one hand it allowed for large parliamentary majorities, more than the two thirds necessary for constitutional amendment. This led to the era of instrumental constitutionalism, where constitutions were enacted by ruling governments and amended to serve their self-interest. This approach to parliamentary democracy led to a certain type of arbitrary government. The extraordinary power that parliamentarians experienced led to the rise of political patronage. Partisan politics was to ensure that the institutions of government would become subservient to narrow partisan ends.

Following the British example, the first constitution contained no Bill of Rights. It did have a provision (section 29) that provided for the equal treatment of minorities, but none of the other fundamental rights were enshrined in the text of the constitution. It was expected that the legislature and the judiciary would follow British precedent, and that custom and judicial precedent would do the needful. Yet the lack of a Bill of Rights was a major flaw. The judiciary was also very weak, being effectively subordinate to Parliament. Unlike in India, a culture of human rights based on the judicial reading of the fundamental rights chapter of the constitution was not established in Sri Lanka. Since the first constitution was based on the British model it did not address the problems of poverty and underdevelopment. It did not spell out an economic ideology, as *laissez-faire* and the workings of the market were seen as outside the realm of constitutional scrutiny.

This constitution governed the country for nearly twenty-five years. However, during its tenure, the country witnessed the rise of Sinhalese Buddhist nationalism and the growing strength of Marxist and left-wing ideology, stressing the need for a welfare, socialist state. These demands came to the fore in the early 1970s and a government commanding a two-thirds majority in Parliament, the United Left government, decided to bring in a new constitution that would give effect to these ideas.

Sri Lanka's second constitution (its first republican constitution), introduced in 1972, combined ethnic nationalist ideas with a socialist ideology. The second constitution was instrumental in the sense that it allowed for the growth of an unbridled executive. With a parliamentary majority, the government could rule with impunity, without any effective checks and balances. Indeed Parliament, or the National Assembly, was strengthened even further, being seen as the instrument of the people's will. The judiciary was weakened and its independence compromised. It did not have the right to scrutinise bills, and it was denied the right to question executive action. A special Constitutional Court was set up to defend the constitution, removing this function from the traditional judiciary, but its decisions could be overridden by a two-thirds majority of Parliament. A drastic reform of the administration of justice introduced by the Minister of Justice further challenged the independence of the judiciary. The independence of the public service was also compromised, with appointments and transfers coming under the Cabinet of ministers. The destruction of an independent public service was to have major future repercussions.

The second constitution introduced a Bill of Rights, but the famous clause 18(2) allowed for a wide array of justifications for their denial.

149

These justifications included such vague clauses as 'in the interest of national unity and integrity' and 'in the interest of national economy'.[2] During the tenure of the 1972 constitution not one fundamental rights case was brought before the courts. In addition the Public Security Ordinance which allowed for the declaration of a state of emergency was elevated from a statutory provision and included in the text of the constitution, allowing the executive to bypass both the legislature and the judiciary during times of crisis. The period of the First Republic was marked by extensive rule under emergency power; the latter was interpreted broadly and used even for normal government functions. The declaration of emergency had no accountability in the courts and was at the sole discretion of the executive. Emergency regulations promulgated under states of emergency were far-reaching, often including censorship and limitations on democratic rights of speech and assembly. The use of emergency power during this period outweighed any other democratic benefits of a republican constitution.

Strong believers in socialism drafted the second constitution. As a result there was a chapter (Directives of State Policy) aimed at guiding the state in areas of economic and social policy. Though the rights contained in the chapter were not justiciable, they paved the way for the articulation of economic and social policy based on the equitable distribution of resources and the redistribution of wealth. The Directives of State Policy articulated the notion of a state socialist economy engaging in import substitution. However, the reality of economic programmes led to low growth and a stifling of the private sector. This lack of growth in the face of the large growth rates of South-east Asian countries led to a great deal of disillusionment with the government, which failed to win a second term in Parliament.

The second constitution governed the country for less than a decade. A blueprint for state socialism supported only by the ruling party, it was cast aside when they were voted out of office. The new regime was interested in a new economic policy and stable government. They wished to replicate the success of South-east Asia and were enamoured of what the Minister of Trade called the Singapore model. They introduced market reforms and a constitution that valued stability over all other political goals.

The third constitution of Sri Lanka, or the constitution of the Second Republic, introduced in 1978, was described by a leading Sri Lankan political scientist as a 'hybrid' between British and French styles of government. The most important institution is the executive presidency, directly elected by the people with a separate electoral base. The President is head of government, head of Cabinet and Commander-in-Chief, and is endowed with emergency powers under the Public Security Ordinance. Though the constitution envisions that the President will govern in collaboration with Parliament and the Prime Minister, in the event of a stalemate the President has considerable power to resolve it in his favour. He can assign ministries to himself; he has a power of dissolution, and the right to defeat the Appropriation Bill. He is also given a large measure of emergency power. Parliament remains in charge of law making and appropriations, but the President is the pivotal figure among constitutional institutions. This new institution of the presidency would define Sri Lankan politics in the 1980s and the 1990s. In addition, the executive presidency led to a cult of personality that would play a major part in electoral politics.

Bowing to demands from many quarters, a Fundamental Rights Chapter was also included, somewhat along the lines of the International Covenant on Civil and Political Rights. In the constitution, executive action can be challenged, but judicial review of legislation takes place only before the Bill is enacted; the judiciary does not have the power to review enacted legislation. Yet the fundamental rights chapter has become an important and dynamic centre of constitutional decision making and has led to a greater respect for the judiciary. In the 1990s, the judiciary became more activist, protecting individuals from torture, upholding freedom of speech and belief, and laying down conditions for arrest and detention. Public-spirited groups and individuals have used the chapter to remedy anti-democratic tendencies and to promote social justice.

The 1978 constitution radically transformed the nature of the electoral process by introducing proportional representation (PR) in place of the previous first-past-the-post system. Pendulum swings under the latter system had resulted in parliaments with large majorities. The drafters sought to bring in a measure of stability by introducing a system that would more accurately reflect the voting pattern of the electorate. This has ushered in a period of coalition governments, since no party is able to win a massive majority. With two-thirds majorities seemingly out of reach, constitutional provisions have become entrenched, and decisive policy making on certain types of constitutional issues is made more difficult. Many feel that this brake on legislative power is a good thing, and operates as a check against unbridled legislatures. On the other hand, it has prevented important constitutional innovations, especially those that would allow for power sharing with minorities.

The 1978 constitution also introduced certain positive features.

Declarations of emergency under the Public Security Ordinance were now subject to approval by Parliament. This prevents the President from ruling the country by decree, using emergency powers. Second, the constitution strengthened the judiciary, as already mentioned, although it still does not have the power to play a full checks-and-balances role. In addition, the constitution introduced certain technical changes, including the establishment of consultative parliamentary committees to assist ministries, which have proved to be a useful innovation.

Both the 1972 and the 1978 constitutions specifically entrenched the concept of a unitary state, reacting against the demands of the Tamil parties for a federal form of government to meet their territorial aspirations. However, after the Indo–Lanka Accord, with India imposing its will on a reluctant Sri Lankan government, the 1978 constitution under its thirteenth amendment introduced Provincial Councils to meet Tamil territorial claims, as well as making Tamil an official language. There were to be eight Provincial Councils spread all over the country, even in areas that did not ask for federalism, leading to the emergence of a second tier of government. Though this was within a devolutionary structure, and Parliament could still override the decisions of the provincial governments, it was a first step in giving Tamil areas of Sri Lanka some autonomy. Yet though the councils were enacted as an answer to the problems in the North and East, because of the civil war they functioned only in the South.

The 1994 parliamentary election was won on the platform of bringing in a new constitution – what would be the fourth constitution of independent Sri Lanka. The government came to power after years of alleged human rights abuses and violent insurrections in the North and South. The ethnic conflict was foremost in the minds of the drafters, as were the human rights abuses committed in the South during a confrontation with the JVP.

The question of legitimacy

Despite all the constitutional activity, constitutions and constitutionalism have suffered in Sri Lanka from a measure of illegitimacy. Constitutions in Sri Lanka have been 'instrumental' in the sense that each government has had the constitution of its choosing, and rarely has this constitution had the support of the other major political party (Tiruchelvam 1998). This has clouded the exercise of constitutionalism in party partisanship and reduced its legitimacy. In addition, once constitutions have been adopted, they have been constantly amended. A study of the amendment process of the 1978 constitution reveals the partisanship of these amendments. Except for the thirteenth and sixteenth amendments, which were responses to the ongoing ethnic conflict, amendments were brought in to give the ruling party a partisan advantage. With the adoption of the PR electoral system amendment has become more difficult, but constitutions are still identified with the party in power and are rarely seen as documents that truly represent the fundamental law of the land.

The second aspect of illegitimacy is that representational democracy was a colonial inheritance sometimes at variance with the cultural practices and expectations of the vernacular-speaking majority. The first constitution afforded no recognition to the cultural renaissance of nationalist forces in Sri Lanka. As a result there was a major revolt against the established political order. The coalition of groups that backed the resurgence included Buddhist monks, rural sub-élites, teachers, native physicians, the Sinhalese-speaking intelligentsia and a certain class of Sinhalese traders. Under their pressure, the second and third constitutions enshrined Buddhism as a specially protected religion, while until the late 1980s Sinhalese was the only official language. These cultural attributes of the constitutions were a testament to the fact that the Sinhalese Buddhist nationalist forces had succeeded in imposing their version of the nationalist agenda on the country as a whole. The constitutions accepted the cultural clothing of a mono-ethnic, mono-linguistic nation state.

The debates on institutional design have also raised fundamental issues about the structure of the state and the different visions put forward by political actors and leaders. The constitutions have retained their basic liberal structure with certain variations. The first constitution enshrined the classical liberal vision of the minimalist state, where custom and tradition would operate as much as the rule of law. The state was seen as essentially providing space for the articulation of points of view and for giving direction to the wishes of the majority. This British concept of the state was challenged by two contradictory viewpoints. The first, put forward by both nationalist and socialist intellectuals, called for the strengthening of the central state. The state was seen as playing a paternalistic welfare role by providing essential services. It was also seen as a vanguard element in the transformative project of leading Sri Lanka into modern nationhood. This transformative project required the state to play an intervening, guiding and regulating role far beyond that imagined by the constitution's initial draftsmen.

The second challenge came from the Tamil ethnic minority, who were also a territorial majority in the North and in some parts of the East. Their conception of the central state was even more minimalist than that of the first constitution. They envisioned notions of shared sovereignty among federal bodies and a self-restrained central government that would leave much of the development agenda to elected bodies at the periphery. In the term favoured by political science literature, their approach tended toward a consociational model of democracy. Their view of the centre was from the perspective of a loose federation, and was directly contrary to the nationalist and Marxist notion of a strong, independent centralised state.

The other aspects of constitutionalism that were greatly contested were those that rested on theories of 'nativeness'. Sinhalese nationalists viewed their position similarly to that of the Malays in Malaysia. They were firm believers that they were 'sons of the soil' and that they should be given their rightful place in the constitutional order. This Bhumiputra attitude is central to understanding Sinhalese intransigence on issues of concessions to the minorities. They locate their praxis in history and the integral link between the Sinhalese and the island that is known as Lanka (Obeysekera 1979). Their influence led not only to the 'Sinhalese Only' legislation of the 1950s, but also to standardisation according to language in university admissions in the 1970s. State-aided land colonisation schemes to redress the demographic balance in the East, where the Sinhalese were a minority, were also seen by Tamils as another aspect of this Bhumiputra vision. Though these preferential policies did not receive constitutional status, as legislation they were powerful enough, and greatly alienated the Tamil minority. The provisions in the 1972 constitution making Sinhalese the official language and giving Buddhism a special place entrenched the viewpoint that sees Sri Lanka as the special homeland of the Sinhalese Buddhists.

The Tamils, too, have developed their own theories of homeland, partly in a defensive reaction to the assertiveness of Sinhalese nationalism. They argue that the North and the East are the traditional homelands of the Sri Lankan Tamils. A great deal of research and argumentation has gone into these contested ideas.[3] Tamil notions of homeland derive from the two-nation theory that was prevalent in Tamil political circles even before independence (Hellman-Rajanayagam 1994). Their argument was that Sri Lanka was home to two nations – the Sinhalese in the South and the Tamils in the North. The constitutional imperatives of such a perception must therefore relate to notions of a shared sovereignty in some form of federal hierarchy. Sri Lankan Tamil nationalism as articulated today sets out the Thimpu principles as the basis for the negotiation of a future constitutional order. These principles, articulated by political groups in Thimpu in the 1980s, see the Tamils as a nation with a right to self-determination. They also regard the North and the East as the traditional homelands of the Sri Lankan Tamils. The Thimpu principles articulate a Tamil notion of 'nativeness'. These principles are anathema to the Sinhalese. Mutually conflicting perceptions not only make the ethnic conflict intractable, but also make constitutional drafting an extremely difficult exercise.

The British liberal vision of constitutions had no room for economic and social policy. There was a belief that the sovereign should stay out of the bazaar and that economic activity should be left to private enterprise and private initiative. Since then constitutional jurisprudence has gone through a sea change. Recent developments initiated by the Indian Supreme Court and the new South African constitution see economic and social rights as not only important but also justiciable, taking a rightful place in the fundamental rights chapter of the constitution. Indian Supreme Court decisions on a minimum wage, caste discrimination and environmental protection prove the point that these rights can be made justiciable. There is a fierce debate on whether to include economic, social and cultural rights along the lines of the International Covenant on Economic, Social and Cultural Rights in the new Sri Lankan constitution currently under discussion. Although the initial draft did not have such a chapter, a revised version included economic, social and cultural rights in the fundamental rights chapter, only for these to be dropped from the penultimate draft. The importance of these rights in the context of youth unrest in Sri Lanka will be discussed later.

Politics of exclusion and the use of force

Though Sri Lanka was often regarded as a successful democracy, the politics of exclusion characterised the actual functioning of the democratic system. This exclusion was not necessarily in formal terms within constitutional norms. However, the functioning of democratic processes in a majoritarian manner and the insensitivity of the system contributed to a great deal of unrest and violence. There were two constituencies that would fight their exclusion from political power-sharing through the use of force. The first constituency was the Tamil ethnic minority living in the North and the East and the second constituency were the Sinhalese educated youth from poorer families. The extra-legal use of force by and against them challenged the fundamental values and premises enshrined in the constitution. Such force tested the democratic system, perverting some of its functions. It also required the system to respond to competing concerns through reform and innovation.

The fault lines of ethnic conflict emerged long before Sri Lanka gained independence. Sinhalese nationalists like Anagarika Dharmapala saw Sri Lanka as a Sinhalese Buddhist nation, with the minorities living at the pleasure of the majority (Ministry of Education and Cultural Affairs 1965). The first manifestation of the triumph of Sinhalese Buddhist nationalism in postcolonial Sri Lanka was in 1956 when the Bandaranaike government adopted Sinhalese, the language of the majority, as the only official language. This led to violent protest orchestrated by the leaders of the Tamil minority. However, it was the 1972 constitution that finally entrenched the ideology of Sinhalese Buddhist nationalism as part of the constitutional order. Sinhalese was made the official language and Buddhism was given a special status in the constitution. In addition the constitution explicitly adopted 'unitary' as a description of the political structure, thus denying any possibility of federalism as an answer to the demands of the minority. The 1972 constitution was drafted in the heyday of Sinhalese nationalism and reflected the political victory of that ideology.

The leaders of the Tamil minority consistently resisted the imposition of Sinhalese Buddhist nationalism on the body politic. After the adoption of the 1972 constitution, their frustration led to the articulation of a demand for a separate state. Tamil constituencies in the North and East returned Tamil members dedicated to a separate state in the 1977 elections, and they became the main opposition party in Parliament. Since then constitutional discourse has been dominated by debate on the type of constitutional order that should be adopted to meet Tamil aspirations while being acceptable to the Sinhalese majority. The debate continues even into the new millennium.

Successive governments negotiated 'solutions' with Tamil political parties only to have pressure from the Sinhalese Buddhist nationalist lobby thwart any attempt to implement these proposals. The first proposal to be negotiated was the Bandaranaike–Chelvanayagam Pact as early as 1957. The Pact proposed setting up directly elected regional councils in the North and the East. Provision was made to enable two or more regions to amalgamate subject to ratification by Parliament. Two or more regional councils were also allowed to collaborate in areas of special interest. The regional councils would have 'delegated powers' over agriculture, cooperatives, land and land development, colonisation, education, health, industries, fisheries, housing, social services, electricity, water schemes and roads. The extraordinary aspects of these proposals were that they were for asymmetrical devolution – only for the North and the East – and that the Tamil notion that these regions were their traditional homelands was recognised in the opportunity left open for the amalgamation of provinces. Sinhalese hardliners have always resisted the East being drawn into the devolution debate, saying that it is multi-ethnic and separate from the North. In addition, in the Pact, the contentious area of land, land development and colonisation was also devolved to the provinces. Many argue that this document was the most far-reaching devolution to be prepared in the postcolonial period. However, the government refused to proceed with the proposals after strong protests from the Sinhalese Buddhist nationalist lobby.

The second agreement was in 1965 between the United National Party (UNP) and the Federal Party, agreeing to the setting up of district development councils on a nation-wide basis as a means of devolution. This agreement ran into resistance and was not implemented either. In 1981, however, the UNP under J. R. Jayawardene implemented the district development scheme as a statutory piece of legislation. This was the first attempt at actually implementing a system of devolved powers. Under this scheme district councils would receive a decentralised budget and be able to guide development in certain areas. However, the conduct of the development council elections resulted in large-scale violence, and after a period the councils in the North and East ceased to function.

The non-implementation of the councils, along with the riots or pogrom of 1983, led to the marginalisation of Tamil parliamentary opposition. The sixth amendment to the constitution, enacted in the aftermath of the riots, outlawed separatism and threw the elected Tamil representatives out of Parliament. They were to remain outside Parliament for over a decade, losing their power of leadership, and many of them were assassinated. Thus the moderate, parliamentary Tamil leadership, committed to liberal democracy, was decimated. In its place emerged the leadership of the Tamil radical groups, especially the Liberation Tigers of Tamil Eelam (LTTE), dedicated to the use of armed force for the achievement of a separate state in the North and East, the traditional homeland of the Tamil people. While the traditional Tamil leadership was drawn from high-caste, Colombo-centred élites, the leadership of the LTTE was purely vernacular-speaking Tamils, who were greatly inspired by Tamil nationalism in Tamil Nadu and retained close links with the latter. With time, through military successes and the assassination of their rivals, they emerged successful and laid claim to be the 'sole spokespeople' of the Tamil nationalist cause.

The next attempt at appeasing the aspirations of the Tamil minority

157

was embodied in the constitutional changes forced on the Sri Lankan government by India through the Indo-Lanka Accord. In 1987, when the Sri Lankan government was implementing a military solution, the Indian government intervened to protect the lives of Tamil civilians. A food drop was followed by intense negotiations, forcing the hand of President J. R. Jayawardene to agree to Provincial Councils as a means of satisfying Tamil aspirations. After the Indo-Lanka Accord, most of the Tamil armed groups except the LTTE came into the democratic fold. The LTTE, however, continued to wage war against the Indian army and then continued its war against the Sri Lankan army once the Indian troops withdrew. Despite brief interludes of negotiations, the war has continued.

The thirteenth amendment to the constitution, adopted pursuant to the Indo-Lanka Accord, instituted a system of Provincial Councils, with considerable devolution of power to the provinces. The amendment was not, however, a federal alternative. The central legislature could still override the decisions of Provincial Councils by a simple majority. In addition there was a provision that the central government had the right to make national policy in all of the devolved areas. The amendment extensively devolved the areas of health and education. However in the areas of land, finance and law and order, the devolution was more complicated. In each of these there was a national commission to be set up to protect the interests of the centre and to ensure a central government presence and central government standards. The Finance Commission would be responsible for the decentralised budget that would be the primary source of income for the Provincial Council. Its capacity to raise independent funding was limited, making the periphery dependent on the centre for most of its finances. The Land Commission was responsible for land allocation in the provinces, and here too the centre had a strong say. With regard to law and order, though there was a provincial police force, representatives of the centre would be an important part of the provincial commissions. The presence of the centre in all these areas prevented the thirteenth amendment from being a truly federal solution. In addition, as in the Indian constitution, there were three lists: the central government list, the provincial list and the concurrent list. The concurrent list provided the centre with the leeway to make legislation and policy in many areas devolved to the provinces.

In addition to the thirteenth amendment, the sixteenth amendment to the constitution made Tamil 'also' into an official language. The ethnic conflict is often seen as having its origins in the 'Sinhalese Only' Act of 1958. Yet the vagaries of Sri Lankan politics had now moved away from the language issue and were concentrated on the question of devolution of power. Strangely, given its initial history, this assertion of equal status for the Tamil language was not opposed by any group, not even rabid Sinhalese nationalists, pointing to a new consensus that government language policy should be broad and inclusive. An Official Languages Commission was also set up to monitor developments under this amendment. Though it has broad powers, the non-implementation of many of its resolutions by the government has led to a sense of frustration among its members.

These amendments led many of the Tamil armed groups and the Tamil parliamentary opposition to come back into the democratic fold. However, Sinhalese nationalist groups fiercely rejected the thirteenth amendment. At the same time, the LTTE claimed that the thirteenth amendment fell far short of its demands and it restarted the war, this time taking on the Indian peacekeeping force that was occupying the North and East. In 1990 there was a period of talks between the government and the LTTE. However, they concentrated on the modalities of a ceasefire and its implementation. Before substantive political discussions could be broached, the talks failed and the war was continued by the LTTE.

The next constitutional attempt at trying to find a political solution to the ethnic conflict were the proposals for a new constitution adopted by the new government headed by President Chandrika Kumaratunga after it came to power in 1994. The moment she was elected she began talks with the LTTE. Again the basis of the talks concentrated on ceasefire logistics and no substantive political matters were discussed. The talks broke down in April 1995 and the government began a full-scale military operation in the North. At the same time, under the slogan 'waging war for peace', the government introduced a draft constitution that attempted to deal with Tamil aspirations through the setting up of a quasi-federal Union of Regions.

The second main challenge to the politics of exclusion came from the deep South, where young, educated Sinhalese took up arms against the state, first in 1971 and then, in a more vicious form, in 1989. Though they also subscribed to a Sinhalese nationalist vision, a great deal of their frustration and anger was due to socio-economic causes, including the inability of the economy to provide jobs and discrimination on the basis of class and caste.

The Youth Commission that was set up to look into the problems of the 1980s attempted to analyse the causes of youth unrest (Report of the Presidential Commission on Youth 1990). Its report was accepted by a bipartisan consensus, and gives an understanding of the social and economic grievances facing young people. Its primary conclusion was that the country's youth had become alienated from the institutions of state and society, at both the national and local levels and even down to traditional institutions such as the family. This lack of confidence in existing institutions was due to the fact that they have been eroded or politicised, engendering an anti-institutional bias among the youth. There was also a belief that these institutions had no sensitivity to youth grievances and representations. The politicisation of political and civil institutions had resulted in merit being ignored and unqualified youth getting jobs over qualified youth. Such discrimination was deeply felt by the educated youths who came before the Commission.

The question then emerges as to why youth took to violence rather than seeking redress through the constitutional process. The answer to this question is complex. There are some scholars who argue that, from an anthropological point of view, despite the Buddhist heritage, Sinhalese society has a propensity to resolve conflicts violently (Kapferer 1988). This thesis is highly contested, but there is a belief that violence has been a traditional way of dealing with enemies. If modern secular forms are not 'legitimate', traditional forms of conflict resolution gain currency and acceptance. Second, there is a strong left revolutionary tradition in Sri Lanka, and many have argued that this legacy has encouraged violence against the class enemy. The JVP inherited much of that logic and its first leaders were inspired by left leaders like Che Guevara and Fidel Castro.

However, the primary reason for the JVP insurrection, especially the second one, was the perversion of the constitutional process by governments in power. The use of democratic and constitutional processes in an unfair manner and the deep politicisation of everyday life had led to youthful contempt for the political and constitutional process. Among the acts of the UNP government that came in for censure was the use of the referendum to prevent general elections, the lack of merit criteria in educational and employment opportunities, the use of thuggery and armed groups by politicians, their close association with criminal elements, and the cynical use of power by powerful urban élite families who see Sri Lanka as their feudal heritage.

The Youth Commission made some important recommendations. One of these was that there be a youth quota at local-level elections; this resulted in the introduction of a 40 per cent youth quota in the choice of candidates by political parties at the provincial level. In addition to youth alienation from democratic institutions, the Commission looked into social and economic grievances, including notably the mismatch between education policy and employment opportunities. The open economy had ushered in an era where private enterprise and the international economy were the growth sectors of the economy. However, university education, especially in arts subjects, resulted in hundreds of graduates expecting jobs in the public sector. Their Sinhalese language orientation and subject choices were more appropriate for a closed economy with a large public sector. With privatisation and retrenchment in the public sector, this avenue of employment was vulnerable and insecure. The Commission made a number of policy recommendations for educational curriculum reform, including the development of technical education and English-language education to enable youth to take full advantage of the open economy.

The Commission was also concerned with what was called *Asardharanaya*, a Sinhala phrase that is used to denote the class anger and the sense of injustice of young people, especially those from rural areas. The youth clearly believed that the current macroeconomic policies were benefiting the English-speaking élites. They spoke of English as *Kaduwa*, the sword that cuts down vernacular-speaking youth. This appeared to be the primary division in their minds. Those who spoke English had enormous access to benefits and privileges. Those who spoke Sinhalese or Tamil only were denied opportunities. The Commission made many recommendations to ensure that governments address this class division, including greater access to English-language education, along with translation of books and manuals into the vernacular.

The second area of discussion was caste, where the Commission found that youth from disadvantaged castes were more likely to take up arms than youth from other castes. Many people spoke of the caste factor in their presentations before the Commission, although it was an extremely sensitive matter in a society where such discrimination is not acknowledged publicly. The Commission suggested that the government deal with the issue frontally and set up a Commission to study the problem; unfortunately, however, its recommendations on caste were completely ignored by the government.

Though government policy does not address the issues directly, class and caste anger are primary causes of youth unrest in southern Sri Lanka. Since the constitution has provided no non-violent avenue for the expression of these concerns, they have been expressed extra-legally through the use of force. It will be interesting to see whether economic and social rights will be made into fundamental rights under the new constitution and whether cases would be brought under these provisions, enabling young people to use fundamental rights jurisprudence to assert equality and fight discrimination without recourse to the use of force. In India, the interpretation of constitutional provisions to include economic and social rights has proved to be a safety valve. It is hoped that the same will hold true in Sri Lanka.

Institutional design and the use of force

For most of the period after independence, Sri Lanka has been ruled by emergency powers. Democratic government in Sri Lanka has often worn an authoritarian face. This has been particularly true since the 1970s. The 1980s witnessed human rights violations that drew the censure of international bodies, including the United Nations Commission on Human Rights. The Public Security Ordinance of 1949 has always been the institutional mechanism for the use of force by the state. In addition the government has made use of the Prevention of Terrorism Act of 1979, which has many draconian features. The civil war in the North and the Southern insurrection of the 1980s led to declarations of emergency in many parts of the country. These areas remain outside the framework of protection guaranteed by the constitution's fundamental rights chapter, which is overridden by its public security provisions. The rights to freedom from arbitrary arrest and detention, along with freedom of speech, are among the rights most affected by the declaration of emergency. Chronicled cases of torture also punctuate international and national human rights reports in the areas where the emergency is effective.[4]

Since the 1980s, there has been a culture of impunity with regard to the actions of the security forces, except in certain documented instances. As a result of widespread abuses, certain institutions have been created to deal with this issue. The first is the Human Rights Commission, with a broad and powerful mandate under the Human Rights Commission Act of 1996. The Commission cannot issue orders but it can investigate complaints and take measures to ensure the protection of human rights throughout the country. Unfortunately the Commissioners have not used their powers to the full and human rights abuses have continued. The Commission was reconstituted recently to make it more effective. In certain areas such as Vavuniya it has been active but in Jaffna, Batticoloa and Colombo there is a belief that it could be more effective. The other institution that has been created is the Anti-Harassment Committee, which deals specifically with human rights violations resulting from the national security situation in the country. It is an informal attempt to help deal with the day-to-day problems of Tamil civilians existing in a climate of suspicion and fear.

Since the 1980s the use of force has characterised an election process marred by widespread violence and thuggery. Independent police officers and election officials have been transferred and state resources have been used to conduct the elections on a partisan basis. The misuse of ballot papers, the impersonation of candidates, the stuffing of ballot boxes and other abuses have emerged as common occurrences (Centre for Monitoring Election Violence 2000 and 2001). Election violence has led to increasing activism on the part of civil society. Widespread protest greeted the conduct of the 1999 presidential election and the use of state machinery to give the ruling party an edge in a contest awash with violence and thuggery, accentuated by the interventions of the LTTE.

In recent times, electoral politics and democratic rights have been increasingly conditioned by the fundamental rights jurisprudence of the Sri Lankan Supreme Court. Until the late 1980s, the Supreme Court was relatively passive in such cases, deferring to the executive on important fundamental rights issues. This changed after the violence of 1988. The Supreme Court has become very active in cases involving arbitrary arrest and detention, thus providing some redress for those whose rights have been violated under emergency rule. In the famous Wadduwa case,[5] where a political meeting in a Buddhist temple was disrupted, the Court laid out detailed guidelines on arrest and detention based on recognised international standards.

Despite the creation of many guarantees and safeguards to prevent the arbitrary use of force, in practice the North and East remain separate from the rest of the country. In these regions there is no civil administration. The North continues to be ruled by a military administration. In certain parts such as the Vanni, where the LTTE operates, there is no military or civil administration, only LTTE administration. In the East, there is a semblance of civil authority but civil and judicial processes do not function properly. Any attempt at civil administration results in the LTTE assassinating the civil authorities.

Military rule, whether by the army or the LTTE, is inherently arbitrary and non-democratic. For a large section of the Sri Lankan population living in the North and the East the constitution and the democratic process are non-existent concepts. Except for informal measures there is no real democratic or consultative process in the North and East. Since 2001, another Tamil militant group with state patronage (the Eelam People's Democratic Party) is operating in the North, thus ensuring there is one more group exerting arbitrary power.

163

In addition, human rights abuses are also perpetrated by the LTTE. The extra-judicial killing of 'traitors', intimidation, the forcible recruitment of soldiers (especially child soldiers) have all been chronicled by human rights groups and even by international representatives of the Secretary-General of the United Nations. Without democratic process and accountable institutions of power, it could be argued that the North and parts of the East are not only beyond the reach of the constitution but also beyond the confines of the rule of law. This has major implications. When constitutional and democratic processes are suspended, there is no obstacle to violence, thuggery and extortion. The population living in the North and the East is subjected to these indignities on a daily basis by the security forces, the paramilitary units working with them, or the LTTE.

In the rest of the country, there is more hope. Political thuggery, media censorship, arbitrary arrest and detention remain, a legacy of the past and a product of the present. Human rights are still an important item on the political agenda and require a great deal of monitoring and vigilance. However, an active Supreme Court and the existence of new institutional bodies like the Human Rights Commission may provide a certain redress. One of the most important developments in recent times has been the emergence of a vibrant civil society. This and the increasing activism of non-governmental groups have now laid the foundation of a more genuine democratic order. There are human rights groups that monitor the electoral and political process and issue reports. Others take cases to court through public interest litigation, and have won some important decisions. In addition, grassroot groups such as the Free Media Movement and the People's Alliance for Free and Fair Elections have mobilised for the protection of electoral and fundamental rights.

The emergence of an active civil society is the direct result of the violence and abuse of power of the past two decades. Citizens groups and NGOs have come forward to protect democratic rights. Their agitation was partly responsible for the change of government in the 1994 elections. They have taken cases to court, and a responsive judiciary has made many judgements in their favour. Nevertheless, the types of political abuse that prevailed in the 1970s and the 1980s, facilitated by large parliamentary majorities and the use of emergency power, still prevail in many parts of the country.

While the South has witnessed the resurgence of civil society in a more vibrant and vigilant form, in the North, where the war and militarisation continue, the opposite has taken place, and there is really no active civil society. Indeed, the type of active civil society that is tolerated in the South is not acceptable in the North, either to the military administration or to the LTTE. While the South has emerged from the years of violence with an aware public, the North's civilians remain silent, polarised between a government military presence and the retaliation of the LTTE. Elected bodies no longer function and even judges have to go on holiday in response to the threats of the LTTE. Electoral politics in the North is a pipedream, and without strenuous efforts by national and international civil society it is unlikely to return to the war-torn provinces in the near future.

Proposals for the future

The final contours or institutional design of Sri Lanka's constitutional framework have yet to be imagined and formulated. Consultations initiated by President Chandrika Kumaratunga's government after 1997 came up with far-reaching proposals for a new constitution, drafted around a 'devolution package' and finalised in August 2000. This followed intensive discussions with the opposition UNP, which ultimately failed, so that the government tried to force through the proposals on a unilateral basis. This too failed, leading to general elections and a presidential election. Though there were attempts at consultation through a select parliamentary committee, there was little public discussion and debate. A South African-style consultative process, recommended by many actors in civil society, did not take place, and instead the constitution was debated by the political parties and a few members of the legal fraternity. Since there was no sense of participation in the constitution-making process, when a draft constitution was finally put forward it did not receive wide public support.

Despite these limitations, the government draft went a major step beyond earlier proposals. The initial 1997 document called for a 'union of regions' and an openly federal structure, with a list of subjects reserved for the periphery and a list of subjects for the centre[6] – although the federal word had been anathema to Sinhalese extremists. In addition, the draft recognised Sri Lanka as a multi-ethnic, multilingual and multi-religious society, a major snub to those who saw Sri Lanka as a Sinhala Buddhist country. The draft constitution gave strong powers to the regions in the important areas of finance, education, law and order and land; in many respects, it gave the regions similar powers to those of the federal units in India.

By the time the draft became an Act to repeal and replace the existing constitution, however, all these provisions had been watered down. The phrase 'union of regions' was taken out and replaced by the strangely worded formulation that the Republic of Sri Lanka would consist of 'institutions of the Centre and of the Regions'. All the advances made in the areas of land, law and order, education and finance were also drastically watered down, with the centre exercising strong control over the periphery. As a result, all the Tamil parties came out against the constitution and campaigned actively for its rejection. The assassination of Dr Neelan Tiruchelvam, one of the main architects of the 1997 proposals, was perhaps among the reasons for the government's reneging on its promises to the Tamil community and its political leadership.

While the Sri Lankan government was finding it difficult to mention the word 'federal', Tamil parties united around the Thimpu principles. These principles, as mentioned above, call for the recognition of a Tamil nation and nationality and for a recognition of the Tamil traditional homelands of the North and the East. The gap between the Sinhala and the Tamil political leadership appears unbridgeable. The only optimistic development since the drafting of the proposed constitution has been the fact that both the government and the LTTE have accepted Norwegian facilitation in an attempt to foster peace talks. Although the talks were stalled by the defeat of the People's Alliance (PA) government in the general election held in December 2001, the new UNP government continued the attempts to open negotiations with the LTTE, assisted by the facilitators, and in February 2002 the LTTE and the government entered into a ceasefire agreement. The implementation of the agreement was being monitored by a committee with the participation of representatives of the LTTE, the Sri Lankan government and Scandinavian countries. If this process (continuing at the time of writing) was to lead to direct talks, however, the constitutional drafters would have to return to the drawing board – since no Tamil party, let alone the LTTE, would be satisfied with the draft constitution presented in 2000.

The draft constitution contains some salutary features, nevertheless. There is a comprehensive chapter on fundamental rights, in line with Sri Lanka's obligations under the International Covenant on Civil and Political Rights and the International Covenant on Economic, Social and Cultural Rights. It returns the country to parliamentary democracy with an accountable prime minister. The draft also provides for a bipartisan Constitutional Council that will appoint persons to independent bodies and commissions, a powerful public service commission and a strong judicial services commission. These provisions were a recognition that independent public bodies are essential for the working of modern democracies. However the chapter on the judiciary is weaker, with presidential and prime ministerial power to appoint individuals to the Supreme Court and no provision for judicial review of legislation over a two-year period. Many civil society groups have strongly advocated a stronger and more independent judiciary.[7] While the democratic aspects of the constitution – those provisions relating to parliamentary democracy, fundamental rights, independent commissions and public bodies – are receiving widespread consensus, the issue of devolution or federalism remains deeply contested. Until there is political agreement on power sharing between majority and minority communities, there will be no finality for any institutional design for a future Sri Lanka.

Conclusion

It may be said that Sri Lanka has witnessed three constitutions and is in the process of entertaining a fourth. The instrumental use of constitutions by successive governments has prevented them from acquiring status as the fundamental law. Nevertheless, the constitutions have shown a gradual evolution away from a majoritarian, Sinhalese Buddhist orientation towards a more complex, pluralistic document. Minority languages and territorial aspirations are being gradually recognised, even if they fall short of the demands of Tamil political leaders. In addition, an active Supreme Court has galvanised fundamental rights jurisdiction in the country and provided for further checks and balances on the system of political decision making. Finally, the proportional representation electoral system has prevented pendulum shifts, denying any side a two-thirds majority and forcing governments to come to power through the use of coalitions. Arguably, this has ensured less arbitrary decision making and a more measured approach to constitutional amendments. Any future constitution must have the approval of all political parties and the people at a referendum. This may force bipartisan decision making and the elusive social contract for which Sri Lankans have waited through years of war and bloodshed.

References

Amnesty International (2000) *New Emergency Regulations – Erosion of Human Rights Protection*, AI-index ASA 37/019/2000, London.

Arulpragasam, A. R. (1996) *The Traditional Homeland of the Tamils: the Missing Pages of Sri Lankan History*, Colombo, Kanal Publishers.

Bandaranaike, S. W. R. D. (1926) 'Federation: a Solution to the Problem of Ceylon's External and Internal Relations', *Morning Leader*, 19 May.

Centre for Monitoring Election Violence (2000) *Interim Report on Election-Related Violence*, Colombo.

Centre for Monitoring Election Violence (2001) *Interim Report on Election-Related Violence*, Colombo.

Government Press (1947) *Public Security Ordinance No. 25*, Colombo.

Government Publications Bureau (1972) *The Constitution of Sri Lanka (Ceylon)*, Colombo.

Government Publications Bureau (1978) *The Constitution of the Democratic, Socialist Republic of Sri Lanka*, Colombo.

Government Publications Bureau (1979) *The Prevention of Terrorism (Temporary Provisions) Act No. 48 of 1979*, Colombo.

Government Publications Bureau (1990) *Report of the Presidential Commission on Youth*, Colombo.

Government Publication Bureau (1996) *Human Rights Commission of Sri Lanka Act No. 21 of 1996*, Colombo.

Government Record Office (1948) *The Constitution of Ceylon*, Colombo.

Gunasekera, P. (1998) *Sri Lanka in Crisis: Lost Generation – the Untold Story*, Colombo: S. Godage Brothers.

Hellman-Rajanayagam, D. (1994) *The Tamil Tigers' Armed Struggle for Identity*, Stuttgart: Fraz Steiner Verlag.

Kapferer, B. (1988) *Legends of People, Myths of State Violence, Intolerance and Political Culture in Sri Lanka and Australia*, Washington DC: Smithsonian Institution Press.

Law and Society Trust (1997) 'Consultation on the Draft Constitution of Sri Lanka', Colombo.

Ministry of Education and Cultural Affairs (ed. Ananda Guruge) (1965) *Return to Righteousness, a Collection of Speeches, Essays and Letters of Anagarika Dharmapala*.

Ministry of Justice, Constitutional Affairs, Ethnic Affairs and National Integration (1997) *The Government Proposal for Constitutional Reform*, Colombo.

Obeyesekere, G.(1979) 'Vicissitudes of the Sinhala-Buddhist Identity through Time and Change', in M. Roberts (ed.) *Collective Identities, Nationalism and Protest in Sri Lanka*, Colombo: Marga Institute.

Peiris, G. H. (1991) 'An Appraisal of the Concept of a Traditional Homeland in Sri Lanka', *Ethnic Studies Report*, 9, 1 (January).

Roberts, M. (1979) 'Introduction' in M. Roberts (ed.), *Collective Identities, Nationalism and Protest in Sri Lanka*, Colombo: Marga Institute.

Tiruchelvam, N. (1998) 'A Tale of Three Constitutions', *Hindu*, Madras, 3 February.

Wriggins, H. (1960) *Ceylon: Dilemmas of a New Nation*, Princeton: Princeton University Press.

Wickremasinghe, N. (1995) *Ethnic Politics in Colonial Sri Lanka*, New Delhi: Vikas.

Notes

1 In the aftermath of the JVP insurgency, the government set up a Presidential Commission to inquire into the causes of this unrest. See Government Publications Bureau, 1990.

2 See article 18 (2) of the 1972 constitution (Government Publications Bureau, 1972).

3 See Peiris 1991: 13, and Arulpragasam 1996 for two contrasting points of view in this debate.

4 Many reports on the human rights situation in Sri Lanka have been produced by international human rights organisations. For a recent example see Amnesty International 2000.

5 This was a case arising out of a meeting held by a civil society group in a small town in the South of Sri Lanka called Wadduwa. The police, on the basis of the proceedings of the meeting and a particular speech, came to the conclusion that there was a conspiracy to overthrow the government and arrested the participants.

6 See article 1 of the draft constitution of the Democratic Socialist Republic of Sri Lanka, 1997.

7 See Law and Society Trust 1997 for an example of these ideas promoted by civil society.

6

Proportional Representation, Political Violence and the Participation of Women in the Political Process in Sri Lanka[1]

KISHALI PINTO-JAYAWARDENA

The failure of a potentially transformative force in Sri Lankan politics

The day before Sri Lanka's provincial council elections in April 1999, a community organisation was bracing itself to face the hustings in a violence-ridden polity split on ethnic, racial and religious lines. The Sinhala–Tamil Rural Women's Network (STRAWN) had several contradictions to its credit. Although it was contesting the Central Provincial Council elections on a gender platform, men nevertheless formed a major part of the organisation, as evidenced by the many male supporters streaming into the line room that cold Monday morning and rather endearingly identifying themselves as belonging to a women's network.

The network fielded fourteen women and six men from widely differing faiths in an effort to provide an inter-religious, inter-ethnic and inter-racial bulwark against the gigantic forces of the country's major political parties, the ruling People's Alliance (PA), the main opposition party, the United National Party (UNP), and the monolithic party of the Central Province plantation workers, the Ceylon Workers' Congress (CWC). A majority of STRAWN's candidates were bilingual, and all of them were community workers in the district. Their excitement was infectious, tempered however by the anxiety that their efficacy at the polls would be marred by intimidation and election malpractices.

Contesting four districts in the Central Province, STRAWN was able to gather a mere 2,335 votes in contrast to the huge vote banks of the mainstream parties. This vote count was meagre by the standards of its membership of 28,500, including a male membership of 5,000. The bulk of the seats in the Central Provincial Council were won by the PA (26 seats) and the UNP (23 seats). The STRAWN leader, Wimali

Karunaratne, blamed widespread intimidation by politicians of the ruling People's Alliance for the defeat. One of the districts which they contested, Walapone, was acknowledged by election monitors to be among those hit worst by election malpractices, including general intimidation and impersonation of voters. Karunaratne herself had been subjected to blatant threats from a powerful opposing candidate in the government ranks to 'rape her in order to shut her up'. She cited the immense financial resources that electioneering within a proportional representation system demands as another major reason for her defeat. Her organisation had only one van to use for its campaigning, and its electioneering was limited to pocket meetings in villages. Even its posters – an essential feature of election campaigns in Sri Lanka – were carefully rationed. The contrast between this humble style of electioneering and the vast amounts of money spent by candidates of the established political parties could not have been clearer.

STRAWN's decision to contest the polls and transform itself from a community organisation into a political force resulted from the failure of successive governments to respond to their lobbying, particularly regarding the problems facing marginalised vegetable cultivators and potato farmers in the area. Realising that community lobbying has its own limitations, STRAWN decided that political action was imperative. In the immediate aftermath of its defeat, the decision appeared to have been unwise. Fuelled by a widespread disenchantment with politics and the deeply corrupt nature of Sri Lankan politics, many formerly enthusiastic supporters of the once immensely popular activist movement expressed doubts about the sincerity of the party itself. It was a feeling of 'they were doing so well helping the people in their own way. Now, they wanted to enter politics and become like the rest of those rascals.' In part, also, the highly visible 'gender in politics' profile adopted by STRAWN backfired among the largely conservative voters of the hill country.

The 1999 defeat of Sri Lanka's first women's party has an interesting postscript. In the general elections the following year, Karunaratne accepted an offer from the ruling People's Alliance to stand as one of its candidates, despite the fact that it was this very party that had subjected her to intimidation and threats of physical violence. Her reasoning was that given the deeply entrenched political culture in the country favouring major parties and the formidable violence practised by them, independent candidates had no chance of success. Her strategy therefore was to use her community influence to win the organisation a seat within a major party, and to lobby to fulfil the objectives of STRAWN from that advantageous position. She was unable, however, to gather a sufficient number of preferential votes required for a seat under the proportional representation system under which the elections were held.

Despite the obvious dangers in idealising STRAWN or generalising too widely from its defeat and eventual co-option into the major party-political process, several questions follow from this experience. Would women's experiences be different if they were contesting under an electoral system other than that of proportional representation (PR) which prevails in Sri Lanka at present? To what extent did PR impact on or contribute to the massive electoral violence that now forms an integral part of the country's electoral process, and in what manner did this contribute to the electoral defeat of women candidates? And are women themselves, in their electoral campaigns, beginning to use violence as a strategy?

PR and its impact on women's representation

Favourable societal conditions will not substitute for unfavourable electoral systems for women to reach their optional representation in parliament and local legislatures. But unfavourable contextual conditions – including cultural biases and discriminatory practices – can be overcome to a great extent by alternative electoral systems. (Rule 1994: 689)

In analysing Sri Lanka's electoral design as far as women's representation is concerned, the key question to be determined is whether the country-specific form of PR has helped or hindered women's representation in legislative assemblies. The broad general argument justifying PR is that plurality-majority systems, and first-past-the-post (FPTP) systems in particular, tend to result in disproportionate legislative majorities. These majorities injure minority interests, riding roughshod over different and under-represented societal interests and compelling parties to put forward a broadly acceptable candidate with the most chances of winning in each particular district. This, in turn, makes representatives of minorities and women less likely to be selected as candidates by male-dominated party structures. In contrast, PR reduces such majorities, resulting in a fairer representation. It allows minority-interest candidates, including women, to access politics more easily and compels parties to use the system to promote the advancement of such candidates, allowing their inclusion into the national debate in a manner that is beneficial to the integrity and development of the country.

Sri Lanka's electoral history amply proved the truth of the first half of this general proposition. The huge majorities that, up to 1977, resulted from FPTP electoral aberrations impacted on national politics in a manner that was distinctly 'minority negative'. In 1970 the United Front obtained well over two thirds of the seats in Parliament, even though its electoral support was less than 50 per cent. Using that mandate, and despite protests from the Tamil United Liberation Front (TULF), an 'autochthonous' constitution was adopted, doing away with section 29 of the Soulbury Constitution, which safeguarded the rights of minorities, and installing Sinhala as the official language in the country. Authoritarian rule then proceeded to exacerbate minority tensions.

Seven years later, in 1977, the pendulum swung massively again when the UNP gained five sixths of the seats, with a popular mandate only a little over 50 per cent. A convoluted constitutional structure was introduced, entrenching an authoritarian executive presidency, while the disproportionate parliamentary majority was kept in place for the following twelve years, far beyond the normal legislative mandate of five years, by the device of a flawed referendum. The following years saw the country plunged into a continuing war in the North-east and a second aborted civil insurrection, with insurgent terror and state counter-terror leaving an indelible impression on the national psyche.

It was during this period that the UNP installed a system of proportional representation, ostensibly to balance representation in Parliament but more cynically viewed as a means of ensuring that the government in power would never be relegated to an ineffective minority in the House. Select committee deliberations during 1983–8 ultimately resulted in a complex system of voting for a political party and thereafter for a maximum number of three preferences from a list of candidates nominated by the party; there were cut-off points and bonus seats to round things off. This shifted the focus from a single-member electorate to a large district-based electorate returning many members (ICES 1997). The first election under PR took place in 1989.

How did these changes affect minority-interest representation in Sri Lanka? How did they impact, in particular, on the nature and participation of women in formal politics, and consequently on the nature of the legal and political decision-making process in the country? While an overview of countries using some form of PR yields positive answers to these two questions, the Sri Lankan electoral experience is notably different. Indeed, the form of PR that the country has chosen led to the system manifesting peculiar internal contradictions as far as minority-interest representation and the political empowerment of women are

173

concerned. These contradictions have ricocheted off each other in a number of ways.

In the first instance, the marginalising of the 'woman' question in the political debate has occurred problematically within the very framework of the 'greater minority representation' argument commonly used to justify PR. Thus, legislatures under PR both in 1994 and in 2000 have seen a positioning of minority parties in greater legislative strength within the House. This minority 'balance of power' has had its own dynamics as far as gender-sensitive law making is concerned.

As this chapter will set out in detail, the Tenth Parliament, elected in 1994, witnessed a great number of instances in which gender-progressive legislation was diluted or done away with altogether on representations made by minority lobbies intent on safeguarding their own cultural and religious identities. This had an impact not only with regard to laws affecting their own communities but also with regard to laws in general. The Eleventh Parliament, with its fragmented composition and greater lobbying power, proved to be even more expedient in law making.

This chapter will argue, second, that the example of STRAWN in particular and the experiences of women in Sri Lanka's major political parties in general manifest the very necessary truth that PR cannot be said, in isolation, to work for the betterment of women in politics. Its beneficial effects are heavily dependent on the type of political party structures and the socio-cultural ethos within which it operates:

> in countries sharing similar political cultures such as Germany and Australia, PR has resulted in three to four times more women being elected. In contrast, in Russia for instance, this generalisation is inapplicable because of the lack of a political culture; specifically, the huge numbers of parties and blocs, their underdeveloped structures, the lack of confidence many women face and political parties' ignorance of women's interests. (Karm 1998:22)

Moreover, there are important qualifications to the general argument that PR benefits women's representation. Reynolds identifies the chief among these to be the level of choice that a voter is given, not just between parties but between candidates as well (Reynolds 1999). The debate is between open list systems (where voters influence the party list through their vote) and closed list systems (which transfer this decision from the voter to the party). In developed countries, open lists have favoured the election of women candidates, but developing countries have found the choice between open list and closed list systems to be far more complicated.

174

Thus, the South African experience of using closed party list systems has been positive. Though women-only political parties do not appear to have met with a marked degree of success in South Africa either (for example, the inability of the Women's Party, led by feminist artist Nina Romm, to secure a single parliamentary seat, despite a low cut-off threshold), the use of a 30 per cent quota for women on the electoral lists in the 1994 and 1999 elections by the African National Congress (whose ranks included a significant number of prominent women's activists), had a ripple effect on other political parties, resulting in a relatively high number of women being elected to Parliament. In this instance, it is argued that the principal value of the PR list system is that it allows progressive party leadership to override traditional sentiments against women's election (Hassim 1999; Goetz and Hassim 2003). The high proportion of women MPs makes the South African Parliament the seventh highest in the world in terms of women's parliamentary representation.

Sri Lanka, on the other hand, employs an open list system with an addition of marking three preferences – a peculiarly local innovation that was introduced into PR, whereby voters are required to vote for one party and then choose three candidates from the party list as their preferred representatives. Despite this adaptation, political and socio-cultural factors within a very violent electoral process have clearly deprived PR of its effectiveness as far as the political presence of women is concerned. Though PR led to a marginal increase of women legislators in Parliament when the system was in its infancy, even this benefit has become progressively diluted through the years.

Within major political parties, PR has, in fact, led to the entrenching of a 'woman unfriendly' political system. Thus, we have seen the post-PR growth of gargantuan party apparatuses subordinating the role of the individual member of parliament. These party apparatuses, without exception, continue to be élitist and gender-insensitive (irrespective of their leaders being men or women) with consequential negative effects both in the nomination of women candidates and the independence that they are allowed from the party whip once elected. Neither has the National List mechanism for appointing representatives been utilised to benefit women.

The post-PR environment of Sri Lankan politics has also become increasingly violent. With the overall breakdown of democratic structures, intra-party as well as extra-party electoral violence has become pronounced. The necessity for each candidate to compete not only with candidates from opposing parties but also with candidates from his or her own party in order to capture one of the three coveted preference votes has contributed to this violence. Immense financial resources are also essential to putting oneself forward as a candidate in a PR system in which electioneering covers an entire electoral district and not a particular electorate. Cumulatively, this has resulted in a bizarre shift from the FPTP to the PR system of the 'most broadly acceptable candidate' syndrome, according to which a party is compelled to choose the candidate who can best hold his or her own financially, as well as in terms of brute strength, against opposing candidates from other parties as well as from the candidate's own party. Inevitably, the candidates thus chosen are either males or (less often) females from established political families, and the entry of politically privileged women into the political process has not led to any significant political empowering of their sisters. This corresponds with the experience of other countries:

> women, because of their gender alone, will not place gender issues on the national agenda. Women in the upper echelons of politics are more likely to become an élite group among women and develop their own vested interests. (Karm 1998: 10)

These issues in turn, have raised the question of the manner in which specific quotas for women should be implemented in national and local legislative bodies. This debate is currently being conducted in the context of a decreasing political will to ensure such representation even at local government level.

In its totality, Sri Lanka demonstrates a clear instance of a country in which specific historical and political forces have led to a fragmented and violence-ridden polity. The rest of this chapter will maintain the position that, from a feminist viewpoint, an experimental electoral engineering has only entrenched a dangerously élitist 'empowerment' of selected women in politics, besides making it even more difficult for women outside this charmed circle to access the political process. The overall result has been a ridiculously low women's presence in the country's legislative assemblies at every level of governance, and a law-making process that is completely devoid of a feminist consciousness.

Sri Lankan women legislators: numerical realities

Eleven years of the proportional representation electoral system in Sri Lanka have not resulted in any significant numerical gain as far as women representatives are concerned, either at parliamentary or provincial/local level. Up to 1977 under the FPTP system, the largest number of women nominated was in March 1960, when 16 were chosen. Out of these only three were successful in getting themselves elected (2 per cent). Prior to 1977, the largest number of women elected under FPTP was in 1970, when six women members succeeded in winning seats in the House (Kamalawathie: 1990).

Following the electoral system change in the 1978 constitution, the new PR system actually came into operation only in 1989. That year's parliamentary elections witnessed the nomination of 52 women out of a total of 1,688 candidates, the percentage of *nominated* women thus being only 3 per cent. However the percentage with regard to women *elected* was higher in this first election under PR: 11 women were elected to a legislative body consisting of 225 members (4.8 per cent) (Department of Census and Statistics: 1995).

Elections to the Tenth Parliament in 1994 and the Eleventh Parliament in 2000 juxtaposed interesting figures of women nominated and elected. Nominations remained low as a percentage, although there were large numbers due to the multiplicity of small political parties which contested. The two main parties fielded only a disappointing 22 candidates between them (*Daily News*, 17 October 2000). The leftist Janatha Vimukthi Peramuna (JVP), now in the thick of mainstream politics with a legacy of anti-systemic struggle, put forward the most number of women on its behalf (23).

The decreasing numbers of *elected* women in 1994 and 2000, however, categorically dispel the myth that PR has resulted in a numerical increase of women parliamentarians. Instead women have all but returned to a pre-PR presence in Parliament (Table 6.1), and their share of ministerial politics has also declined.

Almost without exception, women parliamentarians on both sides of the political divide in the House hailed from families with established political traditions. Out of women in the Tenth Parliament, for example, seven took their seats following the demise or other incapacity of some male member in their families, and with the avowed aim of carrying on his policies. They included President Chandrika Kumaratunge herself, who entered politics to claim the historical legacies of her father and mother, both former premiers of the country, and whose entry into the political race as leader of her party followed the assassination of her husband.

The provincial government situation is worse. Female representation in Village Councils, Municipal Councils and Urban Councils is dismal (see Table 6.2), though the numbers of women nominated to contest these elections increased from 0.5 per cent in 1993 to 5.4 per cent in 1999.

Table 6.1. Women's representation in the parliaments elected in 1994 and 2000

| | 2000 | | | 1994 | | |
	Total	Women	%	Total	Women	%
Members	225	9	4.0	225	11	4.8
Cabinet ministers	44	2	4.5	20*	3	15.0
				28	4	14.2
Deputy ministers	35	0	0.0	26*	5	19.2
				30	3	10.0

* Refers respectively to first and second Cabinet.
Source: Leiten 2000.

In the seven Provincial Councils now functioning, only one woman holds a ministerial post as against 34 men. Two women councillors who won in the Uva and North Central Provinces in 1999 actually stepped down from their positions to enable their husbands, both prominent party men, to take their places and be appointed as Chief Ministers.

The numbers of women in local government are equally disappointing (Table 6.3). There have been only two women mayors and four chairpersons of Pradeshiya Sabhas island-wide. None of the 35 Urban Councils in the country have been headed by women.[2]

Minority women representation has been minimal. Although Tamil women played an important role in the early years of women's suffrage, it was only in 1980, after a long gap, that a Tamil woman, Ranganayake Pathmanathan, entered the legislature after being nominated by the ruling party following her brother's death. Nine years later another Tamil woman, Manohari Pulendran (nominated and subsequently appointed as the UNP member for Vavuniya after the assassination of her husband), was elected to Parliament in 1989, going on to be both the first Tamil woman to hold ministerial office and the single minority woman representative in the Tenth Parliament before losing her seat in the October 2000 general elections. Muslim women were represented by an exceptional figure in Ayesha Rauf: she became a municipal councillor and deputy mayoress, and unsuccessfully contested a parliamentary election. Recently, the entry of Ferial Ashraff, wife of the deceased leader of the Sri Lanka Muslim Congress, into Sri Lanka's Eleventh Parliament has heralded the first Muslim woman parliamentarian, and indeed the first Muslim woman Minister, in national-level politics.

Table 6.2 Women in Provincial Councils

Province	1999			1993		
	Total	Women	%	Total	Women	%
Western	104	2	1.9	104	7	6.7
North Central	34	1	2.9	36	4	11.1
North Western	51	3	5.8	52	3	5.8
Uva	32	1	3.1	34	0	0.0
Central	58	3	5.1	58	1	1.7
Southern	55	1	1.8	55	2	3.6
Sabaragamuwa	43	1	2.3	44	1	2.3
Total	377	12	3.3	383	18	4.7

Source: Ministry of Women's Affairs, 1998, published in *Daily News*, Colombo, 16 March 1998.

Table 6.3 Women in local government

Province	1997			1991		
	Total	Women	%	Total	Women	%
Municipal Councils	252	9	3.4	201	6	2.9
Urban Councils	331	9	2.6	235	6	2.4
Pradeshiya Sabhas	3,137	55	1.7	2,632	42	1.6

Source: Leiten 2000.

This spectacularly low number of women represented in Sri Lanka's legislative assemblies at national, provincial and local level contrasts strongly with an apparent empowerment of the Sri Lankan woman demonstrated primarily through socio-economic indicators. For example, a report on 'Women and Men in Sri Lanka' published by the Department of Census and Statistics in 1995 applauds the impressive improvement in health standards of the country in general as reflecting improvements in the living conditions of women in particular. Fertility has dropped by 50 per cent over the past three decades and high educational levels of women have been noted as a key determinant for this steady decline. Women have entered the labour force in Sri Lanka at a faster rate than men during the past two decades, though women's labour force participation (31.4 per cent) is estimated to be only half that of men. The average age of marriage of women is 25.5 years, indicating that having a family is no longer considered the first priority in a woman's life (Department of Census and Statistics 1995).

Institutional and legal support for women has also been manifest. While a Women's Bureau under a Ministry of Women's Affairs has been functioning since 1978, there has been a 25 per cent quota system for women in the administrative service since 1975. The United Nations Convention on the Elimination of All Forms of Discrimination Against Women was ratified in 1981 and the International Labour Organisation Convention on equal remuneration for equal work in 1993. Between these years there was a steady flow of legislation helping to reduce discrimination against women in the workplace. New laws removed differential wages for selected trades that had been stipulated on the basis of gender by the Wages Board, permitted night work for women not exceeding ten days per month with facilities such as the presence of a night warden and the provision of a rest room, and extended the duration of maternity leave to 84 working days for the first two live births: both private sector and thereafter public sector employees were beneficiaries. In 1993 a Women's Charter was approved, and then a national committee was set up to monitor and implement it.

The commonly held view is that such success stories in the socioeconomic sphere should have led to the formation of a critical mass of women equalling men in the public sphere. Arguing for the effect of development and culture on women's representation, Matland (1998: 29) puts it best when he says that these are presumed to have a consciousness-raising effect:

> Development leads to a weakening of traditional values, decreased fertility rates, increased urbanisation, greater education and labour force participation for women and attitudinal changes in perceptions regarding the appropriate role for women – all factors that increase women's political resources and decrease existing barriers to political activity.

In the case of Sri Lanka the evidence in the political sphere presents a wholly different picture. Even the Department of Census and Statistics, the source of data depicting socio-economic success, seems to acknowledge that in Sri Lanka the acceptance of male supremacy is nurtured by cultural norms (Department of Census and Statistics 1995). It is clear, therefore, that many of the indicators presented by reports like Sri Lanka's Human Development Index (HDI) are highly misleading as far as gender empowerment is concerned.

180

The PR system and a negatively fragmented Parliament

In addition to this extremely low representation of women, the Sri Lankan legislature has not stood out as a positive force in securing women's rights. Sri Lankan law proceeds on the basis of a deficient normative construction of rights with a public/private rationale that validates the law to intervene only in the public sphere of government, the economy and the workplace. Even in this limited intervention, its force is inadequate. This basic deficiency has been compounded by the political realities of a fragmented Parliament produced by the PR system. Under this system most governments have depended on the support of smaller parties, who hold extremely conservative views on a number of gender issues, in order to maintain their parliamentary majorities. The result has been a reluctance to support significant changes on the gender issue.

The legal structure of Sri Lanka postulates a theoretical equality set out in constitutional principles that guarantee a fundamental right of equality of women with men in the protection and enjoyment of human rights.[3] However, these constitutional prohibitions against sexual discrimination have not been significantly used to advance women's rights in Sri Lanka. The one exception to this pattern is the case of action against discriminatory immigration/emigration laws.[4] This inability to use the constitution to benefit women is due in part to constitutional restrictions on social action litigation and in part to perceptions widely held by women that the law is not an instrument through which redress can be obtained for any wrong.

Gender-sensitive draft laws have been caught up in wider political protests. The most striking example of this in recent times was the draft Equal Opportunities Bill. The Bill sought to make unlawful discrimination on the grounds of ethnicity, gender, religious or political opinion, language, caste, age or disability, in employment, education, access to public places and means of transportation and in the provision of accommodation, goods and services; to provide for the formulation of equal opportunity programmes by employers, and to provide for the establishment of an Equal Opportunity Commission and an Equal Opportunity Tribunal. Protests by extremist groups (who saw certain provisions of the Bill as displacing majority rights) and dissatisfaction among liberals over the impromptu manner in which the Bill was put forward, resulted in the draft law being withdrawn from the House.

Where laws concerning the personal autonomy of women are in

181

issue, the opposition of religious lobbies in Parliament has manifested itself mainly through smaller parties like the Sri Lanka Muslim Congress. Thus we have seen laws relating to marital rape diluted beyond practical effect and a reformed policy on abortion completely withdrawn from the legislative sphere in 1995, when efforts were being made to amend eighteenth-century penal laws affecting women. These withdrawals were as a result of protests in the House by Muslim and Catholic lobbies, which saw the proposed laws as offending their religious precepts. Particular issues revolving round this failed legislative intervention deserve special attention.

The 1995 Penal Code reforms were initiated as a result of lobbying by women activists during the 1994 presidential and parliamentary elections that brought the PA government to power. Significant changes were recommended with regard to laws against rape and sexual harassment. The amendments relating to rape enhanced the punishment for this crime by imposing a minimum of 7 years' and a maximum of 20 years' imprisonment, and recognised that actual physical injury need not be established to prove rape. Custodial and gang rape, rape of a minor, of a pregnant woman or of a physically disabled woman were defined as grave sexual abuse, carrying the minimum penalty of imprisonment for 10 years. The court was given the power to award compensation to the victim.[5] The offence of sexual harassment was for the first time legally defined as a crime punishable with a fine and/or imprisonment.[6] The Bill also defined marital rape as a crime punishable by law and recognised the right of a woman to obtain an abortion in situations of rape, incest or foetal abnormality.[7] By the time the Bill went through the House, however, the provisions on marital rape and abortion had been completely revised. The provision on marital rape was limited to situations where husband and wife are judicially separated, and the provision on abortion was completely withdrawn. Not surprisingly, reports of rape and sexual assault have been on the rise since 1995, testifying to the impotency of the legislation passed by the House. Meanwhile domestic violence is still to be addressed by a specific law and continues to be viewed as a strictly private occurrence within the family.

The debate as to the manner and extent to which the Sri Lankan general law can replace personal laws that discriminate against women is also highly contested. This in turn has led to a significant reluctance of the country's legislators to trespass on the ambit of personal laws whenever the general law is changed for the better. Thus, though the age of marriage was raised to eighteen years of age in 1995, marriage under Muslim law, which permits child marriages, was excepted. A similar exception was made when laws raising the age limit for the offence of statutory rape from 12 to 16 were brought in the year before. Attempts to give Muslim women equal access to divorce and to ensure women's consent on marriage have led to similar failure.

An aborting of gender-progressive measures with a direct impact on the participation of women in the political process was flagrantly evident, meanwhile, in August 2000, when a clause in the regional list of the draft constitution that 'election laws shall ensure that not less than 25 per cent of the members elected thereunder to local authorities shall be women' was quietly dropped from revised proposals for constitutional reform following opposition from smaller parties including the Sri Lanka Muslim Congress. Their opposition was on the basis that a compulsory direction to fill 25 per cent of the seats would be practically difficult to fulfil. As a result, the imperative clause assuring a 25 per cent quota was replaced by a tepid provision stating that 'as far as practical' the adequate representation of women shall be provided for.[8]

Explaining the political subordination of women

The party structures

In South Africa, the vibrant presence of women in political parties, most notably the African National Congress (ANC), has injected a distinct women's consciousness into party structures. It was, indeed, the lobbying tactics of the ANC Women's League that led the party to adopt a quota for women on the party's electoral lists, resulting in the overall boosting of women's representation in the South African Parliament. It is interesting that the League took an especially strong stance over women's representation in constitutional negotiations, threatening to boycott the first non-racial elections with the slogan 'no women, no vote' (Hassim 1999). The strong presence of party women also visibly impacted on the manner in which the Women's National Coalition, the umbrella body of the women's movement, was successfully able to combat issues like illiteracy, poverty and spatial marginalisation, political violence and patriarchal control that, it had been feared, would inhibit South African women from accessing the political process.

If the cohesiveness of women within parties in South Africa was responsible for the strong articulation of women's interests in politics, the converse has been the Sri Lankan case. Sri Lanka has boasted women political leaders of singular ability. Thus the executive presidency, the most powerful position in the country's political structures, has been held since 1994 by a woman who is herself the daughter of the world's first woman premier. During one period in recent years, women held the reins of leadership of three major parties in their hands. Despite these apparent signs of gender empowerment, political party structures continue to discriminate against women attempting to access the political process from outside an élite circle.

The Sri Lankan political process, always strongly party-based, has become even more so since the introduction of PR. This, together with the prohibition on cross-overs from one party to another in Parliament (see Chapter 7) has culminated in an almost complete subordination of MPs to the will of the party. This has affected women politicians much more than their male colleagues, given the inherently precarious nature of their entry into politics. With party structures consistently manifesting a reluctance to be gender-sensitive, strong party dominance has impacted negatively on the selection of women candidates and on the space allowed for women to work out their own measure of freedom within party structures.

While all political parties in Sri Lanka have minimal representation of women in their decision-making committees, the privileging of élite women in the political process has ironically led to a second barrier of discrimination within party structures. In many cases, senior party women themselves pose serious problems to younger women striving to make their way within the party. As a local government councillor who wished to remain anonymous said:

> There is a women's organisation in our party. It does not promote young women very much. The reason for that is that most of those in the organisation are elderly women. We do not even know some of the women who hold posts there. Some have dropped from the sky because they know someone higher up in the party. We may genuinely work for the people in our area but our efforts are not recognised by them.

Equally, the women's wing in political parties does not wield much authority in the party hierarchy. Instead, it exists primarily for implementing social welfare programmes and for massing female support during campaign time. In selecting electoral candidates, its voice is minimal.

Many of the women who have entered politics through the mainstream parties have done so because of the political strength and resources of their families, where male members play a dominant role. This process has contributed to the creation of regional and national dynasties where power is concentrated in the hands of regional political élites, with male members of these families retaining seats in Parliament, while promoting their wives to positions of provincial power. This has led to a proliferation of members of political families in Provincial Council politics and some piquant instances where wives of parliamentarians won provincial office but stepped down in order to make way for their husbands.[9]

Contrasted to these categories of women politicians are those women who access politics in their own right. Many of these women have a background in community work, enjoy a good rapport with the people in the area, and have demonstrated a capacity for strong leadership. But they find it difficult to ascend the political ladder because they lack party connections and work under family and financial constraints, heightened by the immense resources needed to campaign in a PR system. If class background and wealth are factors in women who come from political families, these considerations weigh to an even greater extent in the case of women who come from non-political backgrounds. For these women, entering politics is difficult: they face resistance from their family, abuse from rivals, and discouragement from party bosses who fear losing seats if they select them.

The prevalent method of electioneering under PR has aggravated the problems. Politicians justify the selection of 'privileged women' by their nominations committees on the basis that the switchover from FPTP to PR means an inevitable shift in the process of campaigning in an entire district, entailing vast resources. 'We can invest party support only in the member of that area most likely to win the coming elections,' they argue. 'Therefore, the choice necessarily has to be from an economically privileged family, far better a member whose family has traditionally been in politics.'[10] This has resulted in the earlier-mentioned transfer of the 'most broadly acceptable candidate' syndrome from the FPTP system to the PR system.

Neither has the national list mechanism in PR, which allows parties to nominate members on the basis of their proportion of national vote, been used to benefit women politicians. The Eleventh and most recently elected Parliament serves as an example. The MPs selected in the national lists of the two main parties, the PA and the UNP (numbering thirteen and twelve respectively), did not include a single woman. This was despite the PA list containing at the outset the names of three women, who were later dropped from the actual appointments. Again, the jockeying for seats on the PA national list was a direct result of the party being compelled to abide by requests from its coalition partners to accommodate their own appointees on the list. The JVP, however, in a noteworthy departure from the norm, nominated one woman candidate (who also represented a minority community) out of the two national list candidates allotted to them in proportion to the votes that they received.

Perceptions of women on political participation

Voter participation by women has been extremely high in Sri Lanka's elections, yet women have been diffident to cross the political divide and become actively engaged in politics. The political process is consequently left to be accessed only by middle- and upper-class women coming from particular political backgrounds which enable them to make the quantum leap from the private sphere to the public-political sphere effortlessly and indeed almost as a matter of right. This is despite the presence of an almost national agreement that it was beneficial for women to be in politics in principle and for seats to be reserved for them at the local government level.

These conclusions were borne out by a recently concluded study by the International Centre for Ethnic Studies (ICES) on Gender and Governance.[11] The survey respondents in the ICES study possessed an appreciably high degree of literacy, had considerable financial independence and claimed a high degree of personal mobility in their lives. A significant majority of the women respondents asserted a strong participation in decision making within the family in matters such as marriage of children, own marriage, buying and selling property, education of children, resolution of family disputes and even investments.

Despite this, the study showed the manner in which they effectively deny their own capacity for intervention in the public sphere. Entrenched cultural and social norms restrictively legitimise the public functioning of these women in an ironic betrayal of the high rates of literacy and political awareness possessed by them. This behaviour is strengthened by the prevalence of strong family-based voting patterns in the rural areas of Sri Lanka as opposed to voting according to individual preferences (see Table 6.4). Families have tended to vote for particular parties, and only then would individual qualities matter, such as honesty, integrity and leadership.

Crucially, 72.4 per cent of the female respondents stated that even if they had the opportunity to contest an election, they would not do so, and it is interesting that an almost equal number (72.2 per cent) of the male respondents asserted the same. Women respondents cited their not liking politics as the main reason followed (a close second) by the fear that it might interfere with their family responsibilities (Table 6.5). A fair number, however, saw their own lack of ability and 'non-worthiness'

Table 6.4. Reasons for voting decisions

Decision to vote based on:	Female		Male	
	No.	%	No.	%
The way the men in the family vote	35	9.0	–	–
Family has always voted for this person	12	3.1	–	–
Family has always voted for a given family	31	8.0	4	8.7
Family belongs to a party	129	33.1	10	21.7
You support the individual/family/party	59	15.2	10	21.7
Policies of the party	79	20.2	18	39.2
Other	42	10.7	4	8.7
Did not respond	3	0.7	–	–

Table 6.5. Reasons for not contesting an election
given the opportunity to do so

Reasons	Female		Male	
	No.	%	No.	%
No time	12	3.5	–	–
Husband/family would not like	13	3.8	–	–
Financial constraints	9	2.7	1	2.6
Do not like to come forward	3	0.9	1	2.6
Lack of education	33	9.6	5	12.8
Don't like politics	71	20.8	8	20.5
Wish to lead an ordinary life	16	4.7	5	12.8
May neglect housework	65	19.2	–	–
No ability	58	17.1	4	10.2
Can make enemies	8	2.3	1	2.6
Don't like the current political culture	13	3.8	7	17.9
Frightened	7	2.1	1	2.6
Too old/disabled	8	2.3	1	2.6
Violence	10	2.9	2	5.1
Religion/culture	7	2.1	2	5.1
Other	3	0.8	–	–
Did not respond	5	1.4	1	2.6
TOTAL	341	100.0	39	100.0

as a reason, indicating that despite formal education, social habits of negatively positioning women continued to operate as powerful inhibitions. This 'non-worthiness' is again reflected in the apparent inability of the women respondents to powerfully assert their ability to change the present political culture, a possibility that ironically the men interviewed seemed to be more aware of.

The impact of violence

Sri Lanka has a long record of violent conflict. An increasingly brutal culture of social and political violence resulting from a continuing war in the North and East and two youth insurrections has transfixed Sri Lanka's human development during the past three decades. As summed up by one political commentator, the present reality continues to be that 'formal institutions of state power exist side by side with recently emerged "unformalised" agencies of state violence through which questions of legality, constitutionality and accountability of a variety of state practices can be circumvented' (Uyangoda 1996: 119). With these 'unformalised' agencies of violence linked to the rulers and hence to the state, the legitimate agencies of state power have been made increasingly impotent.

This spiralling violence has affected Sri Lankan women in a very particular sense. The crises that the country has undergone in the South in the 1980s, and which it has continued to experience in the North and East for the last two decades, have resulted in deep disillusionment and mistrust of the formal political processes. They have also resulted in the emergence of significant numbers of armed women militants in both the North-East and the South, though this has not extended to their inclusion in the decision-making levels of the militant organisations. In the 1980s, women formed a significant part of the youth insurrection in the South, while Tamil women continue to be successfully mobilised by the LTTE in its fight for a separate state in the North and East, carrying out their roles as suicide cadres with deadly effectiveness.

Ordinary women in the North-East meanwhile continue to be severely affected by the ongoing war. Shortages in basic food items and other essentials, lack of proper health and education facilities, severe restrictions on mobility because of the tense security situation and army checkpoints are facts of life for these women. The research visit by the ICES Gender and Governance team to the East exposed very precisely the hostility with which the people regarded the government in particular and politicians in general. Almost 90 per cent of the respondents from the North and East interviewed reacted either hesitantly or angrily to the questionnaire, refusing to answer questions. Women's participation in these districts is largely limited to informal activities, in order to address day-to-day survival issues such as income generation, trauma counselling and humanitarian assistance.

There is no space for any sort of formal political activity in these areas, and the fear of LTTE reprisals is an overwhelming obstacle. A case in point is the local government elections in the Jaffna peninsula in 1998, held after one and a half decades of non-voting. The militarisation of the peninsula – with the army in occupation, an explicit LTTE threat against all those contesting or supporting the election, and the presence of ex-militants, now allied to the government but fielding arms – devalued the election results significantly. On 11 March the first woman mayor in the history of the country, Sarojini Yogeswaran, was sworn in as mayoress of Jaffna. Four days later she was assassinated, undergoing the same fate as her husband, one-time MP for Jaffna, who had been assassinated by the LTTE some years earlier. The subsequent months saw a worsening of the climate of violence, with the LTTE demanding the resignation of all the local authority members, and assassinating the organiser of a sympathy *hartal* (strike) protesting against Ms Yogeswaran's murder. Thus were the local government elections entirely negated in the North.

The almost total capture of the public space by violence has had an inevitable spillover into electoral processes in other areas of the country as well. Direct electoral violence specifically targeting women to deter them from campaigning, officiating as polling agents, or simply using their votes, has been on the increase since the elections held in the North Western Province in 1999. Women candidates and voters were stripped in some instances, and threatened with rape or with acid being thrown at them. In one case, a 50-year-old grandmother was beaten with iron bars and rifle butts and asked to remove her clothes (*Sunday Times*, 7 February 1999 and 3 March 1999). Those actively taking part in the election campaign were not the only victims. In one incident at Wariyapola, attempts were made to sexually harass the wife and child of a journalist working for a newspaper strongly critical of the government. These incidents of gender-specific violence, extensively reported in the newspapers and in the reports of elections monitors, were seen by election monitors as tapping into ideological weaknesses in the social fabric of the country concerning racism and sexism (CMEV 1999).

Gendered violence was repeated, though not as severely, in the five Provincial Council elections in April 1999 and in the October 2000 general elections. In these elections, what was peculiarly manifest was in-party fighting for preferences, where a number of women party supporters were attacked, while some were stripped and one, at least, had her hair completely shaved.

Electoral violence has made politics even more of a male domain in Sri Lanka than ever before. A woman politician and ex-Provincial Council member who came from an established political family put it thus: '[The UNP] wants women to come [into politics] but women are not coming. For instance, if I knew Wayamba [election] was going to be like this, you can rest assured that I would never have contested. It was the worst nightmare of my life.'[12] In the 2000 general elections, activists isolated violence as the main reason why women remained reluctant to contest the elections (*Sunday Times*, 1 October 2000).

On the other hand, the deepening violence also awoke a certain sense of defiance in some women. These women saw violence as a necessary form of defence. They were no strangers to violence; in most instances they had themselves come to position through the direct intervention of violence, where public outrage had been manipulated in their favour on the death of male relatives. The continuing presence of violence – manifested not only by direct physical violence but also by character assassination, insults, slander, obscene language, etcetera – thus became an indispensable part of their political existence. While deploring the pervasiveness of violence in the present political structures, they did not shy away from engaging in that same violence where such an engagement was essential to their political survival. The necessity of retaining power whatever the cost governed their actions and they appeared to exercise very little individual agency in the manner of their interactions (ICES 1999). In an extension of this logic, women were, in some instances, definitely perpetrators of violence. In the Wayamba Provincial Council election, for example, certain women candidates engaged in election violence to the same extent as their politician husbands.

Strategies for change

Sri Lanka has networks of community-based and voluntary organisations with goals of pursuing community improvement and dialogue across religious and political differences. In general, however, community movements in Sri Lanka profess a desire to disassociate themselves from the prevalent political processes, which they see as 'warped beyond recognition'. Instead, they focus on training women for personal and community leadership positions and on enabling women to become financially independent. Asked whether they found political contacts necessary at a certain point, their response was negative. They pointed out that by mobilising women to assume positions of financial and social importance in the community, visible pressure groups were formed which had to be taken into account by all the politicians of that area.[13]

Economic empowerment groups working in other parts of the country express similar views. Membership of these organisations extends to more than 27,000 in the case of the Women's Development Federation. These women, community leaders in their own right, eschew any direct participation in the formal political processes but apply simple community pressure to achieve limited objectives. Interestingly, findings in the Gender and Governance study buttressed this belief that community mobilisation could be an alternative to direct political intervention.

Unlike in Northern Ireland, however, these activist groups have not provided a means whereby women's needs and interests could be articulated at the national level. Women have not been able to make their way to the peace talks table. Coalitions such as the Women's Action Committee (1983–7), Women for Peace (1984), Mothers and Daughters of Lanka (1990) and the most recently formed Women's Coalition for Peace have all attempted to lobby for peace. But the intervention of women in the peace process and in the constitutional and electoral reform process has been intermittent and lacking in force. Engendering the formal political process has seemingly been given up as a lost cause.

Reactivating this dialogue is currently a primary concern: its goal would be to emulate the achievement of the Northern Ireland Women's Coalition, the fusion of the injustice of women's exclusion from political structures with a broader package of ideas about dialogue and conciliation, equity and justice (Roulston 1998). Discussions on how this could be achieved have recently focused on the question of reservations for women in the political process. The debates have centred on the question of whether reservations for women should be limited to nomination lists, or whether women should press for a specific quota of reserved seats, the latter within a changed electoral system rather than the prevailing PR system. Previous electoral reform with reference to youth representation has been utilised as a precedent for lobbying: consequent to the Youth Commission recommendations following the youth revolts of the 1980s, a 40 per cent youth quota was imposed on political parties in choosing candidates. There had been similar lobbying for reservations for women, but this had not been successful until constitutional reform proposals were formulated by the People's Alliance government on its first coming to power in 1994. Paragraph 42 of the regional list provisions in the 1997 constitutional reforms proposals provided that election laws should ensure that not less than 25 per cent of the members elected to local authorities are women.

In principle, the implementation of a quota for women has drawn favourable reactions nation-wide, as reflected in the findings of the ICES survey. In August 2001, however, the recommendation that reservations for women should be included at local government level was dropped from the most recent constitutional reform proposals. Ironically, this was owing to the opposition of smaller parties, on the basis that they would be unable to find women to fill the required numbers of positions.

Yet the debate on reservations has thrown up several questions. Implementation at local government level would clearly be ineffective without drastic changes in the mandates of local government bodies. Functions entrusted to the local authorities relate mainly to roads and thoroughfares, public health, abetting of nuisance and public utility services. They are also given a general power to do all things necessary for the effective exercise of their powers and duties. In practical terms, the scarcity of financial resources operates as an important limiting factor. There is no specific mandate on women's issues and no allocation of funds for women, unlike at Provincial Council and parliamentary level. This means that even where women at local government level are aware of problems concerning women, they have little opportunity under the current system of devolution of power to address them effectively.

The debate has also raised the question of whether providing for quotas *per se* would ease the prevalent problem of adequate women's representation, or aggravate the prevailing power politics by enabling male politicians to 'pack' the quotas with their own women candidates. As an alternative, women activists have urged that reservations should extend from local government level to national level and that seats should be reserved at least at parliamentary and provincial level through the use of a national list exclusively for women. Currently, a 50-member national list would guarantee approximately 22 per cent of the places in the 225-member Parliament to women; these could be allocated in proportion to the total vote received nationally by the political parties.

Meanwhile, it has been urged that a multi-pronged strategy be adopted to ensure that party committees have gender-conscious representation by making women's policy visible at party meetings and on the public platforms. Organising a monthly question time to put the women's agenda on to the floor of the House, appointing a women's committee within the party to enable selections and nominations, and devising strong and active measures to counter violence against women and men in politics are some of the other suggested strategies.[14]

Conclusion

This chapter has argued that the form of PR introduced in Sri Lanka in 1989 has had a hugely negative impact on the entry of women into a political process seen as wholly violent and corrupt. Despite high levels of literacy, individual mobility and financial independence, Sri Lankan women continue to face deep mistrust regarding their own 'worthiness' to enter the public space. As a result, their capacity to influence decision making is minimal, even on issues concerning their own bodies or their own security, while development efforts have continued to be insensitive to the differences of power and privilege between Sri Lankan men and women.

Fundamentally, Sri Lanka needs to acknowledge that social and political transformation by formal democratic institutions and structures operating under the patronage of a misleadingly benevolent state has hitherto resulted only in a dangerous complacency and no real empowerment of its women citizens. We need to recognise that a more representative legislature should be brought about by specific mechanisms and that attention should be focused not only on fairer minority representation but on committed gender representation as well. In so far as this question remains neglected, the danger is not only that the prevalent gender-lopsided *status quo* will continue, but that it will increase in its ferocity with a progressively negative impact on human development.

Given these specific realities, we need to push for political restructuring that is necessarily linked to social and attitudinal transformation. Without this, a re-evaluation of PR or other wholly formal changes in the country's political system will obviously accomplish very little.

References

Centre for Monitoring Election Violence (CMEV) (1999) *Final Report on Election Related Violence in the North Western Provincial Council Election*, Colombo.

Department of Census and Statistics (1995) *Women and Men in Sri Lanka Report*, Colombo.

Goetz, A. M. and S. Hassim (2003) *No Shortcuts to Power: African Women in Politics and Policy Making*, London: Zed Books.

Government of Ceylon (1978) Results of Parliamentary General Elections in Ceylon (1947–70), in *Report on the General Election to the Second National Assembly*, Colombo: Department of Government Printing.

Hassim, S. (1999) 'The Dual Politics of Representation: Women and Electoral Politics in South Africa', *Politikon*, 26, 2: 210–12.

International Centre for Ethnic Studies (ICES) (1997) *Comparative Electoral Systems in South Asia*, Colombo.

International Centre for Ethnic Studies (ICES) (1999) 'Gender and Governance', unpublished paper, Colombo.

Kamalawathie, I. M. (1990) 'Women in Parliamentary Politics in Sri Lanka', in S. Kiribamune and V. Samarasinghe (eds.), *Women at the Cross-Roads*, Kandy: International Centre for Ethnic Studies.

Karm, A. (ed.) (1998) *Women in Parliament: Beyond Numbers*, Stockholm: International Institute for Democracy and International Assistance (IDEA).

Leiten, Tressie (2000) 'Women in Political Participation and Decision Making', in *Post Beijing Reflections: Women in Sri Lanka 1995–2000*, Colombo: Centre for Women's Research (CENWOR).

Matland R. E.(1998) 'The Effect of Development and Culture on Women's Representation', in A. Karm (ed.), (1998) *Women in Parliament: Beyond Numbers*, Stockholm: International Institute for Democracy and International Assistance (IDEA).

Reynolds, A. (1999) *Women in African Legislatures*, Auckland Park: Electoral Institute of South Africa.

Roulston, C. (1998) 'Did Women Make a Difference? The Northern Ireland Women's Coalition in the Peace Process', *Nivedini*, 6, 1–2, Women's Education and Research Centre.

Rule, W. (1994) 'Women's Under-representation and Electoral Systems', *Political Science and Politics*, 27, 4: 689–92.

Uyangoda, Jayadeva (1996) 'Militarization, Violent State, Violent Society: Sri Lanka' in K. Rupesinghe and K. Mumtaz (eds.), *Internal Conflicts in South Asia*, London: Sage Publications.

Notes

1 This chapter is based on library and archival research with the inclusion of a limited survey component that focused on interviews with selected women both within and outside politics in order to ascertain their views on the targets of the study. It also uses extracts from a recent 18-month Sri Lanka study on Gender and Governance carried out by the International Centre for Ethnic Studies (ICES), Colombo, as part of a larger five-nation study in South Asia. The ICES study attempted to explore the multiple impact of violence on women as an impediment to women's political involvement, how Sri Lankan women define the state, women's interaction with the state, and the state's current limitations and its obligations to women citizens.

2 Pradeshiya Sabhas are the local government units at the lowest level. Statistics from the *Daily News*, Colombo, 16 March 1998.

3 Article 12 (2) prohibits discrimination on the grounds of sex among other specified grounds. Additionally, article 12 (4) declares that laws or executive action that bestows special advantages on women cannot be challenged under the equality provision.

4 Prevalent immigration guidelines discriminate against guidelines for residence visas with regard to alien men married to Sri Lankan women. While a court

ruling recently in a rights application (SC Application No. 436/99 decided on 24 May 1999) directed the immigration authorities to remedy the discriminatory guidelines, no action had been taken at the time of writing this chapter.

5 Sections 363 and 364 of the Penal Code (Amendment Act No. 22 of 1995).

6 Section 345 of the Penal Code (Amendment Act No. 22 of 1995).

7 Section 303 of the Sri Lankan Penal Code enforces the strictest legal prohibition on abortion, permitting relaxation only if it is done 'in good faith' and for the purpose of 'saving the life of the mother'. Punishments for those conducting an abortion range up to seven years' imprisonment and causing death by abortion attracts imprisonment for a maximum of 20 years and a fine according to section 305 of the Penal Code. The 1999 UNFPA Report states that 750 illegal abortions take place a day in Colombo, at considerable risk to the lives of the women.

8 Article 226(4) of the draft constitution (2000).

9 Nalini Weerawanni in the Uva Province and Jayani Dissanayake in the North Central Province, who gave way to enable their husbands to assume office as chief ministers.

10 Interview with PA Deputy Minister Sumithra Priyanganie Abyeweera and UNP MP Renuka Herath.

11 The ICES survey administered 468 questionnaires (with a 25 per cent male control sample). The questionnaires were administered to a target group of females over 18 years of age and below 60 years with a 10 per cent control sample of males of the same age group in nine provinces selected through a stratified, multi-stage purposive sampling design. Respondents from the Northern province were interviewed in the East and in Colombo owing to difficulties of travel to the North. An approximate percentage of 73.3 per cent, 13.2 per cent, 10.3 per cent and 2.8 per cent respectively of Sinhala, Tamil Muslim and Indian Tamil persons were interviewed. The overall study also included two case studies, four focus group discussions and approximately 40 in-depth interviews among activists, politicians from all levels and trade unionists.

12 Interview with Gwen Herath, ex-member, North Western Provincial Council.

13 Interviews with office bearers of the Janashakthi Banku Sangam movement.

14 Indrani Iriyagolle, President of Sinhala Kanthabivurdhi Sangvidanaya.

7

The Political Economy of Electoral Reform
Proportional Representation in Sri Lanka

SUNIL BASTIAN

This chapter focuses on the relationship between the establishment of an electoral system based on the principles of proportional representation (PR) and the political economy of Sri Lanka's capitalism. Its main argument is that one of the principal objectives of introducing PR in 1978 was to take care of some of the problems that the first-past-the-post (FPTP) system of elections was posing to further development of the economy in the direction of capitalism.

Post-independence capitalist development in Sri Lanka can be divided into three phases: the first from independence to the mid-1950s, the second from then to the mid-1970s, and the third from 1977 onwards. The massive electoral victory of the centre-right United National Party (UNP) led by J. R. Jayawardene in July 1977 marked the end of what can be called the 'closed economy' phase of capitalist development in Sri Lanka. This phase, characterised by state dominance in the economy and extreme regulation of markets, had led to an economy that was virtually stagnant. The social consequences were widely felt. On top of this were the political repercussions of a class-based insurgency in 1971. The government's response to the insurgency led to human rights violations on a wide scale. All this resulted in the defeat of the government led by the Sri Lanka Freedom Party (SLFP) in the July 1977 general elections that brought the UNP to power.

With the arrival of the UNP government in 1977 Sri Lankan capitalism began its liberalised phase, which emphasised market forces, private capital and openness to the world market. The role of the state was de-emphasised. Multilateral agencies like the IMF and World Bank began to play a much greater role in the economic policies of the country, both in terms of financial assistance and policy prescriptions. In keeping with the neo-liberal ideology dominant in these agencies, a great emphasis was placed on balancing budgets and bringing about structural changes to promote a liberalised economy.

Parallel to these developments within the economy, the system of governance also went through major changes. The most important of these were the establishment of a presidential form of government under a powerful presidency, which enjoyed a considerable degree of power independent of parliament, and the introduction of proportional representation in parliamentary elections.

Most of the writers who have analysed the establishment of this system of governance correctly credit the first President of Sri Lanka, J. R. Jayawardene, as the brain behind these developments. Jayawardene had been arguing for the need for a presidential system of government and a PR system long before he had the opportunity to establish them. In an often-cited speech to the Ceylon Association for the Advancement of Science in 1966, he argued for a powerful presidency that would be able to act independently of the legislature as a necessary step towards rapid economic development. He put forward similar arguments in support of proportional representation (Jayawardene 1979: 83).

This chapter begins with a brief conceptual discussion of the relationship between capitalism and universal franchise. Then it looks at the political economy of the FPTP electoral system of Sri Lanka. This provides the background for a discussion of the politics of establishing PR and its subsequent reforms. Finally, we comment on the politics of the PR system.

Universal franchise and capitalism

Conceptually the starting point of this chapter is the idea that the establishment of capitalism is a political task. Ruling élites that spearhead this process have to carry out a number of political tasks. Establishing the institutions of a capitalist economy, while managing the social contradictions that this process gives rise to, is one of the principal political tasks that needs to be addressed.

In the case of developed capitalist countries, the political task of establishing capitalism was carried out in a context where there was no universal franchise. As the history of these countries shows, the establishment of universal franchise and the institutions of liberal democracy has largely postdated the entrenchment of capitalism (Therborn 1977). Once the institutions of liberal democracy were established, contrary to the beliefs of liberal theorists, there was an uneasy relationship between the logic of the market and the logic of liberal democracy. As succinctly summarised by Dunn (1992: 254), the relationship between constitutional representative democracy and capitalism is both intimate and deeply untransparent. The historical services which each has rendered to the other over the last two centuries have been profound. But neither, in the end, can be wholly at ease with the other, completely confident of its ultimate fidelity.

In the case of late capitalist developers, the task of building capitalism has to be carried out in a context where demands for democracy have become much more widespread. In many developing societies the beginnings of ideas and institutions of democracy go back to the colonial period when the penetration of capitalist relations in society was at a rudimentary stage. At present, although the practice and impact of institutions of democracy in society might be wanting, there is no doubt that the ruling élite cannot totally ignore the demands for democratic freedoms by the society at large. The establishment of capitalism has to be carried out in such a context.

The uneasy relationship between democracy and capitalism can prove a serious contradiction in such a context. Rising capitalism tries to tame demands arising out of democratisation

by setting boundaries on the evolution of such political institutions as labour unions, parties, parliaments, bureaucracies, judiciaries and constitutions. Political institutions thus come to act as filtering mechanisms between state and society, filtering in some mass social demands as legitimate objects of political negotiations, and filtering out other demands as beyond the legitimate scope of the polity, especially those that may hurt capitalism. (Kohli 1993: 671)

Yet these attempts at setting boundaries will be resisted by various sections of society. How these contradictory processes are worked out depends very much on the social relations prevalent in specific societies. These contradictions need not necessarily be in all societies a zero sum game. There are societies that can sort out these contradictions without disintegration into conflicts. But there are no predetermined paths through which these contradictions are resolved. Therefore, rather than posing extremely general questions about the relationship between capitalism and democracy, one needs to ask more specific questions in each national context, keeping in mind the uneasy relationship between the two and specific historical conditions.

In this uneasy relationship between developing capitalism and demands for democracy, electoral systems are critical institutions, performing a number of functions.

They regulate the transformation of voting preferences into democratically legitimised political power; create political agency by shaping the structure of the party systems; make an important contribution to the management of political, social, economic and ethnic divisions; structure the alternatives with which voters are confronted during elections and lastly contribute to the degree of fragmentation of parliaments and thus influence the creation and durability of governments. (Elster *et al.* 1998: 111)

Thus electoral systems not only determine the 'rules of the game' through which popular will is expressed, but also have an influence on the nature of the political society and the stability of the government.

My central point in this chapter is that in the choice of electoral institutions by the ruling élite the political task of developing capitalism is a key concern. Through the 'rules of the game' determined by electoral institutions, the élite has the objective of managing both the electorate and the social forces reflected in the legislature. In order for the electoral system to be an effective partner in capitalist development, this management has to be done without undermining the establishment of capitalist relations in the economy and the mechanisms of capitalist accumulation. What we hope to do in this chapter is to explore how this has happened in the case of the establishment of the PR electoral system in Sri Lanka.

The FPTP system of elections

Sri Lanka became an independent nation in 1948 with a first-past-the-post system of elections. The preference for the FPTP system was decided when Sri Lanka was granted a universal franchise in 1931, seventeen years before independence. The issue that dominated the discussions during the establishment of the electoral system was whether Sri Lanka should have 'communal' or 'territorial' electorates. Those favouring communal electorates argued for separate electoral registers for different ethnic groups. The élites of politically prominent minorities, especially from the Sri Lankan Tamil community, championed this position. The counter-position was held by the Sinhalese élite, who argued for 'territorial' electorates. This was the demand to divide the country into spatial constituencies and for elections to be held on this basis. This debate was resolved in favour of territorial electorates by the Donoughmore Commission that was responsible for granting universal franchise. In keeping with a vision of a nation state devoid of communal identities, the Commissioners believed that communal representation would prevent the development of a 'true national identity'.[1]

199

During the establishment of the electoral system, the method of selecting the winning candidate was never a part of the Sri Lankan debate. The debates about the flaws of the plural system that are common today did not figure at all when Sri Lanka adopted FPTP. There is no doubt that political leaders right across the political spectrum were ready to accept what prevailed in Britain, the colonial power, without a murmur.

Once the FPTP system was adopted as the method of choosing the winner, the next issue was demarcation of the electorates.[2] Two criteria were adopted for this process: an area-based criterion and another based on population. The area-based criterion allocated one member per 1,000 square miles: 25 members were allocated between provinces on this basis by all delimitation commissions. The rest of the seats were distributed on the basis of population criteria. In 1946 this was stipulated as one member per 75,000 inhabitants. In 1976 this was changed to 90,000. When the population criteria were first established it was assumed that there would be a delimitation process after every census. This would allow the delimitation to take population changes into account. But, in reality, the censuses of 1953, 1963 and 1971 were not followed by a delimitation process. Hence delimitation under FPTP fell out of step with demographic changes.

Political changes were much more important in establishing delimitation commissions. The 1959 delimitation, the first after independence, followed the 1956 elections, when the UNP, the party that inherited power from the colonial masters, was defeated by a coalition of parties led by the Sri Lanka Freedom Party (SLFP). This delimitation was made on the basis of population estimates provided by the Department of Census and Statistics. The 1976 delimitation followed the enactment of the first republican constitution, and its basis was the 1971 census.

The parameters of the two criteria for demarcating electorates were established by constitutional provisions and election laws. The delimitation commissions were given the task of finalising the details: they also had discretion to create multi-member constituencies, where more than one member was elected. Extending the concerns that dominated the pre-independence period, this provision was aimed at those electorates where there was a concentration of politically prominent minority identity groups that were still unable to be represented because of their overall minority position. In multi-member constituencies each voter had two votes, and through this it was hoped that these minorities would be able to count on being represented by at least one member from their community. Until the 1976 delimitation, the legislature also had six appointed members. Here again the objective was to provide opportunities for the representation of politically prominent minority ethnic groups not represented through the regular electoral process.

The fundamental parameters of the electoral system – spatial units as the unit of representation and FPTP as the method of electing representatives – were never questioned during the period when the system prevailed. It was not that there were no reforms to this system, but that the agenda of reform did not question the fundamentals. Even among the radical sections of Sri Lankan society there was never any serious debate at this level. Internalisation of the elements of the system within society at large, and the ability to change governments under the FPTP system ensured its acceptance.

Political economy of the FPTP system

After independence Sri Lanka held eight elections under the FPTP system – in 1947, 1952, 1956, March 1960, July 1960, 1965, 1970 and 1977. Alternate UNP- and SLFP-led coalitions were returned to power in these elections. The electorate voted the governing party out of power five times, and in these terms it was a properly functioning democracy. A closer look at the FPTP system as it operated in the specific social and historical context of Sri Lanka, however, demonstrates certain characteristic features which were not conducive to furthering capitalist relations. In our view it is important to understand these characteristics in order to unravel the link between the electoral system and the political task of establishing capitalism. Proportional representation was meant to rectify some of these outcomes of the FPTP system, and it is not surprising that it was introduced along with the liberalisation of the economy. PR was a product of this particular historical context. The rest of this section will examine the characteristic features of FPTP that provided the background for the introduction of the PR system.

Spatial inequalities in representation

The FPTP electoral system of Sri Lanka showed a high degree of variation in the number of registered voters per elected Member of Parliament. If one takes the 1970 and 1977 elections, for example, the last to be held under FPTP, voters per MP ranged from 16,461 to 70,236 in 1970, and 19,925 to 64,190 in 1977. As a result, sparsely populated, less urbanised rural areas gained an undue advantage from the electoral system.

In order to make sense of these socio-economic disparities, we shall make use of a spatial differentiation of Sri Lanka put forward by Moore

201

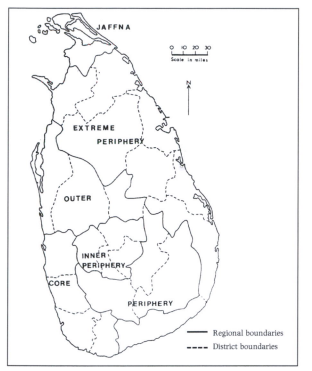

Regional and district boundaries of Sri Lanka

From M.P. Moore (1985)
The State and Peasant Politics in Sri Lanka,
Cambridge: Cambridge University Press

(1985: 126). In this, Sri Lanka is divided into four regions – core, inner periphery, outer periphery and extreme periphery (see map). The transition from core to extreme periphery is based on spatial, institutional and occupational factors. Spatially, the core can be seen as the centre of activities in the country. Institutionally there is a clustering of the more important political, administrative and commercial institutions close to the metropolis. The core areas have a higher population density as well as a dense network of communication channels with the metropolis. Occupationally the rural areas of the core are less dependent on farming than those on the periphery, and practise a very different kind of agriculture. Historically, these are the areas where capital accumulation from economic activities during and after the colonial period was concentrated. The social structures and institutions of these areas have been much more influenced by the penetration of capitalist relations. The areas known as Maritime Provinces during the colonial period, and the central part of the country, which is also the centre of the plantation economy, constitute the core and the inner periphery. As we move to the extreme periphery we have areas further away from political,

202

administrative and commercial institutions, less densely populated, and where the principal occupation of the population is traditional agriculture. Social structures in these areas have been less influenced by capitalist development.

If we compare this regional differentiation of Sri Lanka with spatial disparities in electoral representation there is a considerable overlap between core and inner periphery with the provinces that were disadvantaged by the electoral system. Most districts of the Western, Southern, and Sabaragamuwa provinces both had a high proportion of voters to MPs and fell into the core and inner periphery.[3] In other words, these core areas of capitalism were electorally disadvantaged. In contrast, areas particularly favoured by the electoral system – including parts of the Central Province, North Central Province, Uva Province, Northern Province and Eastern Province – belonged to the outer and extreme peripheries.

These spatial disparities in the electoral system were a direct outcome of the two major considerations that dominated the design of the electoral system in the pre- and post-independence periods. The first one, mentioned earlier, was linked to the issue of minority representation. This is why areas such as the Northern and Eastern provinces, where minorities dominate, figured as areas that had an electoral advantage.[4] The other factor, which came into prominence in the post-independence period, was the overt rural bias that dominated politics. Privileging rural areas was an unquestioned orthodoxy in the politics and development discourses of Sri Lanka. Rural is equated with what is 'authentically' Sri Lankan. Hence 'genuine' development can come only from rural areas and they have to be privileged. These ideas are also part and parcel of Sinhala nationalism and hark back to a romantic past.

These ideas have been upheld by the political leadership, cutting across political ideologies. A significant proportion of this political leadership came from élite families who had made money through ownership of land, either in rural areas or in the plantation sector. They came from upper castes that had privileged positions in pre-modern social relations. The British did their best to protect this élite and nurture them. The electoral base of this leadership was also built up through patron–client networks established within pre-modern feudal relations in rural areas. Based on the argument that rural areas were less developed and needed a greater voice in the legislature, electoral advantages were given to peripheral rural districts, which discriminated against the urbanised 'core areas' of capitalism.

203

Table 7.1 Distribution of the total electorate,
1970 and 1977 general elections

Year	UNP	SLFP + LSSP + CP	Total	Minority parties	Other parties	Indepen- dent	Spoilt	Not voting	Total
1970	31.6	42.2	73.8	6.2	1.2	3.7	0.4	14.8	100
1977	44.4	31.6	75.9	6.1	0.4	3.9	0.4	13.3	100

Political outcomes of the FPTP system

Sri Lankan voters participated enthusiastically within this electoral system characterised by spatial disparities in representation. As pointed out by Amita Shastri, the average voter turn-out of 77 per cent during the FPTP period was extremely high when compared internationally.

It places Sri Lanka tenth, between United Kingdom and Canada, in a ranking ordering of countries world-wide which have had democratic elections continuously since 1945/1950, have population of over 3 million persons and voluntary voting. The Sri Lankan case is noteworthy in that turn-out increased from 55.1 per cent in 1947 to 86.2 per cent in 1977, an astounding increase of 31.1 per cent! This figure puts it far beyond all other increases in turn-out – the highest [other] increase being that in Sweden of 10.6 per cent. (Shastri 1994: 330)

During this period power alternated between two major political formations – the UNP- and SLFP-led coalitions, in which some of the Left-oriented parties participated. As shown by Table 7.1, by the end of the FPTP period, the distribution of the electorate among the major political formations had established an identifiable pattern. The two coalitions led by the UNP and SLFP accounted for an average 74.9 per cent of the electorate, including the bulk of the Sinhala vote. Minority parties accounted for 6.2 per cent and independents 3.8 per cent of the electorate.

Despite an even distribution of the electorate between the two major political formations, the winner-takes-all characteristic of the FPTP system produced governments with huge 'manufactured majorities' for the ruling parties. In 1970 the ruling SLFP–Left coalition, with only 42.2 per cent of the total vote, enjoyed 76.8 per cent of the seats in Parliament. In 1977 the picture was reversed, with the UNP benefiting

Table 7.2 Distribution of seats in the parliament,
1970 and 1977 general elections

Year	UNP	SLFP + LSSP + CP	TC	FP/TULF	Other parties	Indepen- dent	Total
1970	17	116	3	13	–	2	151
1977	140	8	–	18	1	1	168

even more from the system, having only 44.4 per cent of the total vote, but 83.3 per cent of seats (Table 7.2).

Autonomy of the MP and instability of governments

Despite the huge majorities that governments obtained under the FPTP system, it had an element of instability because of the degree of freedom from party control that this system allowed individual members. In the early period of the FPTP system, before political parties became prominent, it was the influence of individuals in their home areas that was key in getting elected. Areas were also small enough for them to secure a political base on the basis of their individual influence. At the beginning many were elected as independents. Later, as political parties became more influential in the electoral process, they still had to take into account the influence of individual MPs in local areas. The freedom that MPs enjoyed from party control contributed to the instability of governments, since it allowed MPs to cross over to the opposition but still retain their parliamentary membership.

In every post-independence government of the FPTP period except one, there were cross-overs from government to opposition, either of individual MPs crossing over to the opposition or of coalition partners moving out of the government (Wilson 1980: 3). In 1964, such a cross-over led to the defeat of the government by one vote during what at that time was called the Throne Speech. The defeat meant that the government elected in 1960 could not complete its full term. Governments in power were thus weakened despite the apparent stability that the FPTP system provided through manufactured majorities.

Social base of Parliament, intermediate classes and state capitalist policies

An unavoidable outcome of universal franchise and the internalisation of the electoral process in Sri Lankan society was the broadening of the social base of the legislature. The politics of the pre-independence period was dominated by classes benefiting from the sources of accumulation provided by the colonial economy; the same classes were heavily represented in the first post-independence Parliament. For the most part, it was the colonial bourgeoisie that inherited political power at independence, and there was a correspondence between economic power and political power (Jayawardena 2000). The major departure from this pattern was provided by those who came into Parliament with the support of the plantation working class and the Left movement

The legislature's narrow class base could not be maintained for long under a political system based on universal franchise and a party system that had to recruit membership and candidates for elections from all over the country. The electoral system provided opportunities for new élites from outside the colonial élite to accede to positions of political power, many of them from rural areas. The predominance of the rural population in the country, the electorate bias towards rural areas, and the particular characteristics of the Sri Lankan rural social structure, in which rural areas were not on the whole dominated by the feudalism of a few landowning families, all made this possible.

Thus in class terms the most important change in the social composition of the legislature during the FPTP period was the entry of 'rural intermediate classes' to the legislature. These included middle-level landowners, sections of the trading classes, minor government employees and vernacular intelligentsia.[5] These intermediate classes became a strong force in the legislature, and their interests became a dominant factor in economic policy making. As in other societies of developing capitalism there was a strong link between the increased influence of intermediate classes within the state and the emergence of state-dominated development policies (Shastri 1983).[6] State capitalist policies provided new routes of social mobility for intermediate classes, as well as new avenues for capital accumulation.

Exploiting the disproportionate share of power given it by the electoral system, the 1970–7 government pushed the ideology of state capitalism to an extreme. The role of the state expanded significantly due to state takeovers of privately owned economic activities and the expansion of the state sector in various spheres. State-subsidised prices and price controls increased. The state rather than markets determined resource allocation. The economy was increasingly cut off from the international capitalist system due to controls and quotas.

If we are to sum up the political economy of Sri Lanka's FPTP electoral system, it was a system biased against the core areas of capitalist development. Due to the inequality in spatial representation and the winner-takes-all features of FPTP, governments could be changed through the voting patterns in sparsely populated rural areas. FPTP also produced both 'manufactured majorities' and a significant measure of governmental instability due to the weakness of party discipline and the ease with which MPs could cross over to the opposition.

The entrenchment of electoral politics brought about a change in the class composition of the legislature, including the rise to political prominence of the rural intermediate classes. By the late 1970s the influence of these class forces had pushed state capitalist policies to their extreme. The power of the intermediate classes in the legislature had to be curbed if Sri Lanka was to move in the direction of capitalist development.

President Jayawardene, the architect of the 1978 constitution, recognised the need to curtail or manage the power of the legislature long before any other politician. His answer was a presidential system independent of the legislature and a PR electoral system. As early as 1966 he articulated this explicitly in a keynote speech to the twenty-second annual session of the Ceylon Association for the Advancement of Science. He argued for a presidential system in which the

> executive is chosen directly by the people and is not dependent on the Legislature during the period of its existence, for a specified number of years. Such an executive is a strong executive, seated in power for a fixed number of years, not subjected to the whims and fancies of an elected legislature; not afraid to take correct but unpopular decisions because of censure from the parliamentary party. (De Silva and Wriggins 1994: 337)

In the same speech he proposed a PR system 'where the voter votes for a party and not for a particular candidate' (ibid.: 378; Wilson 1980: 2). According to him, a FPTP system that gave considerable freedom to individual MPs, including the freedom to cross over, was a recipe for political instability. He was influenced in this view by two government crises in March and June 1960, when governments were brought down before the end of their terms by cross-overs to the opposition.

What is interesting to note is that during the time that Jayawardene advocated these changes in the political system, he also put forward economic proposals remarkably close to what today is called structural adjustment. With the help of an Indian economist he put to the Cabinet of the then UNP government proposals including a balanced budget; a floating rupee (i.e. a depreciation of the rupee); liberalisation of imports and abolition of exchange controls; and removal of all forms of government restrictions imposed on prices, production and distribution.... [H]e recommended a substantial reduction, if not elimination of, consumer subsidies, and a programme of privatisation of government-owned enterprises as measures that would help balance the budget. (De Silva and Wriggins 1994: 169)

However, 'when J.R. recommended them to the Cabinet, he got no support' (ibid.: 169). He had to wait eleven years before he could implement both his economic and his political packages – when the UNP won the July 1977 election with a landslide victory.

Both a relatively autonomous presidential system and a legislature elected on the basis of PR endowed the government with new institutions which potentially could manage the legislature and the social forces represented in it better. It can be argued that one of the major reasons for these new institutions was economic, namely the requirements of the new phase of capitalism. Jayawardene articulated this reasoning in general development terms and proceeded to establish the new institutions once he came to power in 1977. In the following section we shall see how the new rules of the game for the electoral system were expected to overcome the problems posed by the FPTP system that we have analysed above.

Proportional representation in the 1978 constitution

The constitution passed by the National State Assembly[7] on 16 August 1978 instituted a system of elections based on the principles of proportional representation for Sri Lanka. The politics of designing this new constitution was tightly controlled by the UNP and its leader. Making use of the large majority that he commanded in Parliament, Jayawardene moved swiftly to enact the political structure that the UNP had planned. The election was won in July 1977. On 22 September 1977 the government pushed through an amendment 'which radically altered the constitutional structure of the First Republic' (Wilson 1980: 29). It established a directly elected President as the head of the state. Although it brought about a fundamental change in the existing constitution, the Bill was not even discussed by the government parliamentary group. 'It was only taken up at Cabinet level, duly approved, and in addition certified by the Cabinet as a bill that was "urgent in national interest"'(ibid.: 30) and sent to the

Constitutional Court for approval. Under the provisions of the 1972 constitution, the Constitutional Court had to give its verdict within 24 hours for Bills that were 'urgent in national interest'. It duly certified the Bill, which was then adopted by Parliament and certified by the Speaker on 20 October 1977' (ibid.: 30). This was how the presidency, the most important element of the constitution under which Sri Lankans live today, was brought into force.

Although Jayawardene was in a hurry to establish the presidency he was not in a hurry to take up the post. The presidency was established in October 1977, but its implementation was postponed for a three-and-a-half-month period, until 4 February 1978. This allowed Jayawardene to remain in Parliament and be in charge of the next stage of constitutional reform through a select committee established in the Parliament.

This select committee appointed in October 1977 was primarily a UNP affair. The leading Tamil party, the TULF, did not participate because it did not address the issues on the basis of which they fought the elections. The leading party of the previous government, the SLFP, participated at the beginning, but its representatives withdrew later when they realised that they were involved in a process of replacing their own 1972 constitution and not in a process of reforming it. Since it was a select committee of parties in Parliament, none of the traditional Left parties had any influence over it. CWC, the UNP ally that had a Cabinet post, was the only party other than the UNP that participated in the process.

The UNP had no serious plans to generate a public debate on the impending changes, either.

> The Select Committee held 16 meetings in all and based its findings on a questionnaire that had been issued to the general public and the evidence, oral and written, it obtained from various political, economic, social and religious organisations.... Only 281 responses to the questionnaire were received and sixteen organisations and a Buddhist priest presented evidence before the Committee. (Wilson 1980: 32)

The establishment of PR was proposed in the recommendations of this select committee, with a minimum of public consultation.

These recommendations described the principal elements of the system, including the following:

1 A delimitation commission appointed by the President would divide the country into between 20 and 24 electoral districts, their

209

boundaries so far as possible coinciding with the boundaries of administrative districts.

2   This was to be a once-and-for-all delimitation. The boundaries of these electoral districts could not be changed without a constitutional amendment.

3   These were to be multi-member constituencies, with larger electorates than the previous.

4   The new constitution stipulated that the total number of Members of Parliament would be 196, 36 of them distributed on the basis of four per province. The other 160 were to be apportioned before every general election. In order to do so the total number of registered voters was to be divided by 160 in order to arrive at the 'qualifying number'. Then the number of registered voters in each electoral district would be divided by this qualifying number, giving the number of members to be elected from that district. If the total number of seats thus allocated were to be less than 160, the districts with largest residues would be given the remaining seats. The Elections Commissioner was entrusted with this task.

5   Elections were to be on the basis of lists. Each party or independent group would have to present a list of candidates for the electoral districts they wanted to contest. Each list should contain one third more names than the number of members that would be elected from the district. It would set out the candidates from each party in order of priority, decided by the party before the election, and seats would be allocated to the party on the basis of this order of priority.

6   Each voter would have one vote and vote for the list of the party that he or she chose, not having any say in the choice of individual candidates.

7   A party would have to obtain a minimum of 12.5 per cent or one eighth of the total valid votes to be eligible for seats; parties not obtaining this proportion would be eliminated.

8   Next, the party or the independent group obtaining the highest number of votes would be allotted the first seat, or a bonus seat.

9   Then, the votes polled by disqualifying parties would be deducted from valid votes to arrive at what is called the 'relevant number of votes'. The latter would be divided by the number of members to be elected minus one, to arrive at the 'resulting number'. Finally the

votes of each qualified party would be divided by the 'resulting number' to arrive at the number of members elected in each electoral district. If this allocation did not add up to the total number of seats available, then the remaining votes of each party after the allocation of seats would be taken into account, and the remaining seats would be filled according to the method of highest remainder.

10 Members were to be elected through lists as representatives of political parties or independent groups. Once elected from a particular list they would not have the freedom to change their party allegiance. Members selected at the time of the elections would have to adhere to the order. In other cases (if members were to resign or die, for example) the parties would have to choose a replacement from the list but would need to adhere to the priority.

As intended by the UNP leadership, these elements of the electoral system introduced by the 1978 constitution – in particular the principle of proportionality and the new principles of delimitation – did away with the spatial inequalities that had biased the previous system against the 'core' areas of capitalism. The new system greatly reduced regional disparities in representation, including the disadvantage that the more densely populated urbanised areas had in the previous system. Proportional representation thus removed discrimination against the 'core areas' of capitalist development.

Under PR electoral districts became larger and coincided with the districts constructed for administrative and development purposes. Their identities were regional, forcing politicians to think beyond local interests represented by the smaller electorates of the FPTP system, where traditional local-level interests like caste had a greater chance of being influential. Candidates seeking election had to think in regional terms and be familiar with development debates in the administrative districts, which were the units of planning. This increased the likelihood that policy debates on development would be at the centre of electoral politics rather than purely local interests, and was more conducive to promoting market economies.

The stabilisation of electoral boundaries was another step that undermined the influence of local-level interests. Delimitation commissions had previously provided a major opportunity for local-level interests such as caste to be influential in demarcating the electorates. Once-and-for-all delimitation removed this opportunity.

The PR of the 1978 constitution also had the objective of consolidating electoral power within the larger parties. The 12.5 per cent cut-off

211

point would have made it extremely difficult for smaller parties to have a say in politics without coming into coalition arrangements with larger parties. The architects of Sri Lanka's PR system were keen to avoid the common result of PR – a proliferation of smaller parties and their undue influence in the legislature. Keeping out smaller parties would also assure the exclusion of anti-systemic forces. The bonus seat conferred on the party obtaining the largest number of votes was meant to ensure a clear winner in each electoral district, which would invariably be one of the larger parties, thus further consolidating their dominance.

While consolidating the two-party system, the proposed system was also designed to do away with the manufactured majorities that were a feature of FPTP. Given the established voting patterns in the country, it would be difficult for any party to have huge majorities in the legislature under PR. This was considered essential for consolidating the 1978 constitution, and the continuity of the development policies inaugurated in 1977. Finally, the original PR proposals gave the party machines greater control over the members. They decided the hierarchy within the electoral lists. MPs also had to obtain votes from larger areas, requiring more resources and a larger organisational capacity, making party support all the more important. These measures, together with the anti-defection clauses, were meant to ensure the almost complete control of the party over members, and also, critically, to maintain the stability of the government in power. Anti-defection clauses did away with the possibility of bringing down governments before the end of their term. True, the defecting MPs could appeal to the Supreme Court. But, as J. R. Jayawardene agreed, PR established a trend toward dictatorship of the party.

By these means, in sum, the new electoral arrangements were meant to bring the members of the legislature, a large number of whom now came from intermediate classes, under the control of the two major political parties. They would do away with the bias against core areas of capitalism displayed by the FPTP system. They would undermine the influence of local interests like caste, discouraging politicians from campaigning purely on local interests, and encouraging policy debates on development issues. They would consolidate the power of large parties, but get rid of the manufactured majorities that undermined the continuity of development policies.

Reforming the system

The PR system of elections established through the 1978 constitution was a major departure from the system that the Sri Lankan political class had been used to. It replaced the old system with a totally new one. But, remarkably, it did not generate fundamental criticism, except from some of the Left parties not in Parliament. The latter were concerned with the high cut-off point which would make it difficult for them to secure positions in future parliaments. But their criticism was even more fundamental. They saw the constitution, together with PR, as a ploy by Jayawardene to institute an authoritarian system and prolong UNP rule.[8]

Although the major opposition parties made statements indicating that they opposed PR, their opposition was lukewarm. This was characteristic of their response to the new constitution in general. For 'despite strong opposition to what essentially were matters of detail, there was surprisingly a measure of agreement between the two major parties (UNP and SLFP) on the new form of government to be established' (Wilson 1980: 36). This was partly because the opposition SLFP was weak and divided after its defeat in 1977. But it also realised that, being a big party, its position would not be undermined by the new system of elections. After all, it had just been reduced to eight seats in Parliament under FPTP, and a little arithmetic was enough to show that it would have been in a much better position if PR had been operative in 1977.

The other debates on the proposals were within a framework that accepted PR, and concerned specific aspects of PR. The 12.5 per cent cut-off point came under criticism during the proceedings of the select committee itself: the Ceylon Workers' Congress, representing Indian Tamil estate workers, opposed this provision. In 1977, the leader of the CWC had entered Parliament for the first time through a multi-member constituency of the old system. A 12.5 per cent cut-off point would have made it difficult for parties like the CWC to enter Parliament on their own.

Reforms to the original proposals of the 1978 constitution were effected through another select committee of Parliament, appointed in July 1983, the All-Party Select Committee on Franchise and Elections (APSCFE). It proposed reforms in three areas. These were:

- The power given to political parties and curtailment of the freedom of individual members;

- Reducing the influence of local-level interests in the demarcation of electorates;

- The 12.5 per cent cut-off point.

As might be expected, the proposals to bring the MPs under the control of the party hierarchy faced opposition from MPs across the political spectrum. Of particular concern was the list system and the power that was given to the party hierachy in deciding the order in the list, which substantially altered the manner in which MPs had hitherto gained nomination, making them depend on the party machine to an extreme degree.

The recommendations of the APSCFE introduced a system of preferences while maintaining the list system of voting. In the new system the voters could make two choices. First the voter could choose the party and then he or she had the right to cast three preferences for the candidates in the list. The party hierarchy still had a big say in who got on the list, but candidates could canvass support for themselves. This added a new level of electoral competition – between members of the same party in addition to competition between parties.

The proposal preventing MPs from crossing to other parties also came under criticism in the APSCFE. This attempt to control the political allegiance of the MPs had become even more controversial because of two government measures. First the government had passed an amendment to the constitution making it easier for MPs to cross over from the opposition to the government side. Second, Jayawardene, in an unprecedented move, had obtained undated letters of resignation from the UNP MPs of the 1977 Parliament. Both these were perceived as cynical political manipulations by Jayawardene in order to maintain his grip over the 1977 Parliament.

What is surprising, however, is that in spite of the obvious machinations of the architect of the original proposals to maintain control over MPs, and despite the increased power the anti-defection clause gave the party machines, the APSCFE reforms did not abolish the provision preventing cross-over. There were some changes in the procedures for expelling defecting members which, in addition to the provision allowing appeal to the Supreme Court, gave a parliamentary select committee final say in deciding the fate of the MP – but this could actually help the parties in power even more, if they commanded a majority in these select committees. The important fact is that this measure, which changed power relations between individual MPs and political parties significantly, survived the reforms to the original proposals and remains in place, thus abolishing the principal mechanism through which governments were brought down before their time during the FPTP period.

In addition, the APSCFE recommendations further strengthened the hands of the parties by introducing the concept of national list MPs. The select committee proposed the appointment of 29 of them. Each party was to have the chance to appoint a certain number of national list MPs in proportion to the total votes that they secured in the country. Parties had to present the list of names from which these MPs would be chosen before the election. This gave even more power to the parties, especially benefiting the bigger ones.

The other source of opposition to the original proposal had been the establishment of larger spatial units as electoral districts. Pressure to alter the original delimitation proposals of the PR system came in the form of a suggestion to establish a new delimitation commission in order to re-demarcate the most populated electoral districts – those returning more than ten members – into two or more smaller zonal electoral districts.

On the basis of this recommendation of the APSCFE, a constitutional amendment was accordingly passed to appoint a new delimitation commission in 1988 to establish the zonal electoral districts. Following the recommendations of this commission, Colombo electoral district was to be divided into three zones and Gampaha, Kalutara, Galle, Kurune-gala, Kandy and Jaffna electoral districts were to be divided into two zones. In other words, the principal focus of this new demarcation was the 'core areas' of capitalism that we have discussed above, attempting to create smaller zones in order to serve some of the local-level interests in these core areas.

However, the commission's recommendations were never imple-mented, because another constitutional amendment declared this delimi-tation process and its findings null and void. Hence, the new political space constructed through the original PR system still stands, and the attempt to resurrect smaller units that could have created opportunities for more local-level political interests failed.

Thus, instead of reducing the size of the electoral districts, by intro-ducing the concept of national list MPs, (which we have already mentioned), the APSCFE went to the other extreme of paving the way for a new category of MPs who represented the entire country. Since the allocation of 29 members on the national list is decided on the basis of the total national vote, how a party fares in the densely populated areas where the bulk of the vote is concentrated becomes critical in determin-ing its national performance. This has made the urbanised, densely populated areas even more important under PR, consolidating the influence of the 'core' and 'inner periphery' of capitalism.

Finally, politically the most important reform, which reduced the cut-off point from 12.5 per cent to 5 per cent, was effected outside the proceedings of the APSCFE. As already mentioned, there was opposition from the smaller parties to this provision right from the beginning. Politically the most important opposition came from the smaller parties representing minorities. The CWC, representing the Indian Tamil population, opposed this provision right from its participation in the first select committee. The other minority parties took up the same position. In the context of an ethnic conflict it was difficult for the governing UNP to ignore the voices of these parties. In 1988 the UNP was also about to face a presidential election in which the support of the minorities was important. All these factors led to the reduction of the cut-off point to 5 per cent, and the first general election under PR was held under this provision.

In sum, most of the elements of the original proposals survived the process initiated by the All-Party Select Committee, with the crucial exceptions of the reduction of the cut-off point to 5 per cent and the introduction of preference votes. Both these exceptions weakened the political thrust of the original proposals and had serious implications for managing the legislature, which will be discussed below. The national list, on the other hand, is an idea which has strengthened the politics of the original proposals. Apart from these departures the rest of the architecture of the original proposals has remained intact since their introduction two decades ago.

Concluding remarks

The new electoral system has been in operation for four general elections – in 1989, 1994, 2000 and 2001.[9] The average voting rate under PR has been 72.8 per cent. This is low compared to 85.2 per cent and 86.7 per cent in 1970 and 1977 under FPTP. The exceptionally low voting rate in 1989 and the low turn-out in the Northern Province due to the conflict have influenced these figures. The higher rate of spoilt votes has also been a worrying factor. The average rate of spoilt votes for the three elections is 3.9 per cent. This is much higher than the 0.4 per cent for the last two elections under FPTP.

The 1989 general election, the first under PR, was won by the UNP, which was already the party in power. This resulted in the UNP controlling the government for 17 years – the longest that any party has held on to power in Sri Lanka. In 1994, however, true to the Sri Lankan traditions in electoral politics, the UNP was defeated by the People's Alliance (PA). PA repeated its victory in the general election held in 2000. The PA is a coalition of the SLFP and the smaller Left parties. Even in the past this has been the combination that has been the main electoral alternative to the UNP. In the subsequent election, the PA was once again defeated by the UNP. PR, therefore, has not changed the fundamental two-party pattern of electoral politics in Sri Lanka, despite the fact that it is often associated with the proliferation of parties in other political systems.

The most significant change that has an influence on the country's development policies is the disappearance of 'manufactured majorities' in parliament. (Table 7.3 summarises the position of the two major parties in the four elections held under PR.) The end of manufactured majorities has ensured a certain degree of policy continuity. The constituent parties of the PA government elected in 1970 were those responsible for the state capitalist policies of the 1970–7 period. Three of the coalition partners espouse various forms of Left-oriented ideologies. In the SLFP, which is the major partner in the coalition, there are members with a similar orientation. It is true that by the time 1994 elections were held the leadership of the coalition was convinced of the need to change development policies in the direction of neo-liberalism. 'Open economy with a human face' was the slogan that they adopted in the election. If this coalition had obtained the type of majority that the FPTP system gave to governing parties, however, there would have been much greater pressure to change the direction of policies. In fact, on many occasions the leaders of these parties have been critical of the electoral system precisely because of the limited power that it gives them in Parliament.

Predictably, the reduced cut-off point of 5 per cent has allowed smaller parties to play an important role in Parliament. With the two major parties evenly balanced in Parliament, the role of these smaller parties

Table 7.3 Votes and seats under proportional representation

	1989	1994	2000	2001
UNP				
No. of MPs	125	94	89	109
% Votes	50.7	44.0	40.2	45.6
% Seats	55.6	41.8	39.6	48.4
SLFP				
No. of MPs	67			
% Votes	31.9			
% Seats	29.8			
PA				
No. of MPs		105	107	77
% Votes		48.9	45.1	37.2
% Seats		46.7	47.6	34.2

has become significant. PA governments formed in 1994 and 2000 had agreements with smaller parties representing minorities. In 1994 the minority parties supported the government, while remaining formally in the opposition. In 2000 one of the parties representing the Muslim community (Sri Lanka Muslim Congress) joined the government as a coalition partner. This is a trend that has gone against the expectations of the original 1978 Jayawardene proposals.

References

Coomaraswamy, T. (1988) 'Parliamentary Representation in Sri Lanka, 1931–36', unpublished PhD thesis, Institute of Development Studies, University of Sussex.

De Silva, K. M. (1981) *A History of Sri Lanka*, New Delhi: Oxford University Press.

De Silva, K. M. and H. Wriggins (1994) *J. R. Jayawardene of Sri Lanka, a Political Biography, Vol. II, From 1956 to His Retirement*, London: Leo Cooper/Pen and Sword Books.

Dunn, J. (ed.) (1992) *Democracy, the Unfinished Journey*, Oxford: Oxford University Press.

Elster, J., Claus, O. and P. Ulrich (1998) *Institutional Design in Post-Communist Societies: Rebuilding the Ship at Sea*, Cambridge: Cambridge University Press.

Gunasinghe, N. (1996) 'A Sociological Comment on the Political Transformation in 1956 and the Resultant Socio-Political Processes', in Sasanka Perera (ed.), *Newton Gunasinghe, Selected Essays*, Colombo: Social Scientists Association.

Jayawardene, J. R. (1979) *Selected Speeches and Writings*, Colombo: Jayawardena Centre.

Jayawardene, K. (2000) *Nobodies to Somebodies: the Rise of the Colonial Bourgeoisie in Sri Lanka*, Colombo: Social Scientists Association and Sanjiva Books.

Kohli A. (1993) 'Democracy amid Economic Orthodoxy: Trends in Developing Countries', *Third World Quarterly*, 14, 4.

Moore, M. P. (1985) *The State and Peasant Politics in Sri Lanka*, Cambridge: Cambridge University Press.

Perera, N. M. (1979) *Critical Analysis of the New Constitution of the Sri Lankan Government*, Colombo: N. M. Perera Memorial Trust.

Shastri, A. (1983) 'Evolution of the Contemporary Political Formation in Sri Lanka', *South Asia Bulletin*, 3, 1 (Spring).

Shastri, A. (1994) 'Electoral Competition and Minority Alienation in a Plurality System: Sri Lanka 1947–77', *Electoral Studies*, 10, 4.

Singer, M. R. (1964) *The Emerging Élite: a Study of Political Leadership in Ceylon*, Cambridge, Massachusetts: MIT Press.

Therborn, G. (1977) 'The Rule of Capital and the Rise of Democracy', *New Left Review*, 103.

Wilson, A. J. (1980) *The Gaullist System in Asia*, London: Macmillan Press.

Notes

1 See De Silva (1981: 417) for an account of the Donoughmore Commission.
2 One of the little-noticed aspects about the carving out of electoral districts in Sri Lanka under FPTP is the fact that it was done within provincial boundaries. In other words, it was not really a case of demarcating electoral districts in the entirety of the Sri Lankan geographical space, but a case of dividing the provinces into electoral districts.
3 One notable exception to this pattern is the Kandy district. Kandy belongs to the inner periphery but has a lower number of voters relative to MPs, because of the disenfranchisement of the Indian Tamil estate population. This population was counted in the allocation of seats, because population was the criterion in this exercise. But the actual number of registered voters was much lower, resulting in a low voters/MP ratio.
4 I am not arguing here that these electoral mechanisms were able to secure an adequate share of political power for the minorities. The post-independence history of ethnic relations and the conflict that has been devastating this country is adequate proof of the limitations of these mechanisms. But what I am trying to point out is that the interests of the politically dominant minorities did figure prominently in the debates about designing the electoral system and that this was a factor contributing to the spatial disparities of the electoral system. In the case of those provinces where there was a significant presence of the Indian Tamil community – Central Province and Uva Province – the real beneficiary of this spatial disparity was the rural Kandyan Sinhalese population. The disenfranchisement of the bulk of the Indian Tamil population through citizenship laws enacted after independence gave an added advantage to the rural Kandyan Sinhalese. Since the number of 'persons' and not citizens was taken as the basis for the population-based allocation, eligible voters in these areas had an added advantage.
5 The notion of intermediate classes and regimes was developed by the Hungarian Marxist Michael Kalecki in order to explain the growth of state-dominated economies in developing countries. Some writers have used this concept when writing about Sri Lanka. See especially A. Shastri (1983) and N. Gunasinghe (1996) for critical comment on the use of this concept in relation to Sri Lanka. For empirical data establishing the change in the social composition of the political élite, see M. R. Singer (1964) and T. Coomaraswamy (1988).
6 See Shastri 1983 for an exposition of this thesis in the example of Sri Lanka.
7 In the 1972 constitution parliament was called the National State Assembly.
8 The most comprehensive criticism was by N. M. Perera, leader of the Trotskyite Lanka Sama Samaja Party (LSSP) in a series of articles in the party newspaper *Socialist Nation*, later published as a booklet. See N. M. Perera (1979).
9 In discussing how the system has operated in these elections it is important to remember that all the elections have been held in the context of an ongoing ethnic conflict. It has affected the voting patterns in the Northern Province to a large extent and in the Eastern Province to a lesser extent. The 1989 general election was held in an exceptionally violent environment because of an insurgency in the South as well.

219

Electoral Engineering and the Politicisation of Ethnic Friction in Fiji

JON FRAENKEL

In 1997 Fiji introduced a new electoral system that was strongly influenced by prominent political scientists' proposals for 'constitutional engineering' in ethnically divided societies. Post-independence electoral arrangements were identified as having failed to encourage the emergence of multi-ethnic parties or governments. The new preferential voting system, it was hoped, would instead pave the way towards pre-election vote-pooling alliances and robust coalitions between political parties representing indigenous Fijians and Indo-Fijians. Yet at the May 1999 polls the two key political parties which had initiated this constitutional compromise were badly defeated, and a hastily assembled coalition between the former opposition parties took office, led by Fiji's first-ever Prime Minister of Indian descent. The new coalition quickly fragmented, and the government was overthrown after only a year in office by armed ethnic Fijian extremists.

During its 1995–6 hearings, Fiji's Constitutional Review Commission (CRC) consulted with the Australian and New Zealand Electoral Commissions and the United Nations Department of Political Affairs, as well as the world's two leading experts on alternative electoral techniques for ethnic conflict reduction, Professors Arend Lijphart and Donald Horowitz. Ethnic Fijian Prime Minister Sitiveni Rabuka and the main Indo-Fijian opposition leader Jai Ram Reddy strongly endorsed some of the proposed innovative techniques for constitutional reform. As one of the CRC's research papers explained,

> The rules of the political game can be structured to institutionalise moderation on divisive ethnic themes, to contain the destructive tendencies, and to pre-empt the centrifugal thrust created by ethnic politics. There is no assertion that deft political engineering can prevent or

220

eradicate deep enmities, but appropriate institutions can nudge the political system in the direction of reduced conflict and greater government accountability. (Sisk 1997: 4)

The constitution eventually agreed in 1997 combined the three best-known techniques for abating conflict in ethnically divided societies (Reilly and Reynolds 1999: 56). It provided for reserved-franchise or 'communal' constituencies, veto powers for the indigenous Fijian institutions and mandatory power sharing.[1] Most importantly, the constitution provided for the adoption of the preferential voting system in the hope of encouraging inter-ethnic electoral alliances and coalitions and paving the way for the formation of a multi-ethnic government. This was the electoral system recommended by Professor Donald Horowitz as 'perfectly apt' for Fiji (Horowitz 1997: 31). Reilly found that it would 'fit in well with Fiji's existing multi-party system' and 'could well help to promote meaningful accommodation across cleavages' (Reilly 1997a: 16; 1997b: 16). Lijphart subsequently described the adoption of the alternative vote system in Fiji as 'a major practical victory' for Horowitz (Lijphart 1997: 10).

Fiji is the first-ever country to adopt such electoral techniques for inter-ethnic alliance building and, in the past, has experience of some of the other electoral techniques for generating ethnic accommodation now being widely recommended internationally.[2] It is an ethnically bipolar society, with roughly equal-sized ethnic Fijian and Indo-Fijian populations. Post-independence elections became identified with a battle for ethnic control, the CRC argued, because of the winner-takes-all provisions of the first-past-the-post system and because of heavy usage of reserved-franchise constituencies. At district level, populations were identified as widely intermixed on the main islands, with the consequence that Fiji was deemed particularly suitable for Horowitz-type electoral incentives-based solutions (Reilly and Reynolds 1999: 36).[3] Although the country has a history of ethnic friction over land leasing and political appointments, this has mainly been low-intensity conflict, never approaching civil war, making the mild incentives recommended by electoral engineers plausibly more effective than in societies where violent conflict is endemic.

This chapter questions the CRC's analysis of Fiji's electoral history and the assumptions behind the proposal that the country adopt the preferential voting system.[4] The first section examines the background to ethnic conflict in Fiji and investigates the results of elections conducted under Fiji's initial post-independence constitution. The second and third sections look at the CRC's analysis of the defects of that earlier system,

221

and at how this underpinned the proposal to introduce a new electoral system. The fourth section looks at the extent to which the results of the May 1999 polls realised the CRC's objectives, examining the impact of the preferential ordering of candidates and its influence on the formation and dissolution of coalitions. The final part of the chapter considers the plausible impact of alternative electoral institutions and how these encourage or discourage the development of non-ethnically based political parties.

Ethnic conflict and electoral history

The small island group of Fiji was colonised by the British in 1874, after the signing of a deed of cession by leading indigenous chiefs. The first governor, Sir Arthur Gordon, forbade sales of indigenous lands to white planters and restricted indigenous Fijian employment on plantations (Gillion 1962; France 1969). Most Fijians were kept in their villages, obliged to cultivate crops to pay taxes in kind under an officially recognised chiefly system. The workforce for the country's expanding sugar industry was provided by recruiting indentured labourers from the Indian subcontinent. Over sixty thousand arrived between 1879 and 1916, and many stayed. By 1946, Indians temporarily formed a majority of the population, although this lead was subsequently reversed by rapid post-war expansion in the ethnic Fijian population and by the out-migration of some 75,000 Indo-Fijians in the wake of the 1987 coup

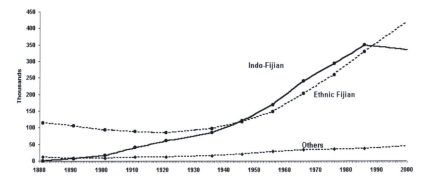

Figure 8.1 Fiji population by ethnic origin, 1881–2000
(interpolated between census points)

Note: Others include Chinese, Europeans, part-Europeans, Rotumans and other Pacific Islanders.
Sources: Fiji Census Report, 1986, Bureau of Statistics, Census 1996, Provisional Results, 21 February 1997.

Table 8.1 Shifts in composition of Fiji's Legislative Council, 1929–97

	1929	1937	1963	1965	1970	1990	1997
Members	26***	31	37	40	52	70	71
Ex-officio	13	16	19	4	–	–	–
Indian							
Nominated	–	3	2	–	–	–	–
Elected							
Reserved constituencies	3	2	4	9	12	27	19
Cross-voting constituencies	–	–	–	3	10	–	–
Fijian							
Nominated	3	5	2	2	–	–	–
Elected							
Reserved constituencies*	–	–	4	9	12	37	23
Cross-voting constituencies	–	–	–	3	10	–	–
European/General							
Nominated	–	3	2	–	–	–	–
Elected							
Reserved constituencies**	6	2	4	7	3	5	3
Cross-voting constituencies	–	–	–	3	5	–	–
Rotuman							
Elected							
Reserved constituencies	–	–	–	–	–	1	1
Open/Common roll	–	–	–	–	–	–	25

* Other Pacific Islanders were first given the franchise in 1965 and included on Fijian rolls from 1965 to 1990, when they were transferred to the 'general' rolls.
** Chinese and part–Europeans were first given the franchise in 1965, and have been included on the European or 'general' rolls ever since.
*** Including the Governor, serving as President.

Sources: Fiji Annual Report, 1929; for 1937 and 1963, N. Meller and J. Anthony, *Fiji Goes to the Polls: the Crucial Legislative Council Elections of 1963,* Honolulu: East–West Centre Press (1968), pp. 15, 18; for 1965, Fiji Constitution Order, 1968, Privy Council; B. V. Alley, 'Independence for Fiji: Recent Constitutional and Political Developments', *Australian Outlook,* 24, 2 (1970): 179; for 1970–1997, election returns.

(see Figure 8.1). Fiji today has a population of just over three quarters of a million, comprising 44 per cent Indo-Fijians and 52 per cent ethnic Fijians.

Gordon's original Legislative Council consisted solely of the governor's nominees, although the indigenous Fijian chiefly hierarchy was incorporated into the running of the district administrations and the British-initiated Council of Chiefs played an advisory role (MacNaught 1982; Ali 1977). Subsequent changes incorporated nominees of the Chief's Council, elected non-official Europeans, and (from 1929) Indo-Fijian representatives who were elected from special 'Indian' constituencies, although effective power remained with the smaller and more exclusive Governor's Executive Council. Further changes in the composition of the Legislative Council are summarised in Table 8.1. All elections were conducted under the British-style first-past-the-post system until the introduction of the 1997 constitution.

From the late 1920s, Indian political leaders repeatedly called for 'common roll' elections and political equality (Gillion 1977: 130). Colonial officials and European settlers, fearful of possible Indo-Fijian political control under a straight majoritarian open-franchise system, upheld racially based electoral rolls. In justification, they appealed to the 1874 deed of cession as a solemn charter of trusteeship and commitment to maintaining the 'pre-eminence of the Fijian race' (Norton 1977: 26–7, 55–6; Lal 1992: 139–43). Nevertheless, domestic Indian agitation and the desire to attract free labour migrants from the Indian subcontinent after the termination of indenture contracts in 1920 made the colonial government responsive to appeals from the Indian government to allow greater political rights for Indians. The compromise eventually reached was an assurance of 'parity of representation', implying an equal number of Fijian, European and Indian members of the Legislative Council, despite huge disparities in the size of their populations.

During the 1960s, steps were taken to move the country towards self-government. In 1965, the official majority was abolished and 'cross-voting' (or 'national') constituencies were introduced, where the ethnicity of the candidate was specified but registered voters from all ethnic communities voted together (British Parliamentary Papers 1964–5: 7). Separate communal constituencies remained in the majority, but votes were required also for members from other ethnic groups. Each voter had four votes – one vote in their own reserved-franchise constituency, and one each in open-franchise constituencies for candidates whose ethnicity was 'Fijian', 'Indian' and 'general'.[5] An extended version of this mixed 'communal' and 'cross-voting' constituency system, coupled with

224

Westminster-style first-past-the-post voting, was the electoral arrangement bequeathed to Fiji upon independence in 1970. The principle of 'indigenous paramountcy' was preserved through a majority of Great Council of Chiefs nominees in the Senate.

The six subsequent legislative elections, running from 1966 to 1987, provide an important source of evidence about the likely impact of open-franchise voting patterns. How did these peculiar election laws influence Fiji's post-independence polity?

Table 8.2 Votes and seats secured by the major Fijian and Indo-Fijian parties since 1966

	Alliance		Federation*	
	Votes %	Seats %	Votes %	Seats %
1966	53.5	64.7	15	26.5
1972	56.9	63.5	33.4	36.5
1977 (April)	43.5	46.2	41.1	50.0
1977 (September)	49.6	71.2	23.5 (18.5)**	23.0 (5.8)**
1982	51.8	53.8	41.1	46.2
1987	49.0	46.2	46.5 ***	53.8

*Renamed National Federation Party before the 1972 polls.
**At the September 1977 elections, the 'flower' and 'dove' factions of the NFP fought the elections on separate tickets. Figures in brackets show the vote for the smaller 'dove' faction.
***A coalition between the National Federation Party and Fiji Labour Party fought the 1987 election.
Sources: Fiji Times, 11 October 1966, 3 May 1972, 7 April 1977, 26 September 1977, 19 July 1982, 13 April 1987.

The first elections under the combined cross-voting/communal electoral system resulted in victory for an alliance between indigenous Fijian political leaders and the over-represented white minority. The Alliance Party, led by Ratu Sir Kamisese Mara, attracted 82 per cent of the Fijian vote at the 1972 general elections and obtained all of the Fijian communal seats (see Table 8.2). The Indian vote, however, went largely to the rival National Federation Party (NFP), which obtained all of the Indian communal seats. Although Indian voters were in a slight overall majority in 1972 (50.6 per cent), the three tiny reserved-franchise seats granted to the solidly pro-Alliance 'General' voters restored the balance. As in all later elections under this voting system, the margin of victory lay in the open-franchise 'cross-voting' constituencies. It was the Alliance Party's ability to command 24 per cent[6] of Indian votes, and therefore win many of the marginal cross-voting contests, that enabled it to secure a majority (63 per cent) of seats in Parliament.

This finely balanced ethnic underpinning of the electoral system allowed many curious results due to variations in the turn-out, changes in numbers of invalid or spoilt ballots, peculiarities of constituency boundaries or split ethnic votes. For example, the largely Indo-Fijian-backed National Federation Party (NFP) won the elections of April 1977, despite obtaining only 41.4 per cent of the overall vote as compared to the Alliance's 43.5 per cent. The key reason was not an increase in support for the successful party. The NFP won 73 per cent of the Indo-Fijian vote, exactly the same percentage it had secured in the previous elections in 1972 when it lost the elections. What was responsible was a marked rise in ethnic Fijian support for the Fijian Nationalist Party, a party that wanted to exclude Indo-Fijians from the top political jobs. The Nationalists took 25 per cent of the Fijian vote, splitting that vote in several key marginal cross-voting seats, so that Ratu Mara lost the election. Ironically, rising support for a more extreme ethnic Fijian party resulted in electoral victory for a largely Indian-backed party.

In the crisis that followed, the appointment of a new administration was delayed by uncertainties within the NFP about the sustainability of a largely Indian-backed government and internal rivalry over the appointment of party leader Siddiq Koya as Prime Minister. Concluding that 'the people of Fiji did not give a clear mandate to either of the political parties', the indigenous Fijian Governor-General, Ratu Sir George Cakobau, announced that the defeated Ratu Mara was nevertheless 'best able to command the support of the majority of the House' (cited Lal 1992: 239–40). Mara was temporarily returned as Prime Minister at the head of a minority government. At fresh elections in September 1977, a fall in the Nationalists' vote and deep divisions in the NFP[7] enabled the Alliance to romp home with 71 per cent of the seats in Parliament.

At the general elections of 1982, two robust, ethnically based political parties again contested the elections. The NFP aligned itself with a small breakaway Fijian party (the Western United Front), which appealed to the hostility of western Viti Levu's chiefs against the dominance of the eastern chiefly élite. It failed to make serious inroads into the Alliance's support base. Again, the margin of victory lay in the open-franchise constituencies. The Alliance continued to command some 14 per cent of the Indo-Fijian vote, enough to tip the scales in the finely balanced Suva cross-voting constituency. Since these key marginal cross-voting constituencies were two-seat constituencies, with a 'Fijian' and an 'Indian' member, the result in Suva was sufficient to sway the election in the Alliance's favour.

At the 1987 election, the precarious electoral balance was upset by the emergence of the Fiji Labour Party (FLP), which fought the election in coalition with the NFP. In the 1980s, the FLP espoused a class-based multi-ethnic platform, an alliance that was tempered by its association with the solidly Indo-Fijian and Gujarati business-backed NFP. The coalition secured 9.6 per cent of the Fijian vote, significantly below the 15 per cent of the Indian vote that the Alliance retained. Nevertheless, this was sufficient to neutralise the Alliance's former advantage in the highly marginal cross-voting constituencies, giving the coalition both the Suva and South-eastern seats. The NFP–FLP coalition secured 46.5 per cent of the national vote, but obtained 53.8 per cent of seats. Mara's 1970–87 government had finally been defeated, and, unlike April 1977 when the NFP responded by attempting to form a Government of National Unity, this time indigenous Fijian FLP leader Dr Timoci Bavadra assumed the premiership.

Within a month, on 14 May 1987, Lieutenant-Colonel Sitiveni Rabuka staged a military *coup d'état* aimed at securing 'a Fiji in which the Fijians will have no fear of being totally dominated by an immigrant race' (Rabuka, cited *Islands Business*, September 1987: 7). Efforts to speedily restore constitutional democracy were derailed by a consolidation of military authority in September of the same year. Subsequent out-migration of around 20 per cent of the country's Indo-Fijian population (75,000), and a new 1990 constitution which reserved the positions of Prime Minister and President for ethnic Fijians, sharply altered the post-1970 electoral balance. The first-past-the-post electoral system was retained, but the distribution of parliamentary seats was arranged so as to guarantee a majority for ethnic Fijian politicians (see Table 8.1). In general elections held in 1992 and 1994, coup leader Rabuka emerged victorious as civilian Prime Minister at the head of the newly formed Soqosoqo ni Vakavulewa ni Taukei.[8] In a move aimed at courting international and domestic legitimacy, reviving foreign investment and enabling Fiji to rejoin the Commonwealth, Rabuka endorsed a review of the 1990 constitution.

The mid-1990s constitutional review and the post-independence cross-voting system

Despite an extensive literature concerned with elections in Fiji, there exists no detailed analysis of the post-1970 British-bequeathed electoral system. Nevertheless, a view of that system's weaknesses underpinned the CRC's recommendation for the introduction of preferential voting in

Fiji.[9] The CRC found that the pre-1987 electoral arrangements had 'not brought about multi-ethnic governments' owing to the problems associated with 'trying to combine the Westminster system with exclusively or mainly communal representation' (CRC 1996: 11). The report identified the following 'chain reaction':

> *the pull exerted by the communal voting system* made people feel that members of their community elected by all voters to represent national constituencies were not really legitimate representatives of their own community. That is why the cross-voting system under the 1970 constitution could not make any impact on the identification of party interests with those of a particular community. To a certain extent, it induced moderation. To get elected a candidate for a national seat had to appeal to the voters of other communities. But, if the appeal was successful, the member thus elected was often seen as not being a legitimate representative of the community to which he or she belonged. (CRC 1996: 11; *my emphasis*)

A similar conclusion had been reached 21 years earlier by the 1975 Street Commission.

> The voter looks to the member of parliament elected for his communal seat as the one who truly represents him, protects his interests and to whom he goes for help and advice. His relation with the other three national roll members is much less close and more impersonal. (Street Commission 1975: 11)

Indeed, this interpretation had initially been suggested by NFP leader A. D. Patel at the time when the cross-voting seats were first introduced in 1965.[10] Initially, the analysis was something of a self-fulfilling prophecy. At the 1966 elections, the Federation Party was unable to obtain European candidates to stand in the general cross-voting constituencies, and Indo-Fijians were encouraged to cast invalid votes in these contests (Alley 1970: 181; Alley 1973: 230–2; Norton 1972: 373). Yet this was no longer the case even by 1972, after which the cross-voting constituencies were just as fiercely contested as the reserved-franchise constituencies. If communal constituency MPs were consistently viewed as the 'true' ethnic representatives, one would expect the turn-out to be higher for these contests. Table 8.3 shows that this was generally not the case. After 1966, both communal and cross-voting constituencies tended to witness parallel fluctuations in turn-out.

Only some of the MPs elected on cross-voting tickets had a 'remote', 'impersonal' and 'illegitimate' relationship with their own ethnic

Table 8.3 Turn-out and invalid votes in general elections held under the 1970 constitution

	1966	1972	1977 (April)	1977 (Sept)	1982	1987
Turn-out (%)						
Reserved constituencies						
Fijian	82.4	84.1	72.1	71.1	87.5	71.2
Indian	89.5	86.1	77.4	75.7	86.4	70.3
General	84.6	84.2	74.1	71.2	81.7	66.3
Cross-voting constituencies						
Fijian	81.4	85.1	74.7	73.0	86.4	70.7
Indian	79.7	85.0	73.8	73.2	86.3	70.8
General	66.8	85.5	76.6	73.1	86.5	70.1
Invalid votes (%)						
Reserved constituencies						
Fijian	3.2	2.0	3.7	7.9	2.0	1.8
Indian	3.2	2.0	2.5	1.6	1.7	1.4
General	0.7	1.7	2.4	1.7	1.7	1.6
Cross-voting constituencies						
Fijian	3.9	2.0	3.7	7.9	2.0	1.8
Indian	4.1	2.4	8.8	6.2	3.1	2.8
General	21.9	2.5	7.8	9.0	2.5	1.3
Difference between reserved and cross-voting constituencies						
Fijian	0.7	0.0	0.0	0.0	0.0	0.0
Indian	0.9	0.4	6.3	4.6	1.4	1.4
General	21.2	0.8	5.4	7.3	0.8	−0.3

Notes: 'Invalid votes' include rejected and spoilt ballot papers, but not other ballot papers received late or not returned (where these are recorded separately).
Sources: *Fiji Royal Gazette*, 25 November 1966, 26 May 1972, 6 May 1977, 18 November 1977, 4 August 1982, 4 May 1987. For candidate's parties, sources as for Table 8.2.

229

communities. In predominantly ethnic Fijian cross-voting constituencies, the Alliance Party had few qualms about asking core-indigenous parliamentarians to stand. Indeed, Prime Minister Ratu Mara himself occupied a 'national' seat, with a 90 per cent Fijian electorate. What was at issue was rather the ethnically specified 'Indian' member for such seats, who was elected mainly on the basis of the Fijian vote. Such MPs were often identified as 'stooges' or 'puppets', with a remote relationship to the Indo-Fijian community. Similarly, the NFP treated cross-voting constituencies with majority Indian electorates as if they were reserved-franchise constituencies, although some efforts were made, without much success, to cultivate indigenous candidates to stand in the 'Fijian' cross-voting constituencies who possessed some social standing or popularity among the ethnic Fijian electorate.

In the peculiarly polarised circumstances of post-independence Fiji, combining cross-voting and reserved-franchise constituencies, under a first-past-the-post system, encouraged a highly divisive style of political campaigning. As Fiji's CRC member Brij Lal noted at the time, 'political success in Fiji is ... contingent upon maintaining solidarity in one's own ethnic community while actively promoting disunity among the opposition's' (Lal 1988a: 90). Only in the more finely balanced, heterogeneous, cross-voting constituencies, where populations were of roughly equal size, were cross-ethnic appeals at least potentially of importance. Yet even here there is little evidence of a strong electoral impact due to the fielding of moderate candidates in these constituencies or of the working of institutional incentives to cultivate a multi-ethnic appeal. Where the key to victory lay in maximising the turn-out from one's own ethnic community, and diminishing the vote for smaller breakaway ethnic parties, playing the race card probably made narrow electoral sense.[11]

There was a further element in the 'chain reaction' identified by the CRC:

> The stress on communal voting means that the parties which make the greatest effort to appeal to other communities are seen as compromising the interests of their own. New parties appealing exclusively to a single ethnic community emerge to fill the perceived gap. In response, parties which were originally committed to multi-racialism are sooner or later driven back to promoting mainly or only the perceived interests of the ethnic community from which, historically, they have derived their greatest support. (CRC 1996: 12; see also Lal, 1988b: 40)

These 'pulls' away from multi-racialism refer primarily to the Alliance Party's reaction to the emergence of the extremist Nationalist Party in

April 1977. This was described by the CRC as an 'effect' of the electoral system, accurately in the sense that splinter parties can split the ethnic vote bringing defeat for the mainstream party under first-past-the-post systems. Yet the key factor here was surely the emergence of the Fijian Nationalist Party, which cannot be accurately described as a simple 'effect' of electoral institutions. Such splinter parties are strongly discouraged under first-past-the-post systems. In any case, a similar threat can be posed by the emergence of ethnic extremist parties under any electoral system, challenging moves towards consensual arrangements with the other ethnic community as a 'sell out' of ethnic interests. Indeed, as we will see, this was also a marked feature of the May 1999 polls, under the CRC's recommended preferential voting system.

Ethnicity-based voting patterns dominated Fiji's post-independence elections, but this was mediated through ethnic loyalty to political parties identified as 'Indian' (NFP) or 'Fijian' (Alliance), rather than personal

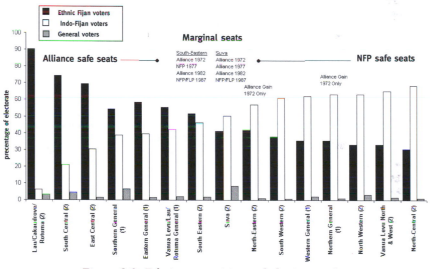

*Figure 8.2 Ethnic composition and election results
in cross-voting constituencies*

Notes: Constituencies organised from left to right on the basis of the ratio of Fijians plus General voters (who tended to vote for the Alliance) to Indo-Fijians (who tended to vote for the NFP) in the electorate, using the distribution of registered voters in 1987. Numbers in brackets show candidates per constituency. The ten dual-member constituencies had an 'Indian' and 'Fijian' seat each. The five General cross-voting constituencies had a single General member. The exceptional election of September 1977 is not shown.
Sources: *Fiji Times* 11 October 1966, 3 May 1972, 7 April 1977, 26 Sept 1977, 19 July 1982, 13 April 1987.

attachments to 'Indian' or 'Fijian' candidates owing to their ethnicity. The Alliance Party never obtained over 57 per cent of the national vote (see Table 8.2), and never secured a single Indian reserved-franchise seat. The NFP (or NFP/FLP coalition) never obtained 50 per cent of the vote, and never won a single Fijian communal seat. These political cleavages were also, for the most part, reflected in voting patterns in the cross-voting constituencies. Leaving aside the exceptional September 1977 elections when the NFP was in disarray, only four marginal 'cross-voting' constituencies ever changed hands under the combined communal/cross-voting system (see Figure 8.2). Two of these were constituencies taken by the Alliance only in the 1972 elections, when it could command an exceptional 24 per cent of the Indian vote. The other two, the Suva and South-eastern constituencies, each with ethnically specified 'Indian' and 'Fijian' members, made the difference between victory and defeat in the elections of April 1977, 1982 and 1987.

The main genuine 'effects' of the post-1970 electoral system were:

- to dampen the normal sharp seat swings associated with the first-past-the-post system owing to the predominance of reserved-franchise constituencies and ethnically homogeneous cross-voting constituencies;

- to institutionalise a disincentive to the emergence of smaller political parties that might threaten the broader ethnic election victories in marginal constituencies;

- to encourage the elevation of parliamentarians who lacked legitimacy in their own ethnic communities, but owed their positions to links forged with the political parties representing the other ethnic group.

What the electoral system certainly did not possess was the main merit usually attributed to the British-style first-past-the-post system: an ability to produce 'strong government' by ensuring greater swings in the number of seats secured by political parties than the swings in the numbers of votes obtained by political parties.

The rationale for the introduction of the alternative vote (AV) system

Fiji's 1995–6 Constitutional Review Commission established as its 'over-riding objective' the 'encouragement of multi-ethnic government', and identified changes in electoral laws as the 'main stimulus for the emergence of a multi-ethnic political culture' (CRC 1996: 310, 309). The 1970–87 electoral system had 'to a certain extent ... induced moderation', but had also possessed a 'divisive effect'. The CRC set out to 'break down the barriers which *force* ethnic parties to take a narrow, communal view of their best interests' (CRC 1996: 277, 20; my emphasis). By endowing electoral institutions with such a determinate role in moulding party orientation the anticipated scope for effective electoral engineering was enhanced. The alternative vote system (AV), with its provisions for parties to swap preferences, it was claimed, would offer stronger 'electoral incentives to moderation and compromise' (CRC 1996: 11–12, 312, 317).

Unlike the first-past-the-post system, AV involves redistribution of preferences until majorities are secured. The system requires voters to list candidates in order of preference. When no candidate secures an outright majority at the first count, constituency results are decided by counting voters' second, third or lower-order preferences. At each successive count, the lowest polling candidate is eliminated and his or her voters' second or lower-order preferences are redistributed until one candidate secures 50 per cent of the vote. Table 8.4 gives an example of how the system operated in the rural constituency of Nadroga in 1999. There, the indigenous Fijian candidate for the governing Soqosoqo ni Vakavulewa ni Taukei (SVT), Ratu Saikusa Makutu, secured the largest number of first-count votes, but was defeated by the Fiji Labour Party candidate who secured a larger number of second- and third-preference votes.

Table 8.4 Redistribution of preference votes in the Nadroga open constituency

Candidates	Party	Counts		
		1	2	3
Kumar	NFP	35	eliminated	
Volavola	FLP	6,239	6,255	7,906
Takolevu	FAP	1,667	1,667	eliminated
Makutu	SVT	6,377	6,396	6,411

Source: Elections Office, *Elections '99*.

The CRC argued that this system would avoid some of the best-known defects of the first-past-the-post system, such as candidates being elected with less than a majority of the vote (CRC 1996: 305). It was also claimed that AV 'generally achieves a better proportionality of seats to votes' than the first-past-the-post system, and that it would ensure governments backed by an overall majority of the popular vote (CRC

233

1996: 306). Most important, the system was embraced as a means of reaching the Commission's 'multi-ethnic' goals. It was hoped that it would encourage the emergence of cross-ethnic allegiances amongst those whose primary loyalty was towards their own ethnic leaders. An Indian voter in Fiji, for example, is likely to give first-preference support to one of the country's two predominantly Indo-Fijian parties. But at second- or third-preference level, that voter might be willing to specify preferences for one of the ethnic Fijian parties. As Horowitz explained, 'the purpose of incentives is to *create* floating voters at some level of preference' (Horowitz 1991: 179).

The Commission's report emphasised still more strongly the anticipated influence of AV on Fiji's political parties. Their need to bid for second or lower-order preferences was thought to encourage more conciliatory party political platforms on ethnically divisive issues (CRC 1996: 316). This also closely followed Horowitz's perception of the consequences of making politicians and political parties 'reciprocally dependent on the votes of members of groups other than their own' (Horowitz 1991: 196).

> Electorally, the way to induce politicians to be moderate is to structure voting arrangements so politicians must rely, in part, on votes delivered by members of a group other than their own. Such incentives are effective because those votes will not be forthcoming unless the candidates receiving them can be portrayed as being moderate on inter-ethnic issues. (Horowitz 1997: 24)

Similarly, the CRC identified party deals accompanying the swapping of preference votes as the pivotal vehicle for fostering a more conciliatory type of politics and echoed Horowitz's assumption that this would encourage gravitation towards the centre ground.

> Only moderate parties with conciliatory policies will agree to trade preferences and will be able to persuade their supporters to honour the agreement. The system therefore encourages the emergence of such parties. (CRC 1996: 316)

Indeed, so important were these electoral incentives for inter-party deals that the Commission introduced a provision for a split format ballot paper, with 'above-' and 'below-the-line' sections (CRC 1996: 320). Those who voted 'above the line' simply had to place a tick next to the chosen first-choice party's symbol. In so doing they delegated decisions about the allocation of second and lower preferences to these first-choice political parties. Since those who voted 'below the line' had to number

75 per cent of the constituency's candidates in order of preference (Fiji Government 1988: Section 116), it is hardly surprising that the vast majority of ballot papers were ticked 'above the line'. Where the counting of preferences proved necessary, such ballot papers were reallocated in accordance with lists lodged by party officials at the elections office.

Finally, the trading of preference votes before elections, it was believed, would lead to durable and politically robust coalitions, alliances that would prove stronger than those 'coalitions of convenience' often negotiated by ethnically based political parties inside Parliament after elections under proportional representation systems. As Horowitz explained: 'the incentive to compromise, and not merely the incentive to coalesce, is the key to accommodation' (Horowitz 1991: 171).

Preference trading, coalition formation and coalition dissolution at the May 1999 polls

Fiji's 1999 election resulted in a landslide victory for the People's Coalition. The Fiji Labour Party emerged with an outright majority. Together with its pre-election coalition partners – the Fijian Association Party and Party of National Unity – the People's Coalition could command 52 seats in the 71-member Bose Lawa (lower house). Rabuka's governing Soqosoqo ni Vakavulewa ni Taukei (SVT) was reduced to a rump of only 8 seats in parliament, while the SVT's coalition ally, the National Federation Party, did not secure a single seat, a crushing defeat for what was formerly the largest Indo-Fijian party. Labour Party leader Mahendra Chaudhry took up the position of Prime Minister, and was sworn in by Fiji's President, Ratu Sir Kamisese Mara. Defeated PM Rabuka addressed the nation, declaring 'loyalty to the spirit of democracy and to the principles of the constitution', but promising defiant opposition.

> If the new government were to use its majority to bulldoze through measures which we see as being detrimental to the best interests of indigenous Fijians, we would oppose these vigorously, both in the House of Representatives and in the Senate, and we will not hesitate to call on the support of the Great Council of Chiefs' appointees in the Upper House. (Rabuka, appearing on Fiji TV, 18 May 1999, cited in *Fiji Times*, 19 May 1999)

The elections witnessed an extraordinary increase in voter registration and in the turn-out. Compulsory registration and voting, backed by the threat of $F50 and $F20 fines respectively, helped to raise numbers of eligible voters on the roll by 32 per cent over the levels witnessed at the previous 1994 elections. Whereas, in 1994, only 73 per cent of registered electors actually cast votes, the comparable 1999 figure was 90 per cent. Voting lasted a week, and the count lasted a further three days, as officials battled with the laborious counting and recounting of votes; 8.7 per cent of ballot papers were declared 'informal' or 'invalid', well above the international average. The cost of the election, not including extensive assistance from the Australian Electoral Commission, was over twice that in 1994.

First-preference voting was solidly along ethnic lines. No significant political party commanded support from voters of different ethnic groups even roughly in proportion to their respective shares in the electorate. Two predominantly Indo-Fijian parties – the Fiji Labour Party and the National Federation Party – together secured 98.5 per cent of Indo-Fijian votes in the Indian reserved-franchise constituencies. Conversely, the five main Fijian parties accounted for 94.3 per cent of the vote in the 23 Fijian reserved-franchise constituencies. Calculating the extent of voting across the ethnic divide in the 25 heterogeneous 'open' constituencies is more complex, but investigations suggest a similar ethnically based division of the vote (Fraenkel 2000a: 96–102).

This, of course, is precisely what Horowitz and the CRC anticipated, which is why they backed *compulsory* preferential voting. To cast a valid ballot, voters were obliged to list three quarters of the candidates in some sensible order, or else to surrender their right to do so, via the 'party ticket' option on the ballot papers, to their first-choice political parties. In May 1999, 92 per cent of all ballot papers were completed 'above the line'.[12] Political parties widely campaigned for this kind of 'party ticket' support, and the required simpler tick next to a political party's symbol conformed to the format of the ballot paper at previous elections. The result was that voter preferences were, where necessary, redistributed in accordance with party-specified lists lodged with the elections office.

These party-controlled preference transfers exerted considerable influence over the outcome of constituency contests and over the final composition of Fiji's Parliament. In nearly half of all constituency contests (46.5 per cent), second or lower-order preferences had to be counted to establish a final result. In nearly a quarter of all contests (22.5 per cent), candidates who were in the lead at the first count were defeated by others leapfrogging from behind. In the 1970s and 1980s cross-voting constituencies, despite their precariously balanced logistics, swings in the number of seats gained by each party were relatively small (other than at the exceptional September 1977 election). Under the new preferential voting system, with a large number of parties entering the contest, open seat swings were potentially considerably higher. The 1999 election witnessed the highest disproportionality between votes cast and seats secured for each party of any Fiji election since 1966 (see Table 8.5).

Table 8.5 Disproportionality in elections since 1966

1966	10.0
1972	6.0
1977 (April)	4.9
1977 (September)	16.7
1982	3.5
1987	5.5
1992	7.9
1994	9.7
1999	19.3*

Notes: Disproportionality is calculated using Gallagher's index to obtain a single figure for each election. The differences between the percentage of votes and the percentage of seats secured by each party are squared and added up. The total is then divided by two, and the square root of this figure gives an index of overall seats/votes proportionality (see M. Gallagher, 'Proportionality, Disproportionality and Electoral Systems', *Electoral Studies*, 10, 1 (1991)).

*Owing to the new voting system operating in May 1999, a plausible objection is that seats/votes differences for each party should be calculated using the final-count, rather than first-preference, vote. Doing this alters the 1999 figure from 19.3 to 16.6 per cent.

Sources: *Fiji Times*, 11 October 1966, 3 May 1972, 7 April 1977, 26 September 1977, 19 July 1982, 13 April 1987, 1 June 1992, 28 February 1994; Fiji Elections Office, *Elections '99: Results by the Count*, Suva, 1999.

The mechanics of the Rabuka–Reddy defeat

The 1997 constitution had initially acquired backing from the indigenous Fijian élite, as a system likely to pave the way to a more internationally respectable era of ethnic Fijian rule, although with Indo-Fijian opposition leader Jai Ram Reddy now assuming the position of Deputy PM. The electoral rewards anticipated as a result of this compromise were considerable. Rabuka's SVT and Jai Ram Reddy's NFP established a tight coalition in the run-up to the 1999 polls, along with the smaller United Generals Party (UGP). These parties appealed to voters principally by highlighting the new constitution itself as an example of the merits of adopting a more conciliatory and moderate political approach to ethnically fractious issues. Each party campaigned separately for the Fijian, Indian and General reserved-franchise seats. In the 25 open

237

constituencies, they made cross-ethnic arrangements to share out seats and exchange preference votes. Yet these architects of the 1997 constitutional compromise were convincingly defeated at the polls.

In the Fijian reserved-franchise seats, Rabuka's SVT faced old adversaries and new rivals. Three established opposition Fijian parties (the Fijian Nationalist Party, the Fijian Association party and the Party of National Unity) captured just over a third of the Fijian vote, close to the share they had secured in 1992 and 1994. But this time around, the SVT's share of the Fijian vote fell to 38 per cent, well below the 65–67 per cent it had received in the earlier 1990s. The key reason was the entry of the new Christian Democratic Alliance (the Veitokani ni Lewenivanua Vakarisito or VLV), which had emerged in the wake of Rabuka's constitutional compromise, accusing him of 'selling out' and betraying 'indigenous Fijian institutions for his own glorification'. The party wanted to turn Fiji into a 'Christian state', supported a ban on Sunday trading and was vigorously opposed to the 1997 constitution. The VLV had considerable strength in many of the SVT's regional strongholds: the eastern part of Fiji's main island, Viti Levu; on the second-largest island, Vanua Levu; and in the urban areas around the capital, Suva. It secured 19.4 per cent of the Fijian vote and, even where defeated, its preferences made the difference between victory and defeat for the SVT in a number of crucial marginal constituencies.

Like the SVT, Reddy's NFP also suffered a decline, failing to retain the 54 per cent of the vote in the Indian communal seats it had secured in 1994. The NFP had initially been a party based in the sugar cane belts of western Viti Levu and northern Vanua Levu, but had gradually lost support in these areas to Labour leader Mahendra Chaudhry's National Farmers' Union. In 1992 and 1994, the NFP had retained a strong backing amongst Indo-Fijians in eastern Viti Levu and in the urban areas. At the 1999 polls, however, its share of the Indian vote slumped to 32 per cent, and even in the urban and eastern areas the party secured below the required 50 per cent. Overseas migration among middle-class Indo-Fijians and the party's association with prominent Gujarati business leaders undermined support for the NFP. Yet these influences were also present in 1994. The main reason for the collapse in the NFP's 1999 vote was the party's willingness to compromise with the former coup leader Rabuka and the governing SVT. Indo-Fijian hostility to the government was considerable, and Rabuka's leadership of the military coup back in 1987, which had dislodged a strongly Indo-Fijian backed government, had not been forgotten (Norton 2000: 57; Lal 1999: 35, 38–9; Sharpham 2000: 296).

The preference-trading system was intended to deliver significant rewards to alliances such as that between the SVT and the NFP. Under the former first-past-the-post system, the Alliance Party had, the CRC argued, been 'pulled' away from multi-racialism by the emergence of the Fijian Nationalist Party. Under AV, the rewards of inter-racial cooperation were supposed to outweigh any potential losses due to the emergence of ethnic fringe parties on the flanks, who denounce the 'sell-out' by moderates. In fact, both the SVT and NFP lost support in their own ethnic communities owing to their shift towards compromise, while both made negligible cross-ethnic gains as a result of their alliance. Vote transfers from the NFP to the SVT accounted for a mere 0.2 per cent of the total in the open constituencies, and those from the SVT to the NFP only 2.9 per cent. (see Table 8.6). The SVT ended up a net total of ten seats short of the number it might have had under a first-past-the-post system. In the Indian seats, the NFP's first-count defeat was so emphatic that no counting of preferences was necessary.

Table 8.6 Percentage distribution of preference transfers between political parties in the open constituencies

From: \ To:	SVT	VLV	FAP	PANU	Nat.	FLP	NFP	Other
SVT		0.3	1.1	0.1	3.3	0.8	2.9	7.0
VLV	0.8		0.8	5.5	3.8	14.9	0.2	2.9
FAP	1.0	0.4		0.0	0.1	21.7	0.1	0.1
PANU	0.0	0.0	0.0		0.0	13.0	0.3	0.0
Nat.	2.8	1.4	1.4	0.0		1.8	0.0	3.9
FLP	0.0	0.0	0.0	0.0	0.0		0.0	0.0
NFP	0.2	0.0	0.0	0.0	0.0	0.2		0.0
Other	1.4	0.6	2.7	0.0	0.4	1.2	0.0	0.5
Total	6.2	3.1	6.0	5.6	7.6	53.6	3.5	14.4

Note: The data show vote transfers to the parties listed in the columns as each of the parties listed in the rows is eliminated, not the first-preference *origin* of all transferred votes. Elections Office data only permit identification of where votes are transferred to as each defeated party is eliminated. Beyond the second count, some redistributed votes will already have been transferred once.
Source: Fiji Elections Office, *Elections '99: Results by the Count*, Suva, 1999.

Formation of a successful moderate coalition, on the Malaysian model, is assumed in the Horowitz/CRC model to generate space on the flanks for the emergence of extremist, ethnically based, opposition parties. The 'rules of the game' are intended to leave such parties at a disadvantage, principally because they prove unable to make arrangements for exchanging preference votes. However, preferential voting provides no guarantee of the sought-after inter-ethnic transfers of loyalties. In a sufficiently polarised situation, voters might simply list candidates from their own ethnic group as 1, 2, 3, etcetera. To avoid this, Horowitz and the CRC backed *compulsory* preference voting.[13] The voter had to list at least 75 per cent of candidates in order or, where parties acquired control of the disposition of votes via ballots endorsing party 'tickets', it was necessary to rank all candidates in some order.

While this obligatory ranking requirement guarantees *some*, indeed *any*, kind of deal aimed at swapping preferences with other parties, by the same token it diminishes the necessity for such deals to reflect some kind of ideological affinity. Even without compulsion, Fiji's electoral history provides numerous examples of curious, ideologically fraught, electoral alliances of convenience. During the 1970s and 1980s, for example, the NFP repeatedly came to deals with Fijian opponents of the Alliance Party, including even the pro-Indian-repatriation Fijian Nationalist Party, simply because of the electoral incentive of splitting the Fijian vote.[14] Compulsory preferential voting strengthens the potential for such odd accords simply because parties are stuck with *de facto* alliances unless they deliberately forge them. It eases the way to the formation of a loose grouping of otherwise fractious opposition parties, who, under a first-past-the-post system, would be unable to arrive at policy platforms conducive to the necessary seat-sharing deals.

The anatomy of the People's Coalition victory

The opposition People's Coalition proved able to take advantage of these anti-incumbent pressures in the new voting system. The FLP, FAP and PANU made deals to exchange second preferences, but without any explicit accompanying deals on party policies. The joint interest in dislodging the Rabuka government proved sufficient. In the Fijian communal constituencies, the main beneficiary was the FAP, which obtained nine of these seats. In the open constituencies, it was the FLP that was the main beneficiary. It received over half of all the open constituency preference transfers (see Table 8.6). Contrary to the assumptions of the CRC, the new 'majoritarian' preferential voting system did not result in the election of a government with a majority of the overall vote. The victorious Labour Party won only 32 per cent of the overall first-count vote, or 38 per cent of the overall final-count vote, including transferred preferences, but 52 per cent of the seats in Parliament.

The first factor accounting for Labour's victory was its fairly evenly spread 66 per cent of the Indian vote, sufficient to acquire all 19 of the

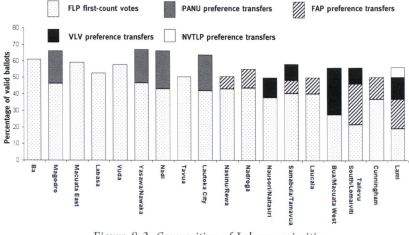

*Figure 8.3 Composition of Labour majorities
in the 1999 open constituencies*

Notes: Constituencies are ranked from left to right in accordance with the percentage of Indo-Fijians in the electorate. Those on the left have predominantly Indo-Fijian electorates, those on the right predominantly ethnic Fijian electorates.
Sources: As for Table 8.4.

Indian reserved-franchise constituencies. The same two-thirds share of the Indian vote was also enough to give the FLP, at the first count, five of the more ethnically homogeneous, predominantly Indian, open constituencies. The remaining 13 open constituencies secured by the FLP depended on transfers of preference votes from the smaller indigenous Fijian parties. These are shown in Figure 8.3. Transfers of votes from defeated candidates from the Party of National Unity (PANU) gave the FLP an additional four open seats in the sugar cane belts in the west of Viti Levu (shown in light grey). PANU was a party sponsored by the Ba Provincial Council, the local government in Fiji's richest sugar cane province.

Preference transfers from Labour's other main ally, the Fijian Association Party, gave the FLP another four open constituencies, most in the more marginal areas of eastern Viti Levu, around the capital, Suva (shown by the striped bars). The FAP has been associated with a more moderate social philosophy than Rabuka's SVT, although FAP parliamentarians attacked Rabuka's compromise over the 1997 constitution and argued for a Parliament dominated by ethnic Fijians (Lal 1999: 29–30; Scarr 1998: 47).

241

The transfer of second-preference votes from these two close allies gave the FLP a total of 32 seats in the 71-member parliament, still several seats short of an outright majority. Most controversially, it was the transfer of preference votes from the Christian Democrats (VLV) that provided the margin of victory for the FLP in another five constituencies (shown in black towards the right of Figure 8.3). As we saw above, the VLV was a militant flank party opposed to Rabuka's compromises over the 1990 constitution. Its call for the declaration of Fiji as a 'Christian state' and for a ban on Sunday trading were clearly not 'moderate and conciliatory' policies aimed at courting support amongst the country's predominantly Hindu and Muslim Indian population.

Considerable potential exists for such curious alliances under the compulsory preferential voting system, particularly where it is anticipated that the government will be re-elected. Assuming that the primary objective of opposition parties is to secure political office, the logical decision may then be to place the governing coalition in last position on preference lists. The position of rival opposition parties, even at the extreme opposite end of the political spectrum, is initially negatively determined by this primary objective.

The most marginal seats won by the FLP, shown on the extreme right of Figure 8.3, were secured solely as a result of negative ranking. In some of the other constituencies where VLV preferences provided the margin of victory, the FLP was listed as the VLV's second preference (Bua/Macuata West) or third preference (Nausori/Naitasiri, Samabula/ Tamavua). But the last two constituencies which VLV party officials delivered to the FLP were areas where ethnic Fijians far outnumbered Indo-Fijians, and could not possibly have been won on the basis of Indo-Fijian first-count votes alone (Tailevu South/Lomaiviti and Lami). In these constituencies, the FLP was well down the VLV rankings. The FLP was listed as the VLV's fifth preference out of seven candidates in Tailevu South/Lomaiviti and in seventh place out of nine candidates in Lami), its position being determined solely by the decision to put the governing SVT/NFP coalition last. Victory in those two constituencies took the FLP over the absolute majority threshold.

Where the People's Coalition made inter-ethnic deals concerning the transfer of second or third preferences, these were not accompanied by any explicit conciliatory agreements on ethnically divisive political issues. The coalition, for example, had no clear policies on the highly sensitive issues of legislation covering the leasing of indigenous Fijian lands or the imminent expiry of leases on sugar cane lands. In Fiji, 86 per cent of land is under indigenous tenure and inalienable, although many of the more fertile of those native lands in western Viti Levu and northern Vanua Levu are leased to Indo-Fijian cane farmers. In 1976, the Agricultural Landlords and Tenants Act (ALTA) had provided for 20-year extensions to leases, thousands of which expired during 1999–2000, with Indo-Fijian farmers being evicted and ethnic Fijian villagers repossessing their ancestral lands. Whereas both of the major Indo-Fijian political parties called for the renewal of ALTA, ethnic Fijian nationalists and many landowners wanted ALTA scrapped, enabling landowners to charge higher rentals and give shorter leases or to repossess lands. Despite the FLP's electoral alliance with PANU, an indigenous Fijian landowners' party, no explicit agreement was forged on this highly controversial issue. Controversies about terms of leases and the eviction of Indian cane farmers proved enduring sources of friction during the People's Coalition's year in office.

Similarly, no political deals were made between the People's Coalition allies on the sensitive issue of 'positive discrimination' in favour of ethnic Fijians in civil service appointments or bank loans. Once in office, the Labour-led government took steps to remove some of these provisions, moves which unsurprisingly stirred up controversy in a country where many argue 'affirmative action' for Fijians is necessary to counter Indo-Fijian dominance in the business sector.

The most symbolically controversial issue was the ethnic background of the Prime Minister, given the 'reservation' of this position for an ethnic Fijian under the former 1990 constitution (it is difficult to identify any 'moderate and conciliatory' alliance that could be formed on this either/or issue). Mahendra Chaudhry's unexpected decision to take the position led to a revolt among the FLP's coalition allies immediately after the election. The feud was halted only after personal intervention by Fiji's President, Ratu Sir Kamisese Mara (Sharpham 2000: 292–3; Keith Reid 1999).

Far from proving politically robust, the People's Coalition began to unravel within days of the announcement of the election result. Pre-election vote transfers became politically irrelevant the moment the polling stations closed. In the wake of the election, all three of the coalition parties engaged in internal power struggles. While some of their leaders took up ministerial positions, backbenchers and grassroots supporters quickly joined the opposition. The general secretary of PANU, Apisai Tora, became the leader of the militant Taukei (indigenous peoples') movement. He headed a Taukei march through Suva on 19 May, the same day George Speight seized control of Fiji's Parliament. Many participants in that march became involved in the subsequent looting

243

and burning of Indian shops in Suva's business district, Toorak. The Fijian Association Party also split, with supporters and parliamentarians from eastern Viti Levu challenging the leadership of the Deputy Prime Minister, Adi Kuini Speed. Most of the FAP MPs joined the opposition during Chaudhry's year in office, including Ratu Timoci Silatolu, who subsequently became Speight's right-hand man. While VLV party leader Poseci Bune retained close links with the Chaudhry government, rank-and-file VLV members were prominent in opposition rallies during 1999 and early 2000, and party officials engaged in continuing discussions with the SVT aimed at forging a united Fijian opposition. Bune was held hostage alongside Chaudhry inside Parliament by Speight's henchmen, where, feeling betrayed, he 'witnessed members of my party coming into Parliament to pay homage to George Speight' (*Fiji Sun*, 20 April 2001).

Those marginal constituencies where the FLP had picked up crucial preference votes, transferred from the smaller Fijian parties, were also precisely the areas which quickly swung behind George Speight's overthrow of Chaudhry's government in May 2000. All nine of those constituencies shown on the right-hand side of Figure 8.3, where preference transfers from the FAP or VLV gave the FLP election victories, were hotbeds of support for the attempted coup. Speight's supporters were strongest in his home province of Tailevu and neighbouring Naita-siri, but also in Lami and the Suva–Nausori peri-urban corridor. Areas traditionally loyal to the ethnic Fijian chiefs from the tiny offshore island of Bau, such as the Lomaiviti Islands of the Koro Sea, also rallied to support Speight's siege inside Parliament, as did chiefs from long-marginalised areas of Vanua Levu, such as Bua and Macuata. Even Nadroga chief Ratu Osea Gavidi, whose interests in Fiji's pine plantations gave him a pecuniary connection with Speight, quickly appeared along-side the rebels inside Parliament.[15] Thus the protest vote which had dislodged Rabuka's administration was quickly turned against Chaudhry's People's Coalition government.

Speight's attempted takeover was eventually defeated, and steps were taken to return Fiji to some form of constitutional democracy. Senior military commanders held out against the hostage takers, eventually arresting and imprisoning Speight alongside other leaders of the putsch. The military nevertheless released a decree abrogating the 1997 constitution, consistently opposed the return to office of the Mahendra Chaudhry-led government, and instead installed an unelected interim administration led by former banker Laisenia Qarase in July 2000. On 1 March 2001, five of Fiji's High Court judges upheld the 1997 con-stitution as the 'supreme law of the Republic of the Fiji Islands', effectively ruling the Qarase-led interim administration to have no legal standing.[16] Having announced that it would accept the court's ruling, the Qarase regime moved forward its timetable for fresh elections. Ironically, the two institutions which could claim the lion's share of responsibility for the defeat of Fiji's May 2000 attempted coup – the military and the law courts – are both institutions entirely impervious to the 1997 constitution's 'electoral incentives for moderation and compromise'.

Multi-ethnic parties: electoral incentives and disincentives

Fiji's experiment in electoral engineering was the third significant effort at forging a multi-ethnic government. The first was the Alliance Party's strategy of creating a Malaysian-style front party, composed of separate Fijian, General and Indian wings. Yet the Alliance's Indian arm was always the weakest, and the emergence of the Fijian Nationalist Party further undermined the Alliance's multi-ethnic strategy. The second was the Fiji Labour Party's effort in the 1980s to cultivate a class-based organisation, with grassroots support in both the Indo-Fijian and indigenous Fijian communities. Yet even in 1987 the FLP obtained less than 10 per cent of ethnic Fijian support and the party's indigenous Fijian vote in the elections of the 1990s was tiny. The third effort was Fiji's 1995–6 Constitutional Review Commission, which attempted to institutionalise electoral incentives for inter-ethnic accommodation. Yet these did not have the intended impact on coalition formation, instead giving the new government an artificially strong mandate and emasculating the ethnic Fijian opposition.

Fiji's mid-1990s constitutional review was initially an exercise in élite conciliation, predicated on the failure of earlier efforts at constructing multi-ethnic alliances. During the run-up to that review, Rabuka – responding to domestic and international pressures to incorporate Indo-Fijians into the running of the administration – repeatedly called for a 'government of national unity'.[17] Similarly, the then Indo-Fijian opposition leader, Jai Ram Reddy, was primarily concerned about the permanent exclusion of Fiji's Indian politicians from political office. He argued in Parliament in 1992:

> Mr Speaker, Sir, you can have multi-racialism in two ways. You can have multi-racialism of the kind that my friend [Labour Party leader, Mahendra Chaudhry] talked about ... multi-racial parties. It occurred to me from

245

experience I gained over a period of 20 years in active politics, that that kind of multi-racialism is, maybe, a bit premature for Fiji, perhaps we are not ready for it. The communal pulls are extremely strong.... We are locked into a situation where we will continue to look into the indefinite future in terms of race.... There is another kind of multi-racialism.... Let us each be in our separate racial compartment.... Let communal solidarity prevail.... Let everyone be united, but from our respective positions of unity, let us accept that we must co-exist and work together.... It may be that that is a more realistic approach. (*Fiji Government* 1992: 730–1)

This perspective is very different to the CRC's proposed exercise in institutionally generated multi-ethnic coalition and party building. It is closer to Lijphart's proposed alternative, combining proportional representation of the different ethnic groups with élite power sharing. What would have been the likely outcome of the May 1999 polls under this, and other, alternative voting laws?

Speculation concerning the likely results of the May 1999 election under an alternative electoral system is fraught with difficulties. Had Fiji's 1999 election been organised under a first-past-the-post system, for example, different political constellations might have arisen. There would have been stronger incentives for smaller parties to stand aside in favour of larger parties with similar political platforms, but with a greater chance of victory. There would have been a greater disincentive to split the vote amongst like-minded parties. Under list system proportional representation, parties would pick up minority votes in areas where they would not otherwise field candidates. Using first-preference votes under the preferential voting system as an indication of likely voting patterns under other electoral systems may, therefore, be misleading. Despite such difficulties, however, it is worth examining the plausible election result had voting, party organisation and campaign strategies remained the same, while the electoral system changed.

The hypothetical data shown in Table 8.7 suggest that the SVT–NFP–UGP coalition would have lost the election under each of the best-known alternative electoral systems. However, the FLP alone would probably not have reached the 36+ seat absolute majority threshold had the election been conducted under list proportional representation (PR) or under a first-past-the-post system. Under list PR, the FLP would still have been likely to form a government, probably in coalition with some of the Fijian-backed parties, whose leverage over government policies would have been strengthened. More importantly, the parliamentary opposition would also have assumed a very different complexion. Rabuka's

*Table 8.7 Hypothetical election result
under alternative electoral systems*

	FLP	NFP	FAP	SVT	VLV	PANU	Others
Alternative vote	37	0	11	8	3	4	8
First past the post	34	0	6	18	2	4	7
List PR	24	11	8	14	7	3	4

Source: Elections Office, *Elections '99*.

SVT would have emerged in a stronger position, with 14 rather than eight seats. With its 32 per cent of the Indo-Fijian vote, Reddy's National Federation Party might plausibly have secured 11 seats in parliament. Given the pre-election complexion of Fiji politics, the result would have been a multi-ethnic opposition, one probably less disposed to use racial appeals as the stock in trade of opposition politics.[18]

Proportional representation is no panacea or alternative technique of 'electoral engineering'. It is plausible that such voting laws would simply 'reproduce ethnic cleavages in the legislature' or enhance the parliamentary power of small fringe parties (Lardeyret 1991: 35).[19] Yet the principal objection of the advocates of 'constitutional therapy' for divided societies is that PR is a 'feeble' or 'no-effect electoral system' (Sartori 1968: 272, 278), under which elections effectively become an 'ethnic census' with little scope for manipulation (Reilly and Reynolds 1999: 30). Along similar lines, Fiji's CRC argued,

The overall effect of proportional systems ... is that, if people vote communally, ethnic parties can expect to succeed in getting a number of candidates elected in proportion to the number of their community members in the constituency, and therefore in the country. This is irrespective of whether they are moderate and seek to reach accommodations with the ethnic parties of other communities. *If a party wishes to appeal to voters in other communities by putting up a multi-ethnic list, it has to calculate whether this will attract more voters from those other communities than the number it will lose from its own....* Any proportional system would, in our view, offer few incentives for parties to become more multi-ethnic in their composition or more willing to take account of the interests of all communities.... In terms of the extent to which it provides electoral incentives to moderation and compromise, we conclude that AV is greatly to be preferred to [proportional representation systems].... *For this reason alone we favour the adoption of AV.* (CRC 1996: 317; my emphasis)

247

What is attributed to PR here is, in fact, an inevitable problem for multi-ethnic parties in ethnically divided societies, under any democratic system. Under the first-past-the-post system, the Alliance Party's multi-ethnic claims were challenged by the emergence of the Fijian Nationalist Party in the 1970s. Rabuka and Reddy had to make a similar calculation in May 1999, but in the event lost more votes within their own ethnic communities than they gained from each other's supporters' preference transfers.[20] In fact, a small multi-ethnic political party, based on political commitment rather than institutional stimuli, would have greater chances under list system proportional representation than under the first-past-the-post or alternative vote systems.

Fiji's 1997 exercise in electoral engineering was an attempt to structure the voting system in favour of a hoped-for multi-ethnic party or coalition – through incentives for preference trading, by requiring voters to complete 75 per cent of the ballot paper and by allowing for a 'party ticket' option which gave party officials control over the distribution of preferences. Yet party preference transfers were not, to any significant degree, associated with political deals on ethnically divisive questions. More important motives included negative ranking of parties that posed the greatest electoral threat, elevation high up the rankings of no-hope candidates or independents who were likely to pose little political threat inside Parliament, personality-specific deals and efforts to make arrangements in the hope of securing ministerial office.[21] There are no neat 'electoral engineering' solutions to the politicisation of ethnic divisions in Fiji. The more modest goal is an electoral system that does not exacerbate divisions and permits the emergence of alternative political currents.

References

Ali, A. (1973) 'The Fiji General Election of 1972', *Journal of Pacific History*, 8: 171–80.

Ali, A. (1977) 'Fijian Chiefs and Constitutional Change, 1874–1937', *Journale de la Société des Oceanistes*, 33.

Alley, R. M. (1970) 'Independence for Fiji: Recent Constitutional and Political Developments', *Australian Outlook*, 24, 2.

Alley, R. M. (1973) 'The Development of Political Parties in Fiji', PhD thesis, Victoria University of Wellington.

British Parliamentary Papers (1964–5) 'Report of the Fiji Constitutional Conference', command 2783, vol. 12.

CRC (Constitutional Review Commission) (1996), *The Fiji Islands: Towards a United Future*, edited by P. Reeves, T. Vakatora and B. V. Lal, Suva: Parliamentary Paper 34.

Fiji Government (1988) *Electoral Act*, Act No. 18 of 1988; Suva: Fiji.

Fiji Government (1992) *Hansard Parliamentary Debates, House of Representatives*, Suva, Fiji, 24 July.

Fraenkel, J. (2000a) 'The Triumph of the Non-idealist Intellectuals? An Investigation of Fiji's 1999 Election Results', *Australian Journal of Politics and History*, 46, 1.

Fraenkel, J. (2000b) 'The Clash of Dynasties and the Rise of Demagogues: Fiji's *Tauri Vakaukauwa* of May 2000', *Journal of Pacific History*, 35, 2.

Fraenkel, J. (2001) 'The Alternative Vote System in Fiji: Electoral Engineering or Ballot-Rigging?', *Journal of Commonwealth and Comparative Studies*, 39, 2.

France, P. (1969) *The Charter of the Land; Custom and Colonisation in Fiji*, London, Wellington and New York: Oxford University Press.

Gillion, K. L. (1962) *Fiji's Indian Migrants: a History to the End of Indenture in 1920*, London, Wellington and New York: Oxford University Press.

Gillion, K. L. (1977) *The Fiji Indians: Challenge to European Dominance, 1920–46*, Canberra: Australian National University Press.

Horowitz, D. L. (1991) *A Democratic South Africa? Constitutional Engineering in a Divided Society*, Berkeley: University of California Press.

Horowitz, D. L. (1997) 'Encouraging Electoral Accommodation in Divided Societies', in B. V. Lal and P. Larmour (eds), *Electoral Systems in Divided Societies: the Fiji Constitutional Review*, Canberra: Australian National University Press.

International Crisis Group (1998) 'Changing the Logic of Bosnian Politics', ICG Report No. 32, 10 March.

International Crisis Group (1999) 'Breaking the Mould: Electoral Reform in Bosnia and Herzegovina', ICG Balkans Report No. 56, 4 March.

Keith Reid, R. (1999) 'Chaudhry: the Man in the Hot Seat', *Fiji Business Magazine*, June.

Lal, B. V. (1988a) 'Before the Storm: an Analysis of the Fiji General Election of 1987', *Pacific Studies*, 12, 1.

Lal, B. V. (1988b) *Power and Prejudice: the Making of the Fiji Crisis*, Wellington: Institute of International Affairs.

Lal, B. V. (1992) *Broken Waves: a History of the Fiji Islands in the Twentieth Century*, Honolulu: University of Hawaii Press.

Lal, B. V. (1998) *Another Way: the Politics of Constitutional Reform in Post-Coup Fiji*, Canberra: NCDS and Asia–Pacific Press.

Lal, B. V. (1999) 'A Time to Change – the Fiji General Elections of 1999', in B. V. Lal (ed.), *Fiji Before the Storm: Elections and the Politics of Development*, Canberra: Asia Pacific Press and Australian National University Press.

Lardeyret, G. (1991) 'The Problem with PR', *Journal of Democracy*, 2.

Lijphart, A. (1997) 'Disproportionality under Alternative Voting: the Crucial –

and Puzzling – Case of the Australian Senate Elections, 1919–1946', *Acta Politica*, 32, 1.

MacNaught, T. J. (1992) *The Fijan Colonial Experience: a Study of the Neotraditional Order under British Colonial Rule Prior to World War One*. Pacific Research Monograph Series, No 7, Canberra: Australian National University Press.

Norton, R. E. (1972) 'Politics, Race and Society in Fiji', PhD thesis, University of Sydney.

Norton, R. E. (1977) *Race and Politics in Fiji* (second edition, 1990), St Lucia: University of Queensland Press.

Norton, R. E. (2000) 'Understanding the Results of the 1999 Fiji Elections', in B. V. Lal (ed.), *Fiji Before the Storm: Elections and the Politics of Development*, Canberra: Asia-Pacific Press and Australian National University Press.

Premdas, R. (1980a) 'Elections in Fiji: Restoration of the Balance in September 1977', *Journal of Pacific History*, 14, 3–4.

Premdas, R. (1980b) 'Constitutional Challenge: the Rise of Fiji Nationalism', *Pacific Perspective*, 9, 2.

Rabuka, S. (1987) interview in *Islands Business*, September.

Rabuka, S. (1999) 'Address to the Nation'. Fiji TV, 18 May.

Reilly, B. (1997a) 'Constitutional Engineering and the Alternative Vote in Fiji: an Assessment', in B. V. Lal and P. Larmour (eds.), *Electoral Systems in Divided Societies: the Fiji Constitutional Review*, Canberra: Australian National University Press.

Reilly, B. (1997b) 'Preferential Voting and Political Engineering: a Comparative Study', *Journal of Commonwealth and Comparative Politics*, 35, 1.

Reilly, B. and A. Reynolds (1999) *Electoral Systems and Conflict in Divided Societies*, Washington DC: National Academy Press.

Sartori, G. (1968) 'Political Development and Political Engineering', *Public Policy*, 17.

Scarr, D. (1998) 'Constitutional Change in Fiji, 1997', *Journal of Pacific History* (Political Chronicles), 47.

Sharpham, J. (2000) *Rabuka of Fiji*, Rockhampton, Queensland: Central Queensland University Press.

Sisk, T. D. (1997) 'Power Sharing in Multi-ethnic Societies', in B. V. Lal and T. R. Vakatora (eds.), *Fiji and the World*, Research Papers of the Fiji Constitutional Review Commission, Suva, Fiji: University of the South Pacific, Vol. 2.

Street Commission (1975) *Report of the Royal Commission Appointed for the Purpose of Considering and Making Recommendations as to the Most Appropriate Method of Electing Members to, and Representing the People of Fiji in, the House of Representatives*, Parliament of Fiji, Parliamentary Paper No. 24.

Notes

1 Parties with 10 per cent or more of the seats in Parliament were to be offered Cabinet positions.

2 See, for example, the policies proposed for Bosnia by the International Crisis Group (International Crisis Group 1998; 1999).

3 In fact, most Indo-Fijians reside in the western and northern parts of the two main islands, whereas the outer islands are almost exclusively indigenous Fijian (or Rotuman).

4 For a detailed critique of the empirical applicability of the Horowitz model to the Fiji experience, see Fraenkel (2001).

5 'General' voters include part-Europeans, Chinese and, nowadays, other Pacific Islanders.

6 This was the percentage of the Indian communal vote secured, which can be reasonably assumed to have been carried over to the cross-voting constituencies (see Ali 1973: 174).

7 Koya's supporters (the 'Dove' faction) and opponents (the 'Flower' faction) stood on separate tickets.

8 These elections are, in this context, of less interest, because there were no open-franchise constituencies and the results were ethnically pre-determined by the distribution of reserved-franchise seats.

9 Two volumes of research papers were published, in addition to the 800-page final report. Yet only five pages of the latter were devoted to investigating the operation of the post-1970 electoral system (CRC 1996: 8–13).

10 See Patel's remarks cited in *Pacific Review*, 28 April 1965.

11 Indeed, contrary to what would be expected if multi-ethnic appeals brought considerable electoral rewards in the more heterogeneous cross-voting constituencies, the Alliance Party's share of the Indian vote was consistently *below* average in the areas of eastern Viti Levu, around the capital, Suva, where the more marginal cross-voting constituencies were located.

12 Fiji elections office estimate, personal communication.

13 Horowitz rejects 'approval voting' on the grounds that although it 'flushes out the second choices', it 'will not produce conciliatory results in divided societies' (Horowitz 1991: 195). 'Even if voters are not prepared easily to contemplate crossing ethnic lines, that is not an insurmountable problem, because second or third preferences could be made compulsory for a valid ballot' (*ibid.*: 190).

14 There is evidence that the NFP paid deposits for Fijian Nationalist Party candidates in the 1977 elections (Premdas 1980a: 195, 196n; Premdas 1980b: 41).

15 Regional support for Speight's putsch is discussed in greater detail in Fraenkel 2000b.

16 *Republic of Fiji vs Chandrika Prasad*, Civil Appeal No. ABU0078/2000S, Judgement, 1 March 2001.

17 See the various documents reproduced in Lal 1998.

18 The CRC seriously underestimated the dangers of creating a single-ethnicity Fijian opposition (CRC 1996: 285–6).

19 The CRC also opposed list system PR because it gave 'too much power to the party and not enough to individual voters' (CRC 1996: 307), a position hard to reconcile with the proposal to give political parties control over the distribution of votes, rather than merely the selection of candidates.

20 As was subsequently recognised by Professor Brij Lal of the CRC, 'Rabuka's

pursuit of moderate, conciliatory politics was always going to risk being outflanked by more extremist parties. Parties which court moderation in a multi-ethnic society tempt fate. Rabuka was accused of selling out Fijian interests, just as Reddy was accused of playing second fiddle to the Fijians' (Lal 1999: 40).

21 The latter is no minor issue in a country where a backbencher's salary is around $F18,000 per annum (around £6,000), while the lowest ministerial salary is over $F60,000 (around £20,000).

9

Building Democracy from the Outside
The Dayton Agreement in Bosnia and Herzegovina

MARCUS COX

The General Framework Agreement for Peace in Bosnia and Herze-govina (the Dayton Agreement) was one of the most comprehensive constitutional modelling exercises ever undertaken. Adopted under intense international pressure on the heels of three and a half years of bitter ethnic conflict, the agreement is a compendium of contemporary thinking on conflict resolution, in particular in its insistence on early elections under international auspices, extensive human rights provisions and the constitutional protection of the three ethnic communities.

This elaborate formula for a new democracy came into immediate conflict with the harsh realities of the post-war environment. The refusal of the wartime regimes to support the new constitutional order left it weak and unstable. Under the pressure of international supervision, Bosnia exhibited many of the forms of democracy but very little of the substance. Frustrated with the slow development of the state, the inter-national mission in Bosnia expanded its role dramatically, assuming the authority to overrule the new democratic organs in pursuit of its peace-building objectives. These protectorate-type powers have allowed for an extraordinary experiment in democratisation through external inter-vention. Although the process is still under way and cannot yet be finally evaluated, it has already generated a wealth of interesting lessons.

The origins of the Bosnian state

The relationship between nations and states on the Balkan peninsula has posed a problem of international order for centuries. For much of its history, domination by the Ottoman and Habsburg empires created a framework in which the region's ethnic diversity could be accommo-dated (Jelavich 1983: 135–6). As the imperial structures collapsed, they were replaced by national self-determination movements which, in territories inhabited for centuries by mixed populations, proved irreconcilable. The resulting fragmentation of the region into hostile nation states with intractable ethnic minority problems led to the coining of the term 'Balkanisation'.

Created in the closing months of the First World War, the first Yugoslavia was the only multinational structure to emerge from the collapse of the imperial order in South-eastern Europe. It was the product of an agreement among existing nations which, though closely related culturally and linguistically, had evolved in very different historical contexts. Serbia's national identity was defined by its long struggle against Turkish occupation, from which it won its independence gradually during the nineteenth century, but within borders which excluded many ethnic Serbs. Croats and Slovenes, by contrast, had been Habsburg subjects, developing national movements only with the collapse of Austria–Hungary. In the instability which followed the war, the creation of Yugoslavia was driven by a common strategic interest in fending off the territorial ambitions of powerful neighbours. Yugoslavia was therefore an aggregate of separate nationalisms, rather than a national project in its own right. In addition to its founding nations, Serbs, Croats and Slovenes, it incorporated various minorities which would, over time, develop their own national identities, including the Slavic Muslims of Bosnia and Herzegovina (Bosniacs), Albanians in Kosovo and Macedonia, Slavic Macedonians and Montenegrins.

Over the course of its seventy-year history, the Yugoslav state displayed a remarkable willingness to experiment with different constitutional structures to accommodate its ethnic diversity. Under communism, the state was structured as a complex federation in which the republics and the ethnic nations were both considered to be component units. While any manifestation of nationalism as a form of political opposition was suppressed, the nations (*narodi*) and nationalities (*narodnosti*)[1] were granted rights to cultural identity and political participation which were considerably more extensive than international standards of the time. The state implemented various policies to prevent domination by any one group, such as an 'ethnic key' by which managerial posts in the bureaucracy and public economy were rotated among the ethnic groups. However, in the absence of any genuine democratisation, demands for national autonomy gave rise to increasing decentralisation to republican level, ultimately creating what Lampe has called 'a confederation of one-party regimes' (Lampe 2000: 22).

With the end of the Cold War in 1989, the Yugoslav federation sank rapidly into constitutional paralysis and state collapse. At one level, its problems were structural, a function of flaws in the political economy and constitutional design of the state. The League of Communists, formerly the backbone of the constitutional order, began to fragment following the death of Tito in 1980 and collapsed with the walk-out of the Slovenian delegation from the party congress in January 1990. Without a unified party at the central level, the excessive decentralisation of the federation prevented it from responding effectively to a series of economic crises, and the country descended into a spiral of indebtedness, unemployment and hyperinflation. As living standards fell dramatically, the republics fought for their share of diminishing public resources in a struggle that became increasingly nationalist in tone. In a process that Hayden (1999) has dubbed 'constitutional nationalism', the republics, led by Slovenia, progressively loosened their institutional ties to the federation and redefined themselves as the nation states of their dominant ethnic groups.

These structural weaknesses created the opportunity for regional élites facing a crisis of legitimation to convert popular disaffection with Yugoslav communism into a xenophobic brand of populist nationalism. From his position as President of the Serbian republic, Slobodan Milosevic used mass demonstrations to try to force the re-centralisation of the state under his own control, encountering fierce resistance from the western republics and destroying what remained of the federal balance. As the constitutional order began to unravel, he shifted strategy, fomenting localised conflicts in order to carve out a Greater Serbia from areas of Croatia and Bosnia–Herzegovina. In Croatia, after the first democratic elections in 1990, the new government of Franjo Tudjman resurrected nationalist imagery from Croatia's short-lived fascist regime of the Second World War period, pushing Croatian Serbs towards open rebellion. After an opening skirmish in Slovenia in June 1991, war spread to Croatia in August 1991 and to Bosnia–Herzegovina in April 1992. In what would become a familiar pattern, attacks by Serb irregulars with the support of the federal army were directed overwhelmingly against the civilian population, using ethnic cleansing in support of territorial claims.

These were the inauspicious circumstances in which the state of Bosnia and Herzegovina first came into existence. Republican elections in November 1990 had led to a power-sharing arrangement between three nationalist parties – the Bosniac SDA (Party of Democratic Action), the Bosnian Croat HDZ (Croatian Democratic Union) and the Bosnian Serb SDS (Serbian Democratic Party). Donia has described an informal agreement among the three parties to share executive positions among themselves on a rotating basis, which operated as a form of 'crypto-constitution' (Donia 2000). This arrangement proved to be the first step in carving the republic into separate institutional spheres. Within a year of the election, following declarations of independence by Slovenia and Croatia, Bosnian Serbs established a series of Serbian enclaves and a separate Parliament, declaring their intention to secede from Bosnia if it became an independent state. By November 1991, Bosnian Croats had declared autonomous regions of their own, insisting that they would cooperate with the Bosnian state only if it became independent of Yugoslavia. Behind the scenes, Milosevic and Tudjman secretly plotted the division of Bosnia–Herzegovina between a Greater Serbia and a Greater Croatia (Silber and Little 1996: 144). Against this background, a clumsy recognition policy on the part of the European Union pushed the rump Bosnian government into holding a referendum on independence in February 1992, which was boycotted by Bosnian Serbs. International recognition of Bosnian statehood followed on 6 April, corresponding almost to the day with its descent into war.

Over three and a half years, the Bosnian war would produce 230,000 casualties and displace 2.3 million people, shattering communities and destroying centuries-old traditions of komšiluk, or 'neighbourliness', among the ethnic groups. The sorry tale of international involvement in the war centred on a long succession of failed peace plans and mediation initiatives.[2] The one principle which the international community consistently defended was the preservation of the international personality of the new state. On internal matters, however, its approach was entirely pragmatic. All of the peace plans proposed to divide the state into ethnically defined territorial units within a weak federal structure. The first map produced by European Union mediator Jose Cutileiro in February 1992 proposed the division of the territory according to which ethnic group had an absolute or relative majority in each municipality, creating a mosaic of non-contiguous ethnic zones. Later maps were based upon the frontlines emerging during the conflict. With the international community restricting itself to the role of neutral mediator, the negotiations themselves created perverse incentives for the warring parties to continue fighting, as any side which captured more territory on the battlefield would strengthen its position at the negotiating table. All three parties negotiated in bad faith, signing off–on ceasefires and settlements they had no intention of respecting in order to achieve short-term, tactical advantages. One Bosnian observer commented at the time: 'The maps of a divided Bosnia–Herzegovina passed around at international conferences have become more of a continuing *cause* for the tragedy that has befallen us than a *solution*' (Kurspahic 1993: 16).

As the horrors of the Bosnian war were exposed in Western media, the international community became drawn further into the crisis, moving up the scale of involvement from the arms embargo, through a range of sanctions measures against Serbia, to international peacekeeping and the first-ever deployment of NATO forces in active combat. A lightly armed UN Protection Force (UNPROFOR) was authorised to protect the delivery of humanitarian aid, and did manage to ensure an average of 750 tons of relief per day (UN Secretary-General 1999: para. 22). However, this purely palliative approach served first as an alternative to serious political engagement, and later as a barrier to effective action. International policy in Bosnia ended in humiliation for the UN when its troops were taken hostage by the Bosnian Serb army, and in tragedy after the fall of Srebrenica and other UN 'safe areas'. In an official report, the UN has acknowledged a degree of culpability for the ensuing massacre:

> The United Nations experience in Bosnia was one of the most difficult and painful in our history.... Through error, misjudgement and an inability to recognise the scope of the evil confronting us, we failed to do our part to help save the people of Srebrenica from the Serb campaign of mass murder.... When the international community makes a solemn promise to safeguard and protect innocent civilians from massacre, then it must be willing to back its promise with the necessary means. Otherwise, it is surely better not to raise hopes and expectation in the first place, and not to impede whatever capability they may be able to muster in their own defence. (*Ibid.*: paras 503–4)

NATO responded by withdrawing the most exposed UNPROFOR troops and conducting prolonged air strikes against Bosnian Serb targets, tipping the military balance in favour of the Muslim–Croat alliance. At the same time, the Croatian army's 'Operation Storm' in August 1995 overran the UN-protected Serb Krajina in Croatia, driving some 300,000 Serb civilians across the border into Bosnia and Serbia. The subsequent joint offensive by the Croatian and Bosnian armies in north-western Bosnia significantly reduced the area under Bosnian Serb control, convincing them that the time for a negotiated settlement had arrived.

The agreement made in Dayton, Ohio in November 1995 was the outcome of a *tour de force* of international diplomacy. US special envoy Richard Holbrooke skilfully exploited divisions between the Bosnian Serbs and the Milosevic regime in Belgrade in order to achieve an agreement.[3] However, at the most basic level, the agreement was made possible because the conflict itself, with the assistance of NATO intervention, had brought about the separation of population and division of territory demanded by the warring parties.

The Dayton Agreement: blueprint for a new democracy

The Dayton Agreement laid out a new democratic blueprint for Bosnia and Herzegovina, complete with elaborate constitutional structures, electoral provisions and human rights guarantees. Rarely can a democratic constitution have been produced in such undemocratic circumstances. Just to gather the warring parties around the table required a combination of NATO air strikes, harsh economic sanctions and the full repertoire of diplomatic threats and promises. Once in Dayton, the parties were confined in close quarters for 22 days while US and European negotiators pressed them with complex drafts on military, territorial and constitutional matters. Bosnia's two neighbours, Serbia and Croatia, whose territorial ambitions had fuelled the Bosnian conflict, were intimately involved in the proceedings, often at the expense of the Bosnian delegations themselves. Although none of the participants had a mandate from their respective parliaments or the Bosnian public to conclude a new constitution, European Union negotiator Carl Bildt comments: 'No one thought it wise to submit the constitution to any sort of parliamentary or other similar proceeding' (Bildt 1998: 139), and it entered into force as part of the peace treaty. The document was drafted in English and, six years later, there is still no official version available in the national languages.

The Dayton Agreement secured the consent of the parties to the existence of a Bosnian state – the element that had been missing at the time of its international recognition in 1992. However, unwilling to engage in any genuine constitutional dialogue with each other, the parties were effectively negotiating with the international community to preserve the maximum degree of autonomy possible within the confines of a single state. The resulting peace agreement bore the marks of this extraordinary process, with numerous contradictions and deliberate ambiguities papering over the lack of agreement on basic principles. It is a curious hybrid document, being at the same time an international treaty and a domestic constitution. It consists of a brief covering agreement between Bosnia–Herzegovina, Croatia and Serbia, in which the latter two acknowledge Bosnian sovereignty and agree to use their influence on elements within Bosnia in support of the peace agreement.

This is followed by twelve detailed annexes covering numerous aspects of the peace process. Integral to the peace agreement was the consent of the parties to a multinational 'peace implementation' force of 60,000 troops, together with a whole array of civilian organisations. In the absence of any real domestic consensus, this international mission became the primary constituency of the new state.

The Dayton settlement was essentially an agreement on internal partition along ethnic lines. Eighteen months before Dayton, an agreement had been achieved on a Bosniac–Croat alliance, called the Federation of Bosnia and Herzegovina, although this had yet to be implemented. There had also been agreement on principle that the division of territory would be 51 per cent to the Federation and 49 per cent to Republika Srpska. At Dayton, the parties adjusted the final military frontlines to match this formula. On behalf of the Bosnian Serbs, Milosevic ceded control of the Sarajevo suburbs and a secure corridor to Gorazde, the last remaining eastern enclave.[4] To make up the balance, the Serbs were awarded an anvil-shaped piece of strategically insignificant territory in north-western Bosnia. The resulting Inter-Entity Boundary Line (IEBL) bore no relation to historical, economic or administrative regions, cutting 48 of 109 municipalities into two or more segments. With 55 per cent of the population driven from their homes, the country was almost entirely ethnically divided, and the transfers of territory agreed at Dayton resulted in the displacement of a further 100,000 people. In previous peace initiatives, the United States had vehemently rejected any proposal which appeared to ratify the results of ethnic cleansing. In 1995, it was partly American acquiescence on this point that made a settlement possible.

Internal division was also the basis of the security arrangements concluded at Dayton. Instead of a common Bosnian army, the Agreement provides for two Entity armies, which operate in practice as three separate forces. These were required to withdraw to their respective territories, and a demilitarised Zone of Separation was created, extending for two kilometres on either side of the IEBL and heavily patrolled by international forces. According to tight timetables, heavy weapons were to be withdrawn to internationally controlled cantonment sites, the armies returned to barracks and demobilised to peacetime levels, armed civilian groups were to be disbanded and foreign forces were to be withdrawn from Bosnian territory. Over the longer term, the parties agreed to a balance of forces across the former Yugoslavia, with an armaments ratio of 5:2:2 between the Federal Republic of Yugoslavia, Croatia and Bosnia, based loosely upon population levels. The Bosnian share was allocated between the Federation and Republika Srpska according to a ratio of 2:1. Given the higher starting point of the Bosnian Serb army in terms of weaponry, this left considerable scope for the federation army to build up to this level.

Integral to the settlement, although not mentioned in the agreement, was the US-led 'Train and Equip' programme, designed to strengthen the Federation forces. The US committed itself to providing US$100 million in training and equipment, to be provided by a private contractor, and a further US$300 million was offered by Turkey, Saudi Arabia and Kuwait. Train and Equip was one of the most controversial aspects of US policy in Bosnia. Many observers saw as distinctly ominous the combination of an arms build-up and a territorial settlement with which all sides were to some extent dissatisfied. As a strategy, the creation of a balance of power between three separate armies seems more suited to peacekeeping between states than to the creation of a common state. In such circumstances, there was a justified fear that the security guarantee provided by the international military presence would serve to enforce partition. As it transpired, for several years after the Dayton Agreement, it was still possible to describe every inch of Bosnian territory as 'belonging' to one of the three parties.

As the price of securing a common state, the Dayton Agreement created an extremely loose federal structural with a minimum of central authority. While it preserved the continuity of the wartime state, some of its symbolism tended in the other direction. The name 'Republika Srpska', under which the military campaign to destroy the state had been carried out, was preserved, while at the same time the title 'Republic' was dropped from the name of the state. The implication was that the continuity of the Bosnian Serb entity was preserved, while that of the state itself was somehow impaired. Holbrooke lists this as a key weakness of the Dayton settlement: 'to permit Karadzic to preserve the name he had invented was more of a concession than we then realised' (Holbrooke 1998: 159).

The new constitutional structure is extremely complex. At the time the Bosniac–Croat Federation was formed, it was anticipated that the Bosnian Serb territories would eventually join. By the time of Dayton, however, the concept had changed and the Bosniac–Croat Federation of ten cantons became a unit of a new federal structure at state level. This two-tiered federal system has four levels of government in one half of the country (state, entity, canton and municipal) and three in the other (Republika Srpska has no cantons), making for an excess of administrative layers in a country of less than 3.5 million people. The new structure is almost entirely novel. Only the municipalities had an institutional history stretching back before the war. All other layers of government had to be created from scratch. Although the Republic of Bosnia and Herzegovina had enjoyed a high degree of autonomy within the old Yugoslav federation, very few of its institutions were incorporated into the new state. By creating a constitutional structure which was both complex and novel, the Dayton Agreement presented an institution-building challenge on a daunting scale.

The Bosnian state is extremely decentralised. The central government has a minimum of functions, conducting foreign affairs and trade, setting customs and monetary policy, and regulating inter-entity communications, transport and crime. The state has no revenue collection powers[5] and is dependent on transfers from the entities. Its few executive functions are presided over by a 'Council of Ministers', rather than a government. So limited is the state's internal authority that, for the first five years of the peace process, it could be ignored by the entities without political or financial cost.

However, the constitution does provide various hooks on which a more workable federal arrangement could develop. It guarantees the free movement of persons, goods, services and capital throughout the state, being the legal basis for the European single market, which could be achieved only through a degree of central regulation. The foreign affairs power has been used to justify a cautious expansion in the state's role, such as taking responsibility for telecommunications and broadcasting, including media standards. In the European context, where states contemplating accession to the Union may take on international commitments to 'approximate' their laws to the European *acquis communautaire*, the foreign affairs power may prove extremely important. Given the potential for expansive constitutional interpretation, the Constitutional Court itself is a key institution. It was created with six national and three international judges, so that any one ethnic group with the support of the foreign members could form a majority in favour of strengthening the state.

The role of ethnicity in the constitution is the most controversial aspect of the peace settlement. The preamble reads: 'Bosniacs, Croats, and Serbs, as constituent peoples (along with Others), and citizens of Bosnia and Herzegovina hereby determine that the Constitution of Bosnia and Herzegovina is as follows'. The implication is that constitutional authority rests on a dual basis of popular sovereignty: the ethnic nations and the civic citizenry. As demanded by all three parties at Dayton, ethnicity is treated as a fixed category and institutionalised as the principal basis of representation. While the Bosniacs are reported to have argued for proportional representation of the ethnic groups, the Croats, as the smallest group, insisted on the political equality of all three peoples, irrespective of population (Burg and Shoup 1999: 361). The concept of 'constituent peoples', which is undefined in the constitution, was later interpreted by the Constitutional Court as 'a principle of collective equality' that 'prohibits any special privilege for one or two of these peoples, any domination in government structures or any ethnic homogenisation through segregation based on territorial separation' (Constitutional Court of Bosnia and Herzegovina 2000: para. 60). The Dayton constitution therefore continues the post-Yugoslav tendency towards 'constitutional nationalism', whereby the state is given an explicit ethnic identity, but avoids ranking the ethnic groups into majority and minority, as found in Croatia or in Macedonia prior to the Ohrid Agreement. However, when combined with internal partition of the territory, this formula simply served to replicate the majority/minority dichotomy at local level.

The three constituent peoples are guaranteed representation across all branches of government. In the upper chamber of the state Parliament (the House of Peoples), the constitution states explicitly that there must be five Croat and Bosniac representatives from the Federation and five Serbs from Republika Srpska. There is a collective presidency of three members, consisting of a Bosniac and Croat directly elected from the Federation and a Serb from Republika Srpska. Ministerial posts and the speakers of the parliaments are divided among the ethnic groups on a rotating basis. These provisions give rise to a number of problems. Reserving representation to particular ethnic groups in specified parts of the country assumes that the population is separated physically along ethnic lines. Non-Serbs resident in Republika Srpska may not be elected to the House of Peoples or the presidency, and nor may Serbs or 'others' resident in the Federation. Partition is therefore written into the structure of representation and the greater the degree of reintegration over time, the more these provisions will operate in a discriminatory fashion. A second problem is that there is no legal definition of the ethnic groups, and no objective criteria could ever be developed to distinguish among them. Electoral laws therefore allow candidates for public office to identity themselves as belonging to a particular ethnic group, and voters may choose in which ethnic list to cast their votes. This is workable only so long as the major political parties are mono-ethnic in nature. Once non-ethnic parties and multi-ethnic coalitions begin to emerge, they are able to pick and choose under which ethnic list to field candidates for different positions, causing the system to become incoherent.

The constituent peoples are further protected through special majorities and rights of veto. Bildt describes the drafters' dilemma at Dayton as follows:

> On the one hand, there was an evident need for a means to prevent decisions taken by a simple majority which conflicted with what one of the ethnic groups perceived to be its vital interests. The country would soon fall apart if there were no such safety device. On the other hand, there was a clear risk that such a device might be abused to block less crucial decisions. There would then be a risk that no decision would be taken at all, and the country would fall apart for that reason. (Bildt 1998: 138)

In the end, the settlement erred in favour of protecting the constituent peoples, tolerating the risk of deadlock. Majority decisions in both houses of Parliament must include at least one third of the representatives from each entity. In addition, a majority of representatives from any one constituent people may veto a proposed decision as destructive of its 'vital interests'. Vital interests are not defined in the constitution, and the provision has been invoked as much for procedural matters as for substantive legislation. Vetoes also apply in the presidency and at Federation level.

Each ethnic group is therefore assured of being able to prevent the state from infringing its autonomy. Superficially, this is reminiscent of the 'consociational democracy' model outlined by Lijphardt (1971), who suggests that proportional representation, rights of veto and regional autonomy are key elements of stable government in divided societies. However, a central feature of the consociational model is missing from the Dayton settlement. Because the state's authority is so limited and its institutions are so easily deadlocked, there is no incentive for the political élites of the three ethnic groups to cooperate in the exercise of power. They are more likely to collude in a power-sharing arrangement in which the state is carved up into separate public spheres, than to participate in a 'grand coalition' at federal level. The Dayton Agreement is therefore strong on protecting the three ethnic groups, but weak on creating the political and institutional ties to bind them together.

It is often observed that the Dayton constitution was drafted by foreigners and imposed on the parties by force of arms. The paradox of Dayton, however, is that it is at the same time firmly rooted in the constitutional tradition of the former Yugoslavia, with all its shortcomings. Its most notable features – excessive decentralisation, a proliferation of weak institutions, complex decision-making procedures prone to deadlock, a lack of workable systems of fiscal federalism and intergovernmental relations, incentives for local politicians to play ethnic politics – are all familiar from the final years of constitutional breakdown in socialist Yugoslavia.

The Dayton Agreement provided that elections would be conducted by the Organisation for Security and Cooperation in Europe (OSCE), no later than nine months after the peace settlement. The parties undertook to ensure 'a politically neutral environment' and freedom of movement, association and expression, and requested OSCE to certify that the requisite 'social conditions' existed for effective elections. Not surprisingly, none of these conditions were satisfied within the deadline, but the international mission nonetheless pressed ahead with elections, for a number of reasons. Convening new public institutions, from the state presidency to municipal councils, had to begin with the election of the first office bearers. On the American side, the haste was driven by the public commitment that US troops would remain in Bosnia no more than a year. There was also an unrealistic assumption in some quarters that elections would automatically alleviate ethnic tension by allowing the Bosnian people to vote against the protagonists of the war. The decision to proceed with elections in the immediate post-war environment was highly controversial, leading to widespread voter intimidation and ethnic engineering through electoral fraud (Bildt 1998: 262).

In its formal provisions the Bosnian constitution is perhaps the most human-rights-friendly of any country in the world. During the Bosnian war, international negotiators had tried to alleviate the ethnic partition aspects of successive settlement proposals by writing in the highest possible human rights standards (Szasz 1995). The Dayton Agreement adopted all of these proposals, incorporating the European Convention on Human Rights directly into the Bosnian legal system with priority over all other law,[6] obliging the state to become party to a further 15 human rights instruments, and guaranteeing additional individual rights in the constitution itself. All public bodies are required to cooperate with international monitoring mechanisms. The Agreement also establishes a network of human rights institutions under international control, including an Ombudsman modelled on the former Human Rights Commission in Strasbourg and a Human Rights Chamber which acts as a formal judicial body, exercising jurisdiction over violations committed by the state or the entities after the peace settlement.

These extensive human rights provisions are the most obviously foreign element of the Dayton Agreement, adopted without significant input from the parties. In the immediate aftermath of the conflict, while the new institutions were being established, ethnic cleansing continued through a combination of violence, intimidation and overt discrimination by local authorities. Domestic courts and public institutions were often implicated in ethnic cleansing or, where they dared act independently of the political structures, were powerless to prevent it. Some observers have noted the contradiction between the extensive protection of individual rights and the constitutional entrenchment of territorially based group rights (Ni Aolain 1998; Pajic 1998). The division of the country into ethnically defined para-states tended to reduce minorities at the local level to less than full citizenship. Whatever the constitution might provide, it would be several years before public institutions could be observed applying the law in favour of minorities.

The Dayton Agreement prohibits any person indicted by the International Criminal Tribunal for Yugoslavia (ICTY) from holding any form of public office. The parties also agree to cooperate with the Tribunal in the gathering of evidence and the execution of arrest warrants. These provisions helped the international mission in its campaign to oust Radovan Karadzic from the presidency of Republika Srpska in 1996, although delays in issuing indictments enabled other individuals now on trial in the Hague to remain in high political office for several years after Dayton. In practice, however, the exclusion of war criminals from the new institutions was severely undermined by the refusal of the international forces to arrest indictees. Concerned about 'mission creep', the Implementation Force (IFOR) accepted the authority but not the obligation to carry out arrests, and on numerous occasions allowed Karadzic and other indictees to pass through its checkpoints, or else took obvious pains to avoid crossing paths with them. Lack of international commitment on this issue undermined the credibility of the ICTY process and there was little or no cooperation from the parties. Later, however, when international forces began to carry out arrests, it had a significant impact on local political development, helping to overcome the climate of impunity in which nationalist leaders operated.

One of the most important elements of the Dayton settlement was an annex guaranteeing the rights of refugees and internally displaced persons to return to their homes. The parties agreed to repeal discriminatory legislation, suppress acts of retribution, protect minority populations and punish individuals responsible for serious violations of human rights. A commission was established to process return claims, with binding authority to determine residential property rights, including reversing transactions made under duress during the war. These strong provisions on the right to return are difficult to reconcile with the basic territorial

265

structure of the Dayton settlement. Prior to the war, the area which is now Republika Srpska had only a slight majority of 53 per cent Serbs (Cox 1998: 611). By the time of Dayton, the distribution of population had become so firmly linked with military control of territory that no one expected a highly autonomous Republika Srpska to tolerate the return of more than 600,000 Bosniacs and Croats. Indeed, the agreement itself was ambiguous, referring to the right of individuals to repossess their homes or receive 'just compensation in lieu of return'. Burg and Shoup note that the reference to compensation was 'diplomatic code for acknowledgement that many refugees or displaced persons were not likely to return' (Burg and Shoup 1999: 358). Since Dayton, Bosnian Serb and Croat authorities have consistently opposed the return of minority populations to territory under their control, while encouraging their own populations to remain in majority areas.

The essential elements of the Dayton settlement can therefore be summarised as follows:

- internal partition of Bosnian territory;

- separation of the three armies by an overwhelming international force and the creation of an internal balance of forces;

- the creation of a loose federal structure, allowing the parties maximum regional autonomy but incorporating elements on which a more effective state could develop;

- formal political equality of the three constituent peoples, backed by guaranteed representation, special majorities and rights of veto;

- elections organised by the international mission as early as possible;

- the exclusion of persons indicted for war crimes from public office;

- proclamation of the highest possible international human rights standards, to be applied by institutions under international control;

- progressive ethnic reintegration through the return of refugees and displaced persons.

As a diplomatic compromise, the Agreement allowed all sides to claim a degree of victory, however contradictory their objectives. However, its many conflicts of principle made it a poor foundation for a new constitutional order. Aware of the fragile nature of the settlement, the Dayton drafters incorporated a comprehensive international peace-implementation mission that would wield considerable authority within the new order.

A force of 60,000 troops (IFOR, later renamed Stabilisation Force or SFOR) was dispatched, with extraordinary powers over local military forces. An international High Representative was appointed, initially with a limited coordinating role but later granted direct legislative powers. The OSCE controlled the electoral process, issuing electoral rules governing matters such as voter registration, the eligibility of candidates and media standards. The United Nations established an International Police Task Force of some 2,000 police monitors deployed across the country, and conducted a comprehensive screening programme to rid the local police forces of war criminals. The United Nations High Commissioner for Refugees (UNHCR) was the lead agency in humanitarian affairs. A network of human rights agencies engaged in monitoring and advocacy, including OSCE, the UN High Commissioner for Human Rights (UNHCHR) and the Council of Europe. The European Commission and the World Bank jointly developed a Priority Reconstruction Programme valued at US$5.1 billion, implemented through a large array of bilateral and non-governmental organisations. By 1998, the database of the International Council of Voluntary Agencies listed as active in Bosnia a total of 18 UN agencies, 18 other international organisations, 49 bilateral missions and 201 foreign non-governmental agencies (ICVA 1998).

Democratisation under international protection

For the first few years after the Dayton Agreement, Bosnia exhibited many of the forms of a democracy but very little of the substance. Despite the elaborate constitutional machinery and a succession of elections under close international control, the country remained trapped in a vicious circle of uncivil politics.

The immediate problem was one of parallel constitutional systems: the new order agreed at Dayton and the remains of the wartime para-states. After three and a half years of conflict, there were few remaining legal or governmental structures spanning the three communities. The Republic of Bosnia and Herzegovina, recognised internationally as the state but representing primarily the Bosniac community, the Bosnian Croat entity of Herzeg–Bosna and the Republika Srpska had become functionally separate states, each with its own political structures, legislature, judicial system, police force, revenue collection and rudimentary public administration. Each used separate passports and identity documents. Companies and public utilities were split into three, creating separate economic spaces. In the case of Herzeg–Bosna and Republika

Srpska, subsidies from neighbouring Croatia and Serbia helped sustain the parallel structures.

Carl Bildt, the first High Representative, has described the three structures as 'warrior states, set up to finance the war and support the armies' (Bildt 1998: 249). They perpetuated the political culture of socialist Yugoslavia, operating as party states. The nationalist parties created their own *nomenklatura*, controlling appointments and privileges across all positions of influence, including in the legislature and judiciary. They controlled the management boards of public companies and exercised a monopoly over financial transfers, enabling them to mix public and party finances. In addition, the wartime imperative of breaking the sanctions regime, raising hard currency and obtaining arms led to the development of complex links between the state and organised crime, which proved difficult to dismantle at the end of the war. In eastern Republika Srpska, for example, a small circle of political leaders close to Radovan Karadzic exercised a monopoly on the smuggling of fuel and other goods, providing the revenue to maintain special police units which were used as a private security service. A raid by SFOR on Bosnian Croat intelligence services in October 1999 found evidence that they were raising revenue through pornography and credit-card fraud (International Crisis Group 2000).

In the face of opposition from these informal power structures, the new constitutional order agreed at Dayton remained largely a paper creation. The three regimes were unwilling to dismantle their parallel systems and transfer authority to new institutions under democratic control. They were able to obstruct the implementation of the new constitution simply by refusing to participate in its institutions. The state Parliament and Council of Ministers were frequently deadlocked by disputes over formal matters such as agendas, the location of meetings or the use of nationalist symbols, and their output in the first three years of the peace process was minimal. Although the three regimes remained hostile at certain levels, they often appeared to collude in frustrating the state-building process.[7]

In order to justify maintaining repressive structures developed during the war, the nationalist parties had an incentive to foster inter-ethnic fear and hostility. They used their control of the media to manipulate public opinion against the peace process. For the most part, the population was war-weary and difficult to mobilise. Incidents of inter-ethnic violence were less common than might have been expected, given the history of the conflict, and on investigation rarely proved to have been spontaneous in nature. However, more than a million people were living in displacement, mostly occupying housing belonging to others. Their insecurity made them a natural constituency for nationalist leaders. Outbursts of extremist rhetoric in the local media were rarely indicative of genuine popular sentiment, but rather evidence that nationalist leaders were trying to mobilise this constituency in order to suppress political opposition.

Against this background, early rounds of elections organised under international auspices produced little change in the political environment. There were no serious electoral challengers to the nationalist parties. Two years after the Dayton Agreement, of 158 elected administrations across the country, only the municipality of Tuzla could claim any significant degree of cross-ethnic support. The weak legal and institutional environment allowed political parties to reward their supporters – for instance through the distribution of humanitarian aid, scarce housing stocks or veterans' and war invalids' benefits – while intimidating political opponents. In addition, the climate of fear and insecurity between the ethnic groups encouraged block voting, which worked in favour of the incumbent parties. Wherever elections did produce results which challenged the existing power structures, they tended to weaken the elected institutions themselves. For example, the Dayton Agreement permitted refugees and displaced persons to register to vote in their place of origin. In municipal elections in 1997, parties representing displaced persons won control of six municipalities under the military control of another ethnic group, as well as substantial representation in 42 others. The OSCE developed electoral rules requiring a fair distribution of executive posts among the parties represented in the municipal assembly, and conducted extensive monitoring to ensure that these rules were implemented. However, where minority parties attempted to exercise their voting rights or executive authority against the interests of the majority élite, the usual outcome was that the municipal institutions themselves became marginalised, while the real mechanisms of power remained concealed.

Thus, elections in the immediate post-war environment tended to replicate the existing power structures. The international mission found itself in the paradoxical position of implementing a far-reaching democratisation process in cooperation with leaders fundamentally opposed to the Bosnian state, yet who were strengthened and legitimised by their new electoral mandates and constitutional authority. By the third year after Dayton, frustration with the slow pace of the state-building process led to a dramatic revision of the international role in Bosnia, which arrogated to itself the power to overrule the flawed democratic process.

SFOR began to adopt a more aggressive posture, and the position of the High Representative was strengthened by the delegation of direct authority within the constitutional sphere, in particular the power to impose laws and dismiss public officials, including elected leaders.[8] Unlike the formal protectorates established in Kosovo and East Timor, where governing authority was vested in the international mission itself, the High Representative in Bosnia acted in parallel to the domestic authorities, intervening in the legislative process as he saw fit in order to advance particular international goals. The scope of the international mission broadened from implementing the Dayton Agreement to pursuing an open-ended reform agenda, including privatisation and economic transition, legal system reform, restructuring the media, creating new central institutions and other initiatives. By mid-2001, the High Representative had imposed over 150 laws and dismissed 75 public officials, making himself a central pillar of Bosnia's real constitution.

By giving itself the capacity to bypass the domestic constitutional process, the international mission was able to act directly against what it saw as fundamental obstacles to peace building and democratisation. The main elements of this campaign can be summarised as follows. First, there were a series of operations to disrupt the wartime power structures. In Republika Srpska in 1997, the international mission sought to exploit a split within the ruling Serb Democratic Party (SDS) to isolate Karadzic and his ruling clique from power and promote a more moderate faction. SFOR was used to limit the mobility of special police, disrupt smuggling operations and, on one occasion, suppress an attempted coup. To prevent aggressive propaganda against the peace process, SFOR troops seized control of transmission towers belonging to the Republika Srpska public broadcaster, forcibly taking the station off the air until the entire management board was replaced. The international mission became directly involved in parliamentary struggles and campaigned openly in elections in support of favoured candidates, threatening the complete withdrawal of international aid to Republika Srpska if the SDS were returned to power. When in 1998 a President from the ultra-nationalist Serb Radical Party blocked the appointment of a moderate Prime Minister, precipitating a constitutional crisis, the High Representative dismissed the President, leaving the candidate favoured by the international community in place as caretaker Prime Minister for two years. Campaigns against the Croatian Democratic Union (HDZ) began in 2000, including raids against intelligence services and the appointment of an international administrator over a private bank in Herzegovina that the international mission believed to be a vehicle for money laundering and illegal revenue flows. These interventions were helped considerably by political changes in Croatia and Serbia in 2000 that led to a decline in external financial support for the parallel structures. The wartime nationalist parties were not discredited or removed from the political scene. They were, however, gradually forced to behave more like conventional political parties.

A second element was an exhaustive campaign to support the return of refugees and displaced persons to their pre-war homes. During the war, under the guise of providing temporary humanitarian housing, all three regimes had erected legal and administrative barriers to return (Cox 1999). The High Representative used his authority to reform the laws and create an administrative claims process for the repossession of property. To overcome resistance from local authorities, several international organisations helped to monitor implementation of the laws, investigating individual complaints and applying constant political pressure. This was supported by a key breakthrough in freedom of movement. In 1998, the High Representative replaced the three ethnically differentiated vehicle licence plates used during the war with a common system, using only letters common to the Latin and Cyrillic alphabets. This led to a dramatic boost in inter-entity traffic. The return process was also supported by over US$700 million in housing reconstruction programmes (World Bank 1999: 85). Over time, this campaign has made possible the gradual return of ethnic minorities throughout the country, even into areas of Republika Srpska which suffered the worst ethnic cleansing during the war. By June 2001, approximately 30 per cent of those who lost their homes during the war had been able to recover possession. With security and ethnic discrimination a continuing problem and economic opportunities in rural areas very limited, many chose to sell their property and live among their own ethnic group. Nonetheless, a limited but politically significant degree of ethnic re-integration combined with the resolution of property rights did a great deal to soften the internal lines of division and remove a continuing source of inter-ethnic tension.

A third element was the use of international authority to create a network of domestic institutions which were to some degree insulated from the dominant power structures. There were many such initiatives. In the police forces and the judiciary, the international mission carried out comprehensive programmes to screen out political appointees and individuals implicated in war crimes or other criminal activity, and introduced reforms intended to reduce direct political interference in personnel matters. There was direct international participation in a number

271

of courts and human rights institutions. An independent Central Bank established under an international governor successfully introduced a common Bosnian currency. An Independent Media Commission was created under international supervision to control media standards. International organisations worked extensively with the customs authorities, tax administrations and public auditors to reduce corruption and increase the effectiveness of revenue collection and public finance control. Independent regulators were created in the banking, securities, energy and telecommunications sectors. At state level, the mission worked to create an independent, professional civil service. In some cases, institutions created under international authority came to perform a useful public service, acquiring domestic legitimacy despite being created outside the democratic process. Dispersing public functions across a network of independent institutions helped stabilise the Bosnian state by making it less prone to being captured by destructive political interests.

Creating a quasi-protectorate structure over the new Bosnian state dramatically changed the course of its post-war development. It helped break down the wartime power structures, creating the space for a genuine political process to emerge. Many specific achievements, from refugee return and human rights protection to the development of new institutions, can be attributed to the use of intrusive international intervention. At the time of writing, however, the use of non-democratic methods to bring about democratic transformation has begun to reveal some disturbing dynamics.

First, the protectorate structure has tended to create dependence. Weak Bosnian institutions have often welcomed the use of international authority, which enables them to evade responsibility for difficult political choices. Pressure from the general public for more effective governance has been diverted away from the domestic organs and towards the international community, leaving the political parties free to campaign on symbolic or identity platforms with little substantive policy content. The weaker the domestic policy process, the greater the pressure on the international mission to use its authority to address pressing economic and social problems. In this vicious circle, there is a clear risk of chronic dependency.

Second, since it acquired the power to overrule the constitutional process, the international community has been drawn into the political fray, expressly supporting 'moderates' over 'nationalists'. This has caused serious distortions in the democratic process. The electorate has become hostile to external interference, and intervention in favour of a change of regime may in fact retard political change. At the same time, political actors under the protection of the international community have come to regard the international community as their most important constituency, neglecting their electorate. As became apparent in Republika Srpska, shielding moderate politicians from the democratic process does not encourage them to behave in a more democratic fashion. Moreover, the use of international authority for partisan ends undermines constitutionalism itself – that is, the development of a political culture in which power is subject to law.

In sum, there may be a value to using protectorate-type powers to overcome deadlocks in a post-conflict democratisation process. International authority can be used to dismantle unconstitutional power structures, guarantee the constitutional order and remove the threat of force from the political sphere. So far as these are preconditions for democracy, then it may be legitimate to use non-democratic methods to achieve them. However, there are obvious dangers in trying to engineer democratic change from the outside. At some point, the international structure has to be withdrawn in order to create the space for a genuine democratic process to emerge – a step which inevitably entails a degree of risk.

Whether this transition from protectorate to constitutional democracy can be achieved successfully in the Bosnian case remains to be seen. Political change is gradually occurring, assisted by changes in the regional political environment, by international security guarantees, by the gradual strengthening of domestic institutions and, above all, by the passage of time. However, with its cumbersome design and inherent contradictions, the constitutional structure conceived at Dayton remains dangerously weak, ill-equipped for the twin challenges of post-conflict reconstruction and post-socialist transition. These problems cannot be circumvented with an international protectorate. Ultimately, unless the Bosnian state itself becomes more effective, the conditions will remain in place for renewed ethnic conflict.

References

Banac, I. (1984) *The National Question in Yugoslavia*, Cornell: Cornell University Press.

Bildt, C. (1998) *Peace Journey: the Struggle for Peace in Bosnia*, London: Weidenfeld and Nicholson.

Bojicic, V. and M. Kaldor (1997) 'The Political Economy of the War in Bosnia–Herzegovina', in M. Kaldor and B. Vashee (eds.), *Restructuring the Global Military Sector: Volume I: New Wars*, London: Pinter.

Bringa, T. (1993) 'National Categories, National Identification and Identity Formation in Multinational Bosnia', *Anthropology of Eastern Europe Review*, 11, 1.

Burg, S. and P. Shoup (1999) *The War in Bosnia–Herzegovina: Ethnic Conflict and International Intervention*, New York: Sharpe.

Chandler, D. (1999) *Bosnia: Faking Democracy after Dayton*, London: Pluto.

Cohen, L. (1999) *The Socialist Pyramid: Elites and Power in Yugoslavia*, London: Mosaic Press.

Constitutional Court of Bosnia and Herzegovina (2000) 'Constituent People's Case', U5/98, www.ustavnisud.ba

Cox, M. (1998) 'The Right to Return Home: International Intervention and Ethnic Cleansing in Bosnia and Herzegovina', *International and Comparative Law Quarterly*, 47: 599.

Daalder, I. (2000) *Getting to Dayton: the Making of America's Foreign Policy*, Washington: Brookings Institution.

de Rossanet, B. (1996) *Peacemaking and Peacekeeping in Yugoslavia*, The Hague: Kluwer.

Denitch, B. (1996) *Ethnic Nationalism: the Tragic Death of Yugoslavia*, Minneapolis: University of Minnesota Press, second edition.

Donia, R. (2000) 'Constitutional Change and Patronage in Bosnia and Hercegovina: a Brief History', unpublished paper.

Donia, R. and J. Vine (1994) *Bosnia and Herzegovina: a Tradition Betrayed*, London: Columbia University Press.

Dyker, D. and I. Vejvoda (eds.) (1996) *Yugoslavia and After: a Study in Fragmentation, Despair and Rebirth*, London: Addison.

European Stability Initiative (1999) 'Bosnian Power Structures', www.esiweb.org

European Stability Initiative (2000) 'International Power in Bosnia', www.esiweb.org

European Stability Initiative (2001a) 'The End of the Nationalist Regimes and the Future of the Bosnian State', www.esiweb.org

European Stability Initiative (2001b) 'In Search of Politics: the Evolving International Role in Bosnia and Herzegovina', www.esiweb.org

Glenny, M. (1996) *The Fall of Yugoslavia*, New York: Penguin, third edition.

Gligorov, V. (1994) *Why Do Nations Break Up? The Case of Yugoslavia*, Uppsala: Uppsala University Press.

Gow, J. (1997) *The Triumph of the Lack of Will: International Diplomacy and the Yugoslav War*, New York: Columbia University Press.

Hayden, R. (1999) *Blueprints for a House Divided: the Constitutional Logic of the Yugoslav Conflicts*, Ann Arbor: University of Michigan Press.

Holbrooke, R. (1998) *To End a War*, New York: Random House.

International Council of Voluntary Agencies (1998) *The ICVA Directory of Humanitarian and Development Agencies Operating in Bosnia and Herzegovina*, Sarajevo: ICVA.

International Crisis Group (2000) 'Reunifying Mostar: Opportunities for Progress', www.crisisweb.org

Jelavich, B. (1983) *History of the Balkans: Eighteenth and Nineteenth Centuries*, Vol.

I., Cambridge: Cambridge University Press.

Kumar, R. (1997) *Divide and Fall? Bosnia in the Annals of Partition*, London: Verso.

Kurspahic, K. (1993) 'Is There a Future?', in R. Ali and L. Lifschultz (eds.), *Why Bosnia? Writings on the Balkan War*, Stony Creek, Conn.: Pamphleteer's Press.

Lampe, J. (2000) *Yugoslavia as History: Twice There Was a Country*, Cambridge: Cambridge University Press, second edition.

Lijphardt, A. (1971) 'Cultural Diversity and Theories of Political Integration', *Canadian Journal of Political Science*, 4, 9.

Lydall, H. (1989) *Yugoslavia in Crisis*, Oxford: Clarendon.

Magas, B. (1993) *The Destruction of Yugoslavia*, London: Verso.

Malcolm, N. (1996) *Bosnia: a Short History*, London: Macmillan, second edition.

Ni Aolain, F. (1998) 'The Fractured Soul of the Dayton Peace Agreement: a Legal Analysis', *Michigan Journal of International Law*, 19: 957.

Pajic, Z. (1998) 'A Critical Appraisal of the Human Rghts Provisions of the Dayton Constitution of Bosnia and Herzegovina' in W. Benedek (ed.), *Human Rights in Bosnia and Herzegovina after Dayton: from Theory to Practice*, London: Kluwer.

Peace Implementation Council (1997) 'Bosnia and Herzegovina 1998: Self-Sustaining Structures', Bonn, 9–10 December 1997.

Ramet, S. and L. Adamovich (eds.) *Beyond Yugoslavia: Politics, Economics, and Culture in a Shattered Community*, Boulder: Westview.

Silber, L. and A. Little (1996) *The Death of Yugoslavia*, London: Penguin, second edition.

Sudetic, C. (1998) *Blood and Vengeance: One Family's Story of the War in Bosnia*, New York: Norton.

Szasz, P. (1995) 'Protecting Human and Minority Rights in Bosnia: a Documentary Survey of International Proposals', *California West International Law Journal*, 25: 237.

Todorova, M. (1997) *Imagining the Balkans*, Oxford: Oxford University Press.

United Nations Secretary-General (1999) 'The Fall of Srebrenica', Report of the Secretary-General Pursuant to General Assembly Resolution 53/35, A/54/549, 15 November 1999.

Woodward, S. (1995) *Balkan Tragedy: Chaos and Dissolution after the Cold War*, Washington: Brookings Institution.

World Bank (1999) 'Bosnia and Herzegovina 1996–1998: Lessons and Accomplishment: Review of the Priority Reconstruction and Recovery Program', Washington.

Notes

1 In socialist Yugoslavia, the 'nations' were the founding ethnic communities – Serbs, Croats, Slovenes, Macedonians, Montenegrins and, later, Bosnian Muslims; 'nationalities' were ethnic groups such as Hungarians, Italians and Albanians whose nation state was in a neighbouring country.

2 For a selection, see Burg and Shoup 1999, Gow 1997, de Rossanet 1996, Silber and Little 1996.

3 For accounts of the process, see Holbrooke 1998, Bildt 1998, Daalder 2000.
4 Carl Bildt notes that this deal, communicated to the Bosnian Serbs only an hour before the final ceremony at Dayton, 'prompted a massive outbreak of rage' (Bildt 1998: 159).
5 In July 1999, the High Representative imposed a law permitting the state to collect fees for certain administrative services.
6 Bosnia has not yet been admitted to the Council of Europe and is therefore not eligible to become a party to the Convention itself.
7 In many respects, there were important differences between the three political structures. In particular, elements of Bosnia's multi-ethnic political culture from before the war survived within the Bosniac regime in Sarajevo. For a more detailed discussion, see European Stability Initiative 1999.
8 The exact legal basis for these powers remains obscure, but rests upon some combination of an expansive interpretation of Annex 10 of the Dayton Agreement, delegation by the inter-governmental Peace Implementation Council and approval by the UN Security Council: see Peace Implementation Council 1997; Security Council Res. 1305 (2000).

10

Managing Ethnic Conflicts
Democratic Decentralisation
in Bosnia–Herzegovina

VESNA BOJICIC-DZELILOVIC

Decentralisation is an ambivalent policy option for accommodating ethnic diversity and promoting democracy, as demonstrated with ample evidence in the literature on the subject (Young 1998; Ghai 2000; Burges and Gagnon 1993; Manor 1999; Horowitz 1991). In some cases it has provided institutional mechanisms capable of balancing contrasting ethnic claims (India) and in others it has failed to do so (Nigeria), while no conclusive evidence either way is available in cases like that of the Papua New Guinea province of Bougainville (Ghai 1998: 62). This suggests that decentralisation's capacity to address the problems of governance in multi-ethnic societies is highly contextual. Consequently, similar institutional solutions can, and sometimes do, result in contrasting outcomes (Young 1998: 59) that can contradict the original aims. Factors other than the shape and the content of the institutions themselves can have a decisive impact on whether decentralisation actually delivers on its promise as a tool for managing ethnic conflict and increasing democratic participation.

Most of the available literature on the subject explores various forms that decentralisation can take, concentrating on the relationship between the central and other levels of governance in terms of the transfer of power, resources and accountability. Within this line of thought, it has been argued that for democratic decentralisation to work well, three conditions are necessary: an adequate transfer of powers to local levels of government, sufficient resources, and functioning accountability mechanisms (Crook and Manor 1998). The argument extends to assert that factors such as the experience in democratisation, the strength of civil society and a well-developed multi-party system may facilitate this process but are not essential to it.

The particular difficulties in decentralisation when the operating principle revolves around issues of ethnic identity and ethnic autonomy have been recognised. Donais (2000: 235) warns that the very cleavages that decentralised political arrangements seek to accommodate may in fact be strengthened. Ghai argues that using decentralisation to solve ethnic problems has both short-term and long-term aspects. The very establishment of decentralisation changes the political and constitutional framework and with it the goals that may have been the original impulse behind it (1998: 62). These effects of decentralisation makes its prospect of providing a framework for peaceful inter-ethnic negotiations in the aftermath of a violent ethnic conflict particularly daunting, suggesting that the relationship between the abovementioned two sets of factors becomes rather more complex. In this context, how decentralisation works in practice may depend more on the relationship between democratic politics and democratic institutions than on the formal provisions regarding the division of powers, revenues and accountability.

This is the key argument I set out to explore in this chapter, using the case of Bosnia–Herzegovina (BiH), a country that has recently emerged from a violent 'ethnic' conflict.[1] The Dayton Agreement, signed in December 1995, sought to accommodate the conflicting claims of BiH's three main ethnic groups through the political reorganisation of space. Thus, in the process, it has created a profoundly decentralised system that combines more-traditional federalism with corporate shares in power and communal vetoes (Ghai 2000: 9). Almost all of the available mechanisms associated with the principle of power sharing among the ethnic communities have found expression in BiH's institutional design. I aim to explore the impact that this new arrangement has had on mediating ethnically based interests and preventing the resumption of violent conflict in BiH. This requires, on one hand, exploring the specificities of the new constitutional design for BiH, and, on the other, looking at how these new structures relate to a particular political and civil society context. In other words, my approach encompasses both the workings of the decentralised structures and the interplay with their enabling environment, which is shaped by factors such as the structure and configuration of competitive party politics, the profile and strength of civil society, and the strength of the local economy. It is concerned with the factors that strengthen the link between decentralisation and democratic results.

I propose to study the complex dynamics of these factors and their conflict mediation effect by exploring the experience of Tuzla and Mostar, two municipalities in the Federation of Bosnia–Herzegovina. They have been chosen because, in spite of many similarities in terms of their respective initial conditions, they have had a contrasting record in managing ethnic conflict. While Tuzla survived as a multi-ethnic community and remained peaceful throughout and after the 1992–5 conflict, Mostar saw some of the most vicious fighting between its three main ethnic groups, was subsequently divided and remains one of the most volatile regions in BiH. The comparison suggests that, within the existing institutional framework, there are alternatives to an exclusionary ethnic politics and that it is possible to provide a political space in which non-nationalist political parties and other social actors elsewhere in Bosnia–Herzegovina could shift the balance of political forces away from the issues of division and confrontation based on ethnic identities.

I begin by looking at the origins and the political context of democratic decentralisation in BiH. The second part describes the structure of democratic decentralisation in the post-Dayton BiH and includes an outline of the electoral system; in the third section I look at how decentralisation operates in BiH, including an in-depth study of the conflict management experience of Tuzla and Mostar. Finally, the fourth part concludes by pointing to the limitations of an approach to decentralisation that is predominantly concerned with perfecting the institutional design at the expense of other relevant factors in mitigating ethnic conflict.

The origins and political context of democratic decentralisation in Bosnia–Herzegovina

The nature of the regime and the underlying political objectives are usually the determining factors in the creation of a decentralised system (Crook and Manor 1998: 13). In BiH this choice was eventually made by the representatives of the international community as part of an effort to end three and a half years of conflict that threatened to break BiH apart. Thus the primary motive for decentralisation as a part of a constitutional settlement was to stop the fighting and prevent the fragmentation of the country under secessionist threats from Bosnian Croats and Bosnian Serbs, rather than to provide an effective mechanism of ethnic accommodation *per se*. In relying on the three dominant ethnically based parties – the Croatian Democratic Union of Bosnia–Herzegovina (HDZ BiH, the main Bosnian Croat party), the Serb Democratic Party (SDS, the main Bosnian Serb party) and the Party of Democratic Action (SDA, the main Muslim party) – as its exclusive interlocutors, the international community had implicitly accepted the view that managing ethnic antagonisms was the key to any lasting peace

279

in BiH. The fact that no other parties or social groups were consulted or involved in negotiations is extremely important because the characterisation of the conflict as 'ethnic' had crucial influence on the ensuing terms of the peace settlement. There was an implied acceptance of the existence of deep ethnic divisions among BiH's three main ethnic groups around which the new institutional architecture was then structured. The ferocity of the conflict and the power of the nationalist parties all seemed to back the argument that BiH's war was about ethnicity and ancient ethnic hatred (a line vigorously promoted by the Bosnian Serbs and Bosnian Croats, justifying their quest to join Serbia and Croatia, respectively) and that it was futile to try to transcend or modify these divisions. These messages were forcefully reproduced by the politically controlled media, especially in the Bosnian Serb and Bosnian Croat majority areas.

Events on the ground seemed to justify the choice of a particular form of decentralisation based on ethnic markers. By the end of 1995, the map of BiH had been reconfigured into three more-or-less ethnically homogeneous territories with populations hostile to each other. Thus one of the preconditions for implementing spatial decentralisation (which in BiH went hand in hand with corporate decentralisation) – the physical concentration of a particular group (see Ghai 1998: 64) – was in place. The creation of ethnically homogeneous territories was one of the principal goals of the nationalist parties in power. They orchestrated population displacement on a massive scale, particularly from the areas under control of the SDS and the HDZ BiH respectively, often accompanied by mass killings and other atrocities. For the Bosnian Croat and Bosnian Serb political élites this was to be but the first step on the road to secession from BiH, an aim which to this day has not been completely abandoned in either of the two communities. We would argue that the very method of securing a correspondence between ethnicity and territory in BiH – through killings and expulsions of the population – has not been without implications for the conflict-mediating outcomes of the new structural framework. It stands in sharp contrast to the experience of those countries where physical concentration of particular ethnic, religious or linguistic groups has been a historical fact.

In devising the new structural framework for BiH, the logic was that, by giving a measure of political autonomy to the territorially defined ethnic groups, an atmosphere conducive to dialogue and compromise as a way of peacefully managing the conflict would ensue. Central to the Dayton Agreement, therefore, was a formula that redefined BiH as a country consisting of two entities and three constitutive peoples, Serbs in

Republika Srpska and Croats and Muslims in the Federation of BiH. With the stroke of a pen new minorities were created: Muslims and Croats in Republika Srpska; Serbs in the Federation.[2] Such was the leverage of the three dominant ethnically based parties that, when BiH's new constitution was being drawn up, BiH's other nationalities, recognised as such while BiH was a part of the Socialist Federal Republic of Yugoslavia (SFRY) and representing some 5 per cent of BiH's population in 1991, were simply left out. This meant that the divisions between BiH's communities created through the conflict, and which were not necessarily the cause of the conflict, had effectively become entrenched in the political and constitutional settlement. This is one of the salient risks of using decentralisation as a mechanism for moderating ethnic cleavages in a society, widely acknowledged in the literature on the subject (see for example Horowitz 1993 and Donais 2000). Rather than moderating the existing ethnic identities, the new structural framework effectively reinforced them; all politics became primarily ethnic politics. The segments of the population that did not feel particularly strongly as Muslims, Serbs and Croats, including Yugoslavs, found themselves having to declare their ethnic identity by all sorts of means for all sorts of purposes.

It is now received wisdom among political scientists that the political élite strives for those institutional choices that best fit its own interests. This tendency becomes more imperative at times of regime change such as those associated with wars and aftermaths. BiH has been no exception in that respect. Since their ascent to power, the SDS, the SDA and the HDZ, the three political parties that dominated BiH's political scene in the period 1991–2000, have relied on a platform of ethnic exclusiveness. They have used the issue of ethnic identity as a vehicle for political mobilisation, managing to centre the national politics around ethnic differences and thus pre-empting conflict along other cleavage lines (Horowitz 1998: 15). They have relied on networks of patronage and clientalism to secure political support, while their economic power base has resided largely outside the realm of formal economic flows, often involving outright criminal activities. They have installed a type of regime in which loyalty to the party outweighs any respect for democratic rules and in which resorting to violence has become a common method of resolving inter-ethnic conflict. They have firmly controlled every aspect of life in the territories with their respective ethnic majorities. It is now clear that, in negotiating the peace agreement, their real political interest had been to secure a framework that would enable them to preserve the power structures they controlled, and that they had little genuine interest in the political compromise needed to rebuild the state of BiH on new foundations – or, indeed, to support democratic procedures. One can argue, then, that the three parties had vested interests in instigating the conflict. This in turn ran counter to one of the main prerequisites for the effective working of the consensual democracy approach applied in BiH – namely, the willingness of the parties in power to cooperate and seek ethnic moderation. This, we hope, will become clear in our analysis of Tuzla and Mostar local government. The fact that the new constitutional framework was not negotiated in a democratic and participatory way (as it was in South Africa), but was imposed by the heavy hand of the international community,[3] was another factor with the potential to undermine decentralisation in BiH.

The structure of democratic decentralisation and the principle of power sharing

Before the war, BiH was one of the six republics of the SFRY. Internally, it was organised into 109 municipalities. Larger urban areas were typically multi-ethnic as 'ethnic' populations were interspersed throughout the country. Both the republic and the municipalities held the status of socio-political communities. This meant that the municipality was responsible for all matters of government except those constitutionally assigned to higher levels of political authority (see Milidragovic 1998: 113). The functional autonomy of the municipality was paralleled by a significant degree of financial autonomy. These features, combined with the experience of a self-management system that brought citizens and other civil society elements into the decision-making process, have left a legacy: the municipality's role as a focus of citizen identity and loyalty. This legacy has been used, depending on the particular circumstances in individual localities, both to moderate communal tensions and to exacerbate them – as the comparison between Tuzla and Mostar aims to illustrate.

Under the new constitution, adopted as a part of the Dayton Agreement, BiH was recognised within its existing borders as a loose union of the two entities. Each entity possesses its own internal legal personality and the highest degree of sovereignty, with minimal functions assigned to the central state. Fiscal sovereignty is also vested with the entities, and the central state budget is financed by contributions from the two entities. The highest legislative body at the central state level is a bicameral Parliament and its internal composition is based on the principle of ethnic parity. The joint three-member state presidency operates on a principle of rotation; this also applies to the executive or Council of Ministers (the chairperson and two deputies of which must represent the three ethnic groups).

While Republika Srpska is centralised, consisting of municipalities only, the powers in the Federation are devolved to the ethnically defined cantons. The cantons have exclusive competencies to perform all functions not explicitly assigned to the Federation. Ten cantons were created in the Federation, five of which have a Muslim majority, three a Bosnian Croat majority and two an ethnically mixed population. A canton is defined as a territory containing all aspects of sovereignty, including its own constitution, legislation and judiciary. Consequently, the Federation also shares fiscal sovereignty with the cantons. Special rules apply to the two mixed cantons, one of which is that decision making is based on consensus and that the principle of 'vital national interest protection' applies (the principle of veto by either of the two constitutive peoples also applies in the Upper House of the Federation Parliament and the Federation government). This principle refers to the right of veto that one of the Federation's two constitutive peoples can evoke when it considers its national interest to be in jeopardy, a right quite frequently used (and abused) by both peoples. The right of veto also applies in the state-level institutions.

Additional mechanisms for the protection of minorities are envisaged, whereby a canton is obliged to delegate or confer some of its responsibilities to its municipalities when the ethnic composition of a municipality differs from the majority in the canton. The Federation constitution established a new municipal organisation of the territories included in the Federation and granted them self-rule in local matters.[4] The powers of the municipality are significantly reduced compared to the previous system: it has virtually no independent legislative function and its self-financing powers have also been reduced – although, in reality, particularly in ethnically mixed cantons, municipalities have continued to play a more significant role than they are normatively assigned. This can be explained primarily by the difficulties in the functioning of the Federation and resistance, especially in the ethnically mixed cantons, to relinquishing the powers concentrated at this level by the fragmentative character of the conflict (a point that will be further elaborated in the discussion on Mostar).

A canton exercises its influence primarily via a mayor, who subsumes all executive powers. The mayor's influence extends to include the appointment of the municipal judges, which obviously has implications for the extent to which the judiciary can act independently – a particularly sensitive issue in a multi-ethnic society (indeed, a weak and unprofessional judiciary has been one of the main obstacles to the country's post-war recovery). The strong role of the mayor in practice enables political parties to exercise important influence at the local level, making the profile of political parties an important factor impacting on local government's effectiveness in mediating conflicts.

This brief overview of the decentralised structures in BiH reveals a complex framework (13 constitutions pertaining to different tiers of government and over 200 ministries) aimed at accommodating BiH's post-war reality. The four constitutionally protected government tiers have unclear and overlapping responsibilities. One of the most problematic aspects of the new constitutional set-up is the relation between the central-level and entity-level governments. Not only has the central government been assigned a minimum of responsibilities commonly associated with a state (even the organisation of the army is under entity jurisdiction), but the entire procedure for exercising them *vis-à-vis* the entities is problematic. This is in sharp contrast to the experience of the Swiss federation, which has often been evoked in BiH as a model to follow. In Switzerland the prerogatives of the central state are clearly defined, requiring negotiation with the cantons if it wants to extend its constitutional and legislative powers. In BiH, however, there is tension between the central state and the entity, with entities attempting to undermine the state and further strengthen their positions. Negotiations over the responsibilities of these two government tiers have as a rule been difficult and proceeded under pressure from the international community representatives. The implementation of the new constitutional set-up was additionally complicated by the fact that the whole structure also lacked clarity regarding the financial needs of the various levels of government. All these problems are also depicted in relations between the Federation and the cantons. Because the prime motive of decentralisation was to provide a degree of autonomy to ethnically homogeneous territories, based on a particular understanding of the nature of the conflict as an ethnic one, redistributive aspects were completely ignored, thus leaving open the possibility that economic grievances could, eventually, be turned into claims of ethnic discrimination. Thus one of the important instruments for enhancing federal solidarity, and a valuable component in creating an atmosphere supportive of inter-ethnic dialogue, is missing from the constitutional formula applied in BiH.

Elections were meant to play a significant role as part of the broader institutional arrangement aimed at mitigating ethnic conflict in BiH.

According to Reilly and Reynolds, three variables are particularly important when choosing an electoral system for a divided society: (1) *the nature of societal divisions* (including group identity, the intensity of conflict, the nature of the dispute and the spatial distribution of groups in conflict); (2) *the nature of the political system* (including the state, the party system, and the overall constitutional framework); and (3) *the process which led to the adoption of the electoral system* (Reilly and Reynolds 1999; 10). In BiH, the closed list proportional representation system was chosen, suggesting that the principal concern of the key actors involved was to ensure ethnic group representation. The electoral system institutionalised ethnic voting and fixed the ratio of the different ethnic groups in the legislature at both state and federal levels. The principle of ethnic parity was duly applied in all public appointments. However, the system provided no incentive for inter-ethnic accommodation as each party could rely solely on the support of its own ethnic group. It effectively encouraged parties to use the issues of ethnicity and territory as the main plank of their election campaigns. One of the Dayton Agreement's inherent contradictions – that it recognised the rights of particular ethnic groups over specific territories while giving the right to return to the population expelled from those territories – provided a legitimating framework for this kind of policy. Two sets of general elections (1996 and 1998) and one round of local elections (1997) that took place under the provisions of the temporary Election Law incorporating the above features resulted in the victory of the ethnically based parties. They managed to secure success through narrow appeals to ethnic solidarity. Indeed, the elections contributed to further ethnic polarisation within BiH's society (Donais 2000: 252). The international community began to introduce changes to the election rules in the run-up to the local and general elections in 2000. Under the new rules, the single constituencies were broken up into multi-member constituencies and the open list system was introduced, enabling preferential voting; any parties underrepresented as a result of the new system were to receive compensatory votes. Another specific change referred to the composition of the Upper House of the Federation Parliament, where the number of seats for 'others' (non-Croats and non-Muslims) was increased.[5] Predictably, the changes had to be imposed by OSCE, the organisation mandated with overseeing the elections, as the SDS, the SDA and the HDZ blocked it in the regular parliamentary procedure. Although this was an important step towards undermining the principle of ethnic voting, it fell short of a substantial change in the electoral system which would reward inter-ethnic accommodation. In

285

addition, the proposed changes, which were subsequently incorporated in the Draft Permanent Election Law, were in contradiction to the eventual changes in the entity constitutions in line with the Constitutional Court's ruling giving each of BiH's three main ethnic groups constitutive status across the country (which is why BiH's Parliament rejected the Draft Permanent Election Law in June 2001).

The April 2000 local elections saw the first major inroads by the multi-ethnic parties in the Federation, a success they consolidated in the general elections of November 2000 that ended the ten-year monopoly of ethnically based parties. The precise role the change in the electoral rules has played in these events is difficult to establish. For one thing, BiH is an international protectorate in everything but name, so the policies pursued by the international community influence the voting patterns. After 1998 the international community stepped up implementation of the property laws, which made the prospect of return to their pre-war place of residence a reality for many refugees. This certainly lessened the attractiveness of the ethnic parties, which claimed to be the sole guarantors of ethnic group interests, including the right to return. The accusations of corruption, clientalism and abuse of public office against the HDZ, the SDA and the SDS was another factor contributing to the electorate's disillusionment. The normalisation of everyday life, which increasingly brought to the fore such issues as jobs, education and health care, worked in the same direction. Thus, while the changes in the electoral rules did help the opposition across BiH to put a foot in the door, a number of other reasons all converged to break the nationalist grip on power.

The new model and its impact on conflict management

Democratic decentralisation in BiH, as suggested before, is a political strategy designed with a view to facilitating the management of the conflict by BiH's three main ethnic groups. The new decentralised institutional framework in BiH has been in place for a fairly short period of time, urging caution in the interpretation of some of the findings. Another important caveat concerns the fact that the new institutional set-up of BiH was not the result of an endogenous evolutionary process underpinned by a social contract, but was imposed from outside. This reflects the lack of what may be an essential ingredient for the success of consensual democracy: agreement on the political community (Joseph 1999). The model applied rests on a number of other assumptions unlikely to be found in the post-war environment, the main one being a political élite prepared to behave moderately. This is a particularly unrealistic assumption in BiH's context, where rekindling ethnic animosity keeps nationalist parties in power. The international supervisor, in the figure of the international community's High Representative, has wide-ranging powers in implementing the basic institutional framework, which restricts the autonomy of local political structures.

The devolved model of government in BiH leaves very little central power to share. Even so, an agreement on the issues under the jurisdiction of the central BiH state has been difficult to reach. While the three-member presidency – typically under extreme pressure from the High Representative or other relevant international bodies – has been known to reach agreement, it is in the main the Parliament that has rejected proposed legislation. The chain does not end here, however; the last stumbling block is the House of Peoples, which has often turned down proposals put forward by the House of Representatives. The key issue has been a difference in approach to the operationalisation of the institutional framework as stipulated in the new constitution. The obstructions came mainly from the Bosnian Serb and Bosnian Croat representatives opposed to the legislation strengthening the role of the central state. The lack of agreement between them complicated the decision-making process, often leading to a paralysis of the central state institutions, and thus undermining the key prerogatives of the central state to maintain the integrity and unity of the country. As a consequence, the High Representative had to impose numerous pieces of legislation by decree, resorting frequently to his powers to replace obstructive officials. This in itself has weakened the responsibility of local political structures and worked against their greater accountability to the electorate, and more generally against promoting democratisation.

The functioning of the Federation was marred by similar problems of centrifugal forces working against the strengthening of its role. The roles of the Federation president and his deputy were marginalised by the Parliament, in which the SDA-led coalition and the HDZ BiH represented a majority right until the November 2000 general elections. For most of this time the Federation remained in legislative deadlock. Policy making in reality bypassed the institutions of the system and took place instead in the parties' headquarters, thus suggesting that the existing mechanisms based on power sharing failed to provide an integrative force.

For most of the period under study, the remnants of parallel wartime institutions controlled by the then two main Federation parties remained in place (separate systems of finance, health, education, pensions, etcetera), which undermined the work of the newly established Federation

287

structures. Clearly, some problems in the functioning of the Federation can be attributed to its design. Although the Federation has been in place since 1994, no clear functional boundaries between the three (or four, including the level of the city) tiers of government have been established. A system of concurrent powers between the Federation, canton and municipal governments has resulted in a lack of coordination, under-financing and inefficient service provision. The tensions within the Federation culminated in the run-up to the November 2000 elections when the Bosnian Croat leadership organised a referendum leading to the establishment of Bosnian Croat self-rule. The agenda behind the move was one of trying to elicit a revision of the Dayton Agreement with two possible options: to create a third entity with the Bosnian Croat majority, or to break up the two multi-ethnic cantons along ethnic lines.

This wider picture of how the new institutional framework operates in practice suggests that the lines of division among BiH's three main ethnic communities, which were created through conflict, have not softened despite elaborate power-sharing schemes. Disintegrative forces remained strong, and ethnically motivated violence, although sporadic, has continued. In searching for explanation beyond the specificities of BiH's constitutional design, we now turn to the experience of conflict management in the two municipalities in the Federation of BiH.

Mostar

Mostar is a city in southern BiH, which, historically, was the administrative, educational and cultural centre of the wider region of Herzegovina. According to the 1991 census, Mostar had a population of 126,000 people, of whom 34 per cent were Muslims, 33 per cent were Croats, 19 per cent were Serbs and 14 per cent were 'others' (a significant proportion of this category were people of mixed ethnic origin who declared themselves Yugoslavs). Until a few years before the war, it was one of the more prosperous parts of BiH, with a fairly diversified industrial structure and a strong export industry. In the first multi-party elections in 1991, the three nationalist parties – the SDA, the HDZ BiH and the SDS – won and entered a coalition government.[6] The government split along ethnic lines soon after the war started in 1992, and the SDA and the HDZ BiH took over the organisation of defence, military provisions and other government functions. Religious organisations – Merhamet on the Muslim side, and Caritas on the Croat side – took the lead in providing humanitarian aid, often excluding members of other ethnic groups. The media came under strict control of the two parties, thus contributing immensely to the escalating tension. Mostar became the stage for some of the fiercest fighting during the 1992–5 war, since the original dividing line between Croats and Serbs (the Tudjman-Milosevic partitioning of BiH) was along the River Neretva, which runs right through the middle of the city. Until spring 1993, local Muslim and Croat forces fought as allies against Serbs, but turned against each other and fought for ten months until the Muslim–Croat Federation was created in March 1994. Croats took control of most of the Neretva's west bank, expelling most of the non-Croat population across the river to the east side and detaining many in virtual concentration camps in the surrounding areas. As a result, the east bank became a predominantly Muslim settlement. The physical destruction of East Mostar was easily the most extensive in all of BiH. The economy was brought to such a complete standstill that, for years after the war, humanitarian aid and donations were still the main source of finance.

West Mostar was much less damaged, which enabled some economic activity to continue throughout the war. Its proximity to Croatia provided various opportunities for smuggling and other illegal activities, with some of the proceeds financing the Bosnian Croats' para-state of Herzeg–Bosna. The West Mostar government also received substantial donations from Croatia. The physical partitioning of the city was mirrored in all social spheres such as education, health, culture and sport. Two separate currencies were in use: the Croatian kuna in West Mostar and the BiH dinar in East Mostar, with the German Mark accepted in both.

Local government: competencies, resources, accountability

As part of the Washington Agreement, Mostar was placed under the temporary European Administration of Mostar (EUAM),[7] which was burdened with the task of overcoming the city's ethnic division through a process of reconstruction and political and social reunification (Reichel 1996). Mostar became the capital of the Herzegovina–Neretva canton, the last of the ten Federation cantons to be established following disagreement between Muslims and Croats. One of fourteen counties, Mostar accounts for some 50 per cent of the canton's population, estimated at some 215,000 in 1999. It was given an elevated position compared to other towns in BiH in that it was to be a second seat of the Federation government and a seat of four of its ministries. Administered as a single municipality before the war, Mostar was in 1995 reorganised as six municipalities – three with a Muslim majority and three with a Croat majority – and a central district.

The central zone, which included most of the area around the partition line, was seen as key to the reunification of the city in physical as well as administrative and political terms. The Interim Statute for Mostar, drawn up by the EUAM, did not specify the competencies of the city municipalities; this was to be defined by an amendment to the Herzegovina–Neretva canton's constitution and law on local self-government, which were subject to obstructions, thus prolonging the rule of war- time power structures. However, the Statute did stipulate that the city municipalities could transfer tasks in their competence to the city of Mostar by a resolution of the city-municipal council – another issue over which bitter struggle between the Bosnian Croat and Muslim representatives was waged.

It was only in March 1998 that the government of the Herzegovina–Neretva canton reached agreement on temporary financing. In reality, much of the funding came from external sources. While sufficient funds were provided,[8] the city administration was not functioning. Most of the projects implemented were defined by donors, reflecting divisions among the local parties not able to reach an agreement.

Establishing the city administration and making it function had been a painstaking job. The first local elections in Mostar, held in June 1996, brought victory to the SDA and the HDZ BiH in the municipalities with Muslim and Croat majorities, respectively. However, the SDA won the elections for the city council, which the HDZ BiH refused to recognise, blocking the work of the governing structures as defined in the Interim Statute. Thus it was only in June 1997, after pressure from the international community, that the six municipal councils and their administrations were formed. From then on, the HDZ BiH representatives staged a concerted campaign of obstructing the passage of the relevant federal and cantonal legislation. The deadlock would remain until July 2000.

The issue of the central zone was at the heart of the dispute. The HDZ BiH saw its establishment and its high degree of autonomy as a sign that a seventh municipality with a Muslim majority would eventually be created (according to the 1991 census, Muslims were in the majority in the central zone). It was only in July 2000, under the threat of sanctions and following two internationally mediated agreements[9] on Mostar, that the law on local government was passed, followed by a law on the distribution of revenues, opening the way for local government structures to operate in line with the constitutional provisions.

The issue of accountability has to be considered within the particular political ambience of Mostar. Until the summer of 2000, the three municipalities with a Croat majority were effectively merged into a single authority, which in itself implied a lack of accountability mechanisms. On the other hand, ten years of unchallenged rule by the two nationalist parties created a culture in which both the accountability of the elected representatives to the electorate and that of the bureaucrats to the officials is, as a rule, poorly upheld. The local Croat power élite in particular showed no accountability either to the citizens or to the higher political authorities; its actions often ran against the interests of the Croat leadership at the Federation level and those of the ordinary Croats who had no influence or control over their officials. For much of the time until the Schwartz–Schilling agreement on Mostar in 1999, Muslim councillors were not invited to the sessions of the assembly of the Union of Croat Municipalities. Although the Interim Statute of Mostar City stipulated that the municipal administrations must include members from minorities, this was rarely the case in Croat municipalities. The municipal governments showed absolutely no interest in matters concerning minorities such as, for example, dealing with property claims. Minorities faced almost insurmountable obstacles in exercising some of their basic rights, such as the right to identity documents. As for the three municipalities with a Muslim majority, they too failed to regularly invite Croat councillors to sessions of the assembly.

Overall, the elections have been the main general mechanism of accountability; the contact between the electorate and the elected officials as a rule stopped after the election campaign was over, suggesting low participation. To the extent that citizens came forward with any demands for elected officials, given the lack of democratic experience and generally poorly developed civil society, it was over issues of refugee returns and displaced people. Much of the funding for the local political élite in the past came from external sources, which also weakened the case for accountability. Failure to establish a functioning and independent judiciary was an additional factor undermining the horizontal accountability (to other institutions of the system) of elected officials.

Clientalism, nepotism and corruption are rife in Mostar, which has reflected on the accountability of bureaucrats to the elected representatives. The circulation of élites, whereby senior officials move back and forth between posts in the municipal government and those in either the private or public sector, is a common practice. The public sector culture is generally very poor, which is to do partly with the heritage from the previous regime and partly with scarce financial resources. The legislation is vague in this respect – it only states that the work of these organs is public, but does not specify mechanisms to achieve public accountability.

The information and interaction between the public administration organs and the governing bodies in Mostar in general remain low-profile and accountability to citizens is still almost non-existent.

Political parties, civic activities and the strength of the economy

Three sets of local elections have been held in Mostar since the end of the war in 1995. The turn-out fell significantly from over 85 per cent in the first elections in 1996 to 60 per cent in April 2000. While the dominant position of the SDA among the Muslims has been challenged by the Social Democratic Party (SDP), the single largest multi-ethnic party in BiH, and the SDA splinter party, the Party for BiH, the HDZ BiH has remained the most powerful party among the Bosnian Croats. The same balance of political power was replicated at the cantonal level in the November 2000 general elections. The political party competition in those areas where the HDZ BiH is a dominant party has been very limited.

Throughout, the HDZ BiH has run on the platform of a divided Mostar, which they see as a capital of the so-called Croatian Republic of Herzeg–Bosna. These demands culminated in a referendum on Bosnian Croat self-rule in the run-up to the November 2000 elections. Similarly, the SDA has had strong support among Muslims in East Mostar. Reunification of the city and the right of refugees to return have been key elements in the electoral platform of its local Mostar branch. Much like the HDZ BiH, the SDA has also exercised firm control over all spheres of social and economic activity in the municipalities it has controlled. It has also played the card of ethnic homogenisation as a bulwark against threats from other ethnic groups. In practical terms, however, the two nationalist parties have worked against a reconciliation between the Muslim and Croat populations of Mostar. On a broader level, one can argue that although the institutional framework has provided for the representation of both Muslim and Croat communities, that has not been the case with the protection of their genuine interests, owing to a particular profile of the dominant political parties.

The firm control of the two nationalist parties over the structures of local authority in Mostar has left its mark on the activities of civil society in general. Overall, the level of mobilisation and the breadth of civic activities in Mostar have been less impressive than in other parts of BiH, notably Tuzla and Sarajevo. This is partly to do with the wartime experience of Mostar, which has reflected negatively on all aspects of the political, social and economic environment considered conducive to civic initiatives, not least on social and human capital. A special factor in Mostar has been the very pronounced role played by associations and groups that may be termed 'uncivil', in the sense that they have been exclusive in both membership and orientation. Among the most active in West Mostar have been the Association of Croat War Invalids of the Homeland War (HVIDR) and the Association of Volunteers and Veterans of the Homeland War (UDIVDR). The two associations although formally representing the interests of war invalids, ex-soldiers and their families, have been actively involved in promoting the political goals of the HDZ BiH. The influence of the HVIDR in particular on local Croat authorities is believed to be significant (for much of the war and post-war period the HVIDR controlled the housing stock acquired through the expulsion of the non-Croat citizens of Mostar, with the tacit approval of local authorities); there are also indications that the HVIDR is effectively the HDZ BiH paramilitary arm. It has been involved in organising violence in Mostar and elsewhere in BiH, and politically motivated attacks on returning refugees and members of the political opposition. It has been the main organiser of protest rallies and marches in support of a separatist Bosnian Croat agenda. The events it organises are usually well attended; however, threats and intimidation have been frequently used to coerce people into participation. The HVIDR is partly financed by personal income contributions in the Croat municipalities in the Federation, thus confirming its links to the regime.

Another special factor in Mostar has been the prominent role of the Catholic church in supporting the separatist goals of the HDZ BiH's hardline faction. Its representatives have regularly attended important political gatherings of Bosnian Croats and issued statements in support of the demands of the faction.

A number of civic associations created on an ethnically exclusive basis have been coopted, in one way or another, by the regime: examples include the Association of Croat Writers; the movement for promoting Croat culture and language, Matica Hrvatska; the Croat cultural movement Napredak, and the Association of Lawyers.

The East Mostar authorities, to a certain degree, have been more tolerant of civil society activities. For example, while trade unions were banned in West Mostar until recently, they operated freely in East Mostar. It is only in the last year or so, however, that trade unions have begun to deal with workers' rights; for most of the period following the outbreak of the war they were engaged in humanitarian work. The political environment in East Mostar has been more conducive to civic initiatives based on inclusiveness. Among the most prominent ones have been women's associations, such as Zene Mostara (The Women of Mostar), Stope Nade (The Steps of Hope) and Bosanska Zena (Bosnian

293

Woman), which have launched a number of initiatives aimed at promoting the spirit of reconciliation. However, the type of initiative that would make civil society a constructive participant in the political arena is still strikingly absent. There has been very little indigenous NGO activity, with a notable shortage of NGOs that focus on work in local communities or deal with urban issues. This is partly the result of a lack of experience in this field and partly a consequence of war, which has to a large extent undermined the concept of local community *per se*. Because of the intensity and duration of the conflict, human capital has suffered disproportionately;[10] this contributes to a lower degree of participation and an underdeveloped associational life in general. Unlike in Tuzla, there is a dearth of organisations focusing on economic development.

The local media, both print and broadcast, have been under the control of the regime and have greatly contributed to fuelling tensions among the two ethnic communities. Split along ethnic lines at the beginning of the war, they have remained divided and disinclined to dialogue and cooperation. Whatever progress has been made has been the result of international pressure.

The economic situation in Mostar remains difficult, particularly in the Muslim-controlled municipalities. There is very little production going on as so much pre-war capacity has been either physically destroyed or rendered useless by a lack of maintenance and technological degradation. Unemployment may be as high as 60 per cent; this fuels an atmosphere of anger and frustration, on one hand, while affecting public finance on the other. Because of stringent public finances the level of public services is low. The local economy in West Mostar is in somewhat better shape, for two reasons: less war-related damage, and access to resources through often clandestine networks of local political and business élites. This discrepancy in wealth heightens the animosity between the two communities. Among both communities, however, there is a pervasive sense of uncertainty of livelihood directly related to persistent ethnic tension and political uncertainty. This has deterred investment and, on the whole, had a negative effect on economic recovery. It has also played an important role in preventing the local population from acting as responsible citizens with respect to local government, which has been under the firm control of political parties whose primary concerns are still to do with issues of ethnic security rather than jobs, education or public services.

As a result of the combined effect of the above factors, the return of refugees and displaced persons to Mostar, an indicator of improved inter-ethnic relations, has been among the slowest in the whole of BiH. While there have been some returns to the suburban zones of Mostar, the return to the city proper, particularly its Croat-dominated sector, has been very thin.

Tuzla

Tuzla is an industrial town in north-eastern BiH, once one of the centres of heavy industry in the former Yugoslavia. Tuzla managed to escape the worst of the economic crisis that engulfed the rest of BiH in the years preceding the war, and was one of the few areas where production, although on a reduced scale, continued throughout the war, thus providing at least some public revenue (for years after the war, revenues collected in Tuzla's Podrinje canton accounted for the bulk of public revenue in the Federation, excluding municipalities with a Croat majority). According to the 1991 census, it had a population of 131,618, of whom 47.6 per cent were Muslim, 15.5 per cent Croat, 14.4 per cent Serb and 21.5 per cent 'other' (BiH Statistical Yearbook). In Tuzla, the coalition of non-nationalist parties (consisting of the Union of BiH Social Democrats or UBSD, the SDP and the Liberal Party) won the 1991 elections. Perhaps one of the most striking contrasts with Mostar in the run-up to the war and during its initial phase, bearing important implications for the conflict-management effectiveness of local government, was the integrity of the municipal authorities. The municipal assembly suspended sessions only very briefly early on in the war; when it reconvened, it did so throughout the war and until the first post-war local elections with a more or less unchanged ethnic composition.

Members of minorities – Croats, Serbs and 'others' – continued to hold key decision-making positions both in local government and in public companies. The defence of the city was organised by the municipal government, which also took care of rationing. The government, with the help of the media, made an extraordinary effort to keep the public informed both of the situation on the ground and of its activities, using every opportunity to encourage people, and minorities in particular, to remain in the city. The police and courts continued to work throughout the war. Citizens' complaints against local government agencies were also dealt with, which maintained public trust.[11]

Early on in the conflict, the SDA tried to undermine the local authorities by winning over some of the very prominent local figures. In response to attempts to stir up ethnic animosities, an association of citizens called the Citizens' Forum was established in 1993, which from then on focused on activities to preserve Tuzla's multi-ethnic character and strengthen democratic processes (the mayor of Tuzla, Selim Beslagic, a charismatic figure who held the post until January 2001, played a key role in these events, lending every support to the Citizens' Forum). Tuzla escaped war destruction on a massive scale, and managed to preserve its administrative, social and economic structures. This provided a more favourable platform for post-war economic and societal reconstruction than many other localities in BiH enjoyed. On the other hand, the Tuzla municipality encountered persistent pressure from the SDA-led cantonal government, which was eager to consolidate its power across the canton with a Muslim majority.

Municipal government: powers, resources, accountability

Tuzla–Podrinje canton was created in 1994 and Tuzla became the seat of the cantonal government. Tuzla accounts for some 25 per cent of the population of the canton, which has both the largest population in the Federation and the highest population density. The canton, which consists of 13 municipalities, has a Muslim majority (like the municipality of Tuzla, with close to 70 per cent Muslims in 1999 as a result of population movement during the war). The constitution of the Tuzla–Podrinje canton is unique in that it places much greater emphasis on human rights protection than the constitutions of other cantons, reflecting one of the main concerns of the political parties in power. The cantonal law on local self-government gives this right to citizens (and not to the municipality, as in Mostar), indicating an institutional framework more favourable to developing and nurturing democratic practices.

Tuzla is organised as a single municipality. One important difference compared to Mostar (and, indeed, elsewhere in the Federation) is that Tuzla's municipality legislation makes the local area committees (*mjesna zajednica*, or MZ), an obligatory form of direct participation in decision making on local matters.[12] Their main competencies relate to matters relevant to citizens' daily needs in their area of residence. There is an effort to strengthen the role of the MZ as a consultative mechanism between citizens and local government, thus stimulating greater direct citizen participation.

Tuzla's relatively stronger post-war economic recovery, when compared with Mostar, has provided a solid tax base. The municipal government has also been successful in raising local funds for projects of particular interest to individual MZ; in 1998, it launched an initiative to provide matching funds for projects that citizens would finance from their own contributions.

296

The fact that most development projects have been at least partly locally defined and funded has certainly had implications for accountability, in the broadest sense. Local authorities in Tuzla clearly had an interest in seeking accommodation with local socio-economic factors, compared with Mostar where much of the funding was externally provided. The difference between Tuzla and Mostar is perhaps most striking in the mechanisms of accountability. Tuzla–Podrinje canton's law on public administration states the precise responsibilities of the public administration bodies to elected officials as well as to the public, listing a number of mechanisms for achieving them. Tuzla's municipal government is a positive example of a public body actually implementing these mechanisms. Particular emphasis has been given to maintaining links with the electorate through meetings, by taking part in local television 'question time' type programmes, through individual meetings with members of the public, and so on. Most prominent in this respect have been the activities of Tuzla's former mayor, who maintained close contact with the public throughout ten consecutive years in office, which to a large extent explains his popularity. The mayor made a particular point of holding discussions over the budget in public, with the participation of MZ representatives so that their preferences could be identified. Another special factor in Tuzla is that the local government monitoring committee has been established as one of Tuzla's municipal assembly committees. Its task has been to assist and promote the work of the MZ, thus underlining the commitment to further strengthen local self-government.

Political parties, civic activity, local economy

The turn-out in both local and general elections in Tuzla has been high. After the UBSD and SDP BiH merged in 1998, the new party, which kept the name of SDP BiH, became the strongest party in the Tuzla municipality local elections in April 2000. In the November 2000 general elections, the SDP BiH managed to defeat the SDA at the cantonal level, too, thus taking over the municipal as well as the cantonal government.

The SDP BiH is a multi-ethnic party that has advocated the reintegration of BiH and the constitutive status of all its three peoples across the whole of BiH. Its success in winning cantonal office is extraordinary, given the SDA's concerted campaign to undermine Tuzla's municipal government. The local HDZ BiH, on the other hand, has been pursuing the general party line of ethnic homogenisation; it has attempted to pressure local authorities in Tuzla to agree to carve a new municipality with a Croat majority out of the present Tuzla municipality. But the municipal government has been united in not permitting reorganisation

297

along ethnic lines, thus reflecting the prevalent anti-nationalist attitude of the public expressed at meetings convened to discuss the proposal. A number of other political parties have also been very active in Tuzla.

Tuzla's somewhat specific wartime experience has provided a much more favourable climate for various civic initiatives and a much higher degree of social and political mobilisation than elsewhere in BiH. Its civil society has demonstrated a significant degree of independence in formulating demands on local government, epitomised by the extremely active Citizens' Forum, formed to express the public's anti-nationalist feelings. During the war, the Forum organised many events aimed at sensitising people on issues of human rights, democracy, peace and reconciliation. The Forum did not allow a single important event that might have serious repercussions on inter-ethnic relations in Tuzla or the political future of the country to go by without responding through public announcements or other appropriate initiatives. Since the end of the war, the Forum has become actively engaged in promoting public debates on crucial local government issues. It organised a discussion on the Tuzla–Podrinje draft law on local government, which provided those at the municipal level involved in drafting the law with valuable suggestions for its improvement. Although the mayor of Tuzla has been supportive of the work of the Forum, the organisation has kept the work of local government in the spotlight, publicly criticising some of its actions, organising public gatherings and initiating petitions to the government.

One of the special factors in Tuzla has been an active engagement of various local institutions, groups and associations in a multitude of projects in partnership with international agencies. Often the projects originated locally, reflecting the genuine needs of local communities and the interest of local actors in formulating and expressing those needs. During the war, the Tuzla municipality established an Office for International Cooperation, which was instrumental in keeping international interest in Tuzla at the forefront, while breaking the sense of isolation many communities experienced during the war (to a certain extent, Mostar was an extreme in the opposite direction, in that the ruling parties nurtured the siege mentality among the local population, thus making it more susceptible to their politically motivated manipulations). The office has been retained in the post-war municipal organisational structure – another of the unique features of Tuzla's local government not replicated elsewhere in BiH.

The relatively better shape of the local economy in and around Tuzla compared to other parts of BiH in the aftermath of the war was one factor conducive to the emergence of organisations dealing with local economic development. Among the most prominent has been the Tuzla Agency for Local Development Initiatives (TALDI). Having successfully implemented a World Bank-sponsored micro-credit scheme, TALDI has continued to support local entrepreneurs and NGOs through various micro-projects aimed at searching for local solutions to development problems. Part of the funding for these projects has come from the municipal and cantonal governments, and been complemented by the donors and private funds.

Civil society in Tuzla has been more locally embedded than in Mostar. Many NGOs, initially starting as an extension of international NGOs, have continued to operate after the departure of their sponors. After Sarajevo, Tuzla boasts BiH's second-largest number of NGOs engaged in a wide range of activities with particular emphasis on inclusive projects. One of the major factors behind the more vibrant civil society in Tuzla is that it managed to preserve its human capital, in which Tuzla University played an important role. Unlike in Mostar, where the university staff was decimated by the war, Tuzla's university managed to hold on to most of its staff, using their skills both during the war and throughout post-war reconstruction. Its staff members include some of the most prominent activists in the NGOs, citizens' organisations and other mobilised groups.

Tuzla's public space also accommodates a range of ethnically based groups and associations – those concerned with the protection and promotion of a particular nation's culture, tradition and language as well as those engaged in lobbying for the political goals associated with the local ruling élite. However, unlike in Mostar, the resort to violence as a means of pursuing their goals has been rare. To a large extent, this can be explained by the fact that the ideas of democracy, ethnic pluralism and tolerance have been a cohesive force within much of the Tuzla's civil society, which has worked against using violence in managing ethnic conflict. These attitudes, combined with effective local government, explain why the return of refugees and displaced people in Tuzla has been substantial and less problematic than elsewhere in BiH.

Another contrast with Mostar relates to the role of religious institutions and the media. In Tuzla, the religious leaders of all three ethnic communities have tried to keep an open dialogue, thus contributing to the conciliatory spirit among the population, particularly returning refugees. The press in Tuzla has been free compared to the strict party control that prevailed in Mostar for much of the time.

The relatively more favourable economic situation in Tuzla, compared with other parts of BiH, has provided local government with steady public revenues. However modest these revenues have been when measured by the vast needs of post-war rehabilitation, they have enabled the government to provide a certain standard of public services that is superior to those in many other parts of BiH. The local government and NGOs have been working alongside each other in attracting foreign donor funding to compensate for lacking funds, particularly in terms of economic development initiatives. While Tuzla shares many of the country's economic problems, in sharp contrast with Mostar it focuses local energies on finding solutions to these problems, based primarily on local human and other resources, reflecting what is essentially an effective local government.

Conclusion

Mitigating the conflict between Bosnia–Herzegovina's three main ethnic communities has been difficult in spite of the deployment of an array of methods of conflict regulation and extensive international involvement. The institutional framework agreed as part of the Dayton Agreement has been successful in ending the conflict, but has failed to provide an effective mechanism for inter-ethnic dialogue. Power sharing in the context of politicised ethnicity and the lack of democratic experience has led to political paralysis of the BiH's institutions of governance.

The comparison of Tuzla and Mostar suggests that decentralisation by itself is not sufficient in fostering democratic processes conducive to conflict management. It points to the crucial role that democratic political culture plays in effectively exploiting the conflict-management potential of democratic institutions. The integrity of local government institutions in Tuzla had a catalysing effect on the way civil society engaged in mediating ethnic conflict, in contrast with Mostar where 'uncivil' forms of mobilisation prevailed, thus heightening the conflict. The wider implications of this case study would be that in those instances where political and civil societies are based on democratic values, are inclined to political and social inclusion, and have populations that embrace anti-nationalist attitudes, the prospects for developing institutions capable of tempering and mediating ethnic conflict are significantly enhanced. Conversely, when the political élite has no interest in inter-ethnic moderation, but uses ethnic exclusion as an instrument to preserve its powers, even a carefully designed institutional framework might in practice reinforce the conflict.

In BiH, decentralisation has been perceived as an opportunity to weaken the state; power sharing based on the primacy of ethnic affiliation has thus, in effect, reinforced centrifugal tendencies rather than provided a framework for multi-ethnic cohabitation. The feasibility and long-term efficacy of democratic decentralisation in BiH have still to be demonstrated, however. The ascent to power of moderate, pro-democracy forces may yet prove to be a real test for the arguments put forward in this chapter.

References

Burges, M. and A. G. Gagnon (eds.) (1993) *Comparative Federalism and Federation: Competing Traditions and Future Directions*, Hemel Hempstead: Harvester Wheatsheaf.

Coulson, A. (ed.) (1995) *Local Government in Eastern Europe*, Aldershot: Edward Elgar.

Crook, R. and J. Manor (1998) *Democracy and Decentralisation in South Asia and West Africa: Participation, Accountability and Performance*, Cambridge: Cambridge University Press.

Donais, T. (2000) 'Division and Democracy: Bosnia's Post-Dayton Elections', *Research on Russia and Eastern Europe*, Vol. 3, London: Elsevier Science Inc.

Ghai, Y. (1998) 'Decentralization and the Accommodation of Ethnic Diversity', in C. Young (ed.) *Ethnic Diversity and Public Policy: a Comparative Inquiry*, London: Macmillan Press.

Ghai, Y. (ed.) (2000) *Autonomy and Ethnicity: Negotiating Competing Claims in Multi-ethnic States*, Cambridge: Cambridge University Press.

Horowitz, D. (1991) *A Democratic South Africa? Constitutional Engineering in a Divided Society*, Berkeley: University of California Press.

Horowitz, D. (1993) 'Democracy in Divided Societies', *Journal of Democracy*, 4, 4.

Horowitz, D. (1998) 'Structure and Strategy in Ethnic Conflict: a Few Steps Towards Synthesis', paper presented at the 1998 Annual World Bank Conference on Development Economics, Washington, DC.

Joseph, R. (1999) *State, Conflict and Democracy in Africa*, Boulder: Lynn Rienner Publishers.

Manor, J. (1999) *The Political Economy of Democratic Decentralisation*, Washington, DC: World Bank.

Milidragovic, D. (1998) 'Polozaj gradova u sistemu lokalne samouprave', *Pravna misao*, Sarajevo, Nos 9–12.

Reichel, S. (1997) *The European Administration of Mostar – Objectives and Achievements, July 1994–July 1996*, Mostar: EUAM.

Reilly, B. and A. Reynolds (1999), *Electoral Systems and Conflict in Divided Societies*, Washington, DC: National Academy Press.

Young, C. (ed.) (1998) *Ethnic Diversity and Public Policy: a Comparative Inquiry*, London: Macmillan Press.

Other sources

Constitution of BiH Federation.
Constitution of Tuzla–Podrinje canton.
Interim Statute of Mostar City.
Official Gazette of Herzegovina–Neretva Canton, various issues.
Official Gazette of Tuzla–Podrinje canton; various issues.
Statistics Bulletin of BiH Federation, various issues.
Statistics Bulletin of BiH, 1991.
Tuzla Citizens' Forum Reports, various issues.

Notes

1 The chapter is based on extensive field work carried out in Bosnia–Herzegovina between September 1999 and August 2000. Although the analysis of the two case studies ends with December 2000, some important more recent political developments receive comment.

2 On 1 July 2000, BiH's Constitutional Court ruled that all three BiH peoples – Muslims, Croats and Serbs – are constitutive nations in both its entities. This will require a change in the entity constitutions as well as an adaptation of government structures (the introduction of a second chamber in Republika Srpska's parliament, for example), thus effectively undermining the ethnic basis of BiH's constitutional make-up.

3 The authority of the international community's High Representative, charged with overseeing the implementation of the civilian aspects of the peace agreements, increased substantially over the years to the point that he became, in effect, the ultimate executive authority in BiH.

4 There is continuing pressure by the Bosnian Croats for the creation of new municipalities with a clear Bosnian Croat majority, in tandem with the creation of the third entity, which would include these municipalities.

5 The HDZ would use the change in the electoral rules to establish Bosnian Croat self-administration in the aftermath of the 2000 general elections.

6 The SDA won some 19 per cent of the votes: given that Muslims represented some 34 per cent of the population at the time, this would suggest that support for the SDA was not all that strong, though the pattern changed throughout the course of the conflict. It possibly provides some explanation why the authorities in East Mostar have been more cooperative than their counterparts in West Mostar.

7 The initial mandate of the EU Administration was for the period July 1994–July 1996, but was extended for a further six months.

8 According to some estimates, some DM4,900 *per capita* in donor aid was spent in Mostar during the EUAM mandate, compared to DM300 in BiH as a whole.

9 One was the Schwartz–Shilling Mostar City mediation of 26 August 1999; the other was the Office of the High Representative (OHR)-mediated agreement on Central Zone of March 2000.

10 The University of Mostar was divided, too; many non-Croat members of staff were expelled from the town and some were murdered. The West Mostar campus has operated as a pillar of the regime established by the HDZ BiH.

11 Particular care was devoted to the investigation of criminal offences against minorities; thus a trial of a group of men who attacked and robbed an elderly Serb couple was held at the height of the conflict. Some 40 citizens' claims were dealt with in 1996, at a time when the government was still switching over to a peacetime working regime.

12 MZ existed in the former system of local government; in Mostar, their role has been reduced to that of subordinate offices of the cantonal government.

11

Conclusion
The Politics of Institutional Choice

SUNIL BASTIAN AND ROBIN LUCKHAM

Writing about the American Constitution in *The Federalist*, Alexander Hamilton argued that the people of the United States had to determine the important question 'whether societies of men are really capable or not of establishing good government from reflection or choice, or whether they are forever destined to depend for their political constitutions on accident and force' (Hamilton 1787).[1]

All six countries considered in this book have passed through periods when their polities have been dominated by 'accident and force'. In all of them constitution makers and citizens have had the onerous task of re-building good government on the basis of 'reflection and choice'.

But in other respects they represent a wide range of historical experiences. Bosnia–Herzegovina has undertaken triple transitions from a socialist ideology, from a planned to a market economy and from authoritarian rule to liberal democracy. Moreover, these transitions have been rendered all the more traumatic by a fratricidal civil war.

All our other case studies are of multi-ethnic states that emerged to statehood after British colonial rule. Their problems and conflicts stem at least partly from the failures and contradictions of the colonial project. South Africa adds a new layer to these historical experiences, as in its case the colonial project culminated in a specific type of white minority rule, which in turn was challenged by a broadly based liberation struggle.

Four of the case studies (South Africa, Ghana, Uganda and Bosnia–Herzegovina) focus upon transitions or attempted transitions to democratic governance. The other two (Sri Lanka and Fiji) analyse the reinvention of existing democratic institutions to resolve or prevent violent conflicts.

What general conclusions, if any, can one extract from their particular national experiences of constitutional and political reform? The following are some of our reflections.

Can democracy be designed? (the question with which we began) has no easy answers. Some of our case studies might seem to suggest it should be answered in the negative. Democratic constitutions do not guarantee democracy; nor, however carefully crafted, do they necessarily reduce conflict. Bosnia–Herzegovina's constitution is described by Cox as a compendium of modern thinking on conflict resolution. It is only the latest of many attempts to craft constitutions in order to accommodate ethnic diversity in former Yugoslavia; and there is little reason to suppose it will be any more successful than these earlier experiments. Similarly, Fiji and Sri Lanka also have long and problematic histories of constitutional experimentation in multi-ethnic societies.

South Africa may be the only clear success story – both of designing democracy and of managing conflicts in a racially and ethnically divided society. Yet its constitution is the outcome, more than the cause, of its process of national reconciliation. And it has drawn relatively little upon the armoury of constitutional devices advocated by the designers of constitutions for plural societies. Uganda's constitution manages the problems of ethnic diversity in part by denying them political expression under its 'no-party system'. Ghana's constitution was drafted to return the country to liberal democracy; there was little attempt to innovate, or to modify majoritarian democratic structures through electoral reform, power-sharing devices or decentralisation. The fact that the country has experienced relatively little ethnic polarisation has much more to do with its political party system and with the judicious deployment of political patronage by its governments, than with its constitutions.

There is a kind of hubris in the idea that constitutional experts, political scientists, donor agencies or even national decision makers can assure democracy or solve conflicts by designing institutions. Indeed institutional design is an apparent oxymoron. Institutions in the sense that many political thinkers use the term[2] evolve, grow, become rooted or become 'institutionalised' – the metaphors are organic – and are not designed. And where attempts are made to design them, history, 'accident and force' and political manipulation may turn them on their heads and produce perverse and unforeseen outcomes, as some of our case studies show.

Nevertheless, there is sometimes no serious alternative to designing or redesigning democratic institutions: for instance, where existing ones have manifestly failed to resolve conflicts, as in Sri Lanka; where there are obvious flaws in the existing constitutional design of the state, as in Sri Lanka or Fiji; where the dominant state structures are oppressive and operate in the interests of a single racial or ethnic group, as in apartheid South Africa; or where state structures have 'collapsed' as in Bosnia–Herzegovina or pre-1986 Uganda. The question in such cases is not whether democracy can be designed. It must be, as the alternatives would be far worse. The real issue is how it can be reinvented, by whom and with what prospect (however meagre) of success.

Institutional choices can be made in a great variety of ways, ranging from entire new constitutional settlements, to piecemeal reforms, to the accretion of small changes, to the *failure* to make appropriate decisions when institutions are failing. Non-decisions may sometimes be as significant as decisions, as shown by the troubled political history of Sri Lanka, which has been hamstrung for many years by its politicians' inability to agree on the constitutional reforms needed to make its polity more inclusive, so as to give it some prospect of resolving its violent inter-communal conflict.

Thus while our own focus has been upon the design of democratic institutions, we need to keep in mind the relatively more cautious view which argues that design is a rare and unlikely mode of change of institutions in general. According to theorists of institutional change there are a number of mechanisms through which institutions emerge and become consolidated. Goodin (1998) looks at three different models of institutional change – accidental, evolutionary and intentional. According to Offe (1998), institutional changes occur due to internal contradictions, total breakdown and internal critiques. For him the 'hyper-rational ideal' of designing institutions is a rare occurrence.

We have argued in Chapter 1 that the consolidation of democracy – where there are both democratic institutions and democratic politics – is a long, difficult and unfinished historical journey. In like fashion White (1998) says 'it is useful to see "democratisation" not merely as a relatively sudden political rupture caused by regime transition, but also as a process of institutional accumulation, built up gradually like layers of coral'. Something similar is expressed by Sklar's notion of development democracy, when he says that democracy 'comes to every country in fragments and parts; each fragment becomes an incentive for addition of another' (Sklar 1987: 714).

Hence although our focus is mainly upon constitutional and institutional reform during democratic transitions, our case studies reinforce the need to be sensitive to the manifold ways institutional choices may be shaped on each country's shifting historical terrain. Often it is not the formal institutional choices that are important, so much as the politics

surrounding them, or even the routines of day-to-day public administration. In the case of Bosnia–Herzegovina, Cox argues that institutional
deadlock created by the Dayton Agreement may eventually be broken by
the re-establishment of central government operations such as an operating Central Bank, judicial institutions and integrated police structures,
and so on. In Sri Lanka, Coomaraswamy emphasises the potential of the
trend toward, greater judicial activism in securing better protection for
human rights, and countering state repression and violence.

*The design of institutions needs to be based upon a proper understanding of
shifting power relations and societal transformations. For this a historical
perspective is needed – both to offset democracy triumphalism and to counter
pessimism over conflict and state failure.* Social scientists all too often write
history backwards, to see in it what they want to see. This has been
largely true of the literature on democratic transitions, which offers
'lessons' about best practice that airbrush out the accidents, traumas
and contradictions suffered along the way. As Hassim and Pottie point
out, even South Africa's extraordinarily successful transition to a more
democratic polity cannot be 'read off' from the preceding crisis of the
apartheid regime. It could easily have ended in more conflict and
bloodshed. What prevented this was a mixture of wise political decisions,
historical contingency, and appropriate structural conditions.

Much the same lack of historical perspective can be seen in the
literature on failing or collapsing states, especially in sub-Saharan
Africa, which tends to see an inexorable march to state collapse and
violent conflict. The three African case studies presented in this volume
serve to lighten this gloomy picture. During the first three decades of its
independence Ghana experienced its full share of political instability and
military coups, though these never escalated into armed conflict. Since
the early 1980s, however, it has enjoyed relative political stability, has
stabilised its economy, and has made a relatively successful transition to
democratic governance. Both South Africa and Uganda have ended
major conflicts, as well as making transitions to more democratic political
systems.

*A great deal depends upon how decision makers use the political opportunities
and spaces open to them at critical junctures in their history, especially at
moments of crisis or transition.* They cannot, to twist a phrase from Marx,
make democracy in historical conditions of their own choosing. They
must respond to history in order to make history. Our research covers a
period in which there were immense global shifts – the collapse of

communism, the end of the Cold War, new forms of globalisation, aggressive Western promotion of liberal economies and multi-party democracy, and the 'Third Wave' of democratic transitions – creating a transformed international environment.

The trajectory of Bosnia–Herzegovina's catastrophic political transition was shaped by the end of the Cold War and the disintegration of former Yugoslavia, which, far from consolidating democracy, erected barriers against it. The transitions in both Ghana and Uganda were undertaken after long periods of corrupt and authoritarian governance. What distinguished the military-populist regimes[3] of Rawlings and Museveni from the regimes of many other African states was how they responded to deep political and development crises, by turning them into opportunities for far-reaching economic and subsequently political reform.

The crisis of the apartheid system in South Africa was brought on by the sustained political opposition of the liberation movements; it was reinforced by an internal critique within the Afrikaner élite; and was accelerated by international changes, including the end of the Cold War. It created a moment of opportunity that was wisely and creatively used by the negotiators of the country's new constitution. Sri Lanka's current peace talks could potentially offer a similar moment of opportunity to create a more inclusive political system. But it is not yet certain whether the country's élite and the Tamil LTTE guerrilla leadership can overcome the burdens of history and the extreme polarisation produced by the war itself.

Institutional choices are never made in a political and economic vacuum; they are often tailored to suit the narrower political and economic agendas of those making them. This is why some analysts (Lijphart and Waisman 1996; Geddes 1996) make a distinction between the hyper-rational ideal of institutional design and the real politics of institutional choice. In a comparative analysis of transitions in Eastern Europe, Geddes (*ibid.*) shows that constitutional choices were to a considerable extent determined by the structure of power and the social bases of party political support in the states in question. In countries where the previous communist parties were strong and confident of winning elections, they tended to introduce majoritarian electoral systems and strong presidential institutions. Parties with charismatic leaders also opted for strong presidencies. But weak parties tended to opt for proportional representation and parliamentary systems of governance. The choices also depended upon the accuracy of the information politicians relied on to calculate their prospects under different electoral systems and government structures.

Among our case studies Bastian's analysis of the politics of electoral system choice in Sri Lanka provides an especially striking example of the use of constitutional and electoral reform in order to promote a particular political and economic agenda. President Jayawardena brought in electoral reforms, including PR, to redress the pro-rural bias of the existing FPTP system, and (along with a presidential system of government) to assure the policy continuity that he felt was needed to push through the government's new strategy of capitalist development.

It does not follow that institutional choices that reflect particular material and political interests are necessarily undesirable in themselves. Indeed institutional designs that leave out or ignore important interests may not be as sustainable. PR in Sri Lanka was arguably a necessary step towards a more inclusive political system that would be better able to represent minorities, even if this was not the main reason it was chosen.

The post-apartheid constitution in South Africa emerged from the fraught process of bargaining between opposed political and economic interests described in Chapter 2. From the start National Party negotiators insisted on PR, mainly because it would guarantee the continued representation of South Africa's white and other racial minorities. The ANC was ultimately persuaded of PR's merits, despite an initial preference for FPTP, for it calculated it would have no difficulty winning large majorities under PR. And its negotiators were wise enough to understand the political dangers of excluding other groups and parties from the political process under a more majoritarian system.

The problematic constitutional and electoral reforms in Fiji described by Fraenkel were initiated after powerful groups on both sides of the ethnic Fijian/Indo-Fijian divide – including the leader of the country's previous military coup – had come to the conclusion that political arrangements to promote power sharing were needed for the country's political stability and for its economic prosperity. The failure of the electoral reforms to foster inter-communal cooperation had little to do with the political and economic biases of the reformers. It resulted mainly from their flawed calculations about the impact of the new AV voting system on the political behaviour of the country's voters and political parties.

In Bosnia–Herzegovina the Dayton Agreement produced an accommodation between the interests represented by the three dominant ethnically based political parties, together with the various mafias, militias and politico-military business groups supporting them. Other groups and interests were simply excluded from the negotiations. The Agreement also satisfied the short-term interests of the international community, including the major Western powers, in ending the hostilities and preserving stability at all costs. In many respects it was a triumph of expediency and of *realpolitik*, against democracy and long-term peace building.

Even though institutional choices emerge from shifting power relations, they also reconfigure and transform these power relations. A good illustration is how South Africa's negotiation process and constitution-making exercise strengthened the ideological centre and marginalised radical options, including both the socialist transformation hoped for by many members of the liberation movements, and the racial separatism and violence advocated by far-right extremists. In Bosnia, by contrast, negotiations and the Dayton Agreement reconfigured power relations in quite a different way, by politically entrenching the ethnic nationalist political parties, and making it all the harder to create viable alternatives to them.

The political and economic forces pressing for reform – and the reforms themselves – may tug in contradictory directions. An especially clear example is the way legislation to encourage women's participation in the political sphere in Sri Lanka, as well as to remove various forms of discrimination against them, has been blocked by the reluctance of governments to alienate political parties representing minority communities, especially the Muslim community – whose influence and capacity to engage in collective political action has been significantly increased by the introduction of PR.

Sri Lanka can also be considered a case where the establishment of a functioning democracy based on a two-party system contained elements that undermined the rights of minorities. The two-party system gave a choice to the electorate and led to enthusiastic participation in electoral politics. But this in itself generated intense competition between parties where ethnic loyalties were mobilised to win votes among the Sinhala majority. In contrast, Uganda's 'no-party' system has been advocated by the government as necessary to prevent ethnically based political competition and ensure stability in a conflict-torn society. Yet Griffiths and Katalikawe argue that it could consolidate autocratic rule, push ethnic tensions beneath the surface and lead to destabilisation in the future.

Even incomplete or politically loaded institutional choices may sometimes create political openings that can be used to expand democratic opportunities or resolve conflicts. The constitutional settlement crafted by the

309

'democratising' Rawlings administration in Ghana, for instance, opened political spaces in which opposition parties could organise and eventually win power, despite flaws in the constitution and government manipulation (initially) of the electoral process. Uganda's new constitution too has allowed for some expression of dissent, through its rights provisions, and the possibility of individual opponents of the regime being elected to Parliament. Yet the restrictions upon political parties under its 'no-party' system, and the authoritarian political instincts of the Museveni regime, have limited the scope for further political transformation. As we have seen, the situation in Fiji has been almost the converse, in that the political openings created through constitutional reforms have been frustrated by the use made of them by extremist politicians.

Institutional reform for conflict resolution is necessarily an open-ended process. Most of our case studies of societies characterised by protracted conflicts have long histories of institutional reform. Conflicts have challenged some of the fundamentals of their institutions and opened up space for new phases of reform. It is difficult, however, to envisage institutional designs that would provide final answers to any of these conflicts. In crafting new institutions, therefore, spaces should be kept open for further institutional innovation.

This is at the nub of debates concerning power sharing, as we point out in Chapter 1. Should the sharing of power be temporary, lasting only so long as is necessary to build peace and restore confidence between communities and among opposed political forces, as during the South African transition? Or should it be constitutionalised as a permanent feature of the political settlement, as advocated by the proponents of consociationalism and found in the constitutions and institutional structures of countries like Malaysia, the Lebanon and (under the Dayton Agreement) Bosnia–Herzegovina?

The problem with the latter approach is that it can easily entrench social divisions between communities, block institutional innovation and diminish democracy. The constitutionalisation of ethnic divisions in communal electoral rolls in Fiji and Malaysia are cases in point. In Cyprus and the Lebanon power-sharing constitutions simply perpetuated communal antagonisms, and did little to prevent the recurrence of violent conflict. The complex power-sharing arrangements in Bosnia–Herzegovia, and its extreme devolution of power to ethnically defined entities, cantons and municipalities, described in chapters 9 and 10, leave little space for significant institutional and political change. Such change will have to come, if at all, from outside the Dayton framework.

There are no universally valid institutional blueprints for broadening democracy or managing entrenched political and social conflicts. Institutional choices made in some contexts have proved ineffective in others. For instance, the PR electoral system chosen for South Africa's new democracy was relatively effective in assuring representation for almost all of the country's ethnic groups and for women. But the introduction of PR in Sri Lanka, though giving smaller minority parties more influence in parliament, failed to prevent the Tamil minority's political alienation. It also made very little impact on women's political representation, in the absence of any serious commitment to the latter by the government and political élites.

The fortunes of decentralisation as a technique for managing conflict have been similarly varied. In Bosnia the decentralisation of powers to the different entities, cantons and municipalities has been especially extreme, far exceeding that in most federal systems, yet for the most part it has ratified ethnic cleansing rather that resolving the underlying conflicts. In contrast decentralisation in South Africa has not made serious inroads into the powers of central government, presupposing a notion of cooperative rather than competitive devolution. In Uganda limited decentralisation has been deployed by the government, mainly as a technique of central government control, to 'resolve' conflict by fragmenting power and preventing ethnic political mobilisation.

Institutional and political variations can exist within as well as between countries. Decentralisation in Bosnia–Herzegovina, as described by Bojicic-Dzelilovic, facilitated the management of conflict in some municipalities, notably Tuzla. But in most of the country it has merely solidified existing inter-communal cleavages – contrary to the conventional wisdom about decentralisation as a 'solution' to inter-communal conflict.

It does not therefore follow that decentralisation will not be appropriate and necessary in other conflict-torn societies, like Sri Lanka, as Coomaraswamy argues. But the kind of manipulated decentralisation that prevails in Uganda, or the cooperative decentralisation implemented in South Africa, would be non-starters, since the Tamil leadership is unlikely to accept anything less than far-reaching autonomy. But the extreme devolution found in Bosnia would be equally problematic, all the more if it simply recognised the political dominance of the LTTE in the North and the East. In Sri Lanka, as in all conflict-torn societies, decentralisation is not a panacea, and must be tailored to the specific requirements of peace building in the country's particular national context.

Institutions per se *will not resolve conflicts or deepen democracy.* The case studies covered in this volume come from a variety of historical experiences. They tell us how institutions operate in specific societies with their own traditions, ideologies and social structures. To understand how institutions work, or do not work, one must look beyond the bare skeletons of institutions, and bring these contextual factors into the analysis.

To illustrate, consider Sri Lanka, where long-established democratic institutions have conspicuously failed to represent women in political decision-making – despite a handful of élite women in top positions – or to facilitate the promotion of gender issues in policy making. The reasons for this, Pinto-Jayawardena argues, do not lie in institutions *per se*. They lie in the nature of political society, in the patriarchal structures determining gender relations and in women's own perceptions of their societal and political role. These factors take us into the realm of dominant ideologies and nature of the political culture, neither of which can be tackled through institutional reforms alone. It is not that institutions are unimportant. They can often be used to create an enabling environment for societal transformation. But our horizons have to extend well beyond them.

Similar conclusions come from the accounts in this book of institutional reforms in Fiji and Bosnia. Electoral reforms in Fiji provide an almost classic example of the limits of constitutional and institutional engineering, where ethnic divisions are historically embedded in the entire fabric of state and society. In Bosnia, Bojicic-Dzelilovic questions the view that an adequate transfer of power, sufficient resources and the presence of accountability mechanisms – the staple prescriptions of the policy literature – are enough to make decentralisation work. The viability of decentralised structures, and their ability to manage conflicts, also depends on the configuration of competitive party politics, the profile and the strength of civil society and the strength of the local economy. All these factors take us well beyond institutions.

A further important feature of democratic institutions is how they intertwine with other societal and cultural discourses. As Dryzek (1998) argues, institutions are always intertwined with discourses. The usual institutional analysis focuses on rules, rights, operating procedures, customs and principles. Discursive analyses make it possible to unravel the multiplicity of discourses surrounding these institutions. For example, Coomaraswamy shows how democracy in Sri Lanka has generated different discourses among different ethnic groups. For the Sinhala majority, democracy has been coloured by the hegemonic discourse of Sinhala nationalists. For them it is a majoritarian notion, according to which those who have history and numbers on their side are entitled to rule. This discourse has proved incompatible with the ideas of democracy held by Tamils, for whom limited government, rights and territorial and group autonomy are considered the essence of democracy. Hence unravelling such discourses, and finding space to overcome the incompatibilities, is a crucial dimension of conflict resolution and institutional design.

The impact on democracy or on conflict management of particular institutions, such as electoral systems, cannot be separated from that of others, such as the structure of the executive, the party system or human rights protections: a holistic approach across the entire spectrum of institutions is essential. Interactions among institutions are the concern of the extensive comparative literature discussed in Chapter 1. A compelling example of how a single key constitutional provision can alter the impact of a range of other institutions – indeed of the entire constitutional framework – is the 'no-party system' in Uganda described by Griffiths and Katalikawe. The ban on party organisation and campaigning instituted under the constitution and its enabling legislation transforms the meaning of the free elections also guaranteed by the constitution, alters the nature of political contestation, bolsters personal presidential rule, affects the balance between executive and legislature, and weakens the effect of constitutional guarantees of judicial and public service independence. These side-effects are of course no accident, but follow from the NRM government's determination to stamp its own particular discourse of democracy and its political predominance upon the country.

It is always important to look at the small print: the specific technical details of grand documents such as constitutions, legislation and judicial decisions that feature in the design of political systems; together with the latent agendas of those responsible for them. What is crucial about Uganda's decentralisation measures is not the way they devolve power – which is rather limited – but how the size and boundaries of administrative units have been constructed to cut across ethnic units and head off the possibility of ethnic political mobilisation (see Chapter 3 and Crook 2001). Likewise it was the specific form of PR introduced in Sri Lanka, and the variant of AV introduced in Fiji (see below), that shaped voter and political party behaviour, as described in chapters 7 and 8.

Even the best-designed and most consultative reforms may not function as expected, and can backfire on their makers. On the evidence of some of our case studies we are almost tempted to suggest a new iron law to complement the 'iron law of oligarchy' Michels detected in democratic political parties: an 'iron law of the perverse consequences of institutional design'. A striking example is Fiji's introduction of a carefully crafted AV voting system, designed to foster cross-ethnic voting and inter-party alliances – only for ethnic extremist parties to use it to secure a disproportionate share of the vote, entering an unstable government alliance, and creating a political deadlock that led directly to a paramilitary putsch.

Externally driven conflict resolution and democratisation have important dangers and limits. An extreme example is the role of the Western powers and the international community in Bosnia–Herzegovina's constitutional settlement, described in Chapter 9. The constitution itself is an annexe of the Dayton Agreement. It was drafted with minimal consultation of local stakeholders (with the partial exception of the nationalist parties), it was not translated into local languages and enjoys minimal legitimacy among the country's citizens. Interpretation and enforcement have mainly been left in the hands of the UN High Representative, creating a *de facto* international protectorate. Without the latter's active intervention to keep the peace and curtail the influence of the extreme nationalist political parties, the Agreement's very complex provisions for power sharing and decentralisation would not work, and the country's semblance of peace would collapse. But this intervention also weakens domestic political processes, leaves too little space for the emergence of political alternatives to the nationalist parties, and discourages domestic constitutional innovation. There are obvious lessons to be drawn for the role of the international community in other post-conflict situations, such as Kosovo or Afghanistan.

Even where there has been a far stronger domestic impetus behind constitutional reform, as with Fiji's Constitutional Review Commission, external advice and assistance have sometimes been sources of controversy. The defects of Fiji's AV electoral system, introduced on the basis of well-intentioned advice from international experts, have already been referred to – although other elements in the constitutional package have proved more positive.

Other case studies also show signs of the growing influence of external mediators and the influence of conflict resolution ideas generated in the West. The most recent case is Sri Lanka, where much hope is placed on a peace initiative brokered by the Norwegians. Even so, our analysis and case studies make us take a cautious view of the attempts to promote democracy and build peace from outside. It is not that external actors should not have any influence. But unless they build upon domestically rooted political processes, and factor in the history and specificity of each national society, their efforts may be counter-productive.

The global economic and political context of democratisation cannot be ignored, and should be factored in. Only one case study – that of electoral reform in Sri Lanka – makes globalisation and expansion of capitalism its entry point for analysing democratic institutions. Yet it is clear that the exposure of developing economies to global economic forces has a bearing on the future of democracy almost everywhere. Bastian uses the Sri Lankan reforms to demonstrate that democratic institutions were reformed primarily to manage the political social contradictions of liberalisation and globalisation, rather than to deepen democracy or resolve conflict.

Other case studies also refer to the uneasy relationship between market forces and democracies. In South Africa, the capacity of demo-cratic institutions to satisfy the demands of the poor, together with the ANC's alliances with trade unions and civil society groups, have proved hard to reconcile with the new market-oriented policies introduced under GEAR. In Ghana, economic liberalisation preceded democratisa-tion, but elected governments have fallen back upon an established political tradition of sacrificing fiscal discipline in order to fight elections, complicating management of the economy. By contrast in Uganda the government has fended off donor pressures for multi-party democracy by raising the spectre of ethnic conflict and political instability that allegedly might threaten the country's development.

Constitutions and institutional designs tend to have distributive consequences: some groups and interests, and some policy alternatives, are favoured; others may lose out. South Africa's constitution confirmed a major power shift toward the black majority. But, as we have argued, it also established the political conditions for the country's participation in the global economy. Much the same could be said of the constitutional settlements in Ghana and Uganda and of electoral reforms in Sri Lanka. In all these cases some have argued that the net losers have been the poor and those most affected by the burdens of economic adjustment.

Also, institutional designs inevitably shape the perceived balance of political and economic advantage in multi-ethnic societies. In Sri Lanka,

315

as we have seen, the existing constitutional framework has marginalised the Tamil minority and will continue doing so unless replaced by more inclusive institutions. The Dayton Agreement in Bosnia and the new AV electoral system in Fiji both in practice favoured the more extreme ethnic nationalists, despite the constitution makers' best efforts to foster inter-ethnic accommodation. In Uganda many Baganda believe – not without reason – that the government's decentralisation policies are designed to divide them and frustrate their demands for a federal constitution. Our point is that such perceptions cannot always be avoided, and must be factored in by institutional designers – preferably by constructing institutions so that all groups feel they can make gains from inter-ethnic cooperation.

The reform process *can often be (at least) as critical as the final constitutional or institutional blueprints.* Among all our case studies, South Africa seems to provide us with the clearest guide to the ingredients of a 'successful' democratic transition. One of these – the primacy of internal political processes and 'home-grown' solutions – reinforces our earlier argument concerning the pitfalls of external influence and advice.

The other two ingredients of South Africa's success have been favourable initial political and societal conditions and participatory and transparent negotiation and reform processes. For the country's transition took place in a context in which political institutions, though exclusionary, were relatively well established. A strong civil society had been forged during the struggle against apartheid. Local technical and legal capacity was highly developed. It was on this historical bedrock that the new South Africa and its constitution emerged.

The transition process alternated between detailed negotiations in closed session between the ANC and the NP government on specific issues, such as the integration of state and guerrilla military establishments, periods of popular mobilisation, especially when negotiations were flagging, and broad-based public consultation, notably during the constitution-making exercise.

There are varying lessons about process from Ghana, Uganda and Sri Lanka. Public consultation played some role in the making of Ghana's relatively liberal constitution, but there was a degree of government manipulation. In Uganda the movement type of politics arguably encouraged somewhat wider participation of the population in the constitution-making process than in Ghana, but with even more regime manipulation and ultimately a more problematic outcome.

Sri Lanka, at least in the past, has adopted a narrower approach to institutional change, driven largely by the political agendas of the parties and governments in power. The electoral reforms bringing in PR saw a notable narrowing of the decision-making arena, in order to better support economic liberalisation. The current process of reinventing the constitution in order to resolve the conflict will of necessity have to be broader – both to assure minority participation and to restore the legitimacy of a weakened constitution and democratic process.

'Collapsed' states might seem to provide opportunities to start afresh and to redesign institutions from scratch; yet post-conflict situations also have their own particular dangers and constraints. Only two of the countries we consider in this book, Bosnia–Herzegovina and Uganda post-1986, have experienced state collapse. The state was challenged and its legitimacy was undermined in Sri Lanka and in South Africa, but this did not bring it to the point of collapse.

Bosnia provides especially poignant examples of the dangers and constraints of state reconstruction. The Dayton Agreement necessarily concentrated on ending the fighting and assuring the compliance of the extremist nationalist parties and their armies. In the process a major opportunity was lost to build a more inclusive and durable constitutional framework, with corresponding popular legitimacy. There was nothing remotely comparable to the broad-based process of peace building and popular consultation that occurred in South Africa.

In Uganda the incoming NRM government sought to be inclusive by representing most of the major political forces and groups in the country in the government, prioritising economic recovery and attempting to reinvent democracy through the movement system, grassroots Resistance Councils and a consultative constitution-making process. All these were easier to initiate because it had emerged as the clear victor in the previous armed struggle. It faced other constraints, however, including donor pressures for structural adjustment and the re-emergence of conflict in the north of the country. In the final event its 'no-party' constitutional framework closed off important avenues for political contestation and debate, giving most priority to the NRM's and President Museveni's own political dominance.

Strategies to neutralise non-democratic politics are almost as essential as strategies to foster democratic politics. In most cases this means treading a delicate balance between working with the perpetrators of violence, incorporating them in 'normal' politics and actively seeking to diminish their military and political influence. It also requires the re-establishment of accountability – including accountability for past and present violence – without thereby reducing the incentives to cooperate in the constitutional settlement.

Even in South Africa peace building and the constitutional negotiations were at one point threatened by violence perpetrated by a motley collection of 'spoilers': rogue elements in the security forces, white extremists and violent elements in KwaZulu–Natal and elsewhere. These could easily have derailed the entire process; though their impact was cushioned by the strong support for peaceful methods by most significant political groups and the majority of the country's population of all racial groups.

In Bosnia–Herzegovina Cox describes the huge gap between the formal democratic structures of the Dayton Agreement and the parallel constitutional and political systems of the country's different wartime para-states, dominated by extreme ethnic nationalist parties, their armed militias and assorted mafias, and linked to their shadow war economies. The office of the UN High Representative has tried to undermine their influence, whilst continuing to work with them (a strategy some critics regard as unrealistic and self-defeating: Chandler 1999). It has attempted to restore the 'normal' functions of government (including its vital police and security functions: see Kaldor 2003) to provide viable alternatives to these parallel power systems. And it has also made efforts to work with and strengthen the country's demoralised and disempowered civil society organisations.

Sri Lanka faces similar potential difficulties if it is to go forward with the current peace process. The LTTE must obviously be a partner in the peace process, but as Coomaraswamy points out, it controls much of the North and East through intimidation and force. Working with it and converting it into a normal political party competing for votes in a plural political system is obviously going to be a long and arduous process. Moreover, there is a more general problem of political violence perpetrated by the security forces, parties and politicians in all parts of the country, which any attempt to ensure accountability for human rights abuses, and to reinvent the country's democracy, must confront.

Spaces need to be kept open for institutional innovation through democratic politics and through responsiveness to civil and political society. Democratic politics are not only necessary to counter violence and non-democratic politics. They are essential for political renewal and innovation.

South Africa's case provides many examples of the way active civil society groups were able to help ensure more inclusive institutions, for instance by providing women with a number of ways of intervening in the political process and in institutional design. Yet Hassim and Pottie also emphasise the limits of this process of women's political empowerment. Civil society *per se* is no more of a universal panacea than democratic institutions. A pertinent example of the limitations of approaches based on civil society is the failure of the efforts of a multi-ethnic Sri Lanka women's group, STRAWN, to convert its undoubted popular appeal into votes (see Chapter 6); partly because it lacked the financial resources to challenge the political parties, but also because of the perception that by moving into politics it was weakening its credibility as a civil society group pressing gender demands.

As we have already argued, it is extremely difficult to come to sweeping conclusions about which institutions are suitable for which types of society and to meet what type of demands. Such definitive answers would ignore the complex way in which civil society and political practice interact with institutions, and would easily be a formula for disappointment.

A more creative approach is to foster continuous institutional innovation. In such an approach there would be no search for recipes that would be valid for all situations. On the contrary, institutions need to evolve continuously. What is critical is how this can be achieved without descending into the kind of violence that rips states and societies apart. Hence we reiterate the central theme of this book, that what is decisive in creating space for the innovative development of institutions is their shifting and creative relationship to democratic politics.

References

Chandler, D. (1999) *Bosnia: Faking Democracy after Dayton*, London: Pluto Press.

Crook, R. (2001) *Strengthening Democratic Governance in Conflict-Torn Societies: Civic Organisations, Democratic Effectiveness and Political Conflict*, IDS Working Paper 129, Brighton: Institute of Development Studies.

Dryzek, J. S. (1998) 'The Informal Logic of Institutional Design', in R. E. Goodin (1998).

Geddes, B. (1996) 'Initiation of New Democratic Institutions in Eastern Europe and Latin America', in A. Lijphart and C.H. Waisman (eds), *Institutional Design in New Democracies*. Boulder, CO: Westview Press.

Goodin, R. E. (ed.) (1998) 'Institutions and Their Design', in R. E. Goodin (ed.), *The Theory of Institutional Design*, Cambridge: Cambridge University Press.

Hamilton, A. (1787) 'Introduction', *The Federalist*, No. 1 (27 October 1787), p. 1.

Kaldor, M. (2003) 'Security Structures in Bosnia and Herzegovina', in G. Cawthra and R. Luckham (eds.), *Governing Insecurity: Democratic Control of Military and Security Establishments in Transitional Democracies*, London: Zed Books.

Lijphart, A. and C.H. Waisman (1996) 'Institutional Design and Democratization' in A. Lijphart and C.H. Waisman (eds.), *Institutional Design in New Democracies*, Boulder, CO: Westview Press.

Offe, C. (1998) 'Designing Institutions in Eastern European Transition', in R. E. Goodin (ed.), *The Theory of Institutional Design*, Cambridge: Cambridge University Press.

Sklar, R. (1987) 'Developmental Democracy', *Comparative Studies in Society and History*, 29, 4.

White, G. (1998) 'Building a Democratic Development State: Social Democracy in the Developing World', *Democratization*, 5, 3 (Autumn).

Notes

1 We are indebted to Vivian Hart, who called our attention to this passage from the *Federalist* Papers. She and Martin Doornbos made many other useful suggestions relating to this book at the final workshop of our research programme in Sarajevo in 2001.

2 See our conceptualisation of institutions in Chapter 1 as 'a socially constructed set of arrangements routinely exercised and accepted'.

3 The NRM/Museveni government, which came to power in 1986 after an armed insurrection, was not a military regime, but Museveni's original and most important political base was the National Resistance Army, and there were several important structural and political similarities to the Rawlings regime that came to power through a military coup in 1982: see chapters 3 and 4.

Index